Margaret Elizabeth Munson Sangster

**The Art of Home-Making**

In city and country, in mansion and cottage

Margaret Elizabeth Munson Sangster

**The Art of Home-Making**
*In city and country, in mansion and cottage*

ISBN/EAN: 9783743407350

Manufactured in Europe, USA, Canada, Australia, Japa

Cover: Foto ©Thomas Meinert / pixelio.de

Manufactured and distributed by brebook publishing software (www.brebook.com)

Margaret Elizabeth Munson Sangster

**The Art of Home-Making**

# THE ART OF HOME-MAKING

## IN CITY AND COUNTRY — IN MANSION AND COTTAGE

### BY MARGARET E. SANGSTER

Author of "Home Life Made Beautiful," "The Art of Being Agreeable,"
' Poems of the Household," "Easter Bells," Etc.

## A Mother's Lullaby

*Sleep sweetly, my baby,*
*Thy mother is here,*
*No chill wind of evil*
*Thy rest shall come near.*
*Oh! soft is thy cradle,*
*And warm is thy nest,*
*Of all life has brought me*
*I count thee my best.*

*Sleep softly, my baby,*
*God-given to me,*
*The angels are watching*
*Thy mother and thee ;*
*Sleep safe, little darling,*
*As bird in the nest,*
*The love that came with thee*
*Sings sweet in my breast.*

—MARGARET E. SANGSTER

## BEAUTIFULLY ILLUSTRATED WITH NEARLY 200 ENGRAVINGS

NEW YORK
THE CHRISTIAN HERALD BIBLE HOUSE
1898

*TO ONE BELOVED*


*AS CHILD, MAIDEN AND MATRON*

*MY DEAR FRIEND*


*ELIZABETH M. CAMPBELL*

# FOREWORD.

*To the Gentle Reader :*

THIS book, which has grown day by day since I first thought of it, till it has reached its present goodly size, is meant for you, Gentle Reader, as a help on the way of life. The old simile, familiar to us from childhood of life as a journey, often uphill, sometimes down the valley, now and then across a level land, is ever more appropriate as experience crowns anticipation or disappointments throng, or love's young dream makes glad the springing steps. Old and young, blithe and sad, rich and poor, prosperous or struggling, we are fellow pilgrims, comrades on the road, and our goal is the Father's House at last. In these simple talks about husbands, wives, parents, children, money, housekeeping, business, study, health, rest, and work, I have kept in view the fact that we are Christian pilgrims, disciples around the Master, and those whom He has honored by calling them Friends. May this book make life happier for all who read its pages!

# CONTENTS.

(7)

# CONTENTS.

CONTENTS. 9

# ILLUSTRATIONS.

(13)

# ART OF HOME MAKING.

## CHAPTER I.

### Falling in Love.

HERE is an old, old fashion which has never yet gone out of date, and which has as many followers in this end of the century as it had in the beginning; or, for that matter, as in any period since the world began. Every generation, as it takes its turn in this strangely mingled life of ours, passes through certain phases, one of which, and not the least important, is the one we call falling in love.

One sometimes wonders why we say falling, as if there were something unexpected and precipitate about the matter; as if it were a sudden thing, against which precautions cannot well be made ; as if, indeed, it were a thing connected vaguely with misfortune ; but Cupid peers over our middle-aged shoulders, laughs in his sleeve, and continues to aim his little darts at young and old, and still his happy victims go on falling in love. One cannot always tell how it happens. The poet says that "in the spring a young man's fancies lightly turn to thoughts of love;" but love has all seasons for its own —spring, summer, autumn and winter alike. One of the certain things in this world of uncertainty and change is that, come what may, people will meet and be mutually attracted ; will fall in love and marry.

Some of the happiest days of life are courting days. Of all futile questions, the most so is this—Why did such a man choose such a woman, or why did this gay girl select for her mate so grave and sober a man? People are apt to like their opposites. The tall, strong man prefers to tuck under his arm the little

2 (17)

slender woman; the short woman does not mind looking up sometimes to quite a
height; the short man chooses a young grenadier of a woman. Equally, the
blonde and the brunette seek one another. The law of love seems to go by con-
traries. The impulsive and impetuous person likes the calm, staid and deliberate
one and vice-versa.

Very slight things are sufficient for love's beginnings. A girl puts on a
pretty gown, knots a blue ribbon at her throat, sticks a flower in her belt, and
goes lightly and thoughtlessly along her way, and that day a man happens to see
the bright cheek and the blue ribbon, and loses his heart. We have all heard of
the maiden who tied her bonnet under her chin and tied a young man's heart
within, and most of us, when we remember cases of love at first sight, see that
what was so apparently accidental had a good deal to do with the matter. As a
rule, young people do not say to themselves, "Go to, I will seek a mate." On
the contrary, they are won by some slight thing; some grace of manner, or
charm of speech, a dimple, a blush, a soft word, and before they know it, all is
over with them, so far as love is concerned.

"Love is strong as death," said the writer of the song of songs, and no truer
word was ever said or sung. Of all forces in this world, love is the strongest,
and the true love of man for woman and woman for man, abiding and constant
and faithful, is the most beautiful and enduring thing in life. Let no one persuade
you that there is anything foolish about love. Love is the truest wisdom. Most
unhappy are young people who take to themselves the philosophy of the cynic,
who are frightened at small means and fear to trust to time and the strength of
one another's affection, and so live lonesome and loveless lives. Many a man
loses a pearl of price because he forgets that faint heart never won fair lady, or
because he is afraid that the girl he admires will not be willing to share his day
of small things. Men do women small justice in this regard. The true woman
is not afraid of poverty; she desires to share the fortunes of the man she loves,
and it is little to her that she will not have fine dresses or fine furniture or a wide
house, if she may share the struggles and the triumphs of the one who seems to
her the best of all.

Young people who have been mutually and strongly attracted to one another
are a little impatient with advice from older ones, unless the advice happens to be
exactly in line with their own wishes; and yet it would seem as though parents
who had watched their children from the earliest days; who had taught them,
worked for them, and for them endured many self-denials, might be trusted to
wish the best for their children. A girl should at least take her mother into her
confidence when she begins to feel that some man who has hitherto been a mere
acquaintance is beginning to be to her something more. When there is a strong
opposition to a match on the part of relatives on either side, young and

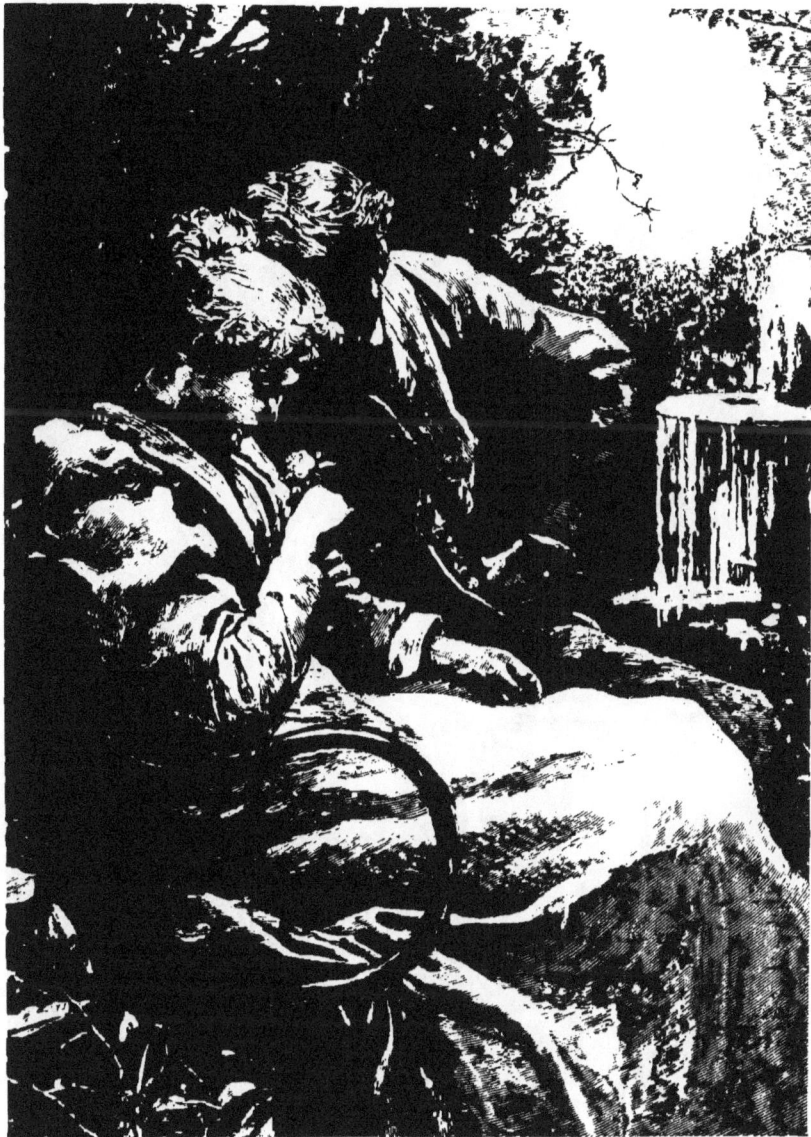

" In the spring-time a young man's fancies lightly turn to thoughts of love." (19)

inexperienced girls should be very sure that they are right before they resolve to go on in the face of friendly opposition.　Equally should men accept counsel in a kind spirit.　I have known very happy marriages which were rushed into in haste, and also some very unhappy ones, which might have been prevented had the parties

"The true woman is not afraid of poverty; she desires to share the fortunes of the man she loves."

thereto been willing to wait and accept good advice given by mature and loving friends.

For instance, a young man on a business journey was once at a certain way-station on a railroad when a beautiful girl entered the car with a package of school books in her hand. She seated herself quite near him, and the man watched with admiring eyes during the miles which stretched between several stations the pretty turn of her small head, the lovely curve of her ear, and the thick coil of nut-brown hair low at the back of her head. By and by a certain station was announced, and the young lady alighted. The young man also found himself at the end of his trip. As he stepped to the platform a friend met him and at once presented him to the maiden whom he had been watching, saying, "Let me introduce you to my sister." Within a week these young people were engaged and in one month from that

" * * * And then the soldier went back to the war."

day of their journey, they were married; and for forty years they lived together in a companionship so sweet, a comradeship so perfect, that wedded bliss in their experience made earth a heaven.

In another instance, during our Civil War, a soldier sitting by the camp-fire one night, received a package of letters and read them by the flickering light of a tallow candle, while his fellow soldiers sat by enviously watching him. Presently, from one of the letters fell a little photograph, the kind we used to call a carte-de-visite. It dropped unnoticed to the floor of the tent and one of the soldiers picked it up, glanced at it and saw the face of a most beautiful girl. He handed it to the owner, who looked up from his letter and said, "Ah ! my cousin Mildred. How sweet of her to send me her picture !" "Where does your cousin Mildred live?" was the question of the man who had been fascinated by a glance at the lovely face. "In such a place in Wisconsin," was the reply, "and when you have your leave of absence, as that village is near your home, I will give you a letter of introduction to her." In those stirring war days of the fife and drum and bugle, girls were not slow to lose their hearts to our gallant boys in blue or in gray, as the case might be. Everywhere a woman's heart throbs quicker at the sight of a uniform, and if it be a uniform to which she is loyal and which she loves, she is very apt to think the man who wears it a hero, and to refuse him little within her power to give.

Days passed and the leave of absence came ; the man went to see the young maiden, presented his letter of introduction, and proceeded to fall violently and with headlong speed in love with the fair girl. His love was returned with equal vehemence ; the courtship was very short, only ten days, and then the soldier went back to the war and the maiden remained alone at home with an engagement ring upon her finger. In due time, she went to him, since he could not come to her ; they were married and their united life for all this world's changes and chances, ups and downs, trials and triumphs, began. They had really known each other ten days—in other words, they had not known each other at all. Their life of thirty years together was a thirty-years' war. They never were happy ; they never were suited to one another ; their whole existence was a scene of storm and conflict, of petty squabbles and undignified quarrels. To their praise be it said, that they held together to the last ; for to neither of them would it have seemed right to seek separation by the too common method of divorce. But they married in haste to repent at leisure, poor, unsatisfied souls.

The fact is, whether young people believe it or not, that courtship, whether long or short, does not necessarily make people well acquainted with each other. A man or a girl who is in love idealizes the other party. Ralph invests Jennie with qualities she never dreamed of possessing; Jennie has an idea that Ralph is the soul of all honor, truth and chivalry. He may be a very commonplace fellow, but she will not admit it ; she may be a very ordinary young woman, but to him she is little short of an angel. The light that never was on sea nor land is floating round them both, and the truth is that they very often do not know one

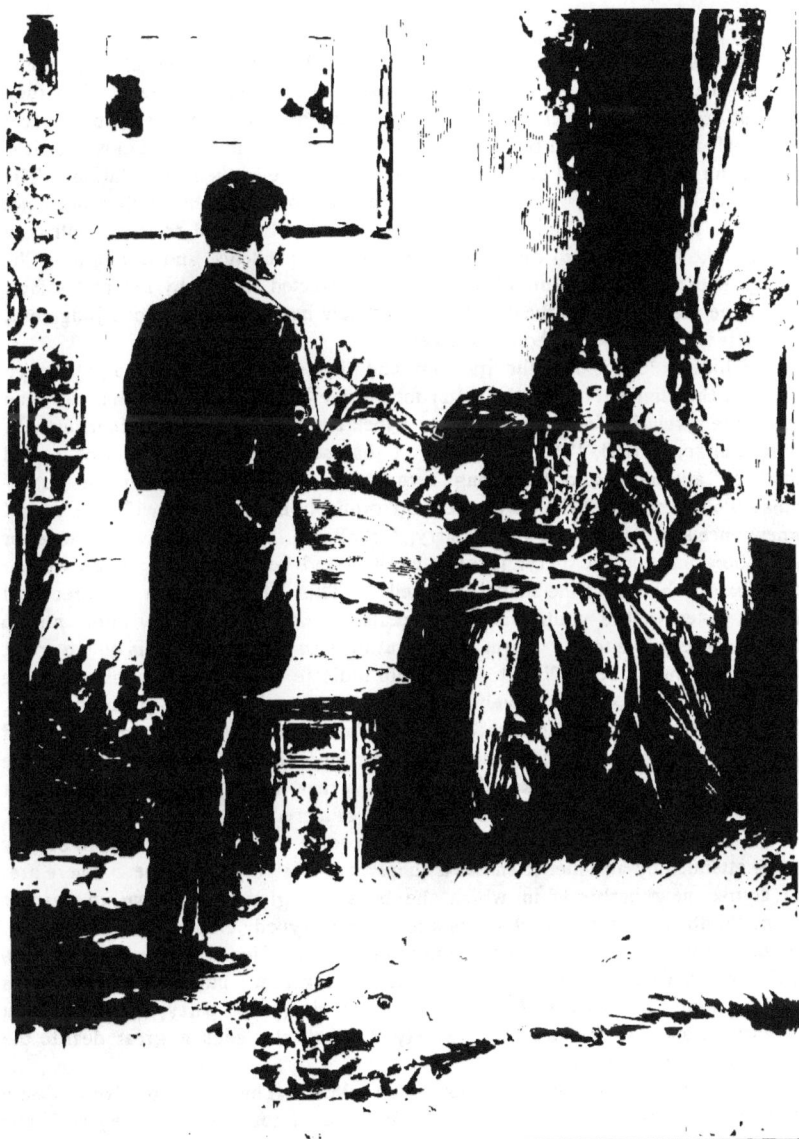

another well until they are married. This is why the first year of marriage is often so hard. People are finding out constantly little peculiarities which they did not dream existed each in the other, and they are much surprised to discover that perfection is far from being where they expected to find it. Therefore, it is as well for those who fall in love to do so with people in their own station. The young woman who consents to elope with a man of whom her father does not approve ; who has not had her advantages of education and training, will very likely wake up too late to wish she had acted with prudence and foresight. The young man who selects an illiterate bride, attracted merely by her pretty face, may have occasion to rue the day that he ever saw her and lost his good judgment, and fettered himself with bonds of steel.

Falling in love is only the first step, and there should be time enough between this and the final arrival at the altar for people to be quite sure that they can stand the revelations and developments which are sure to come after marriage. A wise man once said, "When I marry, I shall seek the good daughter of a good mother," and he was not far wrong, because a girl trained up under the guardianship of a gentle, Christian mother will probably make a good wife. A man I knew once said loftily, "When I marry, I shall not look for beauty, or grace, or education, but for true piety; favor is deceitful and beauty is vain ; but a woman that feareth the Lord, she shall be praised." This lofty sentiment was received by the sisters of the youth with ill-concealed amusement, for they knew him to be very susceptible to the charm of a beautiful face ; as, indeed, it is only a credit that a man should be. They took pains to indicate to him a woman of admirable religious character, but as homely as a hedge-fence, and as clumsy as an elephant. They said to him, recalling his words, that there was the wife whom he would probably like to win ; but, no, he passed her by with indifference, and when he married, he was attracted like other men, by a trim figure, a light step, a bright eye and a graceful manner. And his wife was a credit to the whole connection.

The present custom, which leads young people when they go about in society to be attended by an older friend as a chaperone, is a very good one. There are, of course, neighborhoods in which the boys and girls have grown up together from childhood, where everybody is known to everybody else, where there is not, perhaps, the same need for care in the intercourse of friends that there is in large cities, where comparative strangers are thrown together ; but a chaperone takes nothing from the pleasure of a picnic, an excursion, or a party, and if she be a pleasant woman of tact and true gayety of heart, she adds a great deal to the interest of the occasion.

Even engaged people should not be too selfish. They may not always desire to be in the presence of the family; but they should not too exclusively seek one another's company, nor desire to spend evening after evening entirely by themselves. The requirements of good form to-day are in the line of common sense. It is not for a girl's health, happiness or beauty, to remain hour after hour, evening after evening, in the company of one whom she may truly love, but who should not take her entirely from her parents, brothers and sisters until the time comes when they are to cast in their lot together and become husband and wife. Nor should she be submitted too constantly to a severe emotional strain.

Long engagements are to be deprecated. Quite often they come to nothing. As a rope stretched out too long grows thin in its weakest part, so the engagement which is protracted over years finally becomes a burdensome thing, or the love of one or the other seems to wear out ; and, yet, I knew a couple who were engaged for forty years. They never married. Promptly at eight o'clock in the evening of a certain night in the week, the young man's horse was seen tied at the gate of his ladylove. Time passed ; the brown hair and the golden hair both grew white ; the young people were transformed into middle aged and then into old people, and they were lovers always, he treating her with a grand courtesy and politeness ; she most friendly and beautiful in her devotion to him ; but they never married. Nobody knew why. It was supposed that they thought that while each had money enough to live on alone, neither had quite enough to make it prudent for them to join their fortunes. If this were so, they were a pair of cowards. Nothing mercenary should enter in to defeat the plans of true love. Love, thank God, is independent of dollars and cents. It can and does often flourish in the poor man's cabin ; it sometimes flies from the rich man's palace.

One word more. As a rule, people who fall in love with one another should not have too great disparity of age. We hear of and see very happy marriages sometimes where wife or husband is much older than the other. As a rule, however, it is unfortunate for a man of fifty to fall in love with a girl of twenty or twenty-five. He has had his youth and his time for pleasure, and cares mostly to be quiet and hug the fireside; the wife is still a girl at heart and desires some pleasant excitement and change of scene. Equally, if the wife be the older, the husband may find himself almost in the position of a son to a mother. People should be as to age somewhere near together. The difference of a year or two, of five or even ten years, is not material on either side, although it is better that the husband should be the older. Women grow old somewhat faster than men do and their chances for happiness are greater if the wife be the younger, or if they be nearly of an age.

To look at life from the same standpoint, to have interests in common, to walk cheerily on the road together, keeping an equal pace, to care for the same things, to work and save and share little sacrifices and have common ambitions, and to grow and develop, are the privileges of those who truly love.

"Our little friends try to show how much they love us. A child holds up his hands high, and says, ' I love you all that ! ' Well, there is a measure of human love ; there is a limit—an 'all that.'

"A little boy once called out to his father, who had mounted his horse for a journey, 'Good-bye, papa, I love you thirty miles long ! ' A little sister quickly added, 'Good-bye, dear papa, you will never ride to the end of my love ! '

" This is what Jesus means to say : ' My love has no limit ; it passeth knowledge.'

" Paul, who knew as much about it as most, says, ' The height and depth, and length and breadth '—of the love of Jesus Christ ; it ' passeth knowledge.' "

## The Courtin'.

God makes sech nights, all white an' still
    Fur'z you can look or listen,
Moonshine an' snow on field an' hill,
    All silence an' all glisten.

Zekle crep' up, quite unbeknown,
    An' peeked in thru the winder,
An' there sot Huldy all alone,
    'Ith no one nigh to hender.

A fireplace filled the room's one side
    With half a cord o' wood in—
There warnt no stoves (tell Comfort died)
    To bake ye to a puddin'.

The wa'nut logs shot sparkles out
    Towards the pootiest, bless her !
An' leetle flames danced all about
    The chiny on the dresser.

Agin the chimbley crooknecks hung,
    An' in amongst 'em rusted
The ole queen's-arm thet Gran'ther Young
    Fetched back from Concord busted.

The very room, coz she was in,
    Seemed warm from floor to ceilin',
An' she looked full ez rosy agin
    Ez the apples she was peelin'.

'T was kin' o' kingdom-come to look
  On sech a blessed cretur;
A dogrose blushin' to a brook
  Ain't modester nor sweeter.

He was six foot o' man A 1,
  Clean grit an' human natur';
None couldn't quicker pitch a ton
  Nor dror a furrer straighter.

He'd sparked it with full twenty gals,
  He'd squired 'em, danced 'em, druv 'em,
Fust this one, an' then thet, by spells—
  All is, he couldn't love 'em.

But long o' her his veins 'ould run
  All crinkly, like curled maple ;
The side she breshed felt full o' sun
  Ez a south slope in Ap'il.

She thought no v'ice hed sech a swing
  Ez hisn in the choir;
My ! when he made Ole Hunderd ring,
  She knowed the Lord was nigher.

An' she'd blush scarlit, right in prayer,
  When her new meetin'-bunnet
Felt somehow thru its crown a pair
  O' blue eyes sot upon it.

Thet night, I tell ye, she looked some !
  She seemed to 've got a new soul,
For she felt sartin-sure he'd come,
  Down to her very shoe-sole.

She heered a foot, an' knowed it tu,
  A-raspin' on the scraper—
All ways to once her feelin's flew,
  Like sparks in burnt-up paper.

He kin' o' l'itered on the mat,
  Some doubtfle o' the sekle;
His heart kep' goin' pity-pat,
  But hern went pity Zekle.

# FALLING IN LOVE.

An' yit she gin her cheer a jerk
  Ez though she wished him furder,
An' on her apples kep' to work,
  Parin' away like murder.

" You want to see my Pa, I s'pose?"
  "Wal, no; I come dasignin'—"
" To see my Ma? She's sprinklin'clo'es
  Agin to-morrer's i'nin'."

To say why gals act so or so,
  Or don't, 'ould be presumin';
Mebby to mean yes an' say no
  Comes natoral to women.

He stood a spell on one foot fust,
  Then stood a spell on t'other,
An' on which one he felt the wust
  He couldn't ha' told ye nuther.

Says he, " I 'd better call agin;"
  Says she, " Think likely, Mister:"
That last word pricked him like a pin,
  An'—wal, he up an' kist her.

When Ma bimeby upon 'em slips,
  Huldy sot pale ez ashes,
All kin' o' smily roun' the lips
  An' teary roun' the lashes.

For she was jes' the quiet kind
  Whose naturs never vary,
Like streams that keep a summer mind
  Snowhid in Jenooary.

The blood clost roun' her heart felt glued
  Too tight for all expressin',
Tell mother see how metters stood,
  And gin 'em both her blessin'.

Then her red come back like the tide
  Down to the Bay o' Fundy,
An' all I know is they was cried
  In meetin', come nex' Sunday.—*James Russell Lowell.*

# CHAPTER II.

## Wooed and Married and A'.

GETTING ready to marry is a very practical sort of undertaking, and should enlist the careful thought of both parties in the matter. On the part of a man, it implies self-denial, in order that he may save enough to begin the new home. Perhaps, in the country it means that he will choose a site for a house, clear away the trees, plant the fields, and have what seems to me the most ideal thing in the world, a home of his very own all ready for his bride. In the city, the man will put by as he can, bit by bit, a little money, so that when the time comes, he may be able to pay the rent of a house, furnish it and have something ahead with which to begin housekeeping for two.

Forethought and prevision are very necessary for people about to join their forces in married life. The man's share will be to select the home, furnish it, and be ready to meet whatever expenses come in the way of rent, taxes, or whatever expense properly falls to his part. If by joining a building and loan association, or in some other similar way he is able at once to begin the buying of a home so that he will have a place where the family life may begin on a permanent basis instead of in the nomadic way which many Americans in cities find necessary, the family will be better off from the start.

On the part of the bride, careful mothers usually see that she has a good outfit of linen in all that is necessary—sheeting, pillow cases, towels, napkins, table-cloths, and whatever else in that way is deemed desirable. In French and German families it is quite common for the mother to begin early in her daughter's life, putting aside here and there, as she can, something for her daughter's dowry, so that when the day comes for the girl to go from her father's house to that of her husband, she carries with her a good outfit of all household linen. In some lands it is of her own spinning and weaving.

Brides make a great mistake when they wear themselves out and spend a great deal of time and money in preparing a very lavish outfit for themselves in the way of personal clothing. One would think to see the great supplies of underclothing, the munificent and royally lavish outfit of dresses which some brides think necessary, that they were going at once to emigrate to countries where there were no shops, and that they were never in their lives expecting to have any money to buy the smallest things for themselves again. A girl sometimes arrives at her wedding day thoroughly worn out and exhausted both in body and mind by the incessant sewing and planning and fitting she has undergone in the hands of dressmakers, and all because she has thought it requisite to supply herself with quantities of finery and an immense supply of clothes which she really did not need. A modest outfit in the way of dress is all that any bride needs, whether she be rich or poor.

Every bride requires, if she can possibly have it, a pretty gown for the great day itself. From early times white has seemed the most beautiful color for a bride's dress, and if it seem reasonable and she can manage it, the bride should leave her father's house in elegance, and on her wedding day she should be beautifully arrayed; but simplicity and beauty are not always costly, and a simple gown plainly made will set off a young girl quite as finely as one which is costly enough to stand alone, and richly wrought with pearls and trimmed with priceless lace. It is always appropriate for a girl to wear her traveling gown if she choose on her marriage day, or should she prefer it, the dress which is to be her best one, and which perhaps may be a beautiful gown of silk appropriately trimmed. The rest of her outfit will depend very much on where she is to live; how much company she expects to receive; and what her work in life will be. A farmer's wife doing her own work will need gowns which can be washed, and a plentiful supply of aprons for her work in the kitchen and dairy. A girl going to an elegant city home, where she will have servants to wait upon her, will need beautiful house dresses, which may be as dainty and pretty as she chooses, and she will require also a greater number of changes and things more in the mode as may befit the people with whom she will associate.

Every woman, if she can, should have a black gown as part of her wardrobe, either of cloth or of silk. There are many occasions when one needs a black gown, and there are few occasions in which one cannot wear it appropriately with a little trimming to brighten it up. In Mrs. Ruth McEnery Stuart's amusing story called "The Dividing Fence," she says of the people in Simpkinsville that on all occasions a black alpaca gown in hand was considered an admirable thing for a woman to possess. It might be lightened up with a valenciennes ruffle or a blue ribbon or a red ribbon bow; but the black alpaca, from its first day to its last, was a necessary part of a well-dressed woman's outfit. In that most charming book of J. M. Barrie's, "Margaret Ogilvy," we find that the charming and beautiful old lady considered her black silk gown the one part of her outfit which she would put on when she wished to make a good appearance. "Well," on one occasion said her son, "how would you dress yourself if you were going to that editor's office?" "Of course," said the dear old lady, "I would wear my silk

A GERMAN MARRIAGE CUSTOM.

(31)

and my Sabbath bonnet." In vain her son told her that she would look sweeter in her little gray shawl and her bonny white cap. She shook her head and said positively, "I tell you if ever I go in that man's office, I go in silk." The advantage of a black gown is very great for those who cannot afford many dresses, because other colors are remembered; but one does not recall very much about a decent black dress beyond the fact that it served its turn well.

However, I did not mean to take up all this chapter in talking of such things as dress and furnishing when one is thinking of marriage. When you really consider it, there is nothing so revolutionary in the world as the coming together of two people brought up in different families and under different influences, to make a new home of their own. John has been accustomed all his life to the way his people look at everything; his father, his mother, his brothers and sisters and aunts and cousins all have their own ideas about life. Mary, on the other hand, has come from a different set of people, with different traditions, and her people have their ways, their friendships, their modes of looking at life, which have insensibly passed into her blood. John and Mary must start out for themselves, and they will form together a new household, and their family life is to be a thing by itself and quite independent of what either has known before. So it is just as well for John to make up his mind that his wife, dear and lovely as she will be, is not going to be his mother over again; and Mary may as well remember that her John, though in her eyes perfect, will not be precisely like her own father.

For the first year the two will do well to keep entirely clear of relations in their family life. It is never a good plan for young people, if it can be helped, to form a part of another family, nor should they, except where there is some imperative reason for it, bring in fathers or mothers or other relatives as an integral part of their home. There are exceptional reasons sometimes why a widowed mother or a father otherwise to be left solitary, must come into the new home; but the ideal thing is for a husband and wife to begin quite by themselves. Then there is nobody to notice when they have little tiffs, nobody to take the part of either. Occasionally, asperities which would be like little fires easily fanned into a flame, die of themselves if the two are alone.

Before marriage both parties should think very seriously of the fact that they cannot live any more only for pleasure. There must be on both sides self-denial. In return for the self-denial, there will come a great and hallowed joy in life, but self-denial there must be. Before taking a step which is irrevocable, both man and woman should always count the cost and decide whether or not they are willing to give it. Marriage is in its best estate a service in which there is perfect freedom; but it is the freedom which exists within well-ordered bounds of law and order.

A particular part of fitness for happy marriage is religious faith.  I once heard a good minister observe that if a woman married a man whose principles were not established and who was not a professing Christian, it was usually in her power to win him to the side of Christ; but that so far as his observation went, a man seldom got the better of the case who married a heathen girl.  A Christian man united to a woman who is indifferent or averse to religion, or skeptical, or who holds erroneous views on the most vital of all subjects, will probably lose very much of the spirituality of life and fall away from his own faith.  Husband and wife, to gain the highest there is in marriage, should be agreed on the one great subject; and, therefore, before the time comes when they clasp hands and walk together, it is well for them each to say to the other, we will walk before the Lord in unity.  As a rule it is not well for people of broadly opposing faiths to marry.  A Romanist and a Protestant do not harmonize; the Methodist and the Presbyterian may easily sink their differences, the one agreeing to give something up for the sake of the other.  Whatever the form of religious faith, it will be well for the two who are about to marry to take into account the fact that from the hour of their union they are no longer two, but one.  They should agree, therefore, to attend the same church, and from the very beginning, they should make up their minds to enter upon church life and to take upon themselves certain duties with reference to Christ's work in the world.  If the husband be already established in church work where he is accomplishing good it seems most fitting that the wife should accompany him, rather than that he should leave his work and go with her; but there is no arbitrary rule in a matter of this kind.  Usually, it is to be settled by common sense and kindliness and mutual helpfulness and sacrifice.

In thinking of marriage, each should determine that he or she will begin with no secrets.  I have sometimes been asked whether in case of some sin in the past, or some wrongdoing, it would be right to bury that and start in on the new life without any confession or revelation of that which is a grief in the past of one or the other.  My answer always is that there can be no happiness which is not founded upon perfect truth and candor.  Fortunately and happily, few well-brought up people have any skeleton in their closets, and there are no troubles and trials in the past which ought to be revealed, so far as their own persons are concerned; but wherever there is anything in relation to any member of the family, to anything which has to do at all with the well-being and the good name of either, let there be no reserves.  Confidence is a stepping-stone to happiness.  From the outset, let the two who have joined their hands know all that there is to be known each of the other.  There will then be no danger of disagreeable secrets and revelations in days to come.  It is of the greatest importance, and young people should remember this, that all

NAILING UP THE ROSE-TREE.

through youth the life should be held up to a stern and rigid standard of purity, so that from the very first these two, who out of all the world have chosen each other, may feel assured there is no sin to interpose a barrier between them.

By this I do not mean that a person with an exaggerated sense of duty, and, perhaps, too sensitive a conscience should go over the whole chapter of life that is passed, and think of every little smile and word and innocent flirtation, as if it had been a grave transgression. It is only that in things of grave importance and interest, which have affected the life, there should be no reserves.

This obligation to candor is a duty equally laid upon man and upon woman. When thinking of marriage you are considering a sacrament.

I overheard the other day a bit of conversation between two young men in a public conveyance which interested me very much. They were not talking in low tones, but took the whole car into their confidence. Said one to the other, "I have not arrived at the point where I am willing to surrender my independence. I know a great many nice girls who are fine to have for friends and for helping on a good time; but I have not yet met a girl of whom I could be fond enough to think of spending my whole life with her; always seeing her cn the opposite side of the table; going about with her and not having the chance of going with any other girl." His companion remarked, "Oh, well, there is plenty of time yet. You are young, and when you meet the right one you will throw all your theories overboard." "Well," said the other, "Whatever I do, I will never have a long engagement. I think that is one of the most trying things a person can possibly have." In this I quite agreed with the speaker, as I have said before.

It is worth while to reflect that constancy is an essential part of married happiness; that the man or woman who is married can no longer rove from flower to flower, a bee in search of honey; but that from the time of selection the partner for life is to be the one who receives all the honor, all the reverence and all of the exclusive affection. Ruskin says:

"We are foolish, and without excuse foolish, in speaking of the 'superiority' of one sex to the other, as if they could be compared in similar things. Each has what the other has not; each completes the other, and is completed by the other; they are in nothing alike, and the happiness and perfection of both depends on each asking and receiving from the other what the other only can give.

"Now their separate characters are briefly these: The man's power is active, progressive, defensive. He is eminently the doer, the creator, the discoverer, the defender. His intellect is for speculation and invention; his energy for adventure, for war and for conquest, wherever war is just, wherever conquest necessary. But the woman's power is for rule, not for battle—and her intellect

DEPARTURE FOR THE HONEYMOON.

(37)

is not for invention or creation, but for sweet ordering, arrangement and decision. She sees the qualities of things, their claims and their places. Her great function is praise; she enters into no contest, but infallibly judges the crown of contest. By her office and place she is protected from all danger and temptation. The man, in his rough work in open world, must encounter all peril and trial; to him, therefore, the failure, the offence, the inevitable error; often he must be wounded or subdued, often misled, and always hardened. But he guards the woman from all this. Within his house, as ruled by her, unless she herself has sought it, need enter no danger, no temptation, no cause of error or offence. This is the true nature of home—it is the place of peace; the shelter, not only from all injury, but from all terror, doubt and division. In so far as it is not this, it is not home. So far as the anxieties of the outer life penetrate into it, and the inconsistently-minded, unknown, unloved, or hostile society of the outer world is allowed by either husband or wife to cross the threshold, it ceases to be home; it is then only a part of that outer world which you have roofed over, and lighted fire in. But so far as it is a sacred place, a vestal temple, a temple of the hearth watched over by household gods, before whose faces none may come but those whom they can receive with love—so far as it is this, and roof and fire are types only of a nobler shade and light—shade as of the rock in a weary land, and light as of the pharos in the stormy sea—so far it vindicates the name, and fulfills the praise of home.   ·

"And wherever a true wife comes, this home is always round her. The stars only may be over her head; the glow-worm in the night-cold grass may be the only fire at her foot; but home is yet wherever she is; and for a noble woman it stretches far round her, better than ceiled with cedar or painted with vermilion, shedding its quiet light far, for those who else were homeless.

"This, then, I believe to be—will you not admit it to be?—the woman's true place and power. But do you not see that to fulfill this she must—as far as one can use such terms of a human creature—be incapable of error? So far as she rules, all must be right, or nothing is. She must be enduringly, incorruptibly good; instinctively, infallibly wise—wise, not for self-development, but for self-renunciation; wise, not that she may set herself above her husband, but that she may never fail from his side; wise, not with the narrowness of insolent and loveless pride, but with the passionate gentleness of an infinitely variable, because infinitely applicable, modesty of service—the true changefulness of woman. In that great sense—' La Donna e mobile,' not 'Qual pium al vento;' no, nor yet ' Variable as the shade, by the light quivering aspen made;' but variable as the light, manifold in fair and serene division, that it may take the color of all that it falls upon, and exalt it."

If we accept these wise words of Ruskin, we shall begin our home building on a very firm basis.

" Wherever a true wife comes, this home is always round her."

## Wedded Hands.

The year, sweet wife, is on the wane;
   The happy-hearted year,
Which brought us only tithes of pain,
   And golden sheaves of cheer.

Beside the glowing embers, we
   Need envy no one's pelf;
Content am I to partner be
   In firm of "Wife and Self."

Swift glide away the last low sands,
   Fast fades the hearth-fire's light.
We dare the world with wedded hands,
   Good-night, my love, good-night.

# CHAPTER III.

## Settling the House.

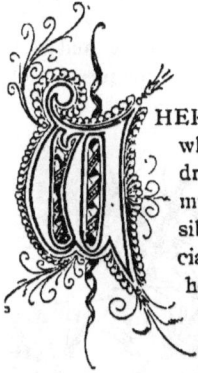

HEREVER the house be which is chosen for the new home, whether in city or country, the first thing to attend to is the drainage. People who wish to live in perfect health and strength must be sure that there is nowhere near them the lurking possibility of anything which will breed germs of disease. Especially in the country one needs to know that the well near the house is good; that there is an outlet for whatever might occasion trouble from a cesspool or anything of that sort. In the city, one must be sure that the plumbing is in perfect condition. This is really a sine qua non for health and consequent comfort and safety. Then the householder must look well to the cellar, especially if the house be one in which other tenants have dwelt before him. Some years ago, in the city where I live, a whole family—father, mother and six children—were stricken down with diphtheria, and in one week the father and five of the children died. This occurrence was in a beautiful street where the houses were exceptionally fine. The local Board of Health ordered an investigation into the condition of the house, and found the cellar so foul that a candle would not burn in it. We need always to look well to cellars, pantries, closets and all shut up places in which the air has been closed, where perhaps careless people have thrown matter which may decay. A mysterious illness broke out once in a community where I was temporarily staying as a summer boarder, and was especially fierce in the house where I had taken my quarters. This house stood in the midst of a beautiful meadow with trees around it, and from the front porch we had a charming view of a mountain landscape. It would have seemed that no conditions could possibly be more favorable for health than those which surrounded us there; but a great many in the neighborhood sickened; several died, and in our own house there were cases of disease approaching typhoid in character. Finally, a rigid examination of the wells took place, and it was found that organic matter in them was the cause of the entire trouble. Perfect cleanliness and everlasting vigilance are the price which must be paid for health. Many deaths are attributed to Divine providence which are due to human neglect.

In moving into a new house, or into a house which is new to you, the first thing to do is to thoroughly clean it. Every woman knows the value of the

broom and the scrubbing brush, of soap and water, of lime, kalsomine, and fresh
paper and paint.   If there is the least suspicion in any room of the presence of
vermin, it is best to have the old paper torn down, all cracks and apertures
puttied up carefully and painted, and then to have
fresh paper on the walls.   One cannot be too careful and too thorough in the cleansing of a house
before putting down carpets and rugs.   The walls
must be thoroughly wiped, the cornices dusted, the
blinds brushed, the windows washed, the paint and
marble scoured, and not a crack or a crevice in a
closet or shelf left neglected.   Then open all the
windows and let a free current of air sweep through
the house, and let the sunshine in, the blessed

"This house stood in the midst of a beautiful meadow with trees around it."

life-giving sunshine. In furnishing the house it is best to begin with the top floor and work gradually downwards, or if the house be an apartment, and the rooms all on one floor, arrange the dining-room, bedrooms and kitchen first, and leave the parlor till the last. Before laying carpets it is best to spread the floor with papers. Newspapers will answer the purpose, but there is a sort of wadded paper which comes for the purpose; and if you wish your carpet to have a very soft feeling under the foot, you can obtain this by putting down several layers of this paper. You may have noticed in hotels how soft and thick the carpets feel under your feet. This feeling is procured by placing several thicknesses of paper lining under the carpets. Cushions or pads should be put under the stair carpet. They save the wear of the carpet and also prevent noise from the rushing to and fro of children and others in the house. If possible, get a carpet man to make, stretch and lay your carpets. It is very unhandy work for novices, and it is better to save somewhere else and not wear yourself out by this labor, if it can be helped. Should your home, however, be in a place where this sort of help cannot be readily obtained, do not fail to let John use his strong arms and stronger back than yours in helping you with the hardest of the work. When people are first married it is very essential that they should begin right. The wife often is inclined in those halcyon days to spare her husband from doing many things, and the husband—bless his heart—while he wishes to save her, will often, from sheer carelessness, let her go on, thinking she prefers to do things which he ought to take upon himself. In the start take for granted that the husband means to lend a helping hand whenever he can.

After putting down the carpets, put up window curtains and shades, and then arrange the furniture in the way you like best. If you are like me you will not be contented to keep it always in the place in which it is originally set. For my part, I like from time to time a change of appearance in my rooms. Many people, however, prefer to find a good place for bed, bureau and sofa, and then to let them stay where they are placed for all the rest of the time. It is merely a question of taste, you see.

In choosing paper for your house, remember that rooms on the north side of the house, where there is little sun, should have lighter and brighter papers and drapery than rooms where there is plenty of sunshine. A bit of yellow in a house produces an effect of cheer and sunlight; so that in a shaded room a yellow hanging or a vase of a yellow color set in a corner will produce an effect of brightness and cheer. Colors are cold or warm, you know. Red gives an impression of warmth; blue and green have a cold and chilling effect; pink is always cheery, and olive and pearl tints and the various shades of gray are very restful. For bedrooms nothing is better than cool pretty matting laid down upon the floor, and this is not expensive, so that the whole furnishing of the house may

be very much lessened if matting is used instead of carpet.   Painted floors, or
hard wood floors, with rugs which can be taken up and laid down with ease,
shaken every week and restored to their places, are favorites with many people in
in these days.   When you are buying bedsteads for your house it is better to
choose either the pretty bedsteads of white iron, or brass, if you can afford them,

"The wife is often inclined to spare her husband."

than to purchase the most expensive bedsteads of wood.   For cleanliness and
durability the metal bedstead far surpasses the ordinary one of wood.   Still,
a great deal is to be said for a beautifully carved mahogany, black walnut
or oak bedstead, if that is your choice, or if you have one as an heirloom.
There has been a return in recent years to the old fashion of having draperies

over one's bed, and it must be admitted that they look very ornamental; but, so far as health is concerned, it is better to have nothing in the way of a canopy, unless you live in a mosquito haunted region, where you must have draperies over the couch. By all means see that you have screens ready for every window, and, if possible, screen doors for your kitchen, so that the swarms of flies which torment the housekeeper in the summer may not drive you from all your patience. Screens also are a great protection against the venomous little mosquito. You need not be like Josiah Allen's wife and spend your whole life in pouncing upon the poor fly who finds its way in. By all means, avoid flies if you can; but if you are unfortunate enough to have them, remember perhaps they are sent to you to discipline you into sweetness of temper and make you less irritable than you would be without them. If possible, have a storeroom or other place into which you may relegate all empty trunks and boxes. Your wood and coal will be put in bins in the cellar or woodshed. Here, too, empty boxes and barrels may be stored.

As far as possible, have the house arranged in a very orderly and systematic manner. A writer on the subject of housekeeping says very wisely: "The individuality of a house is determined principally by its decoration. The necessaries of furnishing are common to all; it is in the minor points of ornament that the house mistress shows her true self." Thus, in the buying of china, one may choose from a great variety. You may have either plain white, which has the advantage of being easily replaced if broken, or you may find quaint Japanese or Chinese patterns, and a great variety of decorated china, much of it at a moderate price. Cut-glass is, of course, very expensive; but pressed glass in these days is found in such perfection that it is almost as beautiful as its more costly neighbor. Plated ware makes a very good show and does not tempt the prowling burglar as solid silver does. I have never understood where the pleasure is in having articles of solid silver, which must be kept in a safe at the bank, and brought out only on great and solemn occasions, because of the fear of robbers; while one may have most beautiful articles in plated ware, which have the effect of the solid silver, and yet which it would not break your heart or bankrupt your purse to part with.

There is room in our bed-chambers for an endless variety of the little touches which make the difference between homeliness and bareness. When you go into a hotel or boarding house you are struck at once with the desolate look of the rooms, because they have only the necessary articles, and no fanciful touches. In your own house you have the chance to use a great many beautiful little articles —table covers, splashers, whisk-broom cases, odds and ends, scarfs, tidies, and no end of cushions.

Let me urge you, if you are about to begin housekeeping, not to be deluded into the purchase of a folding-bed, even if it does take up less room than a

bedstead.   It is neither one thing nor the other, masquerading in the daytime as a
cabinet or a bookcase in a clumsy way and deceiving nobody.  It is always a bed,
and proclaims itself so, even with its mirror in front and its air of standing aside
against the wall.   A divan, which any carpenter will make for you, and which is
a lounge in the daytime, and a bed at night, is very much better.   If you have
one made by a carpenter, give him the dimensions you want.   A plain box fitted
up with springs; over this a mattress which may be covered with pretty rugs in
the daytime, and on which you may have no end of beautiful pillows and
cushions, is itself an addition to any room.   If you choose, you may have a divan
made in such a way that underneath the lid it will be a box, in which you may
keep dresses, blankets, or anything else you choose.

An essential thing in almost any room is a large screen.   This may be plain
or showy, made at home, covered with wall paper, cretonne or satine, or it may
be purchased at a store and may be extremely ornamental.   It serves as a parti-
tion to shut off anything which you wish to hide from the general view; as in
the bedroom, the wash hand basin and its accessories, or it shuts off a draught or
keeps off the too great heat of the fire.

# CHAPTER IV.

## Color and Light.

F you have ever studied the matter at all you have been convinced that color plays an important part in the comfort, as well as in the luxury of life. There are great differences in the degree of appreciation of color which people have, and these differences are determined largely by association and by training. Of the color-blind we are not just now thinking, but of those who misuse color. For instance, you observe in the dress of the Italian peasants who immigrate to our country, a lavish use of what may be called crude and violent color. They wear intense and brilliant purples, scarlets and greens. Very often there is no attempt at harmony or at blending; but the colors, strong in themselves, are just in that sort of extreme contrast which sets one's very teeth on edge, if she prefers harmony and a gentle gradation of tint and hue.

We have learned in these days to value soft shadings of color in our houses; the melting of one dim tint in another, so that our rooms rest us, rather than weary our eyes. Persons who go to Italy to reside tell us that in engaging a furnished apartment in Rome or Florence they find, as a rule, the use of strong primitive colors, which almost swear at one another in walls and curtains. In Germany, there is apt to be less of the startling in combination; but the effect is often bare and cold. The same may be said of Holland. In England and Scotland, a homely comfort prevails; but it is only where people in any country have made a study of color that they are able to show good effects in its use.

An artist tells us that there are colors which are warm and others which are cold. All colors that approach yellow in their tone, are warm. The coldest of all the colors is blue. Red is colder than yellow and warmer than blue. If we mix a little yellow with blue, thus making a somewhat greenish blue, it is a warm blue; mixed with a little red, it approaches purple, but is still a cold blue, but not so cold as pure cold blue that has no suggestion of green. A little yellow mixed with red makes the red warmer; a little blue mixed with red imparts a cold tint. Yellow mixed with red becomes warmer; mixed with blue it becomes a colder yellow. Pure white mixed with pure yellow makes a golden yellow. The purples are cold as they approach blue and warm as they approach red; the greens are cold as they approach blue and warm as they approach yellow. White may be cold or warm; a warm white is yellowish; a cold white is blueish. Lavender is a cold color, being a purple that is much mixed with cold white and blue. Violet is a warm color in comparison, being a purple much mixed with red and a little warm white.

These hints given by an artist may help one in determining the color she will have on her rooms. For instance, a woman is considering of what tone she will have her walls and ceiling. She must think whether the room faces the sun and will be flooded with pleasant sunshine, or whether it has a northern exposure and will therefore be cold and dim. In the latter case, she will do well to have plenty of yellow in the tint she chooses for her papering or her kalsomining, and, if possible, she will hang curtains of yellow silk or cretonne of some thinner yellow fabric in her windows. A great deal of yellow in a room which has little sunlight somehow produces an effect of the sun. In such a room, one may to advantage have wall paper of a warm soft red and a carpet of wood brown, with a glimmer of red in it here and there.

I know of a house in New York City which stands on the shady side of a very closely built street. It has windows only in front; none whatever in the rear, and no sunshine ever gets into the house; yet the whole effect of the furnishing is singularly cheerful. The coloring of the rooms and furniture throughout is white and yellow. All the woodwork is white; the walls are white; the draperies are yellow; the window seats are cushioned with yellow and there is nothing dark or heavy anywhere in the furnishing of the house. All sombre tints and tones are avoided, so that it comes to one as a surprise that the house should be really one which gets no sunlight. The reason that there are no back windows is that the house is built straight up against the side wall of another house on another street. People who live where they have ample room to have windows on every side of the house, and God's free air and sunlight coming at every turn, should not envy those whose lot is cast in the midst of towns. Necessarily, many people in a city like New York have to live, or at least sleep, in dark rooms to which the sunlight never penetrates, and this is a great disadvantage.

In choosing a color of paint or a papering for one's wall, it is well to remember that we have to live a long time with a house dressed in one sort of paint and paper. The papering which looks beautiful in a roll on the counter of the man who sells it, may become terribly trying to you when you are obliged to see it by daylight and candle light for ten or twelve years; and if you are to have a fit of sickness or a period of weakness and nervous depression, it is well to think whether you could then endure it in a room which might be trying to your senses during days when you were shut in from out of doors. It is a good plan to let every member of the family give advice on so important a subject as the furnishing of a house. One person should not force his or her ideas on the rest; but

4        "God's free air and sunlight coming at every turn."        (49)

where it is possible all should have a voice in deciding. A home is a composite affair in which, from the least to the greatest all have a stake.

Kalsomining is so soft and pleasing in the surface it presents, that no one need hesitate in choosing it for ceiling or walls.

A home does not shoot up like Jonah's garden in a night. It is the growth and development of months and years; and one beautiful thing about it is that it is never finished; one may always find something to improve, something to adorn, something to beautify. A home is the one thing on earth which keeps us young and glad, the one Eden left us here below.

In the hanging of pictures in a house, one must be guided a little by the height of the ceiling. As a rule, pictures should not be hung above the level of the eyes. They are better hung too low than too high. It is wise to avoid too much formality in their arrangement; they look better hung irregularly, and the framing may be as varied as the purse or the taste of the owner. One should always have pictures about a house, and they need not necessarily be costly in these days when every illustrated paper and magazine shows designs which lend themselves most beautifully to artistic effect. In a girl's room recently, I was interested to see a collection of extremely beautiful pictures taken from current periodicals and simply tacked up without frames here and there on the wall. With a few photographs, a vase or two, and her hanging shelves, where beautiful books abounded, her room was exceedingly tasteful and pretty, a fit and dainty setting for her sweet self.

What do you understand by the word picturesque? To one person it bears one, and to another a quite different meaning. We talk of a picturesque landscape, of a picturesque house, of a picturesque parlor. My idea of the picturesque is the harmonious, the soft, the restful, the tranquilizing. I do not like to see in any house a jumble of articles carelessly thrown together with no central idea around which they are grouped. The tendency lately has been to multiply objects simply because they are pretty in themselves, with no special relation of each to the other. Therefore, we find some rooms which are filled with a miscellaneous collection of bric-a-brac, rooms which suggest shops or museums much more than they resemble homes. A vase, a statuette, a lamp, should be a delightful thing in itself; then it should be placed where its position in the room shows it to advantage—the lamp on a table in a corner, conveying the idea that people will sit beside it to read or to talk; the vase or statuette against a little curtain or screen which will bring out the purity of its tone and the beauty of its shape.

Nothing is more beautiful in a room than a few plants in good condition, or a cluster of palms and rubber plants, forming a verdant spot on which the eye can rest. It is a good plan to sit down in different parts of your rooms and see how the grouping of the furniture pleases you. Try the effect of a different arrangement. Say to yourself, "How would I like this if I saw it in the house of a friend?" Avoid as far as you can all autumn leaves, crystallized grasses, feathery plumes, all Pampas and Japanese fans stuck here and there. All these things detract from the grace and dignity of a room, and usually give an impression of effort at ornamentation made in an unintelligent way. Besides, they are great gatherers of dust, and the lifelong struggle with "dust" is hard enough without their adding to it.

One of the most beautiful houses in which I have ever been has very few rooms. One large room on the ground floor answers for a parlor, dining room and library, and at need is coverted at night into a bedroom for the lady of the house and her daughters. The color of this room, as to the walls, is a grayish blue; the floor is painted a sort of soft brown; rugs are laid here and there over the floor. One portion nearest the door which leads to the kitchen is used by the family for a dining room, and is simply divided from the rest of the room by an arrangement of movable screens. Another portion, furnished with a desk, some easy chairs, a divan and low bookcases, is also separated from the rest by screens, and is known as the library, where a great deal of pleasant conversation goes on, and where, when

"The lamp on the table in the corner."

she chooses, the mistress of the domain writes, receives her friends, reads or enjoys her leisure. A low tea table with cups and saucers and a burnished copper kettle is ready here for sociable five o'clock tea. Every inch of available space in this room is filled appropriately, and a large family gather in the various parts of it and pursue their various occupations without in the least disturbing one another. Something similar to this will be remembered by visitors to Appledore in Celia Thaxter's day. No one who ever visited the Isles of Shoals will forget the island garden of Mrs. Thaxter's, nor the beautiful, long, low

"One large room on ground floor answers for parlor, dining room and library."

(52)

room in which the lovely poet received her guests. That cottage parlor was in itself a dream of color and beauty, in which the note of bloom and brightness was made by the lavish use of flowers, banked on the mantels, standing in cups and bowls, in vases, in glasses, behind pictures, in fact everywhere, so brilliant, so beautiful and so lovely that no one could help enjoying and admiring the fascinating effect. A poet's garden and a poet's home was that in Appledore.

We are not so afraid of sunshine in these days as people were in the charming story of Cranford. Perhaps you remember what a stir it made in that quaint little hamlet when Miss Jenkyns purchased a new carpet for her drawing room. "Oh," said the writer of Cranford, "the busy work Miss Mollie and I had in chasing the sunbeams as they fell in an afternoon right down on this carpet through the blindless window. We spread newspapers over the places and sat down to our book or our work, and lo, in a quarter of an hour, the sun had moved and was blazing away on a fresh spot, and down again we went on our knees to alter the position of the newspapers. We were very busy, too, one whole morning before Miss Jenkyns gave her party, in following her directions and in cutting out and stitching together pieces of newspapers, so as to form little paths to every chair set for the expected visitors, lest their shoes might dirty or defile the purity of the new carpet."

Quite opposite to this was the course of a friend of mine, on whom a cousin bestowed in a burst of generosity a very rich but very glaring Brussels carpet. My friend was away from home paying a visit. On her return, she found her floor covered with this brilliant and splendid gift. Of its cost there could be no doubt; equally no doubt of the friend's good intentions; but the carpet killed everything else in the room and made the old furniture look shockingly shabby. "What did you do?" I said. "Oh," she answered, "there was nothing to do but first to sit down and cry. Next, I solved the problem by opening the windows to the sunshine, drawing up the shades, and allowing the strong sunlight to pour in on that carpet every hour in the day for days together, until it faded out into something less terrible than it was at first: but it will be a trial to me, I fear, for years to come."

# CHAPTER V.

## Furnishing the Bedrooms.

PON the cheerfulness, good ventilation and convenience of the bedrooms the health of the family very largely depends. A necessity of every chamber in which people sleep is fresh air, and, if possible, light. The furniture of the bedrooms is, in so far as essentials are concerned, limited to a few articles. There must, of course, be a bed, and there should be a bureau, a wash basin, several chairs and a table. No other articles are needed, though others may be added to suit the taste of the owner of the room, according to its capacity. Then a lounge is a pleasant accessory, enabling one to keep the bed nicely made up all day and inviting to pleasant naps at intervals without disturbing the couch. Where there are children the crib or the cradle may stand in the room with the mother's bed. The multiplication of articles in a bedroom is unwise, as they are simply traps for dust, and demand care which might better be given in other parts of the house.

A hard wood or painted floor, with rugs which may be easily taken up and shaken, is by most people preferred to a carpet in these days, although in country houses a pretty tasteful matting makes a very attractive floor covering. The matting may be pure white or figured, and is to be found in many varieties at exceedingly low cost.

It is a mistake to have heavy draperies at the windows of a sleeping room. Shades, either white or ecru, with light muslin curtains are quite sufficient. Unless there are blinds which may be closed at night, or outside shutters, it is also well to have a second pair of shades of very dark brown or green. These can be rolled down at night, and prevent light from falling on the eyes of those who are asleep.

In bedsteads there is room for a wide variety of choice. A brass bedstead is very beautiful, but a white iron bedstead with iron trimmings is equally pretty and costs very much less. In various carved woods, curled maple, chestnut, cherry, black walnut and mahogany there are exceedingly beautiful bedsteads to be found, but the metallic has an advantage over the wooden bedstead in being more easily kept entirely clean.

A wire spring mattress is the first requisite; over this may be placed the best mattress you can afford. Nothing equals a good hair mattress, but there are beds made of moss, excelsior and cotton which are quite comfortable for a time, though less durable than the hair mattress, which may be picked over and remade a number of times, and which is really, when once purchased, a lifelong possession. As so much of one's time is necessarily spent in bed and in sleep, eight hours of the twenty-four being a moderate allowance for most people to be given to this necessary renewal of one's faculties, it is worth while to have as good and comfortable a bed as possible.

Beds of straw and of feathers, once found everywhere, are not now favorites. The straw bed is hard and lumpy, and the feather bed, while to a certain extent luxurious, is very enervating, and in summer exceedingly oppressive. No one can rise from a smothering bath of feathers and feel quite refreshed for going on with the day's work.

The sheets and pillow-cases, bolster-cases, blankets and spreads needed for each bed may be determined by the householder herself. Linen sheets are very luxurious, and most women like to have a pair or two of these in reserve for great occasions, but excellent cotton sheets can be procured, and they form the staple for most housekeepers. A soft wool blanket is much better than a wadded quilt, being lighter, as a rule, and retaining the heat of the body better than the other. A duvet of swansdown or goose feathers is a great luxury as an extra covering for a bed, but equally as good is a soft Italian rug or a knitted afghan.

Pillow shams and lace spreads for the daytime were at one time very popular, but their day is over and only old-fashioned housekeepers are bothered with them now. I cling myself to the old-fashioned idea that a white counterpane and white pillow slips are exceedingly beautiful, but many women in these days prefer a dark silk spread, or a spread made of cretonne, which they throw entirely over the bed in the daytime, covering also a round bolster, and putting the pillows aside until they are used at night. All these things are matters of personal taste, and each one may determine just what she will do for herself.

Have everything about the baby's crib and cradle of the very best that you can get for the dear little sleeper, whose infancy at least should be wrapped in warmth and luxury.

A closet is a requisite in a bedroom, but if one has none, a very good substitute may be made by a set of hooks against the wall, which may be covered with a curtain or hidden by a high screen.

Many lounges serve a double purpose, and when the lid is opened prove themselves long boxes in which garments may be laid away. Window-seats may also serve as boxes for shoes, and ottomans and hassocks often lend themselves to the needs of the householder who has little space and must economize what she has.

The high chiffonier, formerly supposed to belong only to a man and to be appropriate for his use, is now chosen by many women in preference to a lower dressing table and bureau because it has more drawers in which they may keep their belongings. A homemade dressing table may be easily manufactured by a woman who is handy with tools, or who can press her brother or husband into the service. This needs to be simply a pine table covered with silesia appropriately draped with a little lace and some ribbon bows, and above it there may be arranged a looking-glass, beside which the fair lady may sit and comb her hair and survey herself at her will.

The boy's room should not be a repository for all the old things in the house. If possible, let it be attractive so that it may be a refuge for him, a place to which he may retire to study his lessons, or where he may entertain his friends with a feeling that he has a real foothold in the house. The boy will probably like to have his tool chest in his room, if he has a fancy for making articles useful and ornamental, as many boys have. If he is a collector he will keep his cabinet there; if his fancy is for the pursuits of the naturalist, his butterflies and beetles will find their appropriate niche in his room. Whatever the boy's fad or hobby is, he will be apt to let it express itself in this place which is his own. From time to time he should be encouraged in whatever is his specialty by some present which will

"The dainty pretty daughter of the house."

show that the family appreciate his efforts, and it should be required of him that his room should not invariably look as if it had been swept by a cyclone.

There is no reason in the world why boys should throw their things promiscuously around their rooms or about the house for their sisters or their mother to pick up after them. The boy may as well be trained from the outset to keep everything connected with his own peculiar apartment in order. He will be quite as happy, and the family will be much happier if this is required of him.

The dainty daughter of the house usually shows her own taste in the arrangement of her room, and some of the sweetest and prettiest interiors I have ever seen have been in girls' rooms. One sees this in the room of the girl away at school or college; it has an individuality of its own just as it has in her own home. The girl probably will have about her room many souvenirs of friends. She is fond of photographs, and groups them prettily on her walls or about her dressing table. Her combs and brushes, her manicure set, and her dainty toilet appendages testify to her love of neatness and beauty. She will have her little bookshelf with her favorite books and her desk at which she writes her letters, her rocking-chair, her work-basket, and everywhere there will be the feminine touch —the trifles which indicate how much the home means to women.

. A guest chamber, which fortunate people like to have always ready for the occupation of friends, should be, in the first place, entirely comfortable. Let me say in passing that comfort is the prime requisite in sleeping rooms, and that ornament follows a long way after. One may have a guest chamber which is a marvel of beauty in the freshness of the toilet table, in the ribbons and lace and beautiful pin-cushions and pretty knick-knacks scattered about, but in which the facilities for bathing are few and not satisfactory, and in which the bed is hard and lumpy. See that the accommodations which are essential are attended to first and let the decorations follow.

Towels in plenty, not new and slippery, but soft and pleasant to the touch, rougher ones for bathing purposes, also a wash-cloth and delicate toilet soap, should be part of the appointments of the guest chamber. A few sheets of paper and envelopes and a pen and ink, with a postal card or two, should be at the guest's disposal, and if you are very thoughtful you may add a few postage stamps, so that her letters may never have to wait for this convenience. Every bedroom should be furnished with a good strong lock and key or a bolt, as many persons sleep better for knowing that they may safely lock themselves in at night.

A LITTLE girl was going to bed. A dear sister used to sleep on the snow-white pillow beside her. Where was she now?

" Mamma, whom does sister sleep beside in heaven?"

"' There is no night there,' " said mamma.

" She will have her desk, at which she writes her letters."

"Mamma, does a soul have eyes? Will sister know us when we come?"

"'*We shall see as we are seen, and know even as we are known,*' the Bible tells us."

"We shall see them, but our eyes will not be crying eyes; will they, mamma?"

"No, '*God will wipe away all tears.*'"

"There will be nothing to hurt in heaven, and no dark; will there be, mamma?"

"No, dear child, the blessed Bible tells us, '*The glory of God will lighten it and the Lamb* [*our Jesus*] *is the light thereof.*'"

THE following is a very pretty legend to inscribe on a card or banner and hang in a bedroom:

#### A GOOD-NIGHT WISH.

Sleep sweetly in this quiet room,
　　Oh, thou, whoe'er thou art,
And let no mournful yesterdays
　　Disturb thy anxious heart;
Nor let to-morrow scare thy rest
　　With dreams of coming ill;
Thy Maker is thy changeless friend,
　　His love upholds thee still.
　　Sleep sweetly then, good-night.

## Three Baskets.

Bertha's basket: Maiden Bertha, with the merry dancing eyes,
And the brow whereon a shadow would be such a rare surprise—
What has she within this dainty shell of rushes silken-lined,
Where so many maiden musings innocently are enshrined?

Gaily mingling ends of worsted; beads that glitter silver-bright;
Fleece of Shetland, light and airy, lying there in waves of white;
Broidered linen, wrought for pastime in the dreamy summer hours;
And perhaps a poet's idyl, read amid the leaves and flowers.

Bertha's basket: Mother Bertha. Ah, serener light hath grown
In the thoughtful eyes; the forehead hath some flitting sorrows known.
In the larger basket looking, other handiwork we find,
Where the woman's heart its pleasure, love and longing hath enshrined.

" It is they who are storehouses of story and song."

Little aprons; little dresses; little trousers at the knee
Patched with tender art, that no one shall the mother's piecing see;
Flannel, worked with skill and patience; and an overflowing store,
Every size of little stockings, always needing one stitch more.

Bertha's basket: Grandma Bertha; for the years have run their way
And it seems in looking backward it was only yesterday
That the maiden tripped so lightly, that the matron had her cares·
Age slips on so gently, gently, like an angel unawares.

Grandma's work is contemplative.   With the scintillance of steel
Gleam the needles, smooth with flashing off the toe or round the heel,
Leisure days have found the lady; but her face is deeply lined,
And her heart is as a temple, where are hallowed memories shrined.

As along the dusty high-road rise the milestones one by one,
Telling here and there the distance, until all the way is done,
So a woman's basket marks her journey o'er the path of life,
Holding dearest work for others, whether she be maid or wife.
                                   —*From Easter Bells* (Harper & Brothers).

# CHAPTER VI.

## The Dining Room.

THE especial need of the dining room is cheerfulness. Three times a day the family gather around the table for their meals, and as good digestion waits on appetite, and appetite is more or less dependent on good temper, as well as on good food, it is quite advisable to have the dining room a cheerful place. If possible, let it be a sunny room. The daily setting of the table and the making it attractive should be a matter of pride and solicitude in every home.

The table linen need not be fine for common use, but it should be of good average wearing quality, and should always be scrupulously neat and clean. Napkins of different sizes are requisite for the different meals, the dinner napkin being much larger than that which is used for breakfast and luncheon.

In dishes one may choose as she pleases. The advantage of dishes which are entirely white is that if they are broken they can easily be replaced, but few people in these days admire the cold effect of perfectly plain white china. China with a gilt band is always very beautiful, and it too can be easily replaced if a piece is unfortunately chipped or broken. There are very beautiful and not expensive dishes which come in Japanese patterns, or in imitation of the old blue china which used to be seen on our grandmothers' tables, and there is to be found any variety of beautiful decorated china to suit almost any purse. The fad of the moment is to have variety rather than uniformity, and consequently no more appropriate gift can be given from one friend to another than a beautiful bit of china.

Shelves running around the dining room wall about a foot from the ceiling may accommodate jars, vases, and other bits which are perhaps defaced a little or have the handle missing, but which at that height simply become ornamental. Beautiful plates hung up on the wall are highly decorative, and one sometimes picks up at a bargain pieces which answer beautifully for this purpose. Thus, I saw last year a half-dozen magnificent plates which had probably originally cost several dollars apiece. They were slightly injured and the dealer sold them for thirty cents apiece. One of my friends bought them to ornament her room, and very beautiful they looked upon her wall.

Where there is a daughter in the house who has a turn for painting china, she can make very lovely fruit sets and dessert sets which have the charm to her and to her parents of being her handiwork, and which add very much to the beauty of the table when it is set for a gala occasion.

A few flowers in a vase on the centre of the table, or a growing plant, is always an addition. Knives and forks should be bright and in good condition; and the housekeeper who values the peace of mind of the family should look to it that her carving knife and fork are in good order. It is a pity to use the carving knife and fork for anything but their legitimate office, and it is always a mistake to let them be taken for the indiscriminate work of the kitchen; they should be kept sedulously for the use which appertains to them, namely, that of carving meat upon the table.

Equally spoons of all kinds should be kept bright. Any silver in use should be polished carefully

HIS OWN PLACE,

once a week. Silver will be kept in very good order if each day it is dipped into a bath of very hot water, in which there are a few drops of ammonia. If it is then wiped dry with a soft cloth it will not require cleaning so often as if it is carelessly put away without this attention.

Glass and fine china should be washed by themselves. In Virginia and other Southern States, also in old New England, it is the task of the lady to wash her fine and beautiful china. Consequently she is able to keep her sets intact, and the few minutes which she devotes day by day to this work repay her in the neatness of her dishes and in their immunity from breakage.

We should make it a rule never to bring our fits of the blues or our temporary spells of crossness to the dining room. Perhaps you may think it rather hard always to carry a cheerful face to the table, yet it is positively necessary to do this if there is to be real sunshine around the board where the family meet.

"I am not in sympathy with the old-fashioned rule that
            forbids them to speak."

Children should not be permitted to interrupt conversation by frequent questions, yet I am not in sympathy with the old-fashioned rigid rule which forbids them to speak at all. It is very far from agreeable to see children obliged to behave like mutes at a funeral while they are seated at the table with their parents. Besides, it adds greatly to the pleasure of all if conversation at meal-time be joined in by the old and the young alike, always with care that no one is impolite to another, and that the leading part be taken by the older ones. The far too common habit of taciturnity at meals—

people sitting and eating in haste or in solemn silence—is greatly to be deprecated. There should be fun and wholesome enjoyment at our meals, and the parents who take pains to introduce pleasant subjects will find that the behavior of the children will be very much better for the interest and the agreeable talk.

Sometimes indulgent mothers forget that table manners are more than almost any other minor thing important, and that these are formed early in life. To suffer a child to eat in a slovenly or greedy way, to use its knife, to pour milk into its saucer, or do any other thing which is not regarded as polite in good society, is to do the child a great wrong. The manner of eating at once stamps the lady or the gentleman, and in public places, at private tables, in company everywhere, a familiarity with table uses of refinement shows that a child has been carefully brought up among people of good breeding.

In changing dishes for separate courses, if there is a maid to do it, she must take plates and cups from persons separately, not piling everything upon a waiter at once. She will learn to move about with quietness, and to make whatever changes are necessary without disturbing the progress of the meal and without constant coaching from her mistress, who should take pains to teach her servant to wait in the best manner and should insist upon right service when the family are alone, and then never give herself any further concern about it.

Where there is no one to wait upon the table the family may very easily and very comfortably wait upon themselves, and really there is much pleasure in not having any stranger about to hear conversation or to interrupt the pleasant flow of confidential talk. The daughter will then quietly rise and remove plates between courses, bring on the dessert at the proper time, and do whatever is necessary in officiating as her mother's lieutenant. Ease of manner and gentle breeding are shown in many homes where the work is all done by the lady of the house and her children.

In one home where I have visited the tea is always made and served by the father, as he has a fancy that he knows how to make tea better than a woman possibly can, and indeed the quality of his brewing is so fine that the slight innovation is quite pardonable. In making tea, let me observe in passing that it is found to perfection in houses where it is made upon the table—not suffered to stand and steep a long time upon the range.

Of course, for a good cup of tea one needs primarily a favorite brand of tea, either a good blend or an excellent quality of India or Ceylon tea. Nothing on this earth quite equals the delicious flavor of a pure Ceylon tea, which has about it the aroma of flowers, and is quite free from the acrid qualities which some renowned teas unfortunately possess. The next essential is an earthen teapot; then water freshly drawn and freshly boiled. When water stands a long while simmering on the back of a range, the kettle being simply filled up from time to

5

time, the water has a flat taste and does not have about it the life which is needed to make good tea. The water having come to a brisk boiling point, put your tea into the pot the proportion of a scant teaspoonful for each cup, pour on the water,

HER FEW LETTERS WERE SPASMODIC AND BRIEF.

and let it stand for four minutes, not longer. Then pour it off and you will have delicious nectar. It may be served with cream and sugar, or with slices of lemon and sugar to taste—just as one prefers.

Coffee, too, to be served in perfection should be freshly made. It is better to grind the quantity you need just before using it. If you desire to make boiled coffee, mix the grounds with a little cold water and part of an egg. Put this mixture in your coffee-pot and pour on as much boiling water as the quantity of coffee you wish to make. People like coffee in such various degrees of strength that it is well to give but an arbitrary measure. By experimenting you can very soon discover how strong or how weak you like yours, but the beverage must be clear. If the coffee is the old-fashioned boiled kind you simply let it come to the boil on the front of your stove, then push back and allow it to stand about five minutes before serving it.

Delicious coffee may be made in a French coffee-pot without the use of an egg. In this case there are strainers of wire of a fine sieve-like quality which fit into the pot. You put your coffee in a receptacle which comes for it, and pour on your boiling water. The water percolates slowly through the sieve and gets in its passage the full strength of the coffee, losing none of the aroma. If you wish it very strong you will turn it back two or three times, as each time it will acquire more of the strength of the coffee.

Both coffee and tea may very properly and with very little trouble be made on the table if the housekeeper chooses to take the trouble. Both of these are sometimes served after meals in an adjoining room while the family sit about and prolong the pleasure they had at the table by a little social conversation.

# CHAPTER VII.

## The Library.

O a genuine lover of books no house is completely furnished which has not a good many of them, not arranged formally in one room, but scattered all over the house. Still, whenever one can have a library it is a great comfort and pleasure, and the nucleus of one may easily be formed in the early married life. If a small sum be set aside for the purchase of books, and care be exercised in the selection, the householder will find that by degrees the stock of books is multiplied.

A library may very properly open out of a dining room or be the intermediate apartment between the dining-room and the parlor or drawing room. It should have good light. This is very important, as by day those who are reading should not have their eyes unduly taxed, and by night the library is best equipped which has a pleasant central light and two or three good lamps, either in brackets or on tables. Cushioned window-seats add a touch of luxury to a library, and a narrow divan running entirely around the room is also very appropriate and not beyond the most moderate purse, as it may easily be homemade. A few easy chairs, a table in the centre of the room, a desk, and low book-cases in recesses against the walls, and the library has all it needs in the way of what may be called its scaffolding.

But no library is complete until it is furnished with books, and of these there is so great a variety that each house may have its own individuality in this respect. We may regard books in a fourfold aspect. In the first place there are all those useful volumes which are needful for the service of the mind. Prominent among these are school text-books, which are usually admirable compendiums of useful knowledge. They are abridged by careful hands from wider volumes, and in history, geography, applied science, language, rhetoric, and indeed upon every subject one finds a school text-book an exceedingly handy and comprehensive book of reference. One may find in the ordinary school reading books of children, beginning with those which are prepared for the little ones, and going on to those which are meant for advanced classes, what are really stepping-stones to the best literature. Children should be taught to treat their school books with respect, and not to deface them by scribbling or any careless use, but to regard them as important property which is entitled to generous treatment and real regard.

Dictionaries rank very high in the class of reference books, without which no library is really equipped. There are many of these which the scholarly person enjoys having, and no house is complete in which there is not either a "Webster's," "Stormonth's," or other good dictionary. For those who

"It is not always expensive."

can afford it, nothing surpasses either the "Century" or the "Standard Dictionary." The value of a dictionary is not alone in its accurate spelling, but in the fact that it gives a number of meanings of words, and shows by quotations from the best authors in how many ways the word can be used.

A dictionary, though not very consecutive, is really very interesting reading to a student of philology. In the good dictionary we find derivatives, and see how our English tongue has been born from old words; how the Latin and the Greek and the French and Spanish and the Norse tongues have all contributed to it. We acquire a certain reverence for our mother tongue when we study a good dictionary. Beside a familiarity with common words the scholar needs to have acquaintances with the richer and more sonorous and ponderous words, so that his vocabulary need not be limited, but may be rich and full. There are beautiful words which are like embroidery upon silk, and there are short, direct, terse words which have the forceful strength of a hammer's blow. The scholar will need them all, and in the intelligent American household the dictionary should have a high place.

Next in the library should come a good encyclopedia. This may be purchased volume by volume. It is not always necessarily expensive, and there are often chances to get a good encyclopedia without paying an enormous price for it. An atlas of the world, with maps, is another possession worth having; also historical charts of different countries showing the progress in invention and discovery, as well as in freedom and civilization in different countries at the same time.

A dictionary of antiquities, a good reader's handbook and a compendium of quotations will make the reference part of the home library very complete. In mentioning these I do not forget that if you have the good fortune to live in a town where there is a free circulating library you may not need all these yourself, though it will be a joy to have them if you feel that you can afford to so indulge your taste. A doctor, a lawyer, a clergyman always has his own peculiar working library. For the ordinary reader it is not necessary to have books on special subjects, but it is quite worth while to possess some of the works of standard authors, both in English literature and in translations. These books come under the head not of servants but of friends. They will stand by you and be your resource and your cheer all the days of your life.

Have a sprinkling of the poets and the essayists, and do not forget that we all love the story-teller, and that the complete library has a very large amount of fiction on its shelves. Also, do not turn from books of biography. The lives of people are always interesting to others, and one gets a great deal of contemporary history in the memoirs of eminent men and women, as, for instance, in the "Life of Lord Lawrence," and in "The Story of Two Noble Lives," in which one obtains a very clear and succinct statement of the Indian mutiny, or in the lives of the Rossettis, and of Lord Tennyson and of the Carlyles, which incidentally bring in a great deal of the history of the England of their day. Everybody has not a taste for biography. To those who love it it is as the very bread and water by which men live.

A library should be a growth. If we had money enough to purchase a full library at once it would not give us the pleasure that it does when by small accretions and accumulations, day by day and year by year, it grows upon our hands. This book is the gift of a dear friend. We never look at it without

"A doctor, a lawyer, a clergyman always has his own peculiar working library."

remembering the red-letter day when she presented it to us. This other is the autograph copy sent us by an author with whose friendship we have been honored;

money could not buy it. For still another book we saved and planned and did
without, and laid up money a little at a time until the book was our own. We
cannot put a value in dollars and cents on a library which is the development of
slow toil and happy years.

There are people who care a great deal about fine bindings, and their libraries
are rich in stately volumes, which show the finest skill of the engraver, the paper-
maker and the binder; but the genuine book-lover does not always care for style
and costly dress upon his books; he would rather have more books, even if they
were not so elegantly bound. A library in the house presupposes culture, and
greatly assists the intellectual development of the children.

Its greatest foe is that irresponsible person, the borrower of books, who does
not care whether he or she returns this sort of property or not. If you are
generous and kind and lend your books, you will do well to make a little memorandum of the fact of its loan in the presence of the person who takes away your
book. This acts as a check upon the borrower, reminding him or her to return
the book in a reasonable time and in good condition. Should you ever borrow a
book yourself, be sure that you observe every precaution against injury or deface-
ment. A borrowed book should always be covered while it is away from its own
home; and in no circumstances should the person who borrows any volume lend
it a second time without the consent of the first owner.

Susan Coolidge said once that if she had it in her power to bestow a gift
upon the cradle of a babe, she would endow the child with a love of fun and a
love of books. Thus equipped any little pilgrim may set out upon the journey of
life with a very comfortable prospect of making happy progress. No matter how
lonely one is, no matter how much tried and troubled, a good book will prove a
resource, and the love of books will make up for losses of many kinds.

There are always individual treasures in the line of books which should not
be kept away from one's own room. Let the son or daughter, the wife and
mother, have their own little book-shelves in their own chambers, where they may
have the books they specially love and have the sense in them of exclusive and
pleasant ownership.

As for book-cases, I never like mine to have glass doors and locks and keys,
although they are certainly kept from dust by being protected in this way. Still,
I always want my books where I can get at them with ease, and I prefer open
shelves and the trouble of frequent dusting. Silk curtains, or curtains of chintz
or silkoline or cretonne, drape book-cases effectively, and do not give the poor
books the appearance of being state prisoners, as the locked book-case does.
There is opportunity, if you have low book-cases, for pleasant vases and other
objects of interest on the top shelf, and for having beautiful etchings and engravings above them. It is a matter of choice whether your book-shelves shall run to

the top of the room, or whether they shall be low, leaving space on the walls for appropriate ornament.

———————

"Fond as you are of books, there is only one book that you will value at last; and with your head on the pillow you will hardly care to be told that a new

"There is opportunity if you have low book cases for pretty vases on the shelf."

volume of some great history is published, or a marvelous poem, outranking all its predecessors. No, 'Read me the twenty-third Psalm.' 'Let me hear the fourteenth chapter of John.'

"Dear friend, how soon God can make that Bible precious—necessary either for your own support or the comfort of one most dear to you.

"Take the Bible *now* as your best treasure. It will prove green pastures and still waters along your daily way."

———

SAYS a pastor's wife:

"My sunny window with its few greens has been one of my pleasantest school rooms this winter. The lessons of life are often tedious, and we are slow to comprehend, when sometimes a hint of the real meaning will come to us from a familiar and before unnoticed bit in our surroundings. My hardy ivy plant was my first instructor. It had passed the summer in the garden. Evidently it was loth to relinquish its freedom, and resented the confinement of glass and the forced climbing up the window casement, and would not smile by so much as one tender little leaf. For a long time it was sullen and would not acknowledge favors, till at last the warm sunshine has forced a response, and, apparently against its will, each end of a branch is bursting with life, and, creeping up even through restraining supports, is gladdening me with its delicate new leaves.

"Are we not often like the ivy? Resenting transplanting from some sunny garden, and resisting all kindly influences in the new life, because not of our deliberate choosing, we waste many months when we might be enriching other lives by the graces of our own. Our loving Father patiently waits for us to realize the warming influences of His love, which we must feel enveloping us on every side, and in which we live and move and have our being as truly as the plants in the rays of light. Why not respond quickly to His constant care for us, and climb toward the light, stronger because of restraining bands? Then new beauties in our characters will 'prove that we are growing under His tender guidance. 'For the sun meets not the springing bud that stretches toward him with half the certainty that God, the source of all good, communicates Himself to the soul that longs to partake of Him.'

"My ambitious Wandering Jew has been another teacher. In quick and ready response to light and heat, it has grown luxuriantly and has put forth its leaves in rapid succession. But, alas! so ready is it to respond that its strength is failing and the leaves become smaller, till a pigmy colony is flourishing in its vase. What is the remedy, how curb this restless activity? Take from it its sunshine and refreshing showers? Ah, no! but pluck the little new leaves as they peep forth from the last hardly formed ones, before they have time to take any strength from the plant. So my little Wanderer has taught the lesson that, though in a genial atmosphere, it is easy to put forth new efforts, yet to develop in the best and noblest way, we must constantly curb trifling ambitions, lest our time be taken

THE IVY. (75)

up by useless little things and our strength be spent by responding too willingly to every demand on thought and time. The woman of to-day needs particularly this lesson—to be faithful in a few things. Our loving Father is our constant inspiration, but we must study His wishes for us that His garden of our lives be not overrun with useless foliage.

> " ' Books in the running brooks,
>   Sermons in stones, and good in everything.' "

# CHAPTER VIII.

## The Back Door.

THE careful housekeeper is very particular about her back door. That, of course, is not in evidence to the public gaze as is the front door, and she of careless habit and nature indisposed to exertion does not mind whether that part of her domain which comes only under the eye of her family is trim and well-ordered or the reverse. One may set the stamp of capability and niceness exactly by looking at a person's back door. Where one finds a general air of disarray about the back yard, where odds and ends from the kitchen, refuse of various kinds, loose papers, and the flotsam and jetsam of the house are allowed to accumulate around the back steps, it is a sign manual of inefficiency on the part of her who is queen of the house.

Also the health of the family is greatly affected by the care which is taken to keep everything around the back door as it should be. In many country places, where there is nothing in the environment to suggest anything but perfect health, we discover mysterious illnesses breaking out. Often we may trace these to some thoughtless lack of supervision on the part of householders. Who has not seen around wood piles and about the chicken houses and the various barns and outhouses belonging to a house, proofs of absolute neglect? A little daily care given to everything which has to do with the environment of a house means the difference between keeping things as they should be and letting them go to hopeless waste and disorder.

It is hardly fair that the care of the back door, and of all that the back door means, should lie as a burden upon one person's hands. The most fastidious housekeeper in the world may be very much hampered by husband and children and domestics who do not second her efforts. Still, it is worth while for the same care to be given to the back of the house as to the front. Then, too, there is a moral side which presents itself here. Most of us are very careful about our company dress and manners. We like to appear well to the outside world. But are we always as conscious and as heedful in our demeanor to those of our own families? Do we invariably remember that there is a side presented to people who live with us which is not discovered by those who are merely our visitors or our outside friends? We cannot too carefully watch the back doors of life, we cannot too constantly guard ourselves against any heedlessness in that which is generally unseen, but which has to do with the very foundations of good living and high morality.

It is well for each child in a family to have some special duty about the house. In a large family where I am sometimes a guest, I have often been struck with the wonderful celerity with which the daily tasks are accomplished. There seems to be no jarring, no particular effort, no hurry on the part of any one concerned, and yet everything is done. One boy goes at a regular hour either before or after breakfast, or before or after supper, and attends to certain work which he is held responsible for. Another has perhaps the care of the lawn. One sees to the pump, keeping the tank supplied with water. Still another weeds the garden. One feeds the chickens. Each child in the large family moves with almost military precision to his appointed task. I once asked the father of the family how

"One feeds the chickens."

he had managed to get his children into such absolute good order, and how it was that work under him seemed a pleasure rather than a toil.

He said, "My wife and I began right. From the time our children were small we accustomed them to implicit obedience, and as they grew old enough we gave each one some share in the work of the house.

I take it for granted that each of my children will do what he is told to, and should there be any failure to perform a task at the allotted time, that child is sure to hear from me; not in the way of severity, but in a surprise and reproof which he feels. Forgetfulness is not accepted as an excuse, but should a child forget to do something which I had told him, I would expect that he would make it up before going to school or to play. The fact is, Madam, that any place which is governed by law is a happy place, and our home is under the dominion of law even in so small a matter as our back door."

Mats and scrapers save a world of work, and careless boys may learn to use them. The mother builds better than she knows, who brings up her lads to be tidy about the house, and save her needless work and needless steps. The years are flying fast and the boys of to-day will be the husbands of to-morrow. A man's mother trains him for all his life in those early years when he is plastic in her hands as the soft yielding clay. Let her impress on his mind in boyhood the value of seeming trifles, even to the wiping of his feet at the back door.

# CHAPTER IX.

## An Open Fire.

WE lost a great deal from our lives when in the march of modern improvements many of us found that we could dispense with a fire on the hearth. A furnace in the cellar or steam pipes diffusing warmth through the house are certainly very comfortable arrangements for the Arctic cold of our American winters, and where one cannot have these for actual defence against the rigors of the severest January and February weather nothing surpasses a good old-fashioned stove.

But for cheer, for brightness, for making the home alive with sparkle and glow, nothing is equal to an open fire. It may be just a handful of pine knots, or a lump or two of soft coal, or, best of all, a bundle of fagots made of driftwood which has tossed about on the sea and been thrown on the shore, and which is full of all sorts of poetical associations and suggestions of storm and stress outside as it lends itself to comfort within.

Whatever it is, the open fire gives the last touch of domesticity to a home. It is worth the little extra expense it costs to have its daily beauty and brightness, and no one who has ever been able to compass it will ever again do without its joy. In localities where wood is plenty and to be had for the trouble of getting it, people may indulge themselves in rousing fires with a big black log, or a roaring blaze which goes joyously up the chimney and diffuses warmth through a large room.

That is for the dweller in the country. We of the town sometimes have to be satisfied with a mere imitation blaze in the shape of a gas log, and this is better than nothing, but best of all is the real thing itself. An open fire disposes one to pleasant low-toned conversation, to telling stories in the firelight, to sitting with a child cuddled up in one's arms, to retrospection, to all sorts of pleasant dreamings and musings.

Our life is so active, so filled with excitement, that we are much too little given in these days to quiet thought. Anything which tempts one to repose is a great boon. Indeed, there are very few of us who would not be the better for sitting down every day for a half hour, with folded hands, simply for the purpose of thinking, or of letting the mind lie fallow without much effort at consecutive meditation.

(79)

I know how many women will smile when they read this, and will say, " This writer does not know what she is talking about;" but indeed I do. I have led for many years an intensely occupied life myself, and I never in the world would have gotten through one-half or one-quarter of the necessary things if I had not made a point of quite often sitting down, folding my hands, and doing

BEFORE THE FIRELIGHT.

just nothing at all. One acquires a habit of restlessness if one never rests, and deep lines come in the forehead and the voice grows querulous, and the nerves rebel unless one can sometimes rest. Therefore, if possible, have not only the open fire, but what the open fire stands for: a home centre around which pleasant memories may gather as the years go by

As for the fuel to be burned in your fireplace, the question will be naturally between hickory and pine and birch and other woods, and the relative merits of soft and hard coal. You will decide upon that according to your purse, and according to the part of the country in which you live. But do not at once condemn the open fire as an extravagance. When your day comes for canvassing expenses, see if there is not something else which you can do without and indulge yourself in this. All winter long this fire will furnish your room in a way that nothing else can. It will take the place of fine furniture, it will second the welcome you give your guests, it will add greatly to the real elegance of your home, as well as to its comfort, and it will convey to all beholders, as well as to the family itself, an impression of luxury. An open fire, a few books, a few flowers, a lounge, an easy chair or two—and a room is well equipped for the ordinary uses of life.

Besides, on the mere score of health a good deal is to be said for a fireplace in the room. It insures absolutely good ventilation. There are mornings and evenings in the spring and fall when a blaze on the hearth means safety from taking cold, and when you do not at all need a warm fire in the furnace or in the stove; when, indeed, a large fire would mean that the house should be inconveniently heated.

In the sick-room a little fire is very much to be desired. Often the invalid needs only enough warmth to take away the chill from the room. Do not be in your house one of those tyrannical people who never has a fire lighted until a certain day in the fall, and who never keeps fire in after a certain day in the spring. In our changeable climate we cannot have hard and fast regulations of this kind. If we are wise we will not be bowed down in any such iron fashion as this, but we will do what is for the comfort of ourselves and our children.

You know how the baby loves to toast its little toes before the fire ! What pleasure the boys and girls take in roasting apples themselves, seeing them sputter, and finally reach the right turn in the genial warmth ! What a delight to eat apples and potatoes which one cooks one's self by the fire ! The best cooking, let me say in passing, which I have ever eaten in my life was done wholly before a great open fire in a Southern city. Old Aunt Hannah, stately as an African queen, carrying herself with the erectness and aplomb of a woman in society, her bright turban on her head, her little checked shawl over her shoulders, her blue apron around her waist, would make and cook beside this open fire such rolls and corn bread and wheaten loaves as I never expect to taste again in this world. A duck or a piece of meat roasted in this way retained all the juices, and far surpassed anything which our finest modern inventions can show. It seemed hard for Aunt Hannah to lift the heavy pots from the crane, to rake the ashes over her spiders, and to bend as she had to above this great fireplace which cast its eerie redness over the dark kitchen in which it was placed, but she laughingly made light of all

6

the work, and when sometimes in my inexperience I would venture upon directions and suggestions, she would say, in the most dignified and yet affectionate
manner, "You go 'long, honey, into.the house. Your business is to eat things;
my business is to cook 'em. We will both cling to our own side of de house."

Speaking of a cheerful fire leads me to think of cheerful tones, looks and
smiles. A German writer, commenting on these, tells us that "we feel with
every heart-beat the power of that noble, good behavior which can never be
acquired. This power cannot be
defined in words, but whoever
has tried to set it at defiance will
understand in what it consists.

"Is it not an elevating, a
sublime feeling, that it lies in
the power of us parents to endow our sons and our daughters with anything so excellent?
Something which will open to
them the portals of good society
and offer at the same time a
mighty weapon to protect them
against every danger.

"The secret of education in
good behavior and deportment
is more easy to understand than
one generally believes. It is expressed in the sentence: Never
allow in your house a word, a
look, an act that differs from the
words, looks and acts you use in
the best society.

"For instance, the little
words 'please' and 'thank you'
are so quickly said, why do you
only take the time for them with strangers? It is not beneath the dignity of
father or mother to impart every request in an entreating manner, and to return
thanks for what is granted.

"When the mother says to her little daughter, 'Please, Lizzie, pick up my
ball,' and receives the yarn with a friendly, 'Thank you kindly, my child,' then
she can be convinced the child will speak in a similar way to her brothers and
sisters and to the servants.

"This great fire-place which cast its eerie redness
over the dark kitchen."

"When the father jumps up politely to take the heavy basket which the mother holds in her hand, the next time the boy will do it. The servants in such a house will soon be imbued with the universal spirit of politeness, kindness and attention on the part of all the members of the family to each other.

"If you say to your cook, ' Please bring me a glass of water,' she will of her own accord place the glass on a plate, and bring it in a nice manner.

"Light, much light, must be let into even the most remote corners, that should be the rule in all things, and the children who grow up in the clear, sunshiny atmosphere will know how to fill their position in life well enough, whether Providence places them in modest circumstances or gives them a coronet in their coat-of-arms."

## Uncanonized Saints.

Not all the saints are canonized;
   There's lots of them close by;
There's some of them in my own ward,
   Some in my family;
They're thick here in my neighborhood,
   They throng here in my street;
My sidewalk has been badly worn
   By their promiscuous feet.

Not all the heroes of the world
   Are apotheosized;
Their names make our directories
   Of very ample size.
And almost every family
   Whose number is complete,
Has one or more about the board
   When they sit down to eat.

Not all the martyrs of the world
   Are in the Martyrology;
Not all their tribe became extinct
   In some remote chronology.
Why weep for saints long dead and gone?
   There's plenty still to meet;
Put on you wraps and call upon
   The saints upon your street.

CONSECRATION.

And Fox's martyrs were strong souls,
  But still their likes remain;
There's good old Mother Haggerty,
  And there is sweet Aunt Jane.
You know them just as well as I,
  Since they're a numerous brood,
For they are with you all, and live
  In every neighborhood.

————————

## Strength for the Day.

" If it costs me such efforts to conquer
    The hasty or unkind word—
If by each faint breath of temptation
    The depths of my spirit are stirred—
If I stumble and fall at each hindrance,
    When a Christian should conqueror be—
Dare I think—dare I hope—O my Saviour!
    That I could have died for Thee?

" Dare I talk of the martyr's courage,
    And the love that went smiling to death;
I, who fail in such simple duties,
    Forgetting my hope and my faith?"
Then a light broke in on my sadness,
    These words brought comfort to me—
"Accepted in Christ, the beloved,"
"As thy day so thy strength shall be."

————————

## Consecration.

Take my life and let it be
Consecrated, Lord, to Thee.
Take my hands and let them move
At the impulse of Thy love.
Take my feet, and let them be
Swift and beautiful for Thee.
Take my voice and let me sing
Always, only, for my King.

## TRUST.

Take my lips and let them be
Filled with messages from Thee.
Take my silver and my gold,
Not a mite would I withhold.
Take my moments and my days,
Let them flow in ceaseless praise.
Take my intellect and use
Every power as Thou shalt choose.

Take my will and make it Thine;
It shall be no longer mine.
Take my heart, it is Thine own!
It shall be Thy royal throne.

---

## Trust.

I know not if to-morrow
    Shall bless me like to-day;
Of night I sometimes borrow
    Dark clouds and shadows gray;
But sinful, sick, and weary,
    Of this I still am sure:
No clouds or shadows dreary
    Shall my sweet heaven obscure.

Oh, much is left uncertain
    In this strange life below;
But faith lifts up the curtain,
    And sees the inner glow;
And nothing now can move me,
    Nor shake my joy so pure,
For Christ has stooped to love me,
    And of His love I'm sure.

# CHAPTER X.

## The Door-Yard.

HETHER or not one can have any door-yard at all depends, of course, on the place where one lives. I am taking it for granted, however, that you have at least a little patch of ground before your door, which you may plant with hardy flowers, or in which from year to year you may have a brave show of the bright little flowers which come in the spring, or the beautiful and brilliant things which delight our eyes in the fall.

If one has only a wee bit of lawn, that may be planted with grass and kept smooth and velvety by constant care with the lawn-mower, or by attention in watering so that the roots do not become parched or dry. The more space there is for this beautiful green grass rippling up to the very door-step, the better and more beautiful your home will be; and it is quite worth a little care night and morning in the joy it gives you to have this emerald freshness on which to rest the eyes, and to have the sweet reminder constantly before you of the Heavenly Father's love and care.

Think of the millions and millions of grass blades waving in the wide fields all over the land ! Think of the clover, white and red, springing up amid the grass ! Remember how sweet and fragrant is the breath of new-mown hay, and let your mind flit for a moment over the immensity of this provision of God's love. By no possibility can one count the spires in a single small grass plot, and it is as if one would try to measure the sand by the sea, or to estimate the number of stars, when one stops to think of the multitudinous little spears of green grass rising up all over the land every summer through.

Of all this great provision perhaps you and I have just one little bit which we can call our own. That we may make as beautiful as we please. It may be ragged and stumpy looking, or it may be soft and fine, and what it is will depend on our care. Somebody looking at the velvet turf at Oxford in England said, " How do you account for its beauty and its greenness ? " " Oh," was the answer, " it has had a thousand years of sunshine and of rain, a thousand years of cultivation. There are a thousand springs and summers in that green sod."

Of flowers which are beautiful in a door-yard, nothing, to my mind, excels the little pansies, which grow all the more lavishly for being picked; which, indeed, will not thrive and give you generous bloom unless you gather them often, and which with their dear little faces always seem to be saying, "This is a happy world and we are glad to be in it." Then there are four-o'clocks, and lady slippers, and geraniums, and fuchias, and ribbon grass, and carnations, white and pink, and hollyhocks, and larkspur, and love-lies-bleeding, and prince's feather, and the many varieties of roses; the beautiful heliotrope, lavender and sweet william, and ever so many more dear old-fashioned flowers which bloom the

APPLE BLOSSOMS.

summer through.    Early in the spring one may have snowdrop, and crocus, and jonquil, and lilac.

If you have a tree or two, you may have apple blossoms and pear and peach blossoms to make the world the brighter and attract the bees, but if you have no trees in your door-yard, you may still have morning glories running up against the house and garlanding the fence, and making you cheerful the summer through. Then in the autumn come chrysanthemums and salvia, and all the bright and gorgeous procession which bloom defiantly up to the very hour when the frost comes along and winter drops his white coverlet over the land.

"If you have a tree or two you may have apple blossoms."

Do not think that you can have flowers, either in the door-yard or in the house, without giving them some intelligent care. Flowers need attention just as children do. You will have to see that they have the right kind of soil, that at certain times the soil is enriched, that weeds—those foes to flower life —are kept away, that the flowers are picked and brought in to ornament the house, that in due time the seeds are taken care of and the bulbs put in the ground.

Once having started a garden, you will have to give it only a little extra care year by year. The garden will go on growing and blooming and making you glad. What pleasure it is to have a few flowers of your own raising to put on the breakfast table ! a flower for the father's buttonhole, a posy for the children to carry to school, and, above all things, flowers to send to people who are ill or in trouble.

One can always show love and sympathy by sending flowers, for somehow they speak with a certain affection of their own and carry messages which we could not put into words ourselves. As Mrs. Whitney has remarked in one of her sweetest little poems:

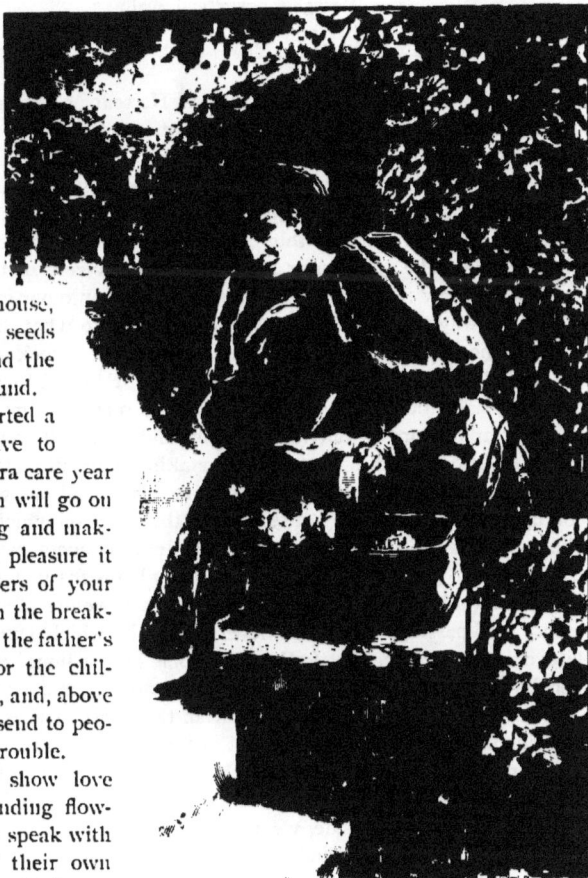

"Flowers which are beautiful in a door-yard."

"God does not send us strange flowers every year.
When the spring winds blow o'er the pleasant places,
The same dear things lift up the same old faces."

And Mary Howitt, speaking in the same way, said:

> "God might have made the earth bring forth
> Enough for great and small,
> The oak tree and the cedar tree,
> And not a flower at all."

But that was not God's way of doing, and He sent us beside the oak and the elm, the loveliness of many a wild flower that lifts its fair face in sheltered places where no eye but God's own ever sees it.

Some of my friends have had great success in making little woodsey gardens in their door-yards, carefully bringing from the forests the little flowers which bloom there, and giving them something of the soil and nurture to which they are used. Still I always feel a trifle sorry for these little denizens of the groves when they are brought away from their own habitat and put into our gardens; it seems as if we are in a way stealing them and doing violence to what they would best like.

One should always have at hand in the house a book about flowers, such as Mrs. Caroline A. Creevey's "Flowers of Field, Hill and Swamp," or Mrs. Dana's "How to Know the Wild Flowers." Even if one is not much of a botanist, there is very great pleasure in studying the looks and ways of flowers, in knowing to what class they belong, and in, so to speak, making their intimate acquaintance.

The door-yard should be an attractive place, and one which gives a pleasant look not only to your own house, but to the street on which you live. In many villages people are now doing away with dividing fences between their homes, so that each door-yard which is well kept really helps the housekeeping of the town, and as one walks through street after street and avenue after avenue, one has the sensation of passing through a lovely park in which homes are dotted about. But we do not all have that feeling. In some old-fashioned Southern towns people even have high brick walls around their gardens, and once inside you enter a wilderness of bloom and beauty, but from the street there is nothing but a forbidding line of wall, which does not add to the beauty of the town.

Our houses and door-yards should in a way help along the place in which we live and add to its general attractiveness. If, however, we have no room for even so much as a flower outside, we may add to the beauty of the street by always seeing to it that we have window boxes filled with green things growing, or with lovely blooming plants, and these will also rest the eye of the passer-by, and convert our homes from dreariness into beauty.

Then one should take pains that all the outside of the house, so far as she is responsible for it, is perfectly clean, neat and shining—door-steps, windows, everything which turns a front to the general public should be made as attractive as possible; and there is really great decoration in simple cleanliness.

" Here she is again, the dear,
  Sweetest vestal of the year,
  In her little purple hood
  Brightening the lonesome wood.
  We who, something worn with care,
  Take the road, find unaware
  Joy that heartens, hope that thrills,
  Love our cup of life that fills,
  Since in Spring's remembered nooks,
  Lifting fair familiar looks,
  Once again with curtsying grace,
  In the same dear lowly place
  God His manual sign hath set
  In the tender violet."

# CHAPTER XI.

## The Kitchen.

T should be the airiest, brightest and most inviting room in the whole house. Here the meals are prepared; here the laundry work goes on; here, if there be no servant, the mother has her own domain, and spends most of her time. Wherever else there is getting along by makeshifts in the kitchen let the provision for convenience be ample. A good range with a good draught, plenty of pots and pans, spiders, spoons, cups and dishes and bowls, will greatly add to the ease of doing the work. The sink should be provided with a large drain pipe. If the water has been brought into the house, the difficulty of preparing food will be lessened, and work will be accomplished with less labor than when water must be carried in buckets full from a spring or well outside. Then the careful housekeeper will see that her stove or range is always bright, that it is cleaned every morning, and the ashes removed before the new fire is made, and she will always keep a quantity of hot water in the kettle.

Says Christine Terhune Herrick, spe aking of the kitchen closet:

"The least used articles should occupy the upper shelves. Tin pails and pans, bowls and cups, should be turned upside down when not in use, to prevent the accumulation of dust. Heavy kettles and saucepans, broilers and frying-pans, should be in a pot closet by themselves. Everything that can be hung up should have its own particular nail. Cake-turners, iron spoons, skimmers, graters, strainers, funnels, egg-beaters, tin cups and dippers, should swing from nails or little brass screw-hooks fastened in the door-posts, or in the edges of the shelves. There should be, if possible, a drawer, where should be kept the knife-box, cork-screw, apple-corer, pastry-jagger, larding-needles, can-opener, skewers, and all the small articles that are liable to be mislaid."

The same admirable writer has given in her volume, "Housekeeping Made Easy," a full list of articles needed by her who would have her kitchen thoroughly supplied with tools for every occasion. They are a formidable array, but many of us can manage with less, and it is interesting to see what we may have if we choose to supply ourselves fully:

| | |
|---|---|
| One spice box, | Two jelly moulds, |
| One Dover egg-beater, | Two small yellow bowls, |

" In the kitchen let the provision for convenience be ample. "

Six kitchen plates,
Six kitchen cups and saucers,
Two large stoneware platters,
One griddle,
One perforated skimmer,
Two stone crocks,
One refrigerator,
One double boiler,
One teakettle,
One teapot,
One coffee-pot,
Knife and fork box,
Garbage pail,
Scrubbing pail,
Scrubbing brush,
Broom,
One one-quart saucepan, agate-ware or porcelain-lined,
One frying-pan,
One soup-kettle, agate-ware or porcelain-lined,
One four-quart tin pail,
One two-quart tin pail,
One one-quart tin pail,
One graduated quart measure,
One half-pint tin cup,
One tin dipper,
One cake-turner,
One corkscrew,
One pastry-jagger,
One wash-basin,
One towel-roller,
One six-quart seamless milk pan,
One four-quart seamless milk pan,
One plain pudding mould,
One two-quart pitcher,
One four-quart pitcher,
Four yellow mixing bowls, assorted sizes,
One split spoon,
Two wooden spoons,
Two iron spoons,
Six kitchen knives,
Six kitchen forks,
Six teaspoons,
Three tablespoons,
One bread-knife,
One meat-knife,
One small knife for peeling potatoes, cutting the meat from bones, etc.,
One larding-needle,
One soup-strainer,
One hair-wire gravy-strainer,
One colander,
One wire dishcloth,
One can-opener,
One apple-corer,
One large funnel,
One small funnel,
One bread-box,
One cake-box,
One potato beetle,
One meat broiler,
One fish broiler,
One toaster,
One vegetable grater,
One nutmeg grater,
Dredging boxes for salt, pepper and flour,
Three pie-plates,
One lemon-squeezer,
One floor mop,
One dish mop,
One bread-board,
One small meat-board,
One rolling-pin,
Two sugar buckets,
One meal bucket.

"In the well-regulated house the sinks, wash-bowls and faucets should receive attention at least once a week. When practicable, all drain-pipes should be flushed daily with hot water, if possible, but when that is out of the question, with an abundance of cold. The human body parts with a great deal of greasy matter in the course of its ablutions, and this is apt to form a deposit on the lining of the waste-pipes that will in time clog them seriously if it is allowed to remain. An excellent compound of potash is sold by druggists and grocers for the especial purpose of cleansing waste-pipes. The same work may be accomplished nearly as successfully by a strong solution of washing soda and by household ammonia. Copperas water, an excellent disinfectant, should be used in connection with these other preparations.

IN THE KITCHEN.

"The marble bowls and slabs must receive a hebdomadal scrubbing, in addition to the wiping off that should be a daily occurrence. Pumice-stone, sapolio, or scourene serves here as upon faucets. On the marble it may be applied with a cloth or a small stiff brush, but for the faucets, stoppers, chains and other plated finishings the brush is preferable, as it carries the soap better into the chinks and interstices. One such scouring as this in a week will keep these platings bright, if it is supplemented by a wiping off with hot water and a rub with a flannel or chamois-skin each morning.

"Lamps, andirons, fenders and fire-irons demand their quota of attention, nor should doorplate, knobs and hinges be neglected."

Our habits of luxury in town life and our relegation of kitchen work to the hired maid, have robbed us of much of the pleasure we used to have in simpler days. But I am sure there are still sunny kitchens in which the cat purrs by the fire, while the brisk mistress steps to and fro, doing her baking and ironing her sweet smelling linen, fragrant with the purest air and the blessing of the light. There the boy studies his Latin grammar and adds up his sums, and the girl tells how she went to the head in spelling, and how the teacher asked her to be class monitor for the day. The dear grandfather pottering about the garden and the barn comes to the kitchen to rest, and to smoke his meditative pipe. The sweet old grandmother sits in the pleasant window with the long gray sock she is knitting, and the baby plays on the floor, or sleeps in the cradle which stands in the darkest corner. Here, in the best of cooking-schools, the daughter learns housewifely management, here the bone and sinew of the land are nourished, here our patriotic American citizens are bred up to stand sturdily for God and their country. The kitchen is the heart of the home, and the mother is queen of the kitchen.

# CHAPTER XII.

## The Parlor.

I HAVE no hesitation in saying that the parlor is the room for which we can longest wait, and which we can most readily dispense with if necessary. Where a parlor is simply a room reserved for company, and seldom used, it may be the pride of a woman's soul, but it is not of much genuine utility. By common consent our parlors are our best rooms, where we keep our richest bric-a-brac, our most beautiful furniture and our most prized possessions. But, why not have instead of a stiff seldom-occupied parlor, a pleasant living room to which everybody turns with freedom and yet with a sense of rest; why not accustom the children to come hither, only enjoining them not to romp and range noisily in this room, but telling them that fine manners befit a fine apartment.

Uniformity was once considered the proper thing for the parlor. I remember when a marble-topped table, a sofa upholstered in horse-hair with chairs to match, a few family pictures and some china vases and sea shells were regarded as the acme of elegance in the parlor. Now, the fashion is for individuality, and we prefer a cozy interior to a formal one. A hard wood floor is liked better than a carpeted one by many women. Rugs are popular. Books lie about. Engravings adorn the walls. Plants stand in the windows. If there is a piano it invites the fingers of the musician; or there is a mandolin or a banjo, and with either a hint of jolly times at home.

The parlor is not shut up and cold and stuffy. It is airy, sweet, bright and winsome. Lively chat is the rule here, and snatches of song, and invariable good temper. It is a room to enjoy but as it is a luxury it may be waited for.

# CHAPTER XIII.

## Order and System.

VERY sensible person knows that the affairs of life are carrie.. on to much better advantage when they are managed with a certain regard to routine than when the duties of the day are left to accident. Especially in the beginning of housekeeping it is a good plan to regulate the various dates according to system: to have certain days for certain work, and as a rule not to vary very much in the schedule laid down. Monday, by time-honored custom, is in most families devoted to washing. If the housekeeper rises early, and has taken the precaution to sort her clothes the night before, putting those which are most soiled into water to soak, keeping the fine and the coarse things apart, and taking this hardest labor of the house with a cheerful spirit, she will find it a good thing out of the way when Monday's sun goes down.

Tuesday again is ironing day. Wednesday may be taken for mending and putting in needful stitches before laying away the freshly laundered clothes. Thursday and Friday divide between them washing windows and sweeping and general cleaning, while Saturday is by common consent appropriated to baking, enough in the way of bread, pies and cakes being easily prepared then for the wants of an ordinary household. If one must bake twice a week, Wednesday is the better day for the second campaign of this kind.

Then, too, in all well-regulated households the hours for meals are a matter of arrangement. Necessarily these are regulated by the business of the man of the house, by the custom of the place where one lives, and also with some regard to the convenience of children going to school. An early breakfast is a necessity in many households. Unless the family rise soon after dawn in winter and about six o'clock in summer, they cannot sit down comfortably to a half-past six or seven o'clock breakfast, which is a needs-be in many cases.

A good deal of the breakfast can be arranged for the night before where one does her own work. Oatmeal, for instance, is the better for being soaked over night in water, unless the housekeeper prefers to put it on in the afternoon and allow it to simmer slowly for a long time on the back of her range, in which case it is very nearly cooked and has only to be warmed over in the morning. All cereals are the better for very thorough cooking. It is a mistake to suppose,

"Needful stitches."

whatever the labels on the packages may tell you, that either wheat or oatmeal or Indian meal may be cooked to advantage in a few minutes. They all need a rather slow and leisurely cooking to bring out their best qualities. Coffee may be ground and placed ready for the morning; potato cakes may be made and set aside; and eggs in any form are quickly cooked. If there is to be a hash for breakfast it is always best to prepare it the night before.

So much of a man's comfort and health depends on his having a good start for the day, that the wife should always feel it incumbent upon her to have his morning meal ready for him so that he need not be too much hurried and obliged to swallow it in frantic haste, and then rush wildly to his train or the place of his work for the day. On the other hand, the man himself, father, husband, brother or son, owes it to the women of the household to get up when he is called, if not before.

Where there are no domestics kept, and fires are to be lighted, it would seem that the man, who is the stronger, should rise first and prepare the fire so that it may be all ready for his wife when she arrives at the preparation of the breakfast. But whatever he does or does not do, it is incumbent on every son of Adam to get up when he is called in the morning, and not to oblige people to rap at his door repeatedly to call him in a voice that might awake the dead. For growing children there is some excuse, and whenever it is possible they should be allowed to sleep their sleep out, but a strong man need not shield himself beside so flimsy an excuse. It is quite in his power to retire as early as he pleases and take the needed sleep before midnight instead of after dawn.

In families where there are invalids, or where there is no occasion for catching a train or going to business early—where, perhaps, nobody goes to business at all —breakfast may be as late as one chooses or as may suit the convenience of the family. I remember a charming visit paid at a beautiful home in the vastness of the Berkshire Hills. Here in this household of luxury, where there was no obligation on any one to stir earlier than he or she pleased, the breakfast hour was most comfortably late and people came and went as they pleased, the maid simply bringing in breakfast to each as he or she desired it. This arrangement is ideal, but it is not possible for us all. Where it is practicable to have breakfast a moveable feast, let the housekeeper adjust her system to the convenience of the family, instead of compelling the family to adjust their convenience to her system. System is to be our servant, not our tyrant. We are very foolish to put ourselves under its control. It is simply an efficient means of aiding us in the work we have to do.

In many parts of our country dinner is served in the middle of the day, and wherever this arrangement can obtain, it certainly is the best for health and pleasure. In cities, however, where distances are great and men do not come home in the middle of the day, the evening meal must be the dinner and the noon meal must take the form of luncheon. This may very properly be for the children

"Where there are invalids."

their heartiest meal, as it is not a good thing for them to eat meat and vegetables or a rich dessert just before going to bed.

Every woman must regulate her household in her own way so far as her means are concerned; also so far as the order of her work is concerned. If she is doing her work herself everything is in her own hands. The daintiest house-keeping I have ever seen has been done by ladies who manage in their own beau-tiful efficient way to suit themselves. They have the great joy of not having their dishes chipped and wantonly broken; their pots and pans last longer than those of others who are dependent upon the help of untaught peasants from other shores; they do not find their towels and dishcloths packed into holes under the sink or wantonly burned—in fact, they find that while they are not quite so much at leisure, they are far more at ease in mind, and are on the whole much more independent than women who have others to help them.

Where, however, as is the custom largely in this country, a maid is employed, or at most two, they should, so far as possible, be made to feel that they are not merely employes but also riends, and they should be treated in such a way that the interests of the family become theirs. I know that this is not a doctrine believed by every one, but I have proved it to my own satisfaction that it is quite possible to have under one's roof women who do one's work and who feel a great degree of responsibility for the well-being of the home, for the management of resources, and for the comfort of all concerned.

A lady who does a large amount of literary work away from home, and who goes to an editorial office every morning, leaving her home at eight o'clock and not reaching it again until six, said to me, "It is possible for me to do my work and do it as well as I do simply because I have had for years the services of two faithful Irish women who behave as well and are as trustworthy in my absence as in my presence."

We need to remember that in many ways the ordinary servant is not more mature than a child, and she will find it a great help if her work is indicated for her in the order in which it should be done. At the same time, the mistress must not be too rigid in insisting that the work shall always be done according to her routine or in exactly her way. The thing after all is to get the work well done, and it can sometimes be managed much better if there is a little elasticity.

For children system is invaluable. Nothing could be worse for a small boy or girl than to be allowed to go to school or stay at home according to the childish pleasure, to play all day when lessons should be learned, or to feel no sense of responsibility in the house. Every little child and every older one should have some little task or duty which belongs to him or to her, and for which father and mother hold the child responsible. Country children have a great advantage over city children in this respect, because in the country there are more simple tasks about the house, garden and fields than there are in our town houses. Perhaps that is one reason why our greatest men and women so often come from the

HELPING GRANNY. (103)

country, with its peace and seclusion, its chance for individual homes and for natural development, than from the crowded streets of our great towns.

A fad of the moment is what is called the Don't Worry Club, and we find many fashionable women, as well as many plainer ones, enlisting themselves in these circles who take for their motto " Don't Worry." But long before the days of clubs, and long before the present thought of repose and serenity as factors in home life, we were told by one who spoke with infinite wisdom that "sufficient unto the day is the evil thereof. Take no thought for the morrow, for the morrow shall take thought for the things of itself."

The wise housekeeper needs to avoid two foes of health, happiness and beauty: the name of one is Hurry, and the name of its twin brother is Worry. Nobody can be contented who is in a state of rush and tug and whirl; nobody can be at peace who is distressed lest things will not come out as they should. We must neither hurry nor worry if we wish to retain our good looks, but go cheerfully and gladly on our way through life. Worry writes wrinkles on a woman's face and furrows deep ruts in her mind, and after all what good does it do? We often find that the very thing about which we have worried most turns out quite well, and that we might have spared ourselves all needless anxiety.

In that good old book "Pilgrim's Progress" there is a story of the pilgrim walking along and afraid to enter a beautiful house because he saw on each side of it a ferocious lion standing on guard. When at last, however, he made up his mind to walk up to the house he found them perfectly peaceful and quiet, and when they saw his approach they paid no attention to him. So when Daniel, God's servant of old, was thrown down into the den of lions, God sent His angel to keep them from harming him. We must sometimes in this world be like Daniel, thrown down among raging lions of trouble, care and sin; perhaps temptation will assail us; perhaps there will be trial which it is beyond our power to meet. But do not let us be afraid; God can always send His angel in the hour of our need.

When you think of it, friend, the worries,
The troubles that wear you out,
Are often the veriest trifles,
That common sense would flout;
They write the forehead with wrinkles,
They bow the shoulders with care,
Yet a little patience would show you, friend,
Just how the weight to bear.

"Every child should have some little task."     (105)

# CHAPTER XIV.

## Ourselves and Our Neighbors.

ERHAPS we might call it an American peculiarity to care a great deal about what our neighbors think of us. More than any other people in the world we are influenced in our style of living by the style which obtains around us. People are disturbed if their shades and curtains, their carpets and furniture, are less elegant than those of others residing in the same vicinity, and often the householder is tempted to extravagance in these directions simply that she may put the best foot forward and appear to as much advantage as the resident across the street or next door, whose income may be double or treble her own.

When we think of it, this entails an amount of needless anxiety and a stretching after effect which is very indiscreet, and which does more than any other thing to rob us of the joy and peace of life. So far as the mere environment is concerned, the furniture, the richness or the plainness of our homes, we should preserve an entirely independent attitude. Nobody should fear to be considered singular. Each person has a right to spend or to save as seems best to himself, and it is both weak and silly to attempt more than our income warrants. No one cares any more for you because you live in a beautiful house or in a small cottage. The friends who really love you, and whose friendship is worth having, will go to see you if your home be in an obscure neighborhood just as eagerly as they would if you lived on a splendid avenue.

Often, too, people lose more than they gain by putting on a style which does not belong to them. For instance, a man starting out in life sometimes loses opportunities because older and more sagacious people, observing the manner of his life, say "A or B is going beyond his means; he cannot keep up at that pace; we do not want in our employ a man who is living at such a rate." I have known instances in which a man's whole future was injured because his wife or his children, or his general style of living, challenged a degree of fashion which in his case was very unfortunate. Mr. Micawber's famous remark that "if your income is twenty pounds, nineteen pounds, nineteen shillings and six pence spent means bliss, while twenty-one shillings means poverty," remains true to this day. We must never let our neighbors unduly influence us as to what we spend. On the other hand we need not be, as people too often are in our cities, wholly unaware that we have neighbors at all.

The decline of neighborliness is one of the sad features of city life. One may even live in the same house with others and know nothing of sickness or death which has occurred to the other family; and it is not infrequent for us to find

FATHER'S LITTLE DAUGHTER.

that some one who lived a few blocks off, and whom we occasionally have met but meet no longer, has passed away. In village life this can never happen. Each household knows every other. A smaller town or a village is decidedly the better place for a home on this very account, that it somehow is like a great family, where everybody knows something about and cares something about everybody else. Here in the smaller town if a maiden is to be married every one is interested. During the days of her engagement people regard her with friendly eyes, and when the bridal day comes the whole place is stirred up to do her honor and the village assumes the air of a fête. If there is illness in any home all homes feel it, and friendly offers and kind hands are extended to help those who are in need of assistance. If a lad gains a prize at the High School all his neighbors are pleased, and they congratulate his father as he goes to business, or stop and speak to the boy himself with pride because he has brought honor not only on himself but on the whole place. When a girl goes away to college all the other girls and the other girls' mothers feel an interest, and her first letter home is discussed in more houses than her own. Just so if one family have a windfall of fortune, the cordial good wishes of all their neighbors add to their pleasure. And if disaster and misfortune are the portion of any, every one shares in sorrow that the calamity has come. Blessed is the sweetness of this neighborly contact, and true indeed is the word that was said of old, that "Better is a neighbor that is near than a brother that is far off."

Among little neighborly offices nothing ever seems to me more beautiful and significant than the simple passing of a covered dish from one house to another. Shall I ever forget my home just after the war in a lovely Southern town, where often in the morning as I sat down to my breakfast table a friend living on one hand or the other would send me in a plate of hot waffles, or of biscuits breaking like snowy puffs under their brown covers, or perhaps a saucer of golden honey, or some other pleasant reminder that I was thought of in a loving way by the housekeeper who lived next me.

This sweet neighborliness was recalled to my mind when on a recent visit to Tennessee I found everywhere the same loving thought and kind attention. At the house in which I was staying there occurred suddenly a death, and instantly three or four charming women whom I knew but slightly, having met them for the first time but a few days before, came to invite me to be their guest and stay under their roof with them. They filled my life while with them with sweet and friendly offices, and when at last I left, the parting guest was speeded on her way with loving words and kind attentions, and the very last thing that was done was to give me a beautiful box of such a lunch as one seldom sees, to be taken on the train. Here were sandwiches and beaten biscuit and fried chicken and beautiful cake and salted almonds, all put up in the most dainty way for the traveler's comfort—and this for one who had been a few days before an entire stranger. Do you wonder that I remember and always shall recall with the greatest affection these angels unawares, who have made me understand again that in the South at least the old sweet neighborliness has not been forgotten?

Equally, visiting last summer in a family of New England, I found there the spirit of good neighborhood just as ready to brood with tender kindness over the wayfarer, and the loveliness of the sweet word and the kind act and the spontaneity of goodness shown in just the same friendly way. Alas for us that this

" If a maiden is to be married." (109)

spirit seems to have shaken the dust of her feet from our great and bustling towns.

———————

"DID you ever think how every part of your house can remind you of the great truths which Jesus Christ taught about Himself? The corner-stone or

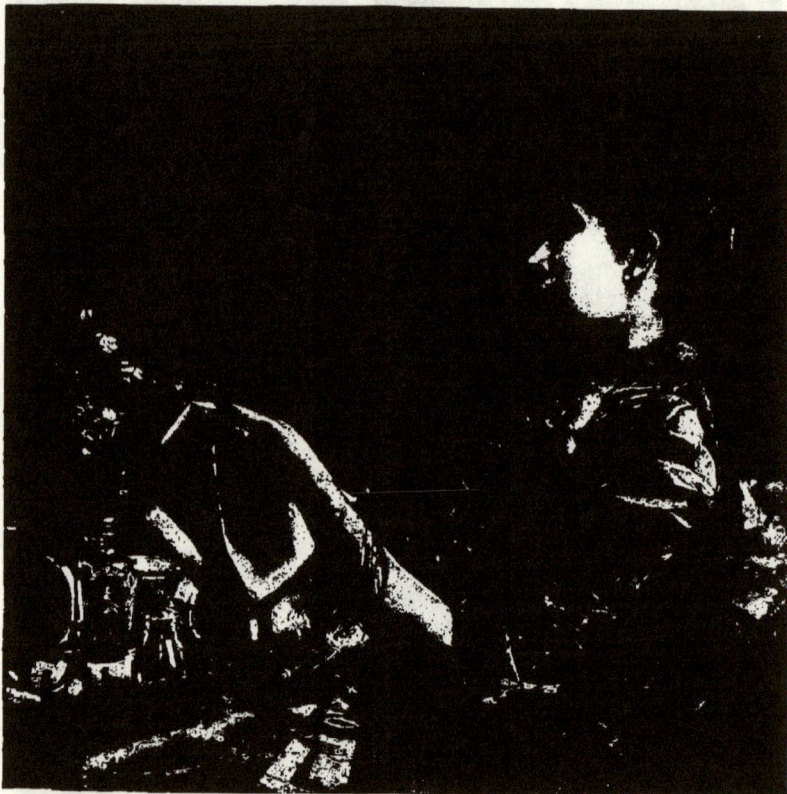

HER FIRST LETTER HOME.

foundation, says, 'Christ is the corner-stone;' the door, 'I am the door;' the burning light, 'Christ is the light of the world.' You look out of the window, and the sight of the starry sky bids you turn your eyes to 'the bright and morning star.' The rising sun speaks of the 'Sun of righteousness, with healing in His wings.'   The loaf on your table whispers 'I am the bread of life,' and the water which quenches your thirst, 'I am the water of life.'   When you lie down, you think of Jesus who had not where to lay His head, and when you get up you rejoice that Jesus is 'the life.'"

---

WISELY and pithily says John Ruskin:

"Now the man's work for his own house is, as has been said, to secure its maintenance, progress and defence; the woman's to secure its order, comfort and loveliness.

"Expand both these functions.   The man's duty, as a member of a commonwealth, is to assist in the maintenance, in the advance, in the defence of the state. The woman's duty, as a member of the commonwealth, is to assist in the ordering, in the comforting, and in the beautiful adornment of the state.

"What the man is at his own gate, defending it, if need be, against insult and spoil, that also, not in a less, but in a more devoted measure, he is to be at the gate of his country, leaving his home, if need be, even to the spoiler, to do his more incumbent work there.

"And, in like manner, what the woman is to be within her gates, as the centre of order, the balm of distress, and the mirror of beauty; that she is also to be without her gates, where order is more difficult, distress more imminent, loveliness more rare.

"And as within the human heart there is always set an instinct for all its real duties—an instinct which you cannot quench, but only warp and corrupt if you withdraw it from its true purpose;—as there is the intense instinct of love, which, rightly disciplined, maintains all the sanctities of life and, misdirected, undermines them: and must do either the one or the other; so there is in the human heart an inextinguishable instinct, the love of power, which, rightly directed, maintains all the majesty of law and life, and misdirected, wrecks them."

# CHAPTER XV.

## The Management of Money.

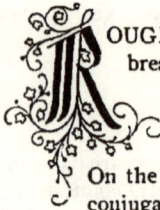

ROUGHLY speaking, in most households the husband is the provider or bread-winner, and the wife is the administrator of the income. A great deal of unhappiness, however, is caused and much unnecessary friction by a lack of proper management of the family resources. Is the wife a licensed beggar or a business partner? On the answer to this question depends more of married felicity or of conjugal misery than the unthinking can ever know.

Most wives dislike unspeakably to ask their husbands for money, and many otherwise excellent husbands make their wives perfectly miserable by the churlish or disagreeable way in which they dole out necessary funds for the maintenance of the family life. It would be well in the very beginning for people to arrive at some conclusion as to this important matter of domestic finance. Where the man has a salary, or brings home every week a certain stipend in the way of wages, it is quite easy for him to know how much he can afford to spend for house rent, for pew rent, for fuel, for his own and his wife's clothes, for table expenses, for traveling expenses and for the necessary items which come into the affairs of every day. He may sit down with his wife and they may together amiably apportion the various parts of the income intelligently, leaving a margin free for doctor's bills and for any sudden emergency which may occur. If they cut their coat according to their cloth, they will have great peace of mind and much comfort; and, just here, if the husband will give the wife a certain allowance for her personal expenses, so that she will not be obliged to go to him when she wishes to pay a visit; when she wishes to make a little contribution to a charity; when she wishes to buy herself a pair of gloves, he will find, and she will find, that their mutual happiness will be greatly increased. The lack of money wears out many an apparently well-to-do wife.

Most men have a notion that women are not to be trusted with money. They are willing to trust their wives with everything else; with things which you would consider more important than money—their good name; the reputation of the family; the care of the children—in fact, with everything which has to do with the actualities of life, and yet they say, "My wife, dear child, does not know how to manage money." How is she ever to learn unless it is given her to care for? Are you going to keep her a child till her hair is gray?

There is often peculiar hardship in this aspect of the case when a wife has during her spinsterhood had an income of her own. As a young lady, she perhaps taught, and had her quarterly salary, which was absolutely her own to use as she pleased, or she was a clerk and brought home her weekly wages, or as a stenographer, or in some other position of responsibility she earned a fair living. When it comes to having no money at all except what John chooses to give her; when she has to ask this same good John for five cents to ride in the cars, or for the price of a pair of shoes, or a new gown, or a feather for her hat; when she cannot put her name down as a subscriber to a periodical or give a dollar to the missionaries, or do anything else she is inclined to without first consulting him, life becomes very bitter and the taste of married happiness is not so sweet as it well might be. This is most unfortunate, because if husbands could see it in the right way, they would be only too glad to try the business arrangement, and they would find in most cases that their wives, far from taking advantage of their justice—not their generosity—would prove themselves admirable financiers.

A woman's self-respect and her ability to take a fair view of matters is greatly increased if she is treated as an equal by her husband; and certainly the money which comes into the home is the joint property of both. The wife, though her duties are indoors, does as much toward the saving of the income and toward the presenting of the family in a right light to the world, as her husband can possibly do in his business.

There are instances, it must be conceded, and not a few, where it is by no means plain sailing to thus manage: as when a man has no certain fixed income and cannot always tell how he is coming out at the end of the year. It will be necessary for him to watch very closely, indeed, the relative obligations of income and outgo; but the true wife is willing to share his anxieties and does not wish to increase his burdens. Often the man makes the great mistake of not letting his wife know just how he is situated and so she incurs expenses which she would scorn to do if she were treated fairly.

People living on farms and not needing to handle very much money often find a different arrangement necessary and convenient from that which prevails in town life; but there is a great unfairness in that sort of management which enables the husband to hire all the help he wants in the fields, and to hold the purse strings very tightly, while the wife toils faithfully year after year and never has a cent to call her own. Always for him the pocket-book, for her the empty purse. It is not fair.

About the whole question of domestic finance there should be perfect confidence and a sensible division of the money in hand, with always a prudent forethought for the rainy day. It is unwise to live up to the full extent of one's income. There will always be breakers ahead for people who do this. As soon

8

as possible, one should begin to lay up something for the day of sickness; the day
when the education of children will call for greater outlay; the day of old age.
To live without thrift and with great improvidence is a sin as well as a blunder.
If possible a man should have a life insurance, the premium of which should be
punctually paid, as any deficiency in this will invalidate all that has gone before.
To keep up the premium may sometimes mean a good deal of self-denial for all
concerned; still, it should always be done, for if in the changes and chances of
this world, the bread-winner be taken away, he will be happier to know that he is
leaving his wife not unprovided for in a cold and stormy world.

People are of different minds as to what proportion of their income should be
given to the service of God. In the old Hebrew economy the tenth at least was
always laid on the altar of Jehovah. It would seem as if the Christian would
desire to appropriate a share of what God gives for God's service. All that we
have and are we owe to the divine blessing, and we may well say when we offer
our gifts in the temple of God, "Of Thine own we give Thee." There is a
sporadic giving which is impulsive and enthusiastic; there is an unsettled giving
which amounts to very little; there is a way of contributing to the church and to
benevolence prayerfully and according to system, and this way in the end brings
down a blessing on one's self and helps forward the coming of the heavenly
kingdom in the earth. Singularly, one never misses that which is given to the
Lord. It always brings back its return in full measure from His loving hand.
We must not forget that we are stewards and that often the only thing we can
offer to our dear Lord, showing Him how much we love Him, how much we desire
to serve Him, is our money.

The pastor of a church in New York City once told me that in his congregation there were no rich people, and very few who could really be called more than
poor; but, he said, "My people have consecrated their means to the Lord, and the
result is that they give largely on all occasions. They put aside week by week,
as God prospers them, what they can spare, and the result is that our collections
are always wonderfully generous and often surprise me by their aggregate. Not
long ago," he said, "I preached a sermon in which I urged that a liberal contribution should be given to our foreign missionary fund. This was in the morning of the Sabbath, and in the afternoon, as I walked through the Sunday-school,
a young lady beckoned me to her and handed me a roll of bills. She said, ' My
sister and I wish to contribute this to the missionary cause.' When I counted the
amount it was one hundred dollars. I said to her, ' Are you justified in making
so large a contribution?' She answered, ' Yes; this is what we have been putting
aside from time to time as a gift to the Master.' " Another very poor woman,
earning her living as a laundress, during a winter of unprecedentedly hard times
was not called upon as usual by the collector of the missionary society, for the

reason that the pastor thought that it would not be right to ask her to give anything that year. She was ill and could not go out, but she sent one of her children to her pastor's house asking for a visit. When he came she put her hand under her pillow, produced a little purse and said: " Here is my dollar and a half which I have been saving, but which they forgot to call for. This is my offering to God, and I should be very much disappointed and very sorry if it did not go in the way that I meant it to." There is a lesson here for all of us. Let us never forget that, whether we have much or little, a certain proportion of it is always due to the Lord, who loves us and who bought us with His own blood; who kept nothing back when He came to this world to save us, and who accepts the gifts of our love as we make them in His name. " Freely ye have received, freely give," is a motto for every Christian.

" Imogen," said a friend the other day, " has developed an amazing capacity for business management since David's death. David never consulted her at all. His large fortune comes to her as a great surprise, but she shows a wonderful capacity for handling it wisely, and she is most able and clear-headed." So would other women prove if they had the chance.

In illustration of our theme we quote an admirable story from *Harper's Bazar:*

### Fidelia's Purse.

" If only I had some money of my own! I envy the maids when they reach the end of the month and receive their wages. I envy old Aunty Jane, the char-woman, as she goes in and out of the apartment-house over the way, for *she* earns her bread, and buys it with her earnings. As for me, I am a pauper in velvet and silk, and I don't think I have much reason to boast myself concerning my clothes. I'd as lief be a beggar in rags and be done with it."

" But, Fidelia," urged her sister, " why don't you tell Benjamin how you feel? Benjamin loves you dearly; he worships the ground you walk on; he does not want you to have a wish ungratified. Look at this drawing room, a bower for a queen; look at your carriage, a dream of luxury; your horses, your coachman, your footman, the service which waits on your every step! My dear Fidelia, if the people up in Greenbrier County saw all this, and heard your complaints, they would think you had lost your senses."

" I'm likely to lose them if things go on as they're doing now," answered Fidelia, firmly. " When I was a girl in Greenbrier I had one white frock, which I had worn to parties for five years. The tucks were let down as I grew taller, summer after summer. The lace on the waist had been washed and mended; my slippers were homemade; my gloves were cleaned till they gave notice on their own account that they wouldn't stand it any longer. I had a black alpaca for school wear, both as teacher and as pupil; I thrummed on an ancient piano, I rode

an old plow-horse, when he wasn't wanted in the field; I visited the sick, I sang
in the choir, I did as I pleased, and I was happy. That last year at home my
salary was two hundred dollars. Two hundred dollars! Think of the wealth, of
the independence, of the joy, of the sense of something accomplished, something
done, which earn's a night's repose! I was happy then, Marion—happy; and I
am not happy now. I am wretchedly discontented—a bird beating against the
bars of my cage. Why, this gown I have on now cost a hundred dollars, and my
fur cloak would pay the salary of the Greenbrier schoolmistress—bless her soul!—
for five years. I wish I were she."

"Do you never have money?" inquired Marion, perceiving that Fidelia was
very much in earnest, and divining that this outbreak was more than a passing
caprice. Ever since she had been with Fidelia, enjoying with the fresh and eager
zest and enthusiasm of a country girl for the first time in her life away from home,
and for the first time a guest in a great house in a great city, the operas and
theatres and concerts and parks and promenades and mornings of music, and
drawing rooms where elegant women assembled to listen to charming lectures on
every subject under the sun, and luncheons, dinners, pleasures of every kind going
on, she had been aware that Fidelia was dissatisfied. But she had not been able
to comprehend the reason at the core of the discontent. Fidelia's husband was
devotion itself; and though, as a busy professional man, he gave comparatively
little time to his home, still, when he was there, he was so kind, considerate,
suave and deferential that Marion, albeit she was accustomed to good manners in
the men she knew—as every Southern woman is—could find nothing to criticise.

"I never have anything to call money," Fidelia answered, solemnly, her
large eyes filling with tears, which she dashed away. She was a beauty, Fidelia,
with her great violet eyes, her golden hair, and her daintily poised head, and
Marion was used to seeing her have her own way. Tears in Fidelia's eyes because
she had no money, when she lived in elegance and splendor, quite confounded
Marion, who put down her embroidery and went across the room to bring the
smelling-salts.

"Nonsense, sister! I'm not ill," exclaimed Fidelia; "I'm simply out of
sorts, and disgusted with a disagreeable situation. I ought to be ashamed to
make you uncomfortable because I am, but I'll tell you how it is. I have carfare
if I choose to ride in cars, though Benjamin prefers my going out in greater state,
and the horses need exercise, and altogether he does not like my patronizing the
public conveyances, when I can be seen in our own equipage. I have a little
change for emergencies. Once in a great while I have a five-dollar bill. But I
want my own bank account; I want liberty to manage my affairs as best pleases
me. I desire to make a present to mamma without consulting my husband, to
pay little Jennie's music bills out of savings of my own; I don't wish to be treated

like a child, and made to ask for what is my right as Benjamin's wife—his honored and trusted wife.

"You see, Marion, the only thing Benjamin will not leave in my care is

"Fidelia's husband was devotion itself."

enough money to give me a certain freedom, and the power to spend or to save
without consulting him at every point.

"Benjamin defers to my taste in household furnishing; he concedes my prerogative as to the selection of servants and the administration of the domestic economy; he is proud of me as his wife. If we had a child, or children, he would allow me to have entire charge of their training and education. It is in just this one particular that I am a mendicant.

"Yes, of course I buy things and send him the bills. I have accounts at the stores, and my husband audits them, and wonders or smiles, as his mood happens to be, at the sum total of my shopping; for indeed, Marion, I am extravagant and reckless, and order the things for the mere fancy, as you would do, too, if you were treated like a baby or a plaything. And to-day, when the lady called and wanted me to subscribe for St. Mary's Guild, I had to put her off until I could talk it over with my husband; and it will end in my giving nothing, for Benjamin likes to be consulted about charities, but always concludes with the remark that we are doing enough in the line of benevolence already. Marion, my child, never marry. You are much better off as you are."

Marion blushed, a lovely seashell flush warming her ivory skin, until she looked almost as beautiful as her sister. Marion was the plain one of the family. Plain girls are not without charm, however, and she had her own happy secret—a *fiancé*, whose stock-farm of many acres, and plain, low-ceiled, wide-verandaed house, awaited the coming of a mistress. In Greenbrier the problems which vexed Fidelia's soul and took the sweetness from her life would not annoy Marion; for her home, leagues back from the railroad among the primitive mountains, would be carried on without much actual gold and silver; and as for barter, the butter and eggs and honey would be hers, to do with as she chose. Marion could not imagine herself in the pitiful case of Fidelia.

Being a sensible maiden, and one of those persons whose disposition is not to drift along at the mercy of the wind, but to act with decision, and set matters straight if they are crooked, the little girl from Greenbrier began to speak in a common-sense manner to her distressed sister.

"Fidelia, all I have to say is that you are behaving very foolishly. Benjamin, poor fellow, hasn't an idea that you are taking this thing seriously to heart. Until you talk it fully out with him, and persuade him to try another method, you have no right to suffer martyrdom as you do. Let us drop the subject now and go out for a walk and some chocolate creams; I've been wishing for chocolates all day."

"Oh! have you, dear?" sighed Fidelia. "I am sorry, but I can't get them for you, unless I go somewhere and have them sent home, C. O. D., with strict orders to let the delivery be between six and seven in the evening. I might have them charged, it is true, but I would not like to send a bill for a pound or two of chocolate creams to Benjamin's office."

"Come, my dear," said Marion; "I'll relieve your difficulty this time."

Meanwhile, Benjamin, unaware of the conflict in Fidelia's mind on a subject which to him seemed of very slight importance, was sauntering slowly homeward, intent on bringing his wife, after the fashion of loving husbands everywhere, some agreeable votive offering. Now it was a new book, some charming story about which people were talking; now a photograph; again a bunch of violets or a cluster of roses; occasionally his evening gift took the form of bonbons.

Passing a brilliantly arrayed and ornamented window, it suddenly struck his fancy that women liked sweets, as was proved by the procession of female figures flitting to and fro at this particular corner. Benjamin determined to procure for his wife and her sister a large box or a ribbon-bound basket of choice conserves and confections, sure that "the girls" would be pleased. He entered, stood before a counter, and gave a lavish order, paying for his purchase royally from a large roll of bills.

He was about leaving, when he heard a faint little familiar voice behind him, saying, "Pardon me; we might as well go home together, dear."

It was Fidelia. And Marion was with her, smiling and unembarrassed. Fidelia seemed a trifle disturbed.

"You are driving?" inquired Benjamin.

"Not at all," answered Fidelia. "We are taking a constitutional, and Marion has been treating me to chocolates."

"And pray, dearest," asked Benjamin, "why did not you treat Marion?"

"I? How could I? I never have the means to do those spendthrift things. I leave such vagaries to my betters."

Benjamin stared. A man seldom understands the intricacies of the feminine mind. All he did comprehend was that something had happened to put Fidelia out. He hated to see her out of temper. So he hastened to soothe the perturbed spirits of the lady by his side; he never forgot that she was a lady, and to be studied and treated as such, though she was his wife, and therefore privileged to snub him if she chose.

"Well, Fidelia, I've just bought five pounds of bonbons apiece for you, and you may play the Lady Bountiful with yours if you like."

This remark did not appeal to Fidelia. She received it coldly. The trio walked briskly through the crisp evening air, and in silence arrived at the house, which, lighted and cheery, sent out its cordial welcome to them as they went in. A perfect dinner was prepared, and after it, what with a glowing open fire, soft-footed servants, and the peace which falls tranquilly on a civilized household when it has dined, Benjamin was partly conquered beforehand, when Marion suddenly took him to task, playfully at first, but presently with great seriousness of purpose and manner.

"Brother, do you know that I have discovered a skeleton in Fidelia's closet?"

"You don't tell me! Pray, when? And what can it be? Fidelia is the most absolutely contented woman in New York."

"You think so, but it is a mistake. Fidelia is extremely discontented, and has a very legitimate grievance."

Benjamin looked grave. He laid down his newspaper and flicked away the ashes from his cigar. "What do you mean, Marion? Do not speak in riddles."

"Fidelia wishes a private purse, and you do not allow her to have one."

"Excuse me, Marion," said Benjamin, stiffly, "but surely Fidelia and I can arrange our finances to suit ourselves."

"Certainly, if only you will do so," answered Marion, going to the music-room, and playing, softly and dreamily, waltz, sonata, measure after measure of silvery melody; marches with long thrilling chords; cradle tunes, such as children love—while by the fire, beyond her hearing, the married pair carried on a low-toned conversation.

"Fidelia, you know that all I have in the world belongs to you and is altogether at your service. We can have no separate interests. I do not like the idea of dividing our united life by the entering-wedge of an apportionment to you of any stated sum. You have my purse always, and may command what you will."

"In other words, Benjamin, I am a licensed beggar."

"Why put it in that way? One cannot beg for what is her own by right. What practical basis can you suggest which would meet your views and make you altogether satisfied?"

Fidelia did not hesitate the fraction of a second.

"Give me a stated sum every month for my personal use, entirely apart from housekeeping or other expenses connected with our home; let this be deposited in my name in some convenient bank, let me have my own check-book, and you will never hear another complaint from my lips. I ask only a small sum, dear; but I wish the knowledge that there are funds which I may control—the pleasure of my own private purse."

"In short, you prefer an allowance—an allowance—to the unrestricted use of your husband's income?"

"I do certainly; for the latter phrase, though beautiful, has no practical significance. If the allowance is to cover all my needful expenses of dress, traveling and other incidentals, it will have to be larger than the one I am pleading for—which is simply money enough to come and go on, without feeling always like a mendicant who has no hope of brightening her fortunes."

"We'll try it for a year, Fidelia," was Benjamin's conclusion, and Fidelia stooped and kissed him. She was standing by his chair, and she swept her fingers caressingly through his hair, and looked as pretty and animated as she used to do at Greenbrier in their courting days.

"Women are enigmas," said Benjamin, musingly. "It never entered my brain that you cared so much about so small a thing. Why, it might easily have been arranged in this way from the beginning."

"I wish I had dared to speak sooner," said Fidelia. "I have tried, but you never would really listen, and lately I've felt desperate. You wouldn't like the situation, dear, if the cases were reversed."

"I own that I might not. You may prefer the old way, my love. This is only an experiment."

"An experiment worth trying," cried Fidelia, gaily, while Marion's music surged up into a triumphant march.

And "Women are queer," thought Benjamin, applying himself again to the evening paper.

## The Sin of Omission.

It isn't the thing you do, Dear,
  It's the thing you leave undone
That gives you a bit of a heartache
  At the setting of the sun.
The tender word forgotten;
  The letter you did not write;
The flower you did not send, Dear,
  Are your haunting ghosts at night.

The stone you might have lifted
  Out of a brother's way;
The bit of heartsome counsel
  You were hurried too much to say;
The loving touch of the hand, Dear,
  The gentle, winning tone
Which you had no time nor thought for
  With troubles enough of your own.

Those little acts of kindness
  So easily out of mind,
Those chances to be angels
  Which we poor mortals find;

# THE SIN OF OMISSION.

They come in night and silence,
    Each sad, reproachful wraith,
When hope is faint and flagging
    And chill has fallen on faith.

For life is all too short, Dear,
    And sorrow is all too great
To suffer our slow compassion
    That tarries until too late;
And it isn't the thing you do, Dear,
    It's the thing you leave undone
Which gives you a bit of a heartache
    At the setting of the sun.

# CHAPTER XVI.

## Boarding versus Housekeeping.

YOUNG couple often find it convenient to board during the first years of their married life. There is something to be said in behalf of this arrangement. If they are starting with a very small capital, they can more definitely manage their expenses at first, and by careful economy can lay up enough to begin in their own house later on. If they have the good fortune to get into the right kind of house, especially if they can be accommodated in the home of some pleasant people, who do not take other boarders, the arrangement may turn out an exceedingly agreeable one for all parties. Still, boarding, no matter how ideal it may be, is only a step toward the home-making, and is not like home itself. It is living in a tent instead of setting up a home.

People who board seldom have a sense of permanency in their domestic life. They live in trunks and their aim is to have as few portable possessions as possible, so that they may break camp and change their quarters, if needful, at a moment's notice. There is a delightful sense of privacy when one turns the key in one's own latch, and sits down at one's own table, and lives under one's own vine and fig tree, which one cannot have in the nomadic life of the boarding house or hotel.

Of course, if people who board have a sufficient income to warrant their making their abode in a large and beautiful hotel, they will be saved much of the drudgery and many of the inconveniences of life in their own house. In a hotel you touch a bell; and, presto, an obliging person is at your elbow to know what your serene highness may desire.

Everything is brought to you; you sit down at a table a queen might envy, and order a sumptuous repast from a bill of fare varied enough to make a banquet for princes and great people generally. You fare sumptuously every day, and to suit the splendor about you, you wear neat attire and cannot be seen at any time out of your own room in a negligée costume. The whole thing has much the aspect of life in an Arabian night's entertainment, where obedient genii are always ready to come at a call and furnish everything the traveler can possibly desire. And you must be always on dress parade to some extent.

But even with all this, hotel fare becomes monotonous, and the bustle of hotel life is not so satisfactory as the retirement of a home of one's own. In the smaller

"Lives under one's own vine and fig tree."

boarding houses conveniences are, of course, much more limited; service is not always up to the mark, and even at the best of times, the menu palls upon one's appetite.   One learns that Monday's, Tuesday's and Wednesday's bill of fare is regulated by a law exact as that of the Medes and Persians.   One grows tired of seeing the trim maiden ladies and the elderly widows in black gowns, and the nice

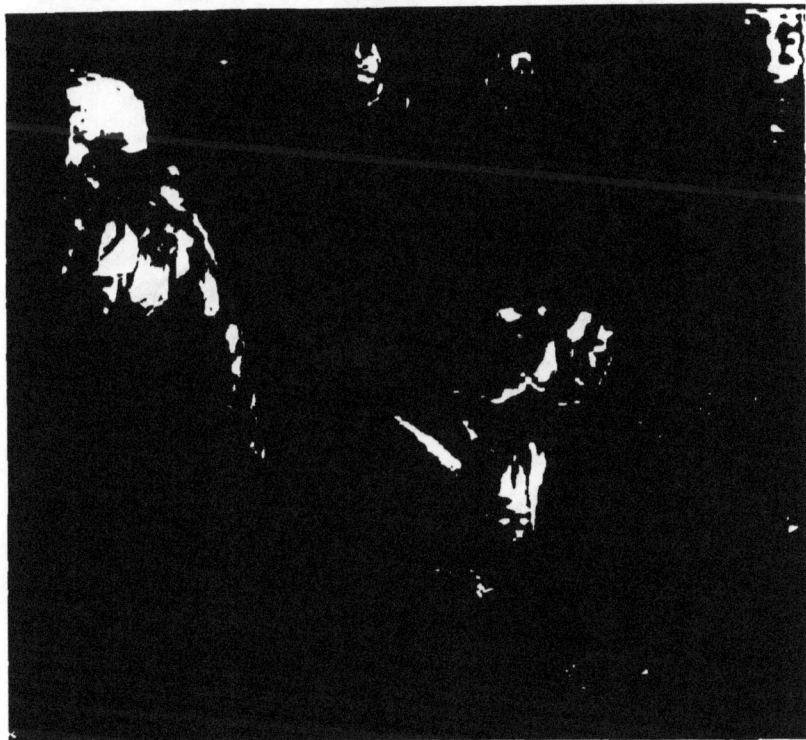

"Cannot be seen at any time out of your own room in negligée costume."

young men, and the pretty belles, who make up the coterie around the boarding-house table, and one sighs for a little place of one's very own.

The women whose homes are in the boarding house, having comparatively little to engage their attention, become interested in small things.   They talk on trivialities; the talk sometimes grows personal; there are feuds and opposite sides,

"And you must be always in dress parade to some extent."

and altogether the life is not invariably elevating. For a bride with little to do all day while her husband is at business, or for a young mother, the boarding house is hardly so fitting a shelter as the simplest home. It would seem, all things being equal, that it is usually wiser not to dread the day of small things; but to begin at once as one hopes to go on. Even if there is not very much money, if there is a good deal of love; if there is common sense and prudence and loyalty, the two will start better under their own roof than they will under the roof of a neighbor.

The wife, particularly, may as well grow used to marketing, catering, cooking and doing the various things which are implied in housekeeping for two, finding even her inexperience full of lessons and learning by her very mistakes. Nobody should fear housekeeping because she has had no practice in it. Whatever people may tell you, there is nothing occult or difficult about the simple processes of housekeeping, and nothing at all which a sensible, intelligent, average American girl cannot master in six weeks if she gives her attention to the matter. I speak on this subject with feeling, because when I began myself I did not know any more about practical housewifery than a child of six, and my attention had always been given to things quite opposite the mysteries of the kitchen and dining room; but I found very speedily that if I had to show other people, I must know how myself, and so there was nothing for it but to start right in and learn how to broil a steak, bake a loaf and do whatever was to be done about the house.

There are many manuals which greatly assist the young housekeeper; but that which aids her beyond all else is the determination not to be daunted by difficulties, but to prove herself equal to any situation, and superior to any emergency, let either be what it will.

I take it for granted that most young wives have mothers who can advise them as to the best ways of management, and all husbands have mothers who have been patterns of perfection. The man does not live who will not tell you that his mother's doughnuts, his mother's pies, his mother's puddings, and viands in his mother's house generally, surpassed anything he will ever again find on the face of the wide earth. Do not take exception to this very natural feeling on his part. The man looks back through the glamour of a happy mist and he forgets that in the days when his mother's cooking melted so sweetly in his mouth, he brought to the homeliest fare the appetite of a hungry, growing boy. Besides, men, as a rule, are more or less given to exploiting their relatives to their wives, and to boast of their wives' wonderful attainments to other people. Many a wife would be surprised to hear how genially her husband praises her when he is out of her sight and hearing. At all events, it is quite a good plan for the young wife to ask advice and accept assistance wherever she can get it. We learn a great deal in this world by keeping our eyes open and observing what is going on; also we learn a good deal by the simple method of asking questions. Nothing is ever learned without attention and industry, and in the science of housekeeping it is quite worth while to study the ways of those who have gone before us, and to gain by what they have to give.

A good cookery book is a friend in need and nobody should think of beginning housekeeping without one or without several of these useful advisers. The best housekeepers and the most expert cooks are those who follow implicitly the

"It is well to have a formula."

directions laid down in recipes. Of course there are people who seem to cook by nature, and who throw things together with apparent ease and produce results which justify their hap-hazard way of cooking. These people belong to the order of cooks who are born, not made. The most of us, however, must pursue a different method, and we will find it to our advantage to have a formula and to follow it literally.

My dear and honored friend, Marian Harland, one day in her kitchen said to her Irish cook: " Do you know where 'Common Sense in the Household' is?"—this being her own famous manual of cookery.  The book was not at hand and was sent for, and while Mrs. Terhune waited for it the cook took occasion to remark in a lofty manner: "It's a poor cook that needs a receipt book."  This was very amusing, addressed to a woman who stood at the head of the house-keeping profession in America, but it was the attitude of the mind of ignorance, not of knowledge.  Besides, there is no use in our burdening our memories with a lot of useless luggage.  Why should we remember things which we may just as well have set down in a book, to which we can refer at need.  If you are to make a dessert, whatever it be, simply look at your recipe and follow it exactly, and if you are careful to have everything just as the book tells you you should, your result will probably justify the pains you take.

Housekeeping for two implies smaller quantities than are usually given in the ordinary cook book, and therefore it will be necessary for you quite often to halve or quarter the amounts which you find in the recipes.  This, however, is an easy matter.  One needs to bring to bear on everything in life common sense and judgment.  The bill of fare in the simplest home is usually more varied than that which obtains in a boarding house, for the reason that the housekeeper does not suffer herself to fall into a rut.  There is an art, too, in buying.  In this country we are given to laying in large quantities of things.  We might easily take a lesson from the housekeepers of France and of Italy.  In Paris one buys exactly what she wants for a meal.  The purchasing is done in very small quantities, and everything is carefully counted down to the fraction of a cent.  Here we are very apt to despise small economies, the result being that our purses are lean and in most households we waste enough to support another family.  When, some years ago, there was a great war debt to be paid by France, the people found themselves quite equal to the added strain because they were a nation of great frugality and everybody was able to bear his proportion.  In dry groceries, such as sugar, flour, etc., there is sometimes an advantage in purchasing in the larger quantity.  Soap gains by being kept on hand, as it hardens and does not waste away so fast as when first made, when it is soft and easily melts away in the water; but there are many things of which it is best to buy only what you want at the moment.  The housekeeper's rule should be to keep her living expenses well within her income.  Only thus can there be real comfort and the absence of anxiety in domestic life.

Above everything else, avoid debt.  It hangs around one's neck like a mill-stone, it fetters hands and feet, and it robs one of all self-respect.  Nobody can look himself in the face in the looking-glass, without a blush, unless he " owes not any man."  Retrenchment, self-sacrifice, honest poverty, are far to be preferred to debt.

9

# CHAPTER XVII.

## Florilla's Sanitarium.

OU can't stay here by yourself, Florilla. It will be too desolate. Rent the old house for the summer, and come to New York with me. There must be many things which a clever girl like you can find to do in a big city."

"Perhaps there are, Aunt Adela, but I don't know of any. In the meantime I must live, and it costs less to live here than it would in town. I have grandmother's little legacy as a nest-egg, the garden will furnish me with fruit and vegetables, the bees will give me honey, and old Keziah would be homeless if I went away. She takes the heaviest end of the work, and I think I cannot do better than to stay right here among the people who have known me since I was born. I shall miss dear grandmother terribly."

"She has been a great care," said Aunt Adela, "and very hard to get on with for the last two years, but you were very patient, Florilla."

"Well, Auntie, it isn't hard to be patient with one you love. And if the young and strong cannot bear with the old, and make allowances for their weakness, I think they are very poor creatures; very unworthy of respect. Grandmother had been active so long that she felt being laid aside more than most people do, and somehow, toward the end, I had two sorts of love for her: the love of a child for a mother, and the love of a mother for a child. I shall miss her, dear grandmother."

"I never knew her very intimately," Aunt Adela replied after a pause. "I never met your father's people much till I came back from Italy, after your mother died. But your grandmother was a good woman, Florilla. The thing which troubles me, though, is leaving you alone, and I must take the first train back in the morning. I have been away as long as I can be spared from home."

"I haven't had time for planning yet, Auntie, but this is what I have thought of. Here is this pretty house with the hills in the background and the lovely lake in front; here is the comfortable furnishing, the airy rooms, and the good beds are here, and a plentiful supply of linen; everything, in fact, that a house needs. I am not a trained nurse, but I am accustomed to an invalid, and I have a practical knowledge of what the sick want. Keziah is devoted to me. I think I will carry on a sanitarium in a very modest way here in my home."

(130)

"You can but try," said Aunt Adela. "It will be hard work, and if you should not succeed, you can always come to me and rent or sell this place. For my part, I have lived so long in the stir and bustle of New York, that I don't care for the country, except for a little while in the summer, but you have grown accustomed to it, I suppose, and it does not seem so lonesome, so dreary."

"I love it, dear, I just love it. I love the fields and the flowers, the old apple trees in the south meadow, the willows by the lake, the silence and the sweetness, and the kind neighbors who call me Florrie as they did when I was a little girl. I could not be contented where trolley cars were clanging and elevated railroads thundering along all day."

"Tea is ready, Florilla," said old Keziah, putting her head in at the parlor door. Keziah would not have thought of prefixing a "Miss" to the name of the young woman she had carried in her arms as a baby, though she served her as loyally as a baroness of the middle ages was served by her maidens. A strong old woman and capable, Keziah Sinn might be depended on to guard Florilla Dawes.

The two ladies went out to a country tea of fresh eggs, scones, honey, and cream so thick that a spoon in it stood straight up, like a sentry on duty. Aunt Adela, looking about her at the old-fashioned luxury of everything could not but admit to herself that her niece had at least the environment suited to her purpose.

"But, dear me," she thought, "what is five hundred dollars, and that is all Florilla has, besides the house."

To Florilla the five hundred dollars seemed a large sum. She had rarely had five dollars in her pocket-book at one time, in her whole life, and she had never yet needed money, living in a place where barter covered most of the simple transactions. There was no mortgage on the house, and Florilla had not a debt in the world.

After she had seen her Aunt Adela off the next morning she went down the long village street to the doctor's house, and told her old friend what she wished to do. To Dr. Sanford there was nothing fanciful or absurd in Florilla's proposition. On the contrary, he thought well of it, as a practical notion which could easily be carried out. He told her that he had an old classmate in town whose specialty was treating nervous patients and those in need of a rest cure, and he volunteered to write to Doctor Lawrence at once, in Florilla's behalf.

"You get your house-cleaning done, child," he said. "Not that you are not always as neat as a pin, but women aren't satisfied unless they turn the whole house out of the windows every spring and fall."

Three weeks later, when the faint golden-green of the April orchards had deepened to a richer tone, and the land was everywhere a tossing sea of pink and white blossoms, Florilla Dawes received a thick letter from New York. The great physician wrote to her about a patient of his whom he proposed sending to her, a lady who would require very peculiar care and treatment, and for whom he desired such an atmosphere as she would find in Florilla's home. She had been under a long strain, had been in the midst of exacting duties, and must have absolute tranquillity for weeks to come. "Twenty-five dollars a week will not be too much to charge for her," he added, "as during her stay you must have no other sick people. But you need not exclude one or two quiet cheerful guests in addition, if you hear of them. Miss Lillie Fairchild will give no trouble that she can help, and your house is just the place for her."

Arrangements were soon completed, and one lovely afternoon Florilla, borrowing a neighbor's phaeton and leisurely old horse, drove to the station to meet Miss Fairchild. A maid had accompanied her on the journey, but left by the return

" She went down the long village street," etc.

train. Florilla was attracted at once by the sweet refined tones and the gentle high-bred air of her new inmate, and though she discovered that Miss Fairchild was accustomed to much service, and expected to receive it, she was more than ready with her ministrations. She had rubbed and bathed her grandmother, and Miss Fairchild found her able to give her restful massage, and not averse to doing anything an invalid required.

Old Keziah had her private opinion of a woman who looked well but had her breakfast in bed, took something to eat—an egg, or a glass of milk, or a cup of broth every two hours in the day—and had to be rubbed before she went to sleep at night; but she felt pleased that Florilla was paid for the lady's fancies, and she, too, was won by the invariable softness and charm of Miss Fairchild's manner.

LANDSCAPE.

If the two country-bred women had known it, that same charm had captivated the most fastidious people in very exclusive social circles; it was Miss Fairchild's distinction that, added to beauty, she was both sympathetic and exceptionally well bred.

Florilla, quick to receive from her associates, insensibly learned certain graces of speech and manner from her guest during the three months of her stay.

Two rather elderly ladies and a young girl were added to the household before the summer was over, and Keziah's niece, a farmer's daughter, sixteen and studying for college, came to help in the increased work of the family. The ladies were teachers taking their vacation and needing a quiet spot where they could sit on the porch, read and knit, go for long walks, and drive about the country at their will. A gay place was their aversion. The stillness and peace of Florilla's home suited them precisely. The young woman was another patient from town, recommended like Miss Fairchild, by her physician, to the sisterly care of Miss Dawes.

"All very well for summer," wrote Aunt Adela, "but do you suppose, Florilla, that you'll have visitors coming to you in the dead of winter? Then you'll have to shut up the house and try something else."

"I am saving so much, dear Aunty," Florilla wrote, "that I'll be able to rest when winter comes. Besides, I am living by a good old rule, in a good old book, ' Take no thought for the morrow; the morrow shall take thought for the things of itself. But my dear doctor tells me that people are often sent to the country in the winter, in these days, and Miss Fairchild has promised to speak to her friends for me."

Miss Fairchild kept her word. And if Florilla could have heard her, this is what she would have been told about herself:

"Florilla Dawes is a sensible, amiable, merry hearted woman, whose house shines with neatness, whose rooms are all used, who has good springs on her beds and excellent hair mattresses, whose cooking is of the best, and who knows how to make people thoroughly comfortable. Plenty of clean towels, plenty of good milk, no jars or friction. I can recommend Florilla's little sanitarium. It is kept by a sweet, loving, lovable young woman, who has tact, kindness and common sense."

The doctor's statement was verified. Winter and summer alike Florilla had all the guests she could care for under the old roof, where she had learned her profession in nursing a feeble and querulous grandmother.

----

THE walk is not in the valley but through the valley: Ah! then it must be a straight and plain path, and one that leads somewhere. It must be a direct journey to a distinct destination. Yes, I am assured that it is, and that the destination is nothing less delightful than heaven itself. How, then, can I fear when once by faith I have connected the valley with the heaven to which it leads? This going must be like the flight of a bird through some dark cloud, and then out into the full light of the sun. It must be like some traveler journeying through a deeply shadowed canyon between the mountains, and then coming out into the broad and smiling country where the sun is shining in its glory, and where every green herb and beautiful flower is springing up to bless. Surely, if it is only a quiet walk through the sheltered valley, and the valley itself opens out full and broad in the shining fields of heaven, why, indeed, should I fear?—*G. B. F. Hallock, D. D.*

"The trivial round, the common task,
   Will furnish all we ought to ask.
Know to deny ourselves, a road
   To bring us daily nearer God."

# CHAPTER XVIII.

## Music in the Family.

HE bond of the family is love. The expression of love may be practical or it may show itself in a more spiritual way—in affection. Music may be taken as the symbol and expression which unites these two features. The tangible part of music is practical, addressing itself to the eye, the ear, the hand, the voice. Its ethereal aspect takes us at once out of the realm of the senses, and carries us into a toneworld of surpassing beauty. Music is a fitting symbol of that very inner spirit of love which is the characteristic of every true family.

A single sound alone is but a noise. Yet each single sound can be fitted into the gamut, out of whose seven notes all music is constructed. Browning speaks in his "Abt Vogler" of the three sounds which create, not a fourth sound, but a star! It is those starry effects of harmony or associated sounds which so fittingly represent the family. Each adds an essential note, which would be wanting without that particular member of the home circle. Union of different temperaments forms the fascinations of the family. And music in grouping and binding a diversified family into a unity about so lovely a centre shows one of its most charming powers.

Music is so wide a realm that it takes into its magic enclosure the gifted and also the undeveloped, the young but latent lover of song and sound, and the mature connoisseur and master of its science and art. The great palace of music opens wide doors to those who love and long for the divine in sound. Of all our art-loves, this is the most ethereal. It speaks indeed a mystic language and one of other spheres. But we comprehend it.

If jarring, discordant sounds sometimes fall into rhythm, as we are told the incoherent noises of a great city are reduced to tranquilizing, lulling, musical effects, by distance, so may the sometimes unavoidably disturbing elements of family life glide softly into forgetfulness in the family music in which all join.

" Given," says Syndey Lanier, " the raw material—to wit, wife, children, a friend or two and a house—two other things are necessary. These are a good fire and music. And inasmuch as we can do without the fire for half the year, I may say that music is the one essential. After an evening spent around the piano or the flute or the violin, how warm and how chastened is the kiss with which the family all say good-night ! Ah, the music has taken all the day cares and thrown

MUSIC IN THE FAMILY.

them into its terrible alembic, and boiled them and rocked them and cooled them, till they are crystallized into one care, which is a most sweet and rare and desirable sorrow—the yearning for God. We all, from little **toddler to** father, go to bed with so much of heaven in our hearts, at least, as that we long for it unutterably and believe it.''

Next in importance after the attitude of the family toward God is the keeping its spirit gentle and affectionate. Travelers tell us that the atmosphere in St. Peter's, Rome, is like a celestial climate, always equable, never too hot, never too cold. So the temperature of our homes should be serene, life-giving, always charged with the tranquillizing, yet uplifting, ever-reigning spirit of love.

Music will help to effect such a desirable state. Even with its most rudimentary beginnings, there steals into the home a sense of something above and beyond the life of the senses, differing in its nature from the three meals a day, and the routine of economy or of pleasure.

Intercourse with an ethereal world is let down upon us, a supra-mortal language is spoken to us, a new and mystic world is revealed to us—dimly, perhaps, at first, but gradually drawing us toward itself with more and more powerful charm.

"A man," says Drummond, "cannot be a memoer of a family, and remain an utter egoist." And music in the family, by the family, draws each one out individually, and yet each one must subdue himself to the harmony of the whole. One egotist can destroy much family music. And the willingness to fall into the secondary place, to accompany another who takes the first place, is one of the unselfish acts which music requires and promotes.

Into the family life is brought, and should be brought, everything which concerns each member, be it sad, joyous or neutral. But, in fact, very little is of a neutral nature in our American homes. Everything is vital, from the getting off to school in the morning, to the seeing of the last one in at night. We lead highly vitalized lives, and for this reason, quite as much as to relieve tedium and monotony, we need the controlling and adjusting, the tranquillizing effect of music. It is not possible, without a greater expense and trouble than our average families can afford, to call in musicians from the outside. For most of us, if we are to have music in the home, we must depend upon ourselves for it. To forego such a boon is not to be thought of. It can always be obtained by effort and determination. This latter is even more important than musical ability. Every family should have music in some form, even if no other than singing together without an instrument, among its purposes and its achievements. An instrument, presumably a piano, is much to be desired, but much can be effected without a piano, especially if the father or one of the sons has some knowledge of the flute or violin. The rent of a piano may not be money thrown away. But taking the instrument for granted, that one in the family who has the most musical skill and ability should take the lead, and gather the others around the piano as a centre, and should try to bring out, even if most feebly at first, whatever talent is dormant or cultivated in each one.   The less musical should be most encouraged!  And great gentleness should be used in training and helping each.   What is a false note now and then, or the failure to keep time, compared to the serenity and sweetness that is lost by friction and unpleasant, personal remarks?  Music evaporates and disappears as religion does, when the spirit is ruffled and hurt.   In such music as we speak of, where no one is a virtuoso, there will be imperfection, and it is not a question of faultlessness, but of endeavor.   The imperfection must be made good by the harmony of spirit felt and expressed by each attempting it. Certainly if the father or the mother can be the Choraegus of this house-band, it will be most likely to succeed.   But let the leader be a child, if he is more competently gifted.   To begin with singing some song which is perhaps simply a popular air is as easy a way as any.   Buying two or three copies will interest the children to follow the notes.   If the means of the family allow instruction for one or two of the children, this will greatly serve to keep up the interest from week to week.

The chief benefit, however, will arise not so much from absolute knowledge gained as from those flitting, beautiful, elusive and mysterious emotions which fill a child's soul when music is heard. · These emotions form a soft mould which takes on and gives out again lovely impressions which never can be forgotten or erased from the soul.   The world of the infinite rises upon us when we hear good music, and because a child says nothing about it, and cannot and does not give expression to his feelings when music surrounds him with its penetrating sweetness, it is no sign that he is not receiving some magical power and some soothing and controlling influence into his inner being which is to remain with him through life as a sweetener and a comforter.   The associations of the young should be with the bright and innocent and joyous things of life.   If these speaking impressions of something supersensuously beautiful are not presented to the mind in childhood, they may never exist at all.   And, indeed, the lack of such early and delicious impressions may account for the imperviousness of many in later life to the pure sense of beauty, and the witchery and mystery of the emotional world.

The finer qualities of the spirit need (in this hardening world) constant cultivation.   We cannot begin too early with our children to provide that which shall evoke the diviner and more subtle part of their nature.   We must give them a true sense of gentleness by that

> " Music that gentlier on the spirit lies
> Than tired eyelids upon tired eyes."

The pervasive, all-enfolding resonance of noble music may give a deeper conception of the ever-present being of God than many words.   Infinity itself may surge into a very young spirit on the

"Tides of music's golden sea
Setting toward eternity."

We know not which one of our children or youth is to be "the reed through which all things blow into music." His musical director said of Lanier:

"To him as a child, in his cradle, music was given—the heavenly gift to feel and to express himself in tones. His human nature was like an enchanted instrument, needing but a breath or a touch to send its beauty out into the world. It was, indeed, irresistible that he should turn, with those poetical feelings which transcend language to the penetrating gentleness of the flute, or the infinite passion of the violin."

The dormant and the latent must be awakened by placing our children in the environment to educe that to which their higher and finer nature will respond. And the love of music is too heavenly a gift to lie in lasting sleep within our children for want of a home surcharged with the sweetness of loving and life-giving family music.—*Mrs. Merrill E. Gates.*

MRS. LOUIS KLOPSCH AND HER DAUGHTER MARY.

# CHAPTER XIX.

## The First Baby.

THE coming of the first little one marks an event of great importance in family history. During the months which precede the baby's arrival the mother must of necessity undergo an amount of self-denial and seclusion, which are really no sacrifices in the eye of a loving and conscientious wife and mother-to-be, for surely it is true that beyond all other women in the world she is blessed to whom is sent from heaven the gift of a little child to be her very own.

The reluctance which married women sometimes feel and express to assuming the duties of maternity is not to be explained on any ground except that of singular and unwomanly selfishness, unless, indeed, they fear to bring into the world a child inheriting morbid and diseased tendencies. In a case where there is danger of this sort the husband and wife should have considered very solemnly whether or not they had a right to marry, because it is a crime to deliberately bring into the world beings who will be freighted with evil tendencies, or compelled to bear in their bodies sorrow and sickness all their days.

Persons closely related to one another by ties of blood and kinship, as, for instance, first cousins; persons of scrofulous tendencies or with a disposition to insanity latent in their blood, should not marry. They should have the courage to say, "This great evil which I unfortunately have inherited shall die with me; I will not be a partner to prolonging so great a burden in the race." Granting, however, that parents are strong and healthy, they should not feel a hesitation about any obligation which the married state involves. The birth of offspring is one of the obligations to which people become liable when they fall in love and marry.

During the nine months in which the mother carries her little one as a precious trust under her heart she is in a sense a sanctuary. She should be careful to guard herself from any violent outbreaks of passion, and above all things from anger and fear. For the sake of the little one who is coming she should let her speech be gentle, her mind peaceful, and she should remember that the whole future of her infant may depend on the mental state in which she is usually found during the earlier portion of her pregnancy.

(141)

A mother is sometimes in her early youth too ignorant to know that she may almost make or mar her child's future in this early time, and yet this is true.  I remember hearing a wise elderly woman once say to a friend whose first baby was expected:  " My dear, if you wish by and by to have peaceful days and nights take all the quiet rest you can at this time.   Do not suffer yourself to be nervous.

**FIRST BABY.**

or to be fluttering here and there and getting tired.   Take all the exercise you comfortably can, but remember that if you wish to have a quiet little one, who will be a real comfort to you during his baby days, you must provide beforehand for this sort of disposition."

The mother, too, must be careful about the food she eats.   If, for instance, she refuses all meats and vegetables, and lives exclusively on fruits and salads and stimulants in the way of tea and coffee, her child will come into the world physically weak—very probably plump and well-formed, but with soft limbs which have not in them enough quality of vigor to make the baby well either during its infancy or in its later life.

Very many of the disturbances which are trying to the mother during her pregnancy may be overcome by care on her part and patient discipline of her system. For instance, the nausea which is a distressing symptom in the morning during the first three months usually disappears at the end of that time. Very often it can be overcome by simply taking a cracker and some warm drink before rising, or by the persistent use of lemonade or some other remedy which a physician will advise. The physique of a healthy woman accommodates itself to the new state of affairs, and usually after the first few weeks there is not very much trouble or pain to be borne, but it is wise for an expectant mother to place herself early under the care of her physician, and from time to time to have advice, so that she may go through the months which precede her baby's coming with a quiet mind and a body somewhat at ease.

American families are unfortunately growing smaller and smaller. Where once people had from six to ten children they are now contented with two or three, and these at long intervals. Yet there is no sight in the world so beautiful as that of a large family, and a crowded nursery is not unlike a crowded nest with the little fledglings close together under the mother's brooding wing. The children, when they come at shorter intervals, really help the mother in bringing each other up, and even if it means for some few years a time of greater struggle to the parents, the large family usually turns out quite as well in the end as the smaller one.

In sewing for the little one who comes to your care there are certain necessary articles which the loving prevision of the mother will prepare, but an immense outfit of baby clothes is by no means necessary. Everything which a baby wears may be bought in our large shops, but where the mother can make the little garments herself she will take pleasure in having an additional daintiness about them, and they will cost her very much less than if she simply sends an order to a merchant. Besides, handmade clothing is always more beautiful and gives more satisfaction—at least in garments for little wearers—than that which is made by machine, if only as a matter of sentiment.

The baby's first garments will include six little bands of soft flannel, which will be simply laid over and feather-stitched at the edges—a hem is apt to make a hard place which may hurt the delicate skin of a baby; six little undershirts which open in front, and which may be either of silk and wool or of wool and cotton, are the next necessity. Four of these may be very small, and two of a larger size to allow for the baby's growth. What is called a little barrow coat is also a

"The coming of the first little one marks an event of great importance."

necessity. This is a flannel skirt which is fastened to a muslin band and which opens in front. Two of these at least are requisite. There must be a supply—several dozen at least—of soft linen and cotton diapers, and one dozen of these should be made of old linen table cloths or something of that sort, as they are soft and absorbent. Do not use a rubber napkin upon a baby; it is better to be watchful and change the diapers frequently.

Little socks are so pretty and dainty that every mother will require a supply of them for the little feet at first, and almost always friends like to give these as presents. The same may be said about the dainty little knitted and crocheted sacks, which finish prettily a baby's dress. The supply of slips and skirts which are prepared for the little one will depend on the mother's time and her purse. Not very many are needed, nor should they be very long. A beautiful embroidered christening robe is often an heirloom in a family, and is passed from mother to children. I know one family in which all the grandchildren have been christened in the robe in which their grandmother received upon her brow the drops from the baptismal font.

One thing is over all essential, that your little one comes to a home hallowed by love and fragrant with prayer. Be glad that your baby is coming. Let it be born into an atmosphere of Christian love, of Christian influence. Make up your mind from the first that it is a gift of God, and that you cannot be too joyful to receive this gift from His hands.

The first weeks of a baby's life should be spent in a dim, hushed world. The baby needs sleep, and must have it in abundant measure. The principal requisites at this time are that the little thing shall be kept warm and comfortable, shall be fed at regular intervals, and shall be allowed to lie in his own little cradle and not be continually held in people's arms and jumped and bounced about or passed from hand to hand. Care taken during the first few weeks to be very regular in the treatment and management of a little baby will make it much easier for him and his parents when he begins to develop, to feel his little feet, and to realize that although he has no language but a cry, yet that by crying he can get what he wants.

The old-fashioned way was to dose a baby with catnip tea and other remedies, to feed him whenever he cried, to carry him up and down, to and fro, and in every possible way to make of him a little tyrant. All this was not to baby's permanent advantage nor at all to the comfort of those who had to care for him. The modern method of doing everything according to rule, of refraining from injudicious over-loading of the tiny stomach, and of keeping the baby warm and quiet is very much better. From quite an early period the little creature may be taken out every day into the open air. The healthiest babe I ever saw lived in the open air all the time, its carriage standing out of doors in all but extremely

HAPPY CHILDHOOD DAYS.

stormy weather, and the little inmate taking its naps in the fresh air and being kept as much as possible out of the house.

The nursery world should be a tranquil one. Loud tones, scolding, all sudden violent explosions, such as the slamming of doors, screaming, and things of that kind, should be kept away from this enchanted spot. Too strong light should not be suffered to fall upon a baby's eyes. Mothers sometimes, in their desire to have a pretty perambulator for their little ones, forget that a glaring white sunshade is not at all the thing, and that a hooded carriage somewhat darkened with green or blue would be very much better to keep away the sunlight.

The mother cannot too sedulously care for her little one herself. Even if she employs a nurse she must herself take the supervision; no hired hands can be trusted wholly, however responsible they may be. This little being may owe all its health, happiness and usefulness in the world to the constant tender care it receives in babyhood. I have known a mother to find out when too late that an unscrupulous nurse had night after night put sleeping drops into the baby's milk, so that she would not be disturbed nor her rest broken by his stirring in his sleep. The result in the deadening of sensibility, in impaired nerve force and lessened vitality could not be reckoned perhaps until manhood, but all the same nature would make its reprisals.

It is quite as well that little children should not be indiscriminately kissed. Of course every one wishes to kiss a baby, but it is not for the child's best good that it should be thus brought into close touch with all sorts of lips, and the wise mother will prefer to forbid too much kissing on the little rose-leaf face. "Hands off!" is a good rule for babies and for small children.

> Baby, my baby, I love you so,
> I cannot be sad whatever winds blow.
> For you are safe in my cradling arms,
> And nought shall come near that my baby harms.
>
> Hush, my babe, lie still and slumber
> Holy angels guard thy bed,
> Heavenly blessings without number
> Gently falling on thy head.

# CHAPTER XX.

## The Nursery Group.

HEN instead of one beloved child the mother has around her several little ones of different ages, there is nothing more beautiful in the world than the sight of the children growing up. In the morning when they rise flushed and rosy from their happy sleep, all day as they play, at night when they are taken away to rest, the mother may be tired, but she is happy; her little ones are under her eye and hand; she can attend to their bathing, dressing, and watch their development day by day.

Nothing ever seems so wonderful, almost miraculous, as the rapid improvement of children from the hour they begin to make sounds until they talk plainly. Their vocabularies grow as if by magic. A little child can learn without difficulty several languages at once. A baby of eighteen months or two years will acquire French and German and English all at the same time, and the different words do not seem to jostle in the little brain. All this, however, must come naturally. Children are imitative creatures and they prattle as the birds learn to sing; they copy without apparent effort the tones of the voice, the accent, and the words of those about them.

A little child who can hear easily learns to talk, and in most cases the period of baby talk and broken speech which some persons so much admire will be very much abbreviated if people simply use ordinary grown-up speech in talking with the nursery group. For my part, I think it much more attractive and interesting to hear a quaint little maiden or laddie speaking correct English than using a jargon which nobody can understand.

The moral education of children begins very early, and they can be taught to give up their little playthings to one another, to share their pleasures, to refrain from the angry frown or demonstration of violence in the way of kicking or slapping, if all around them there is an environment of gentleness. When a child falls and bumps his head on the floor, it is the foolish mother who runs and beats the floor. The wise mother diverts the child and makes light of the little tumble. It is the more than foolish—it is the wicked—mother who teaches the little child by example and speech to be afraid of a poor innocent worm, to go into spasms at the sight of a mouse, or in any way to show symptoms of terror.

In every possible manner we should teach children to be strong and bold, and not
to go through the world tied down by bonds of graven fear. Early impressions
are very enduring, and the foundation for much nervous terror and distress may
be laid by unwise parents in the years of babyhood. Let the little child fear
nothing. Surround it with kindness, let its play be unselfish, and from the first
try to inculcate the golden rule.

" When instead of one beloved child the mother has several little ones."

After the child reaches the age of four years the kindergarten will prove an
excellent assistant to the mother. If there be no kindergarten to which she can
send her little child or children, the mother will do well to supply herself with a
kindergarten magazine and with some of the games which the little ones use in
that loveliest of nursery schools. Children who are taught in kindergartens

before going to the primary school have their perceptive faculties trained, and although reading and writing form no part of kindergarten instruction, yet they reach these useful studies in a state of preparation which is not to be found among children who have not had kindergarten advantages. The pricking patterns into paper with pins, moulding and modeling in clay, and the various occupations of the kindergarten employ the little hands, while the plays and games are really educational and the child learns without knowing it. Then the little children are taught truth, kindness, love and generosity, and their manners insensibly take on

IN THE NURSERY.

a stamp of goodness. They learn many little facts about natural history, and are prepared unconsciously for the school-room at a later date.

The bed-time of little children should be a very happy hour. Never should a little head be laid upon the pillow except peacefully; and the habit of some mothers of going over the faults of the day and reproving or punishing the children at bed-time is a serious blunder, not far from a crime. The tender mother tucks the little ones in with gentle hands, hears them say their prayers, and sends them off to dreamland happy and glad. Among the little prayers appropriate for children to say at night none surpass the familiar

"Now I lay me down to sleep,
  I pray the Lord my soul to keep,
  If I should die before I wake,
  I pray the Lord my soul to take;
  And this I ask for Jesus' sake.  Amen."

There is a little morning prayer corresponding to this:

"Now I wake and see the light,
  'Tis God who kept me through the night;
  To Him I lift my voice and pray
  That He will keep me through the day,
    For Jesus' sake."

Children can appropriately learn the Lord's Prayer, and have whatever other religious instruction their parents choose to give them. Do not postpone the time of indoctrinating children into the creed of your life. Before the child is six years old he is made or marred for the Kingdom of Heaven. Little children early taught about God and duty, and the simple things which every child should know, receive them into honest hearts where doubt has not yet intruded. They will not be turned in after days from the faith of the fathers if this faith is taught them carefully at a sufficiently early age.

Children are educated more than we sometimes think by their little play-mates. A grandmother seated one day at her sewing heard the conversation of two little tots behind the screen in the room. One said to the other, "To-morrow will be Good Friday." "What is that?" was the inquiry. In reply the first child said, "Why, don't you know? It is the day when our blessed Lord died upon the cross for our sins, and all Christians go to church on Good Friday and remember how the Saviour gave Himself for them." "Oh," said the other child, "I never heard about it; do tell me." And so as they sat over their play the one child told the other the story of the Lamb of God who taketh away the sins of the world.

There is often implanted in childish minds some thought which you would not desire to have there. Especially as children grow older they learn things which are impure from children who have not been carefully trained; and the sum of the matter is that a mother should know who her children's playmates and associates are. Do not select them chiefly or even at all on the ground simply of their being well dressed. The little ragged boy or girl may not prove so unfit an associate for your child as another royally clad little creature who has been neglected.

One of the saddest stories I ever knew was of a little girl who lived in a large boarding house, and whose parents seemed to care nothing for her. They went away every day on their own pleasures, leaving her by herself to roam about the

"Now I lay me down to sleep."

halls and parlors and find such care as she could from strangers in the house or from maids. One day she said to a friend of mine, "I wish my papa and mamma cared for me, but I never go near them that they do not say, 'Run away, dear, don't bother me.'" At last little "run away, dear" did not bother them any more, for she sickened and died, and they followed her little hearse to the cemetery. It is to be hoped that no more children came to those cruel people to be thus shamefully neglected

---

With flare of trumpet and roll of drum,
Tho' never a stick have we,
 And never a horn save a dimpled hand—
 A roistering, rollicking, warlike band,
Right valorous soldiers three.

Our line of march through the parlor dim,
And out to the open hall,
 A step and a stamp and a fearless stride—
 And a paper-knife strapped to each valiant side,
Then way! we are heroes all.

Shall it be a charge on the rocking-chair?
Or a siege of the balustrade?
 Or a slow, strategical night-attack
 On the castle walls of the old hat-rack,
Or merely a dress parade?

'Tis one I vow to the soldiers three,
Polly and Prue and I,
 With never a horn save a dimpled hand,
 We'll march all over this Downstairs Land
Till the stars peep out in the sky,
And the moon says bed-time's nigh.
    *—Charles Edward Thomas.*

# CHAPTER XXI.

## Going to School.

TURN in memory with a sort of wistful and loving thought to the first school I ever attended. It was a little red schoolhouse in the country, and it stood on a hillside under spreading trees. Whittier has described a similar place in his well-known poem,

> " Still sits the schoolhouse by the road,
> A ragged beggar sunning."

The teacher's desk and chair stood in one corner, and the children of all ages sat before him, from little rosy-cheeked tots of five or six up to young men and women. I remember my triumph one day when a very small child I was told to go up head because I had known how to spell "measles" when all the others had missed it; and I remember, too, how we used to play out of doors on broad stones beside the brook, where we had our oak-leaf cups and saucers and ate our luncheons in the middle of the day with a zest which no appetite of later years has surpassed. That school is a dim and distant dream.

Much better do I remember the beautiful seminary for young ladies which I attended when somewhat older—a long, low building which stood on the banks of the beautiful Passaic River. Here three women, long since gone to heaven, presided over a most excellent school. We called them Miss Anna, Miss Lizzie and Miss Jane, and early in the mornings the children gathered in groups before the door, ready to enter when Miss Anna, coming there with a little silver bell in her hand, gently rang it and called us in. Some of the lessons taught in that school abide with me still and always will. Our desks were green, and as we sat by them we could look out upon the river and see its pleasant life.

Once a furious thunder storm came, and many of the children were frightened, but the young teacher told us to put aside our books, and we turned and sang with her a German hymn,

> " It thunders, but I tremble not,
> My trust is firm in God,
> His arm of strength I ever sought
> Through all the way I've trod."

Another favorite hymn which we often sang at the opening of school was,

"I'm a pilgrim, and I'm a stranger,
I can tarry, I can tarry but a night."

We were obliged at the end of the day to give in our own reports, and the roll being called, each scholar frankly stated her marks for the day, whether she had been perfect or imperfect in lessons or in behavior. We were thus put upon honor, and a very good lesson was inculcated, because any child in that school would have been ashamed to be untruthful. I still have some of the little cer-

THE SCHOOL-ROOM.

tificates for good conduct which it was my proud privilege to take home at the end of the term, setting forth in the delicate writing of Miss Jane what my standing had been during the term just ended. These were written on note paper, with a beautiful lace-like edge, not unlike our modern valentines.

The choice of a school is a very important thing. In these days, when graded schools and excellent public schools abound in cities, many parents at once send their children there.   There is, however, a choice among these, and a choice also between public and private schools.   For some children the smaller private school is far better during the first years, and where parents can afford to pay for their children's tuition, they should hesitate long before sending a little child into the crowded classroom where one young teacher is obliged to train as many as fifty or sixty children, which frequently happens in our large cities. This objection of overcrowding does not exist to so great an extent in grammar as in primary schools.

It is of course always much better that a child should attend school than that he or she should stay at home, but individualism is the thing to be sought in early education.   Try to keep as much as possible in touch with the teachers while your child is under their care.   There should be no strife between teachers and parents. Both have at heart very strongly the good of the little ones, and the conscientious teacher desires nothing so much as that the child shall improve in knowledge and wisdom; and to this end the co-operation of the parents is extremely necessary.

If children have lessons to learn at home the parents should see that they are prepared in time, but no parent should without protest allow her child to have so much school work to do at home that his hours of recreation or of sleep are infringed upon.   Both are essential to a growing child.

The school luncheon, too, is a very important thing.   Where the school is so near home that a child may at the noon hour have a hot meal at the mother's table the situation is ideal, but distance often makes this impossible.   Mrs. Van de Water, writing in *Harper's Bazar* on this subject, gives mothers some excellent hints which do not come amiss here :

" The school luncheon is a matter upon which the girl and her mother find it difficult to agree.   The desire that her child shall eat nourishing digestible food leads the parent to frown upon such indigestible and toothsome dainties as tarts, fruit cake, doughnuts and crullers.   Too often when the girl's lunch box does not contain that which her sweet tooth craves, her mid-day ' snack ' is supplemented by a piece of pie from the nearest baker's, or by a handful of nuts and raisins from the corner grocery, which are indeed very indigestible.

" The mother and daughter should learn that, to be digestible, an article of food must not of necessity be unpalatable, and that there are many things that do good and taste good.   One can fully sympathize with the rebellion of the girl whose lunch for five days of each school-week last winter consisted of three thick slices of buttered Graham bread and what Miss Woolson calls ' a large, cold apple.' We understand how even the healthy young appetite revolted at this fare, so that the mother was informed that if the lunch box must contain Graham bread and apples. or nothing,' the owner ' would prefer nothing.'

"A little forethought and planning on the part of the mother will lead to a vast improvement in the contents of her daughter's lunch box. Among the many articles of food which can be readily transported to school come, first of all sandwiches. These are of so many varieties that one cannot weary of them. In days of old the filling for these popular dainties usually was of ham, tongue, cold chicken, or cold meat. Now fish, flesh and fowl, vegetables and fruit, are used in their preparation.

"Salmon sandwiches are easily made and eagerly eaten by the average schoolgirl. They are of Graham bread, cut very thin, and spread with cold boiled salmon which has been picked fine then rubbed to a soft paste with salad-oil, the yolk of an egg, a little lemon juice and salt and pepper. This mixture is made particularly delicious by the addition of a few chopped olives, and will be keenly relished.

"Although the girl in her teens seems to cherish a prejudice against sensible. nourishing food, she may be persuaded to eat sandwiches made of whole wheat bread cut into waferlike thinness, and delicate slices of rare roast beef spread lightly with French mustard or with cream horseradish.

"Occasionally in the lunch box can be put a joint of cold roast chicken or a slice of turkey. As the meal taken during the noon recess cannot be hot, it should be as nourishing and tasteful as maternal love and ingenuity can make it. In some schools hot chocolate can be bought by the scholars at noon. Our girl must be urged to drink this with the lunch she brings from home. The desire for sweets after eating is a natural craving of the stomach, to satisfy which plain cake, cookies and fruits of various kinds may be supplied. Pastries, rich cakes, fried sweets, nuts and raisins are as much out of place in the lunch box as in the stomach of a growing, studying girl.''

---

## In School Days.

Still sits the schoolhouse by the road,
　　A ragged beggar, sunning;
Around it still the sumachs grow,
　　And blackberry vines are running.

Within, the master's desk is seen,
　　Deep scarred by raps official,
The warping floor, the battered seats,
　　The jackknife's carved initial.

＊　　＊　　＊　　＊　　＊　　＊

Long years ago a winter sun
  Shone over it at setting;
Lit up its western window-panes,
  And low eaves' icy fretting.

It touched the tangled, golden curls,
  And brown eyes full of grieving,
Of one who still her steps delayed
  When all the school were leaving.

For near her stood the little boy
  Her childish favor singled;
His cap pulled low upon a face
  Where pride and shame were mingled.

\*   \*   \*   \*   \*   \*

He saw her lift her eyes; he felt
  The soft hand's light caressing,
And heard the tremble of her voice,
  As if a fault confessing.

" I'm sorry that I spelt the word;
  I hate to go above you,
Because,"—the brown eyes lower fell, —
  " Because, you see, I love you !"

Still memory to a gray-haired man,
  That sweet child-face is showing;
Dear girl ! the grasses on her grave
  Have forty years been growing !

He lives to learn, in life's hard school,
  How few who pass above him
Lament their triumph and his loss,
  Like her,—because they love him.
          —*Whittier.*

## The Old Schoolhouse.

Set on a rounding hilltop
  And weather-stained and gray,
The little mountain schoolhouse
  Looks down on the lonesome way.
No other dwelling is near it,
  'Tis perched up there by itself,
Like some old forgotten chapel
  High on a rocky shelf.

In at the cobwebbed windows
  I peered, and seemed to see
The face of a sweet girl teacher
  Smiling back at me.
There was her desk in the middle,
  With benches grouped anear,
Which fancy peopled with children—
  Grown up this many a year

Rosy and sturdy children
  Trudging there, rain or shine,
Eager to be in their places
  On the very stroke of nine.
Their dinners packed in baskets—
  Turnover, pie and cake,
The homely toothsome dainties
  Old-fashioned mothers could make.

Where did the little ones come from ?
  Fields green with aftermath
Sleep in the autumn sunshine,
  And a narrow tangled path
Creeping through brier and brushwood
  Leads down the familiar way;
But where did the children come from
  To this school of yesterday?

Oh, brown and freckled laddie,
  And lass of the apple cheek,
The homes that sent you hither
  Are few and far to seek.

But you climbed these steeps like squirrels
    That leap from bough to bough,
Nor cared for cloud or tempest,
    Nor minded the deep, soft snow.

Blithe of heart and of footstep
    You merrily took the road;
Life yet had brought no shadows,
    Care yet had heaped no load.
And safe beneath lowly roof-trees
    You said your prayers at night,
And glad as the birds in the orchard
    Rose up with the morning light.

Gone is the fair young teacher;
    The scholars come no more
With shout and song to greet her
    As once, at the swinging door.
There are gray-haired men and women
    Who belonged to that childish band,
With troops of their own around them
    In this sunny mountain land.

The old school stands deserted
    Alone on the hill by itself,
Much like an outworn chapel
    That clings to a rocky shelf.
And the sentinel pines around it
    In solemn beauty keep
Their watch from the flush of the dawning
    Till the grand hills fall asleep.

# CHAPTER XXII.

## The Spoiled Child.

HAT is a spoiled child, and who is to blame for his condition? The first question is easily answered, for few of us are so fortunate as never to have met poor little specimens of a most disagreeable and unpopular genus. The spoiled child cries and whines and sulks and storms when it cannot have its own way. It is stubborn, greedy and selfish, or it is saucy, disobedient and rude. All its sweet juvenile beauty, its pretty winsomeness of babyhood are clouded over and obscured because it has been spoiled, that is to say, because it has been both untrained and mistrained. The pity of it is the greater, that the thing is wholly unnecessary. Coming to its parents a wee bud of humanity, with every trait in embryo, the baby is theirs to make or to mar, to do with absolutely as they will, and it is one of those blunders which are very near being crimes, which causes them to spoil it, either by foolish and weak over-petting and indulgence, or by equally foolish and cruel severity.

Let one word be said, which cannot be contradicted. No child is ever spoiled by too much love. Not love but folly, not love but cowardice, not love but laziness spoils children.

But you, dear anxious mother, you, fond proud father, spoilers though you are, cannot always be held responsible for the unhappy results in your particular cases. Society, as you have seen it, has helped along. American children have been too much reared in public, too early forced, as plants are forced in a hot-bed. Their lives are not sufficiently simple.

We hear mothers asking babies of two-and-a-half or three years, whether they will have this or that dish? As if choice of food should ever be made by such a tiny creature. We ask a mother why her nursery brood are not in bed and asleep early in the evening, and she smilingly replies, "I wanted them to go at six o'clock, but they *wouldn't* go!" As if they should have been so much as consulted! You hear mamma and papa glibly repeating the clever speeches of Florence, aged four, and Claude, aged six, while the two cherubs stand by, eagerly drinking in and enjoying the surprise and applause which gratify their vanity. As if a child could escape self-consciousness, whose ears heard these pleased and proud comments on his own precocity!

11          (161)

Children should be children, not little ladies and gentlemen, not little puppets to be displayed on a stage, and not premature men and women. From infancy they should be taught obedience by gentle and loving, but consistent and patient authority. Harsh punishments and loud scolding and fretful nagging are as bad for children, and as unnecessary as are inane and silly yielding to their little whims.

I knew a baby of two years who had been so spoiled that he made life a burden for his doting father and mother. One morning these two grown up idiots

WAITING FOR SANTA CLAUS.

came down to breakfast completely worn out. Sammy had refused to remain in his crib. He had elected to pass the night in their big bed. But once there, the diminutive despot determined to occupy that vantage-ground by himself, and so his mother took the sofa and his father took the floor, and thus the trio wore away the hours between midnight and the dawn of day. Was there ever anything so absurd as this performance of a spoiled child and his complacent slaves?

A child is none the happier for being thus ruined in temper and behavior. Children enjoy a tranquil atmosphere. They thrive best where they are under a loving rule; restraint gently exercised is pleasant to them, and they are entitled to it as a privilege of their period in life. In the nursery and the early school-days they need few rules. To mind when spoken to, to come when called and to tell the truth are rules enough. They do not spoil themselves. They are not to

"WHAT IS IT FATHER?" SHE ASKED.

blame for being either prigs or rebels. The work lies at the door of their mistaken parents.

Now if you have been a sinner in this regard, don't, I beg of you, turn sud-denly around and exchange your limitless indulgence for a contrasting and far more to be avoided severity. On the whole, children are not injured by a little wholesome neglect.

## A Fellow's Mother.

"A fellow's mother," said Will the wise,
With his rosy cheeks and his merry eyes,
" Knows what to do if a fellow gets hurt
By a thump or a bruise, or a fall in the dirt.

"A fellow's mother has bags and strings,
Rags and buttons, and lots of things;
No matter how busy she is, she'll stop
To see how well you can spin your top.

" She does not care—not much I mean—
If a fellow's face is not always clean;
And if your trousers are torn at the knee,
She can put in a patch that you'd never see.

"A fellow's mother is never mad,
And only sorry, if you're bad;
And I'll tell you this: if you're only true,
She'll always forgive you, whate'er you do.

" I'm sure of this," said Will the wise,
With a manly look in his laughing eyes;
" I'll mind my mother, quick, every day—
A fellow's a baby that won't obey."

                          —*From Little Knights and Ladies.*

# CHAPTER XXIII.

## The Children's Sunday.

THIS nation was founded by the fathers with a certain strong leaning toward truth and justice, with certain well-defined principles, and in steadfast opposition to tyranny over the conscience.

"What sought they thus afar?" wrote Mrs. Hemans in her beautiful poem, on the landing of the Pilgrims, when

"The breaking waves dashed high
On a stern and rock-bound coast;
And the woods against a stormy sky,
Their giant branches tossed,
And the heavy night hung dark
The hills and waters o'er,
When a band of exiles moored their barque
On the wild New England shore."

Then she goes on to say that they sought not wealth, nor spoils, nor anything but "Freedom to worship God."

One of the broad planks in the platform on which the fathers built was the respect for the Lord's Day. They founded a Sabbath-keeping nation.

In the last few years we have seen a decline from the old reverence for the Sabbath, people have allowed themselves more license than once. Children are not so strictly brought up. Socially, in our cities, the Sabbath is more and more treated as if it were a holiday and not a holy day. Since wheelmen and wheelwomen have grown to be a numerous class, there has been noticed a growing tendency to use the sacred day for the amusement of bicycling. Young men and young women, who formerly attended church and Sunday-school, now excuse themselves for absence from both on the plea that their weekly occupations debar them from fresh air and exercise, and they fancy that they are doing right in first considering their own health of body. But our Lord said:

"Seek ye first the kingdom of heaven, and all other things shall be added unto you."

We need a return to the happy home Sabbaths of other days. Perhaps some of our ancestors erred in being too rigid; if so, the swing of the pendulum is

(165)

now confessedly toward the other extreme. There is such a thing as keeping the day holy, and yet having it a very happy day too.

Little children may early learn that there is a difference between weekdays and Sunday. The Sunday is not for the rough play of the week. There may be Sunday toys, Sunday books, Sunday talks with mother, Sunday walks with father, a Sunday treat in the way of candies and desserts not allowed on other days, a Sunday indulgence in sitting up a half-hour later at night, and Sunday evening singing by the whole family.

The little ones who are old enough may go to Sunday-school, and to church. They will never be sorry in later life if they were early taken to the sanctuary. Though they understand little of what they hear, they will gradually form the habit of listening to the sermon, and they will get more positive good and instruction than parents fancy possible by simply being in the house of God.

Religious instruction must begin early, be regular, thorough, and dogmatic, if it is to sink deeply into the juvenile mind and influence life and character. Is there on this wide earth a more beautiful sight than that of fathers, mothers and children attending the house of God together?

We are told of our blessed Lord that He came to Nazareth, where He was brought up, and as His custom was, He went into the synagogue on the Sabbath day. Commenting on this passage, Dr. Deems pithily remarked:

"Any hint of the every-day life of Jesus Christ is peculiarly valuable to the careful student of His history. Very instructive, therefore, are the words of this verse, for they plainly teach that Jesus was in the *habit* of what we now call church-going; He was not an irregular attendant; every Sabbath day saw Him in His accustomed place, none more profound in homage, as none were more eager in attention. If Jesus Christ could not do without public worship, can we? If Jesus Christ was not ashamed of the house of God, should the young of this day be negligent of the sanctuary of their fathers?"

Then, pursuing the congenial theme, this wise pastor and preacher goes on, and adds:

"We are not to think that in God's family are to be found only the old, and those who are grown up men and women. A large part of God's family consists of *children*. Just as in other families you find young and old together; so it is in God's family; and just as in other families the children are not the least dear and beloved of the household, so it is in God's family.

> "'There is room for the child, who His doctrine adorning,
> To Jesus his heart and his service has given;
> And still in the beauty of life's early morning,
> Has chosen his part in the kingdom of heaven.'"

Within the banner: GLORY TO GOD IN THE HIGHEST AND ON EARTH PEACE GOODWILL TOWARDS MEN

CHRISTMAS CAROLS.

People sometimes hesitate about leading the dear little children early into the kingdom. But Jesus called the little ones to Him and said, "Suffer them to come and forbid them not." One easy upward step in the Christian life is the step of Sabbath-keeping. And little feet easily learn to take this, and to tread in the uphill path that, straight and narrow though it be, leads by moor and fen, by rough and smooth, right to the Father's house.

"To take a Sunday walk with father."

Apropos of the familiar question, "Are you ready for church?" some one has said very beautifully:

"Up the stairway of a quiet New England parsonage used to come this question, Sunday after Sunday, asked by the minister in his calm, reverent voice as he came from his study, where he had been pleading for a blessing upon the day's labor, and down would float the various replies in careless, girlish voices: 'Yes;' 'Almost;' 'No: don't wait for me, I'm not nearly ready.'

"And still after the lapse of many years, in the calm of the blessed Sabbath mornings, do I seem to hear the same old question. The same and yet not the same, for with the passing of time the meaning has broadened and deepened, going far beyond that which takes note of the outward adorning alone, for the words now come to my soul and the speaker seems to be 'One whose form is like unto that of the Son of God,' and again, as in the long ago, do I ofttimes have to make sad reply, ' No, I'm not nearly ready.'

"In this experience do I walk alone? I fear not, and in the lack of individual preparation, it seems to me, may be found the reason why to so many of us the prayerfully, carefully prepared services of the Lord's house on His day prove to be ' flat, stale and unprofitable,' when they might glow with divine power, leading our souls into 'green pastures and beside still waters,' so refreshing us spiritually that throughout the week we would be

"'Plying our daily task with busier feet,
Because our secret souls a holier strain repeat.'

"If special preparation would lead to this result, would it not be worth our most earnest endeavor? Is it too much to ask that we who are called to present ourselves before the King of kings and the Lord of lords should make ready? The simple rule in physics, that no two things can occupy the same space at the same time, holds good in spiritual matters as well, and we who would truly commune with God on His day must first be from 'our worldly cares set free.' We are so constituted that we cannot rush into His presence and be calmed and quieted instantly. While we are striving for a restful soul condition precious time is being wasted, and long before we have found the desired help the benediction is pronounced, and we go from the house of prayer hungering and thirsting for that which we might have had.

"In order to gain the most from this God-given day of rest, worship and service we need to preface each one with six days of earnest preparation. Without this daily living in touch with God a few special hours of devotion will avail little. But those whose lives are most in accord with that of the great Teacher are the very ones, seemingly, who most feel the need of adding to this weekly preparation a special time when they may, as it were, begin their ' day of rest and gladness' before it really comes by a quiet season alone with their God.

"There are many housekeepers who could do some of the extra work, which seems of necessity to precede the Sabbath, a little earlier in the week. If we only thought so, there are times other than Saturday evening which could be used to reduce the pile of clothes in the mending basket. These and many other ways will suggest themselves to those whose steadfast desire is to make of these earthly Sabbaths foretastes of the heaven above. In this, as in all other debated questions

John H. Bacon

(170)          PLEASURES OF MEETING THEIR TEACHER.

of right versus practicability, the wise old saying, 'Where there is a will there is
a way,' will prove itself true, and the blessing of the Lord will surely rest upon
every effort to gain for one's self and others the most good from the right use of
sacred times and seasons.    Try for one month the plan of coming to this 'day of
all the week the best' rested in body, strong in mind, calm and peaceful in spirit,
and thus be able to answer 'Yes' when the question comes to your soul, 'Are
you ready for church?' "

---

## The Dear Little Heads in the Pew.

In the morn of the holy Sabbath
  I like in the church to see
The dear little children clustered,
  Worshiping there with me.
I am sure that the gentle pastor,
  Whose words are like summer dew,
Is cheered as he gazes over
  Dear little heads in the pew.

Faces earnest and thoughtful,
  Innocent, grave and sweet;
They look in the congregation
  Like lilies among the wheat.
And I think that the tender Master,
  Whose mercies are ever new,
Has a special benediction  .
  For the dear little heads in the pew.

Clear in the hymns resounding
  To the organ's swelling chord,
Mingle the fresh young voices,
  Eager to praise the Lord.
And to me the rising anthem
  Has a meaning deep and true:—
The thought and the music blended,
  For the dear little heads in the pew.

When they hear "The Lord is my Shepherd,"
  Or, "Suffer the babes to come,"
They are glad that the loving Jesus
  Has given the lambs a home,

A place of their own with His people;
  He cares for me and for you;
But close in His arms He gathers
  The dear little heads in the pew.

So I love in the great assembly,
  On the Sabbath morn to see
·The dear little children clustered
  And worshiping there with me;
For I know that the gracious Saviour,
  Whose mercies are ever new,
Has a special benediction
  For the dear little heads in the pew.

———————

THERE is no harm, by the bye, in providing for the entertainment of very little children during the hours of public worship, by keeping in the pew a story-book, or a Bible history with pictures, or a pad and pencil, so that they may quietly employ themselves, when the sermon is going on above their little heads. Only little children will require this resource. Older ones will not find an ordinary service wearisome.

# CHAPTER XXIV.

## Mothers and Sons.

KNEW a mother years ago who, living in a place where hired help was simply not to be had, even if her means had allowed her to engage it, did her own work with the aid of her husband and her boys, and in addition prepared the sons for college. I used to receive her long, bright chatty letters from the little far-away inland town, where her home was a haven of peace to my thoughts, oftentimes written by snatches as she waited for the loaves to brown in the oven, or taken up when she laid her mending aside for a moment's rest. She sometimes told me of the blue-eyed laddie at her knee reciting his Latin grammar, which was propped up before her as she washed dishes and made bread, or explained an incoherent sentence by the fact that her husband had called her into the study to listen to a report he was about to send to a ministerial committee, in the very mid-current of her friendly letter.

A hard-working, cheery, useful life was hers, far-reaching in its influence, too, as the lives of good mothers always are. Now that she has gone, her sons, trained in pure and noble ways, are repeating her in countless blessed endeavors —sons, perhaps rather than daughters, carrying most of the mother with them through this world.

To speak of the mother-brooding which enfolds the opening years of a man's life as the dearest experience which life will ever have for him may be in a sense untrue. Man goes through many experiences and tastes many a cup divinely brewed. There are for him sacramental days which lift him almost to the plane of heavenly joy all along the road here and there in his progress. The day when he decides for Christ against the temptations of lower ambition and mere temporal advantage is one starred forever after in happiest memory. The day when he finds his ideal enshrined in a fair woman, and she returns his love in sweet trustfulness and gracious surrender, is henceforward a glad anniversary.

The day when the cry of the first-born is in the house and the sweetness of heaven haloes the mother's face is set apart as a day of the solemn feast, of the crowning and the laurel. But yet always, and more and more as time goes on and youth yields to the pressure of lengthening age, the heart of the son goes yearning back to the golden dawn when his mother made his childhood a dream of delight.

There is something of the woman nature in every complete man as the finest and strongest women have in their souls, too, a strain derived from their fathers. Each sex complements the other in a mysterious but evident exchange of gifts and graces, so that a wholly feminine woman, could we find one, would hardly please us, and would probably be of somewhat tenuous fibre, while a wholly masculine man might have too arbitrary, not to say inclement and even brutal, a nature. In the highest types of men and women we find the human element compounded of the best in both halves of the race, and daughters are often most like fathers and sons like mothers, from a law which goes deep into the primitive conditions of being.

The mother who would have her sons grow up worthily must count not her life dear in the years when they are under her moulding hand. She must take an interest in whatever engages them, from the era of balls and tops to the era of falling in love. Never to lose a boy's confidence is the wisest counsel which can be given a mother. But how is she to attain this end? Only by putting her boys first and keeping them first. Only by subordinating other engagements, of pleasure, of society, of church work, of philanthropy, to the more important engagement she has in the nursery, the playground and around the evening lamp. Her boy's associates and comrades must be hers, too. She must share his life and know his aims, and keep with him hand in hand.

A woman whose sweet face rises on my thought has done this thing for her boy, though she has been handicapped by continual bondage, literal bondage, to a couch of pain. During the long years when she has been unable to walk a step, or to turn in bed without assistance, her indomitable will has kept her from casting a shadow on the wholesome sunshine of her boy's youth. She has kept pace with him in his studies and in his games, has been able brightly and constantly to stimulate him in the best ways, has given him a saintly ideal of what womanhood may be when tried in the furnace and seven times refined.

If a woman worn with bodily pain and spent with weakness may do much, what may not one accomplish whose life is unfettered and who may go and come as she chooses? Under God, a mother may make her boy what she will.

Here is a good bit of advice: "An active boy must have some chance to let off his extra activity. If a boy does not have this opportunity legitimately he becomes moody and restless, and is likely to vent his superfluous energy in some unlawful manner. It is a great mistake to repress the energies of boys, or, for that matter, of girls. The active games to which boys naturally turn are not merely for exercise; the boys must work off their extra power. What is often considered mischief is nothing but the inevitable blowing off. They will outgrow it, and their natural energy will soon enough be piped, like the natural gas of the coal fields, and made to be useful. Their invention in mischief is only the prophecy of genius in practical life. Mothers worry needlessly over active children. Little children are called good when nothing is meant but quiet."

THE MOTHER'S BOY.

And this quotation, from a sensible writer and child lover, is applicable to fathers and mothers, too. We never outgrow the need of a word in season.

I want to tell you about a lovely little mother whom I met in a crowd.

We were standing, she and I, beside a great engine, a mighty thing of multiplied cogs and wheels and bands, which neither she nor I in the slightest degree understood, but which we could look at with wonder in our eyes and admiration.

She had come from her home in the quiet mountains, her first outing in thirty years.  On her dear gray head she wore a sunbonnet, with finely hemmed ruffles and shirrs, and a deep cape.  Her black gown was old in fashion but of excellent stuff, and it draped her figure in severe straight-hanging folds.  She carried a little bag and an umbrella.  By her side, ever silent, attentive and watchful, strode her son, a fine-looking, bronzed young farmer, who had brought his mother to the fair, and meant that she should miss nothing that was worth seeing. Between the two, both reserved, both unused to being in great crowds of strange people, there passed looks of perfect mutual understanding, and once I perceived for an instant on her beautiful old face the expression which I remember, the sweet, proud, confident, restful look which glorifies motherhood, see it where you may.

.   "Honey," I heard her say, "I'm glad you persuaded me to come.   It's fine."

"Yes," he answered, "it's great!"

Curious, is it not, the bond between mother and son.   In some ways it's more close and intimate than the bond between mother and daughter.  A good man always has a bit of his mother in him, and is apt to be sympathetic and tender in home relations because of the woman-part of his nature.  Sons "take after" mothers in many subtle ways, just as daughters favor fathers.  It's a beautiful thing to see a boy playing the part of lover to his mother, lifting her burdens, making life easier for her, and seeking her as his comrade on a journey for pleasure and recreation.

Seeing that mother's face made me think about a mother's heart.  What a composite thing it is, so full of passionate sacrifice, so devoted, so unselfish, so full of self-forgetfulness and self-abnegation.  Half the time we mothers are not aware that we are making sacrifices; it is joy to us merely to have the chance to go without and do without and stay in the background that our children may have every possible opportunity for advancement.

In every line of that dear old mother-face at the fair I read the story of the mother-heart, and I carried away from the great and beautiful exhibition the sweetness and the glory that I saw there.   After all, what did it matter that she knew the hard side of life, that she often had felt loneliness and sometimes sorrow! She had her boy!

One day last summer, in quite another part of the country, I sat on a farmhouse porch and talked with the mistress of the dwelling.   Near us played on the

HELPING MOTHER.                    (177)

grass a slender, delicate little boy, who was the last remaining child of six born in that cottage, and carried from there to the graveyard. In that mother's face were furrows made by grief. A woman is never just the same again after she has buried a child. The scars of the old wounds are there, and the wounds ache in the night. This mother clung to her little laddie, toiled for him, studied with him in the long winter evenings, and walked with him to Sunday-school over the rough, steep road, a walk of three long miles, every week, because Jack must go, and she wouldn't send him by himself.

"Jack is a great comfort, isn't he?" I said.

"Jack is a good boy," she answered, "and he's all father and I have to live for. But I can give him up, when the time comes. I don't want him to live his whole life hemmed in by mountain walls. We'll send him out to have his chance in the great world."

A mother's heart, you see, has its ambitions!

Our Civil War is so long over that its animosities are forgotten, and its old battlefields blossom with roses and lilies of peace. In Nashville there is a story told to-day, and a bust is shown carved with rare art, the sculptor's tribute to Sam Davis. The mother who bore so noble a son must have been proud of him, tragic and terrible as were the circumstances of his death. Not quite twenty years old, this son of the Tennessee mountains went into the war and became a Confederate spy. Captured by the Union forces, and sentenced to meet a spy's death, he was promised life and liberty if he would tell from whom he had received the information found on his person. The youth was too noble to betray an enemy, and brave as either Nathan Hale or Major André, he went, with sealed lips, to the gallows. It is a pathetic tale of heroism and gallantry, and to-day women from the North and the South, women with mother-hearts throbbing in their breasts, look with wet eyes on the marble which shows the strength, sweetness and courage of this Southern lad.

Pertinent questions arise as we consider the ever-present problem of child-training. It is in maternal hands for the first and most important years of life. How shall we rear our children? What shall we do that they may be developed in goodness, in valor, and in truth? First, we must ourselves be transparently true, true in the spoken word, true in the outward expression of character, true in our very thoughts.

Next we must be resolute. Weak and silly women will have children like unto themselves. We must take a position and keep it. We must sometimes perhaps be stern, for sternness and tenderness are not always in opposition. We must hold firmly to the right in all cases, without compromise.

Then, lastly, we must bring up our children in the fear of God. Grand men and women are built only on sure foundations. The next generation, if it is to be worthy of the period and of this great and splendid land, must honor and revere Almighty God. Rudyard Kipling struck the right note in his recessional hymn:

> "Lord God of hosts, be with us yet,
> Lest we forget, lest we forget."

"How can I secure perfect obedience from my child?" This question is daily agitated by thousands of well-meaning fathers and mothers. . Various answers might be given, to suit various cases, all of which would be more or less helpful, such as "Don't nag," "Don't demand too much," "Don't punish in anger," "Give the child a chance to exercise a right of choice," "Trust your boy," "Show your faith in his good intentions," "Sympathize with him in his weaknesses,—some of which he may have inherited from you, and which he sees in you," "Treat him as though his youth were not his fault, and don't let it debar him from obtaining simple justice."

But there is one answer which is above and beyond all these; in truth, it lies back of them and includes them. The shortest and surest way to get obedience from your child is to think less about what you are going to get, and more about what you are going to give. Think less of yourself as his master than as his helper. God's truth is a unit, and the infallible rule against self-seeking applies in this as in every other sphere of life. It applies in God's own dealings with His creatures. His whole nature is outgoing. Humanly speaking His first concern is for His children.

"But," replies the inquiring father, "I don't call that self-seeking. Paul says that children ought to obey their parents; and, as a parent, it is my duty to train my child to do what he ought to do."

Good father, you and Paul are right; but it makes a great difference whether, in your general desire to so train your child, the burden of your anxiety falls most upon your deserts as his father, or upon his deserts as your son.

Of course, the child must understand that it is under authority, and it must grow by doing for and serving you; but that is quite apart from your indulging yourself in the despotic delights of "my authority" as the finality of your parental thinking. The man who lies awake at night over the proposition, "How can I get obedience?" is not likely to think beyond that obedience when he gets it by fair means or by foul. He will rest satisfied in the ultimate achievement of his purpose to be obeyed. And if the demands that he makes upon his child for obedience are unreasonable, not to say immoral, he will still have reached the goal of securing obedience,—which was what he started out to do.

And what about the obedient child's character in the meantime?

"Oh!" answers the good father, "I wouldn't make unreasonable demands, and, of course, I purpose to be morally correct in my rulings."

Let the moral question pass.   Are you sure you would not be unreasonable?
Are you sure that you could not misunderstand your child some time, that you
could not be unfair to him, could not slight him, could not even be impolite to
him?   Are you sure you are fallible in everything except this one business of
being your child's master and ruler?

"Oh! certainly I should make mistakes," replies the father; wouldn't you
yourself?"

Undoubtedly I might.   But, other things being equal, when my child's due
was my first thought I should be in far less danger of making mistakes than when
that thought was for myself.   Now let me tell you a good old secret: "Nature is
commanded by obeying her."   Child nature is one of God's forms of nature.
Study it,—it will take about all the brains and heart and time that you have to
spare.   In dealing with little children we obey God, so far, by obeying child
nature,—that is, complying with natural conditions.   Work from that point of
view, and you will be surprised to find how naturally your child obeys God by
obeying you.   Get by giving, but don't give for the purpose of getting.   Obedience to you is the child's business.   If you do your part faithfully toward the
child, he will easily do his part toward his father.   When he fails in his duty, as
occasionally he will, it will not be too soon to look back of his failure for your
own.   Obedience can be obtained through fear, or the mechanism of so-called
discipline.   But obedience for love's sake is the easiest to obtain, and is worth
most when you get it.

"It was the late Henry Drummond who once said to a great company of boys:
'Boys, if you are going to be Christians, be Christians as boys, and not as your
grandmothers.   A grandmother has to be a Christian as a grandmother, and that
is the right and beautiful thing for her; but if you cannot read your Bible by the
hour as your grandmother can, don't think that you are necessarily a bad boy.
When you are your grandmother's age, you will have your grandmother's
religion.'

"Now, there is a deal in the above for a boy to take to heart; for some boys
have the idea that they will be expected to put aside most of their propensities, if
they take upon themselves the duties of Christian boys.   This is a mistake.   No
one expects, no one wants them to give up the natural rights and feelings of
boyhood.   They are not to be in the least grandmotherly or grandfatherly, but
they are to be happy in the way that God intended all youth should be happy.

"One of the truest-hearted Christian boys I know is also the merriest.   No
one would think of calling him 'grandmotherly.'   He reads his Bible, too, and
goes regularly to church, to Sunday-school, and to prayer-meeting.   He is at the
same time such a good ball-player that he is always chosen first when the boys
are choosing sides for a game.   And no boy of his age can excel him at football
or at tennis.   And they always say of him: 'Harry plays fair; he does!'

" No boy can excel him in foot-ball or at tennis."

" He is the life of the social gatherings he atteuds, and his reputation for absolute truthfulness is such that the teacher of the school he attends told me, not long ago, that on one occasion, when the boys on the playground were hotly discussing a certain matter, and there had been charges of falsehood made and still more hotly refuted, one of the boys said:

"' Let Harry M——— tell the straight of the story.   He knows all about it, and he'll tell the exact truth.'

" It is a fine thing for a boy to have a reputation like that in a community in which he lives.

" At another time, the pupils in Harry's room had met to select some one of their number to present a certain request to the principal of the school, and Harry was immediately chosen, 'because he is so sort of gentlemanly,' as one of the boys said.

"This was a tribute of the unfailing power and influence of real courtesy, and true courtesy is a marked trait of Christian character.

" Harry is a Christian boy in a boyish way, which is quite as charming and impressive as the grandmotherly way of being a Christian.   All Christianity is based upon right thinking and right living, without regard to age.   Each decade of life has its own particular joys in the Christian life.   They are all God-given, and none are sweeter than the joys of true Christian boyhood."

# CHAPTER XXV.

## Fathers and Daughters.

HERE is a very delicate bond of sympathy and friendship between the father and his daughter. From the very first the baby girl twines her arms very closely around her father's heart, and as she grows older he regards her with an admiration almost lover-like. Fathers are usually much more stern and rigid in their demeanor toward their boys than they are in their bearing to the little girls who seem to them so sweet and flower-like, and who enlist the tender qualities of their nature. As a young girl grows up she recalls to her father the attractions which her mother possessed in her girlish days, and the father dislikes very much to disappoint or in any way deny a wish expressed by Mary or Jennie, while he has no hesitation in saying "no" to John or Frank.

A girl should prize her influence with her father very much, and should use it always in the best way. The ordinary father works hard and constantly for his family. He takes few holidays; he spends and is spent for them. All that he can earn goes to the maintenance of his household, the education, preparation for life, clothing and caring for his sons and daughters; and when you think of it, the amount he personally uses out of all he makes is very little. His life, health and energy are all used—and used on his part without a thought of sacrifice—for his wife and children, and this is as it should be.

But on the other hand, much should be done to make home a happy and cheerful place for him, and the loving daughter can do a great deal to this end. She it is who can meet her father when he comes home at night, find for him a comfortable seat, see that he has the sort of dinner he likes, hover about him with pleasant attentions, and altogether make him feel that life is still an Eden, where roses bloom and joys abound.

If the daughter is fond of music, her father will like to hear her play in the evening. I often think that we undervalue the piano as a household fairy. We have grown so fastidious as to musical excellence that we expect too much and do not sufficiently estimate the pleasure which can be given by very simple, old-fashioned playing. The child who has learned to play the waltz or the march,

(184) "The baby girl twines her arms about the father."

the daughter whose playing would not be highly regarded by those who understand classical melody, may still make the family very happy by her airs and variations and her simple songs.

Some of the fathers and mothers whose heads are growing gray remember when we used to sit down by the piano and sing "Nellie Was a Lady, Last Night She Died," "Maggie by My Side," "My Old Kentucky Home," "Rest for the Weary," and other sweet and somewhat sentimental songs which gave us a great deal of very innocent delight.  I have seen a plain, hard-working man look exceedingly bored when a fine musician was rendering Mozart, Chopin and Schumann, simply because his ear and taste had not been educated up to the standard of the great composers, but he brightened up immensely when a little girl went to the piano and began merrily playing "Yankee Doodle" and "Hail Columbia." It is always worth while for children and young people to be entertaining to those who have passed the meridian, and it is an especially beautiful sight which we see when a father and daughter are in the best sense of the word "chums," understanding one another, and enjoying the pleasure their relationship brings.

A daughter is sometimes very thoughtless, and imposes burdens on her father which he should not have to bear.  If he is rich and there is no need of her lending a hand in the support of herself or the family, it is quite right that she should take whatever he chooses to give her, but if in his long bearing of the burden and heat of the day he has not been able to accumulate a competence, it is not kind or daughterly in a young girl to add to his cares after she has reached maturity.  She would very much better enter the ranks of the bread-winner and support herself.

I saw an instance of this sort of selfishness one day which went to my heart. The father was pallid and middle-aged, and rapidly growing old.  He bore on his face the marks of evident care and anxiety.  His pretty daughter hanging on his arm as he went away in the morning said: "Now, papa, you will be sure to bring me that fifty dollars to-day for those furs when you come home, will you not?" He said: "Ethel, dear, papa will do his best, but he may not be able to let you have the furs this week." A cloud instantly settled on the pretty face, and the young girl, frowning and all her pleasure gone, exclaimed, "I never can have anything like other girls.  I suppose it will be the same old story.  There is never any money to spare for me.  And if I cannot appear as well as the girls do with whom I go, I may as well settle down and be an old woman at once." The father went away with a heavy sigh.

A few days after I saw the young woman looking very dimpled, rosy and beautiful in her new furs.  A business friend of the father said to me: "John will soon go to pieces; his family are too extravagant, and he has not the strength of

"Looking very dimpled, rosy and beautiful in her new furs."

will to restrain them. He is borrowing money right and left and has great trouble in meeting his notes. He will soon go under, and I am convinced that his family are partly to blame."

Surely no daughter who loves her father will be willing to have such a record as this; to help ruin his business prospects and break him down in health and spirits. I am glad to know that such instances are exceptional, and that most young girls really enjoy entering the ranks of self-supporting women. Indeed, when I begin to think of all the bright and lovely, refined, and altogether charming young women I know who are supporting themselves, I am sure that on very few of them can rest the stigma of being selfish and thoughtless.

Sturdy and plump and clean and fair,
With big blue eyes and a tangle of hair,
There's a little lassie who runs to meet
Her father's step that rings on the street,
As, day after day, at the set of sun,
Father comes home when his work is done.

Making money for wife and weans,
Few are the sheaves the good man gleans;
All day long he is busy down-town,
Snowflakes sift where his hair was brown;
But he starts for home at an eager pace,
And love lights up the care-worn face.

For there at the window watching out
Is the little maid whose merry shout
Of " Daddy is here ! " in his ear shall be
Swift as he turns his own latch-key.
And glad is the heart at the set of sun
When father goes home with his day's work done.

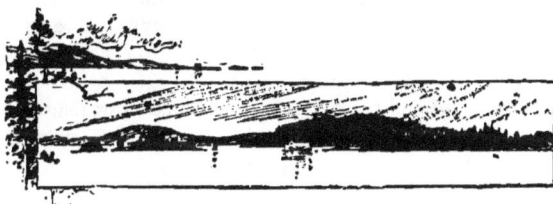

# CHAPTER XXVI.

## A Talk About Dress.

OOKING over old fashion plates one cannot but be struck with the way in which history, so far as clothes are concerned, is forever repeating itself. Ten centuries ago, or for that matter twenty centuries ago, Orientals dressed exactly as they do now. The women in Rebekah's day covered themselves in veils, as they do to this hour, and the sheikh in the desert is dressed in 1898 as Abraham and Isaac and Jacob were, before the pyramids were built or Rameses passed away.

But Occidental fashions constantly change. Wide skirts one year, narrow ones next. Balloon sleeves to-day, tight sleeves to-morrow. Poke bonnets and picture hats this season, cottage bonnets and trim toques next. Only nuns and Quakers wear anything like a uniform.

I was looking over a set of fashion plates this morning, and I saw a dame of the sixteenth century dressed in the identical costume we have worn this year. Frills, ruffles, waist, collar, sleeves, skirt, every detail of trimming are repeated in the gown and general effect of the toilette by our maidens and matrons now. The hat is just the same. The hand on the dial has completed the circle, and in the end of the nineteenth century we dress as women in good society did in Europe in the middle of the fifteenth.

A fanciful writer discovers some interesting points of resemblance between dress and architecture. Thus he tells us that "a house is a garment; it is raiment in stone or wood which we put on over our vesture of linen, wool, velvet or silk, for our better protection against weather; it is a second garb which must mould itself to the shape of the first, unless indeed it be the first that adapts itself to the necessities of the second.

"Are not, for example, the pictorial and emblazoned gowns, the cut-out, snipped-up costumes of the Middle Ages Gothic architecture of the most flamboyant kind, just as the more rude and simple fashions of the preceding period belong to the rude and severe Roman style?

"When stone is cut and twisted and made to flash into magnificent sculptured efflorescence, the more supple textile fabric is cut and twisted and made to

THE ROMAN STYLE OF DRESS.                    (189)

effloresce also.   The tall head-dresses which we call extravagant are the tapering tops of the turrets which rise from everywhere toward the sky.   Everything is many colored, for the people of those days loved bright tints, and the whole gamut of the yellows, reds and greens is employed.

"How superb they were!   Those belles of the Middle Ages with their long, clinging gowns, ornamented profusely with gold and silver.   At this time, and for long after, there were edicts which restricted women in their dress.   Philip the Fair issued very peremptory enactments forbidding ermine and miniver to common people, and prohibiting them from wearing golden girdles set with pearls and precious stones.   One pair of gowns per year was, in this sovereign's opinion, quite enough for a young woman of ordinary fortune, and two pairs sufficed for a woman of independent means."

The history of fashion is full of interest and romance.   The farthingale, or wide skirt, supported by some mechanical contrivance, came in and has held its own for three hundred years.   Pannier, hoop, crinoline, bustle, pouf, we have had it in its various phases, and have not seen the last of it yet.

We are at present very independent in one sense, and very far from free in another, as regards our dress.   No law threatens us with penalties, let us wear what we will, and fashion equally wins its way with the queen and the humblest wage-earner.   Each may wear what she chooses.   Each must be ruled only by her sense of what is fit and appropriate, and by her purse.

We require a ceremonious and formal dress, an elegant dress, ornate and sumptuous for great occasions, for the wedding and the stately dinner, and the evening party and reception.   For every day and business wear a short, simple serge answers every purpose.   For the kitchen nothing surpasses calico and gingham.   A dress has no beauty unless it is suited to the occasion and to the wearer.

As a general rule, a lady should not try to produce too youthful an effect in her clothing.   Her face should be younger than her bonnet.   Excessive gayety in feathers and flowers, a straining after the lost bloom and an overloading of finery, accentuates wrinkles and calls attention to the fact that old age has arrived.   A grandmother must not array herself like a young lady in her teens.

Long and trailing skirts, while very beautiful in the house, are suitable only for the drawing room and have no place or propriety in the street, the office, or the shop.   They are inconvenient when they must be carried in one hand lest they touch a pavement, and they are a menace to health if suffered to come in contact with sidewalks and roadways, where all sorts of germs abound.

The sensible and judicious woman wears a short walking dress, devoid of needless trimming, on her excursions abroad and on the rainy day.   To church also she goes very plainly and very simply attired.

If women who wish to be well dressed would spend less time and thought on their gowns and wraps, and more on their bonnets, gloves and shoes, the effect

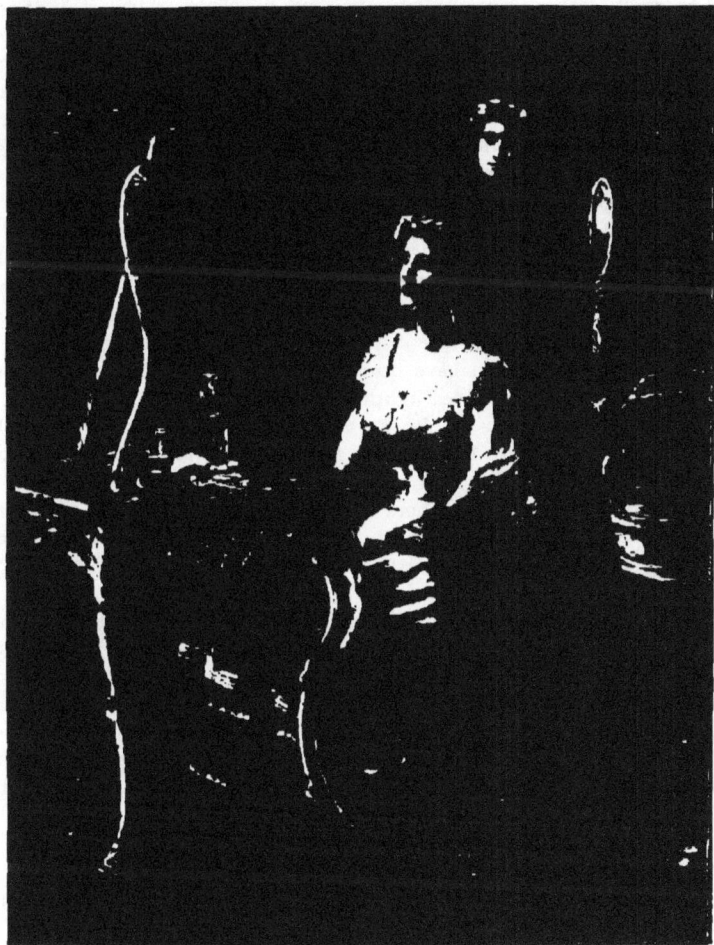

"And the evening party and receptions."

they desire to obtain would more easily satisfy them. The gown is of course important, but the richer it is the more necessary is it that every detail of its trimming and finishing—every little thing about the costume—should match it.   The whole effect of a beautiful afternoon toilette can be marred by a soiled or tawdry-looking pair of gloves, by shoes which do not suit the dress, or by a hat which is apparently meant for somebody else than the wearer.   The best dressed women in the world, from an artistic point of view, are those who have adopted a certain style—a uniform which they wear all the time, as, for instance, the Friends, with their beautiful shades of dove color and gray, or certain orders of charitable sisterhoods, whose dress is appointed for them.

One sometimes wonders why women of middle age so often blunder in the choice of their gowns.   For instance, a lady approaching fifty, rather short and stout, with hair turning gray, who would look well in a solid color or in black, has nothing better to do than to buy for herself a checked dress or a staring plaid, or, worse still, a limp wool material of some kind with gay and garish flowers stamped all over it.   I remember the pride with which a friend of mine showed me one day a purple gown she had just bought, on which were green and yellow flowers.   The material would have been pretty for some upholstered chair or for a portiere in a room which needed lighting up because it had not enough sun, but made up for its wearer it was simply shocking, and set her at once out of harmony with everything in the room in which she sat, and with everything in any room. The same lady simply dressed in a black gown would have looked refined and elegant.   This is why it is sometimes an immense improvement to a woman to adopt a mourning dress, the severe outlines and solid hues of which are not so trying to her as the glaring contrasts into which her lack of taste suffers her to fall.

Speaking of gloves, those which wear best are of a dark shade of brown or a pronounced shade of tan; pale yellow, ecrus and the white gloves stitched with black which have been popular recently, soil with provoking celerity; and a soiled glove does not look ladylike.

As for shoes, for outdoor wear in cold weather they should be thick, with broad, comfortable soles, and the shoe should be a little longer than the foot. For indoor wear any light, thin shoe may be worn, but it should not be used out of doors.

Bonnets are, upon the whole, the most trying accessories of a woman's costume.   Sometimes they are immense, like coal scuttles or three-decker ships, and then again they are little tiny affairs which rest on the head like a flake of snow. Women have been known to go serenely down the street unaware that their hats have blown off in the days when these were very small.   Our present fashion, however, of fastening on our hats with long pins makes this catastrophe less dangerous than once.   In choosing a bonnet one must not be guided by the milliner's taste alone.   The shape of the head should determine the kind of bonnet worn, and some concessions should be made to the age, complexion and general style of dress of the wearer.

It may be remarked in passing that men frequently blame women for extravagance when they see women beautifully dressed, the fact being that very well dressed women often spend only small sums on their wardrobes. For instance, a lady the other evening appeared at a dinner in a gown so beautiful that her friends who were intimate complimented her about it afterward. They supposed it to be a creation of the present season, whereas she explained that it was really ten years old, and had gone through several changes from one year to another, having just come out from the latest transformation with its white lace and new ribbon, so bright and pretty that it really looked as if bought yesterday.

# CHAPTER XXVII.

## Anniversaries in the Home.

O we always make as much as we might of home anniversaries? Every birthday should be a home festival. When the wedding day comes round, it should be kept as a gala day in the home life. If there is some signal event in the family life which you wish to remember, always keep the day of its recurrence with a special gift or greeting. There are homes in which the humdrum routine of life is seldom broken, and where birthdays come and birthdays go, and nobody is the wiser. In other homes, the cake, with its birthday candles, the gifts upon the child's plate at breakfast, the flowers, the little extra feast, the company invited in, and the general air of a holiday about the house, signalize the time as something very sweet and pleasant, a time of gladness and gratitude.

It goes without saying that in all Christian homes Easter and Christmas are kept with appropriate and joyous feeling, and that the children are made especially happy when these great days come round. Christmas is, of course, more than any other day in the year, the children's day of supreme felicity, but from eight to eighty we may all be children when we celebrate the world's greatest birthday —that of Christ, our Lord. His resurrection day is equally a time of joy and gladness. Among our American anniversaries the Fourth of July naturally holds high place, and patriotism can be kindled and encouraged by our celebration of our national independence day. Then we have Memorial Day, when we lay flowers on the graves of our dead heroes; and Washington's Birthday and Lincoln's Birthday, which we celebrate in memory of two of our greatest men— two of the greatest men the world has ever seen.

We need not fear the multiplication of holidays. Life is more or less a grind for most of us, and whenever there comes a blessed little break in the routine, we may be thankful for it, and avail ourselves of it with all our hearts. Thanksgiving Day is peculiarly a national fête day for Americans. Begun by the Pilgrim Fathers, when they had wrested the first scanty harvest from the reluctant fields of New England, it was an acknowledgment of the kind and fostering care that had led them over the sea and brought them safe to shores where their freedom to worship God could be unchallenged. It has more and more become a home day,

(194)

WHAT SANTA BROUGHT. (195)

kept perhaps more universally in the Middle States and New England than in the West and South, and yet it should never be suffered to lose its character, nor be passed by carelessly in any part of our broad land.   One of its special characteristics is the gathering of people in the morning of the day to acknowledge God's goodness in public worship.   After this comes the home gathering, and for days before Thanksgiving every train is filled with people returning to the old roof-tree, so far as New England is concerned.   You see the boys grown gray returning from California and the West to sit beside the dear old father and mother in the homestead, and there are merry groups of children and grandchildren all gathered around the table, and keeping up the mirth till the evening shades fall.

Our character as a nation is apt to be a trifle too grave and sombre.   We are prone to be thoughtful and sedate, but sometimes we may unbend, and we cannot better do so than on occasions of either national significance or on the simple home anniversaries, which each family may keep for itself.   The fact is, we work pretty hard, and work takes the mirth out of us.

A children's party is by no means a difficult undertaking, nor need it cost very much money, but it makes a child supremely happy.   A children's party should be given in the daytime, or if in the evening the early evening hours should be chosen.   From four to eight is a very good time to choose.   Let the invitation for a birthday party be written either by the child's own hand, or by that of mother or sister.   Where a child is old enough to do this for herself or himself, it is very proper to commit the task to him or her.   The invitations may be very simple, and, preferably, should be written in the first person; the third person being too formal.   They may, however, be written in the third person if the mother prefers this style, as, " Miss Edith Bartley requests the pleasure of Miss Mary Howard's company at a birthday party on Monday, April 11, from four to eight o'clock."

When the little children come they may have games and other pleasing entertainment; as, for instance, a story told by an older young lady; forfeits, or anything which presents itself as agreeable to the mother.   A peanut hunt or a game of hide-and-seek to find presents, which have been tucked away in different corners, is very interesting.   The birthday supper need not be elaborate, but children like to have on such occasions besides the birthday cake, bonbons, mottoes, and what to most little ones is a treat—ice cream.   A candy pull is always popular at a birthday party.   Should you decide to have this, provide the children with large aprons to wear over their best clothes, so that they will not become spoiled with molasses or flour.   Then let them flock into the kitchen, provide them with flour to keep the candy from sticking to their hands, and let them pull at their discretion.

I heard the other day a very pretty little story regarding a birthday party given to one of her children by a beautiful and popular lady, the wife of an

COMING TO SPEND THE HOLIDAYS.

ex-President of the United States. Her home is in a little town where class
distinctions are very marked. Invitations were sent to many little girls, among
them being the daughter of a poor man who had been asked with the others; where-
upon one priggish child seeing this little girl, who was not in her particular set,
said: "I do not think mamma would like me to associate with such a little girl
as that." This child was accompanied by a maid who took upon her to remon-
strate with the hostess: "I think Mrs. Blank would not like her daughter to
associate with that child." The lady very properly answered: "If that is the
case, you are quite at liberty to take your little charge home, but I invite to my
house to meet my little daughter any one I please."

From un-American and undemocratic ideas instilled into babes and sucklings
we can but cry with all our hearts, "Good Lord, deliver us !"

Beside the anniversaries which we keep among our friends and at the fireside,
most of us have other days sacredly set apart which, it may be, only God knows of,
and of which we do not often speak. A little mark in our every-day book, a
penciled line under a text, a furrow in the earth where a bed has been made for all
that was mortal of one of God's saints, a date which means for us more than for
others, and the whole past awakens, the present drops away, we are back again
in the sweet fields of youth. A waft of perfume, a strain of music, a chance
word in conversation have power to revive a whole sheaf of memories at any time,
but our special personal anniversaries do no require these reminders. Always for
some of us there is a month, and a day of the month, and an hour in the day when
life is sadder colored than its usual wont, when we have need to lay hold on
strength that is greater than ours, and when, indeed, we enter into our closets,
and shut our doors, and pray to our Father who seeth in secret.

Few lives there are which, having been extended beyond youth, have not
known the moulding touches of pain. In God's economy pain comes as the gracious refiner, so that the noblest and most lofty souls we know seem to have had
most of its discipline. Pain accepted as God's gift, pain looked upon as God's
angel, in the last analysis brings out all that is best and most abiding in character.
Only when we fret at pain and gird at it, quarrel with it and resist it in fierce rebellion does it produce bitterness and sharpness rather than sweetness and strength.

Of these heart anniversaries the larger part have to do with gloom and sorrow
of some sort. There was one, dear as our own lives, but the time had not come
for the love to be told to the world, and even our own world of home knew nothing, suspected nothing. To friends and acquaintances the attentions seemed mere
commonplaces, and no deeper sentiment was so much as thought of, so that when
death came suddenly there was no knowledge that one was taken and the other
left—the other left, not to the royal purple of widowhood, but to the sober gray
of a life out of which color and flavor had gone, but which must be quietly borne

alone. There are such bereavements, and their anniversaries are kept all the way
on till old age comes and death reunites.

Some of us must number among our heart anniversaries the mistakes of
judgment into which we were once impulsively led, and which, so far as we were
concerned, had results impossible to foresee and were stepping-stones to inevitable
disaster. "If I could only put myself back where I stood one summer day, ten,
twenty years ago, at the parting of the ways, how thankful I would be, and how
differently I would act." We say this, but the summer day will never dawn
when we can retrieve our mistake. Always, as it returns with the scent of honey-
suckle and the song of the robin, we live it over and are troubled in spirit, and
sometimes remorseful, and sometimes half-despairing.

But about such an anniversary it is better to heap violets of tender penitence
than to wreath it with the bitter rue. After all, we probably acted as we then
thought best, and with what light we had, and as our ways and words are under
God's overruling providence, it is not right to mourn too heavily over anything
which is done with. To leave it with God is better, and to go on, to "act, act in
the living present, heart within and God o'erhead."

"Such or such a one has gotten over her grief," we remark, observing that
the grief is put bravely in the background where, after the first, it should always
be, and that the sufferer has taken up her life again. But nobody ever quite gets
over a great grief or is ever the same again, even though she wear a smile and
join in mirth and walk with uplifted head. A great grief sets its stamp on the
life once for all. Nobody speaks of little Aleck or Joe, who was snatched away
so suddenly seven years ago, but his mother keeps both his birthdays always in
her heart—the one when he came to her arms and the one when he began the
heavenly life. The father remembers, though he seldom speaks of the son who
passed from his side in the pride of his early manhood. The wound heals, but the
scar remains, and the effect is visible in the readier tact, the gentler compassion,
and the more loving art in dealing with others who are stricken or tried.

---

## The Dear Little Wife at Home.

The dear little wife at home, John,
　With ever so much to do,
Stitches to set and babies to pet,
　And so many thoughts of you—
The beautiful household fairy,
　Filling your heart with light.
Whatever you meet to-day, John,
　Go cheerily home to-night.

For though you are worn and weary,
  You needn't be cross or curt;
There are words like darts to gentle hearts,
  There are looks that wound and hurt.
With the key in the latch at home, John,
  Drop troubles out of sight;
To the dear little wife who is waiting,
  Go cheerily home to-night.

You know she will come to meet you,
  A smile on her sunny face;
And your wee little girl, as pure as a pearl,
  Will be there in her childish grace;
And the boy, his father's pride, John,
  With eyes so brave and bright;
From the strife and the din to the peace, John,
  Go cheerily home to-night.

What though the tempter try you,
  Though the shafts of adverse fate
May bustle near and the sky be drear,
  And the laggard fortune wait?
You are passing rich already,
  Let the haunting fears take flight,
With the faith that wins success, John,
  Go cheerily home to-night.

----

## Comfort.

Be not disheartened, brother,
  Though weary the task you try;
Strength will come with the toiling—
  You will finish it by and by.
Then sweet in your ear at sunset,
  When the day's long course is run,
Will sound the voice of the Master,
  And His word of praise, "Well done!"

Be not disheartened, brother,
  Though you lose your precious things—
Though the gold you gained so slowly
  Fly as on the swiftest wings.
There are better than earthly riches,
  And loss is sometimes gain;
Wait for the Lord's good hour,
  When He'll make His meaning plain.

Be not disheartened, brother,
  In the dark and lonesome day,
When the dearest and the truest
  From your arms is caught away.
The earth may be bare and silent,
  But heaven is just before;
And your path leads up to the splendor
  And the love in its open door.

Be not disheartened, brother,
  However you may fare;
For here 'tis the pilgrim's portion,
  But the song and feast are there.
There in the dear Lord's presence,
  There in the halls of home,
You will one day hear Him call you,
  And cry with joy, " I come!"

Be not disheartened, brother,
  For every step of the road
Is under the eye of the Father,
  Who measures the weight of the load.
He cares for the tiny sparrows,
  And how much more for you!
Look up and never doubt Him—
  His promises all are true.

# CHAPTER XXVIII.

## The Family Medicine Chest.

HAKESPEARE'S famous advice to throw physic to the dogs is not without its sensible application to us in all vicissitudes of life. The habit of frequently taking medicine is as unfortunate a one as can well be imagined, and in its train come marching swiftly many disasters to the human frame. Certain illnesses the flesh is heir to, no doubt, but taking the days as they come, those people are in the best health and spirits who give nature a fair chance, look at life in the attitude of Wordsworth's pilgrim, who was a man of cheerful yesterdays and confident to-morrows, and who, on every occasion, *expect* to be well. Optimism pays in the long run.

An old colored Auntie whom I knew in the South just after the war, and who was really a picture of vigor and strength, would never confess to being anything but ill, and her invariable reply to all inquiries about her health was "Miserable, thank you." There are even people who boast of enjoying poor health, but their number is fewer than formerly, and most of us have learned that it is creditable to be well, and a matter for sympathy and regret to be ill.

Many common illnesses and some serious diseases are largely within our own control. We may have them or not, as we please. Diphtheria and typhoid fever, for instance, are diseases born of unfortunate sanitary conditions, and are preventable by attention to the laws of drainage and by inexorable cleanliness about our habitations. Most diseases which are carried about by germs—and we have learned to know that germs fly about on the wings of the wind—may be avoided by keeping the body in a state of poise and of comfortable health. It is when we are tired, for instance, that we most easily take cold. When we are faint and famished the evil thing seizes upon us as it does not when we have been well fed and nourished.

All this being acknowledged, it is still a good thing for every family in which there are young children or old people to have on hand a simple medicine chest in which are certain remedies, time-honored and efficient, which may be turned to in the hour of need. Where there are children who are always by the way of having accidents, and who may be burned or bruised or cut, it is a measure of precaution to have on hand something which may be applied in case of need before the doctor comes. Thus linseed oil and lime water is an admirable remedy for burns; flour instantly applied to a burned or scalded place shuts out the air and gives relief.

There should be on hand a supply of old linen and lint, also of absorbent cotton, in case these are needed; sticking plaster and some good salve, either of domestic manufacture, or else some such thing as salvacea or vaseline, or other tried and approved emollient; and an excellent cold cream or camphor ice will be handy to have in the house. Paregoric is an old-fashioned remedy, useful in certain conditions; camphor is of almost universal excellence; essence of peppermint poured upon camphor gum makes an excellent remedy for toothache; and extract of witch hazel should always be on the shelf, as also tincture of arnica for the relief of pain.

Mustard leaves which come ready for use are admirable in cases of nausea, applied to the pit of the stomach, and are also excellent for relieving pain. The ordinary homemade mustard poultice should always be mixed either with molasses or white of egg to keep it from blistering a sensitive skin, and it should be made in the proportion of one part mustard to two parts flour or corn meal, unless a very strong plaster is required, when equal parts of the mustard and flour or corn meal may be used.

Because one has these things close by and within reach it does not at all follow that they will be in frequent use—they are only admirable as helps in time of need. A supply of alcohol, a small teakettle and spirit lamp, and a hot water bag—and the domestic machinery to fight sudden illness may be considered almost complete. There are charming little water bags to be had now, just large enough to hold against the face when there is earache or toothache, and remember that a few drops of hot water very carefully dropped into the ear often soothe an obstinate earache. Also, most old-fashioned mothers are aware that the roasted heart of an onion is a very admirable prescription for earache, applied, of course, while hot, the chief efficacy being in the amount of caloric an onion with its many involutions can retain for an almost indefinite period.

Children should be accustomed to make light of their little tumbles and accidents. There is a brave way of bearing pain which may be learned in early life, and the habit of self-control once acquired stands one in good stead in the various hours of physical trouble and distress which are bound to come sooner or later.

Speaking of cuts and scratches, burns and bruises, and other minor ills which happen in the family, Mrs. Dinah Sturgis, writing in *Harper's Bazar*, has given directions which are well worth observing in every household:

" First and foremost in point of frequency is the scratch. It often comes smartingly to light without one even knowing whence it came to be. On some skins a pin-scratch will disappear as easily as it came; other skins poison more

CHILDREN'S ACCIDENTS AND TUMBLES.                    (204)

quickly, and a scratch means, if allowed its own way, a painful ridge that may suppurate if the scratch be a deep one. One of the simplest remedies is to bathe the afflicted part in spirit of camphor, a bottle of which should be always on hand. Do not soil the contents of the bottle by dipping even the cleanest fingers in it each time it is opened. Instead, pour a few drops upon a piece of clean old linen, and gently moisten the scratched surface of the skin. The first momentary sting will pass off at once. Repeat the camphor bath once or oftener according to the nature of the wounded surface.

"A drop or two of spirit of camphor dropped into a half-glass of cold water and drunken will often dislodge a headache that comes from a disordered stomach. A few drops of camphor poured upon a handkerchief and held to the nose will frequently dissipate a headache more efficaciously than many of the patent remedies, and is far safer than to swallow drugs unless they are administered by one's physician. It is not necessary to pay the price asked in the drug-shops for spirit of camphor. Break into a clean bottle some camphor-gum, the ordinary gum of commerce, and add proof-spirit of alcohol to make a saturated solution (one that will not take up any more of the gum). For use pour a little of this into another small bottle, and dilute with a fourth more alcohol if it is not liked so strong.

"From scratches to cuts. If any cut bleeds profusely in jets or spurts of bright red blood, tie something tightly above or below the wound, to bring the ligature between the cut and the heart, and meantime send for a physician; a cut artery, which is what this state of affairs indicates, is not within the province of the amateur to treat. In the case also of an extensive cut, or a painfully deep and jagged one, a surgeon's services should be asked for at once. But the common slight cut, such as Young America, and very often the house-mother herself, suffer frequently, serious as it may be if not treated properly, can be very well taken care of at home with a minimum of discomfort.

"First allow the wound to stop bleeding. Iced applications will control profuse bleeding; so will holding the hand, if that be the injured member, above the head. If the cut is on one of the lower extremities, lie down and elevate the foot. The flowing of the blood is an excellent provision of nature for washing the wound clean in case any external matter has been carried into the cut along with the blade, so do not allow the sight of the blood to excite apprehension. As soon as the flow is controlled, hold the wound over a basin and pour over it slowly from a pitcher water as hot as can be borne by the skin; this water should have been boiled and allowed to cool off in the same vessel to the using temperature. No matter how careful a housekeeper has washed the pitcher which receives the water from the heater, see that it is rinsed in boiling water and not wiped before the water to douche the wound is poured into it. This precaution is necessary to insure cleanliness as the surgeon understands cleanliness—namely, a condition in which the bothersome microscopic germs that cause suppuration and other evils cannot live.

"Sterilize the fingers in hot water, and then press the edges of the wound together, bringing about a perfect union, and when every particle of oozing has stopped, dry the wound and paint the injured surface with a coating of flexible collodion, which should be applied with a fine camel's-hair brush. A small bottle costs but a few cents, and if kept wrapped in dark blue paper and stoppered with rubber, will last a long time. Assist the first coating to dry by gently blowing upon it, and as soon as it is dry apply another coat, and if the wound be a large one, a third one. It will assist in keeping the wounded member quiet, and give the edges of the cut a chance to unite by 'first intention,' meaning

."What do you think, Doctor?"

without drawbacks, if a small bandage is added. This should be of thin woolen material in preference to cotton fabric, as the woolen is more porous, and being elastic, fits better.

"When Bobby comes screaming with a poor little palm all cut and scratched by a fall on the street, with gravel clinging to the inflamed and maimed surface, the domestic surgeon has a labor of patience as well as one of love and mercy upon her hands. Hold Bobby's hand over a basin and rinse it with a long-continued douche of water prepared as outlined above for washing a cut. Those bits of gravel or splinters that refuse to be washed out must be helped out gently with a needle. Sterilize this first by passing it through an alcohol flame or boiling water, and do not rub the fingers over it before it touches the wound. When the bruised and scratched and cut surface is quite clean, cover with a little carbolized vaseline, that may be had cheaply of any druggist, and over it lay a piece of old linen, very soft, or a layer of lint, and a cover of gutta-percha tissue similar to that used by dentists for dams in filling teeth. It costs but little, and is very useful in dressing wounds, as it protects the clothing from a moist dressing and retains the moisture for the benefit of the injury. Wax-paper or any light-weight water-proof material can be used in place of the gutta-percha. Do not tie a bandage on with thread. Use elastic yarn, or, better still, sew it on with a few long stitches.

"Burns are divided by the surgeons into half a dozen grades, and even those of the first or slightest degree are looked upon by them as serious if any considerable portion of the body suffers. Therefore, for any burn that covers a large surface, a surgeon's care is imperative, the resulting shock being a dangerous thing, although the surface of the body may not seem to have suffered deeply.

"The usual household catastrophes in burns come within the first two grades of the surgeon's list—first those that redden the surface merely and smart painfully, and second, those that blister the surface burned either in one large or several little blisters.

"The sudden great rise in temperature of the portion of the skin that is exposed to steam or flame or a highly heated surface injures the exposed ends of the sensory nerves, hence the exquisite pain. The main thing to do is to at once protect the surface from the air, the skin being now supersensitive to every breath. A homely but not-to-be-laughed-at remedy in a slight burn is to dredge the part with flour. Do not heap and pack the flour on, but sift it on lightly till the surface is well covered. Flour is always at hand, so should be remembered as at any rate an immediate relief. Better still, spread a piece of linen (very soft and old) with vaseline enough to completely cover the surface burned, and lay over it another covering of gutta-percha.

"One of the best applications for a burn is Carron oil, so called from having been first used to dress burns at the Carron furnaces. It is made of equal parts of linseed oil and lime water. So beneficent a remedy should be kept in the house, and it can be made at home very cheaply if the oil and a piece of quicklime can be had. Slake the lime by dropping it into water. A white powder will be precipitated; drain off the water, and put the powder into some cooled boiled

"Call on the family doctor at once."

water and shake; when the water has taken in solution all of the lime that it will hold pour off the liquid into a clean bottle, and the lime water is ready for use.

"To dress a burn with Carron oil, wet a piece of linen in it and lay on the wound, cover with gutta-percha tissue; as soon as the linen dries wet it again, and continue to keep the burn wet until the 'fire' is out of the wound. Protect the skin of a burn until it loses all sensitiveness, as if once abraded it heals very slowly.

"If the burn blisters, and the blister is small, let it alone, as the skin will absorb the fluid in the blister in time. If there is a large blister, or several small ones, open them very carefully on the lowest dependent point, never on top. Make a very small opening with a needle that has been sterilized before it is put into each blister, and it is wise to introduce the point of the needle under a bit of uninjured skin next the blister, and then gently to express the fluid. Then cover with a moist dressing made of the Carron oil. Exquisite care is necessary to prevent carrying even microscopic dirt into an open wound, since this external interference of germs is more apt than the original injury itself to make mischief.

"When Betty falls and bumps some portion of her rolly poly body the doctor, if at hand, would order a cold application, and as a moist one is better than dry cold, pound a piece of ice and fold it in a towel. If there is no ice at hand wring cloths from cold water, fold in several layers and apply to the bruise as often as the cloths become warm; continue the cold application for three or four hours in case of a bad bruise. Follow this treatment with hot applications, and here again moisture is desirable; so, instead of the hot-water bag, wring cloths from hot water and lay on as often as they cool. It is difficult to keep a child still and under treatment after the first pain passes off; but if after the nap which usually follows cessation from pain, and during which the ice can be applied, baby gets up and trots about, the bruise can at least be bathed several times with very warm water, and this will reduce the discoloration. Gentle massage will help restore the circulation impeded by the blow, and prevent a 'black eye' or 'black-and-blue spot,' but the pressure of the ice or cold and hot cloths is often all the handling a bruised surface can bear. The old wives' notion that a person should not be permitted to sleep after a fall is moonshine, and has no scientific reason for being."

Speaking of remedies, there is nothing of more universal excellence than just plain hot water. A hot compress laid on a child's chest will soothe a fretting cough, and a hot water foot-bath, with mustard, is a time-renowned preventive and magical helper in domestic crises, before the doctor is sent for. Often the child who comes in from school with aching head and limbs will be all right if given a hot bath and put to bed. Simple and prompt action will save doctors' bills. In real illness call on the family doctor at once.

# CHAPTER XXIX.

## A Chat About Photographs.

REMEMBER very well when daguerreotypes and ambrotypes first came in. They were the predecessors of the photographs which are now so common and which have been brought to such wonderful perfection. The first sun-pictures, as we called them, were enclosed in little leather cases, and the centre-tables of those days, way back in the forties, used to be adorned with piles of these little embossed cases which were among the precious possessions of every family.

By swift degrees these pictures were superseded as the fine art of the camera was better understood. During the war we had the little carte de visite, as well as the imperial photograph, and many times as the soldiers sat by the camp-fires and read the letters which came from home out from among the folds would drop the pretty little picture sent by a sweetheart, wife or sister, or maybe it would be the baby's picture for her father to see and to notice how she had grown since he went away.

In these times almost everybody can afford to have pictures taken often, and our boys and girls carry kodaks and have great success in taking likenesses of those they love and beautiful interiors. Wherever one can do it, it is well to have frequent pictures taken of children, for these darlings of the home change a great many times as they grow up, and it is interesting to watch the development, both of body and mind, as the little rosy, dimpled baby face changes to the older countenance of school-boy or school-girl, and then as that gives place to the look of the youth or maiden, and finally as the face takes on the beauty of maturity.

Nothing is a more interesting or welcome keepsake to send to a friend away from home than a picture of one's self or of some member of the family. Always an acceptable Christmas or birthday gift, one may be sure of making no mistake in thus remembering a friend; and when the cost of the ordinary photograph is compared with that of almost any other gift, it is really trifling.

In sitting for a picture one should remember that it is not so much the dress and costume which are to be seized and put upon the background of the picture as the expression of the face. A plain every-day gown often takes better than a more elaborate toilette, and often people sacrifice real beauty and successful effect in a desire to show off a handsome new gown. The hair should be a little rough,

(210)

rather than too smooth, and should be arranged in a natural way. The artist who takes the picture can usually tell what colors are most becoming, and it is always a good plan to ask advice if you are anxious to have the photograph particularly good.

Looking over an old photograph album some years after the pictures have been taken one is very much struck with the swiftly changing fashions. For this reason do not have your picture taken in a bonnet or hat, unless you expect after a while to have it appear very old-fashioned. Be a little conservative as to wearing anything in the extreme of fashion. A standing position is as a rule less desirable than one in which you are seated naturally in a chair as you would be in every day life.

There is an amusing poem by Lewis Carroll which describes Hiawatha, a wandering photographer, taking an English family group. Each member of the family is determined to pose, and from the father, who strikes an attitude holding a roll of paper in his hand, and the mother, who is determined to have a big bouquet shown prominently, down to the youngest member of the group, a sturdy freckled boy, each person is so determined to produce an effect that the result is entire disappointment, except in the case of the boy, who, not caring how he looks, looks pretty well. A pretty effect is sometimes produced by a drapery of lace over a high comb, or by a soft scarf of liberty silk brought loosely around the shoulders.

Miniature painting has become very popular during recent years, and I have seen some beautiful old pictures reproduced successfully in this way. A young girl with artistic taste, if she can secure the necessary training, can make an excellent livelihood by painting miniatures; and women have succeeded remarkably in photography when undertaking it as a business. They seem unusually skillful in arranging details and in catching likenesses, and the whole business is well adapted to womanly taste, and comes well within the round of occupations most congenial to the gentler sex.

## An Episode in Child Life.

Our delightful New England romancer, Mary E. Wilkins, in a charming story about children—"Mehitabel Lamb" is its title—has a sketch showing the curious reticence and martyrlike fortitude possible in a very young child; showing also the ease with which grown people may blunder in their dealings with children whom they love very tenderly. Mehitabel, a little dimpled girl who still plays with her doll, has been solemnly bound over to an older girl not to tell a certain thing.

"I s'pose," says Hannah Maria, "you'll go right straight home, and tell my mother just as quick as you can get there."

Mehitabel said nothing.

"You'll be an awful telltale, if you do."

"Shan't tell," said Mehitabel in a sulky voice.

"Will you promise, ' Honest and true, black and blue, lay me down and cut me in two,' that you won't tell?"

The child promised, repeating the gibberish over after her friend.  From that moment until the next morning her little life enters into a cloud of misery

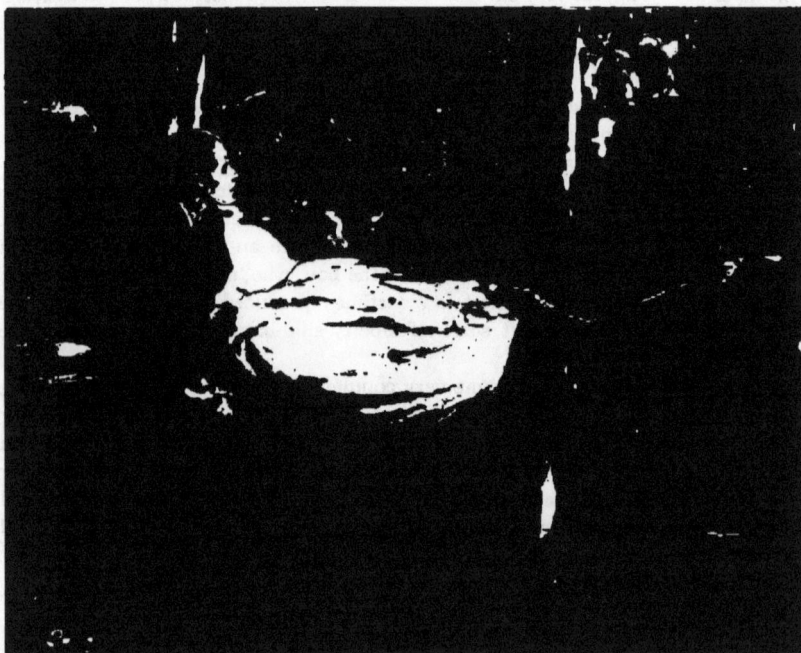

" Mothers, pray for your children."

and wrath.  For Hannah Maria has started to walk to her Uncle Timothy's, supposing it merely a little way up the road, and it is five miles, and when she reaches the place her uncle and aunt keep her all night, and her parents are distracted, and the town rouses itself to go in search of the lost child, and the well is dragged, and little Mehitabel is scolded and punished and drenched with bitter thoroughwort tea, and makes no sign.  A Christian martyr of the first century could have shown no more invincible courage than the poor baby whose mother whips her for the first time in her life, but who would have died sooner than tell that she knew that Hannah Maria Green had set out to walk to her Uncle Timothy's.

Reading this plain little story the other day, I was struck anew by its insight; and again, as often before, I was impressed with the singular color-blindness of many grown-up people with regard to the mental processes of children, with the astonishing lack of comprehension which is displayed by many parents in their intercourse with their beloved little ones. I am not sure that even now, when a wave of interest in what is termed "child-culture" has swept over the land, children will be very much the gainers. There is the danger that we will treat our delicate small girls and boys as the botanist treats the flower he wishes to analyze; that before our ruthless scrutiny and our rigid search-lights the sweetest thing in childhood, its unconsciousness of self, will disappear.

The whole duty of children in the old days is epitomized by Robert Louis Stevenson in his "Child Garden of Verse":

" A child should always say what's true,
And speak when he is spoken to ;
And behave mannerly at table -
At least as far as he is able."

Much more than this, which is elemental and simple, is required of our little ones to-day, and the peril is that while we are requiring so much of them and of ourselves, we shall forget that after all the thing is not so complex.

"Suffer the children to come unto me, and forbid them not, for of such is the kingdom of heaven," said our blessed Lord.

We suffer the little ones to come when we so bring them up that our homes are full of the love-light from above; when we do not comment on their faults in their presence, nor on their remarkable attainments either. To make a child's own performances of any sort the theme of conversation before the child is most injudicious. We must often leave to time and nature passing phases of child-life, knowing that some developments which give us anxiety will drop away from the unfolding life, and be seen no more. We must remember—alas, we too often forget—that childhood is a period of imitation, and that our example, our life lived purely and sincerely, our high-mindedness or our low ideals, will surely tell, and tell as vitally in the end as the process is imperceptible, upon the child's welfare and character for two worlds.

And, mothers, whatever else you leave undone, do not cease to pray much for the children whom God has given you. For as you pray, you will receive help straight from that heaven where "their angels do always behold the face of our father."

# CHAPTER XXX.

## The Kiss Deferred.

TWO little cousins once there were—
   Mary Ann and Mary Jane;
The first one lived in Boston town,
   The second down in Maine.
(But as the town of Boston stood
   So very far from Maine,
The cousins yet had never met,
   Which caused them much pain.)

And Jane she wrote a little note:
   "Dear cousin"—thus wrote she—
'Dear Cousin Ann, I've made a plan
   That you should visit me;
For you are the one, the Ann unknown,
   I've always longed to see.
They say that you have eyes deep blue,
   And a face all lily fair,
While round your face, with many a grace,
   Doth curl your golden hair.
Now I, they say, have eyes of gray,
   And the puggiest little nose,
A little round chin with a dimple in,
   And cheeks as red as a rose.
Let me tell you this, that I'm saving a kiss,
   And a dear good hugging too,
For the cousin so fair with the golden hair,
   And the eyes so brightly blue.
So pray, dear Ann, come if you can,
   And bring your dolly, dear;
My dollies all, both great and small,
   Will make her welcome here.

And we'll sit upstairs in our little low chairs,
    And dress them all so gay;
And we'll hunt for flowers in the woods for hours
    And I know such a pretty play!''

Wrote Ann to Jane:  ''I'd come to Maine
    And play with you, I'm sure;
'Twould be so good, if I only could,
    But my pa he's too poor.
When his ship gets home, then I may come,
    He says, for that will bring
All it can hold of silver and gold,
    And clothes, and every thing.''

            *     *     *     *     *

The years flew on; young maidens grown
    Were Marys, Ann and Jane;
Still dwelt the first in Boston town,
    The second down in Maine.
(But as the town of Boston stood
    So very far from Maine,
The cousins yet had never met,
    Which caused them much pain.)

And now Jane wrote a perfumed note,
    All in a perfumed cover;
And thus it ran:  '' Do come, dear Ann,
    Do come and bring your lover.
I've a lover, too, so tender and true—
    Oh! a gallant youth is he.
On a moonlight night, when the moon shines bright,
    How charming it will be
To pleasantly walk and pleasantly talk,
    Or for you two and we
Together to roam where the white waves foam
    All down by the sounding sea!''

Wrote Ann to Jane:  '' That visit to Maine
    Must longer yet delay,
My cousin dear; for soon draws near
    My happy wedding day.''

            *  .   *     *     *     *

More years had flown; much older grown
    Were Marys, Ann and Jane;
Still dwelt the first in Boston town,
    The second down in Maine.
(But as the town of Boston stood
    So very far from Maine,
The cousins yet had never met,
    Which caused them much pain.)

And once again Jane took her pen:
    " Dear cousin," now wrote she,
" Won't you come down from Boston town,
    And bring your family?
Bring all your girls, with their golden curls,
    And their eyes so heavenly blue;
Bring all your boys, with all their noise,
    And bring that husband too.
I've a pretty band that around me stand—
    Six girls—my heart's delight!
They're as lovely a set as ever you met,
    And all remarkably bright.
There's a kiss—don't you know?—that since long ago
    I have been keeping warm for you, dear;
Or have you forgot that first little note
    I scribbled and sent you from here?"

Thus Ann did reply:  "Alas! how can I
    Set forth on my travels, dear Jane?
I've too many to take, yet none to forsake,
    So sadly at home must remain.
If your kiss is warm still, pray keep it until
    You see me come jaunting that way.
I've a loving kiss too, that's been saving for you
    This many and many a day."

       *     *     *   ·*     *

Time onward ran; now Jane and Ann
    Were old and feeble grown;
Life's rapid years, 'mid smiles and tears.
    Had swiftly o'er them flown.

Thin locks of gray were stroked away
  From the worn and wrinkled brow;
Their forms were bent, their years were spent,
  They were aged women now—
  Lone, widowed women now.
One, young folks all did "Aunt Ann" call,
  The other one "Aunt Jane;"
Still dwelt the first in Boston town,
  The second down in Maine.
(But as the town of Boston stood
  So very far from Maine,
The cousins yet had never met,
  Which caused them much pain.)

Sudden one day—one winter's day—
  Aunt Ann said, "I must go
To Cousin Jane, who lives in Maine,
  In spite of ice and snow."
"Why, grandmother dear! This time o' the year?
  Oh, what a foolish thing!
You are far too old to go in the cold;
  We pray you wait till spring,
When the skies are clear, and flowers appear,
  And birds begin to sing."
"Children," said she, "don't hinder me.
  When smiling spring comes on,
The flowers may bloom around my tomb,
  And I be dead and gone.
I'm old, 'tis true; my days are few;
  There lies a reason plain
Against delay. If short my stay,
  I must away to Maine,
And let these eyes, these mortal eyes,
  Behold my Cousin Jane."

    *    *    *    *    *

As Aunt Jane sits and quietly knits,
  Thinking her childhood o'er,
The latch is stirred, and next is heard
  A tapping at the door.

"Come in," she said, and raised her head
  To see who might appear.
An aged dame, who walked quite lame,
  Said, " Cousin, I am here !
I'm here, dear Jane; I've come to Maine
  To take that kiss, you know—
The *kiss*, my dear, kept for me here
  Since that long, long ago !"


In glad surprise Aunt Jane she cries:
  " Why, Ann, can this be you ?
Where and Oh where is the golden hair ?
  Are these those eyes of blue ?"
"And where," Ann said, " are your roses fled,
  And your chubby cheeks, I pray ?
This, I suppose, was the little pug nose;
  But the dimples, where are they ?
Are the dollies up stairs in the small low chairs,
  Dressed out so fine and gay ?
Shall we gather flowers in the woodland bowers ?
  Shall we play that pretty play ?
And the lover, too, so tender and true,
  Who walked by the light of the moon;
And the little band that around thee did stand—
  Are they gone, all gone, so soon ?"


They turned their eyes to the darkening skies
  And the desolate scene below,
Where the wintry sun was sinking down
  Behind the waste of snow,
As they spoke with tears of their childhood's years
  And the hopes of long ago.


Thus sitting there, long talked the pair
  Of those they loved that day;
How some were dead, and some were wed,
  And others far away;
How some had proved true, and of erring ones who
  Had sadly gone astray;

Of the brides they had dressed with many a jest,
  Though with many a secret sigh :
.Of the fair and the brave they had lain in the grave
  Too fair, too brave, to die !

Slow fades away the winter's day,
  Its last faint gleam is gone ;
Shadows deep now o'er them creep,
  But still the tale goes on ;
The smiles and tears of buried years
  Are smiled and wept again ;
And marriage bells and funeral knells
  Are mingled in one strain.

And thus at last, a lifetime passed,
  The cousins met in Maine.

  —*Anon.*

## A Way of Escape.

From the turmoil, the trial, the conflict of life,
  From the hour of darkness, the hour of tears,
From the struggle, the sorrow, the anguish, the strife,
  Which we meet and we dread in our fast-fleeting years,

Thank God ! there is ever a way of escape ;
  We may fly from the din, we may step from the mart,
Our course for the day may in quietness shape,
  Our looks may grow bright in the peace of the heart.

There is always the comfort of leaving the load
  At the foot of the Cross that stands hard by the way ;
There is always the gladness of walking the road
  With one whose dear words are our strength and our stay.

There is work to be done, there are lessons to learn,
  There are nobler things waiting than heaping up pelf,
And ever, as flowers to sunlight that turn,
  We may turn unto Jesus, forgetful of self.

Though life be a battle, though sometimes defeat
  And sometimes sore wounds be our portion and grief,
Yet this is our comfort—we shall not retreat
  At the end of the fight if we follow our Chief.

In the stress and the pain, in the languor and woe,
  By the pattern He set us our course we will shape;
Whatever the peril, the issue, we know,
  Is safe in His hands, and the way of escape,

Which He marked from the first, will be ours at the end;
  So victors we tread, though the marching be steep—
We are led by our Captain, our Master, our Friend;
  Though the battle be stubborn, the rest will be deep.

---

## Good Intentions.

The wonderful things we have planned, Love,
  The beautiful things we have done,
The fields we have tilled, the gifts we have willed,
  In the light of another year's sun,
When we think of it all we are baffled,
  There's so much that never comes true,
Because, Love, instead of our doing,
  We're always just meaning to do.

The friends we are wanting to help, Love,
  They struggle alone and forlorn,
By trial and suffering vanquished,
  Perchance by temptation o'erborne;
But the lift, and the touch, and the greeting,
  That well might have aided them through
The perilous strait of ill-fortune
  They miss—we're but meaning to do.

We dream of a fountain of knowledge,
  We loiter along on its brink,
And toy with the crystalline waters,
  Forever just meaning to drink.

Night falls and our tasks are unfinished,
  Too late our lost chances we rue;
Dear Love, while our comrades were doing,
  We only were meaning to do.

---

## The New Year.

The clock struck twelve in the tall church tower,
  And the old year slipped away,
To be lost in the crowd of phantom years
  In the House of Dreams that stay
    All wrapped in their cloaks of gray.

Then swift and sweet o'er the door's worn sill
  Came the youngest child of Time,
With a gay little bow and a merry laugh,
  And a voice like bells achime,
    Challenging frost and rime.

He found there was plenty for him to do,
  The strong and the weak were here,
And both held out their hands to him
  And gave him greetings dear,
    The beautiful young new year.

You must bring us better days," they said,
  "The old year was a cheat."
Which I think was mean when the year was dead;
  Such fate do dead years meet,
    To be spurned by scornful feet !

"I bring you the best a year can bring,"
  The new-comer stoutly spake,
"The chance of work, the gift of trust,
  And the bread of love to break,
    If but my gifts you'll take !"

The noblest thing a year can lay
  In the lap of you or me,
The brave new year has brought this day,
  It is Opportunity,
    Which the wise are quick to see.

# CHAPTER XXXI.

## The Daily Papers.

IF we are to keep in touch with the world about us we must of necessity read the journals which report current happenings in the world. Every home has its relations to the village, the state and the nation. In order to have our minds well furnished and alert we must be aware of what is going on around us, not only in our own community, but also must keep abreast of the wider thought of the world.

History is a record of events which are past. We are making the history of the future in our daily lives. Interesting as it is to take up such a story as Motley's "Dutch Republic," or Merivale's "Ancient Rome," Gibbon's "Decline and Fall of Rome," Hume's, or Macaulay's, or Greene's "History of England," essential as it is that we shall know the whole wonderful story of the past upon the earth, it is quite as important that we should have a grasp of the doings of to-day. We are living in thrilling and exciting times; certain leaves are being turned in the pages of the world's history on which the scholars and thinkers of the future will dwell with wonder and awe. Of all this we are a part.

While excessive reading of the newspapers tends to little profit, yet all intelligent people must make it a part of the business of their daily lives to peruse and ponder on the contents of these wide-awake and stirring periodicals. We may have our choice among them. Of different political beliefs and traditions, each household and family has a right to select that paper which best represents its own ideas; but, apart from the teachings of the editorials and of the various writers who contribute to daily and weekly journals, the gathering of the news alone is a matter of great moment. Reporters are sent here and there all around the globe, the telegraph keeps us informed of that which is happening in remote corners of the globe, and the day has come when the word of prophecy is fulfilled, that knowledge is diffused over the whole earth, and they that run may read.

There is an excellent method of reading the paper, as there is of doing everything else. It would not be a bad idea for children in schools to be taught how to use the newspaper to advantage. In the first place, it is well to ascertain whereabout in the paper, if anywhere, there is a summary of the daily news. Certain excellent papers so arrange their material that one can turn at once to the things he or she wants, and need not waste time on that which is of little moment.

It is unfortunate that so much space is given to details of dreadful crimes and to minute and sensational relations of things on which the curtain of oblivion should be dropped. If we cannot wholly avoid hearing and knowing the story of the wickedness in the world, yet we need not dwell upon it, and we may pass it over lightly and not make it the subject of conversation.

Women are supposed always to read first the notices of marriages and deaths, thus showing their interest in that which is personal and individual. Curiously, we do feel an interest in accounts of weddings and engagements, even when we do not know the people concerned, and often we have a compassionate regret for the hearts that ache when we see the account of a death. I once heard of an old farmer who put the morning paper down with an air of disappointment, saying, "Nothing interesting in this to-day; there is nobody dead that I know." But that is not the mental attitude of most of us. Generally, we do not express it in precisely that way, even if we have no special relation to the sorrows of which we read. All good citizens feel an interest in legal enactments and in all phases of legislation which involve the welfare of their township, county or state. In law-abiding communities we turn at once to our legislators to protect us in our rights, and we invoke the protection of law for our own property, as, for instance, in a New England State which this spring has passed a resolution forbidding all persons for one year to pick the beautiful trailing arbutus, because the wholesale picking of former years had almost deprived certain forests and woods of this prime favorite of the spring.

Then, also, in certain townships women have been prohibited from wearing large and obtrusive hats in public places, especially of amusement, because the community was law-abiding and could thus protect itself from thoughtlessness on the part of the ladies. We find it entertaining to read of such little things as this, and also amusing to study the comments made on these and similar occurrences.

In a larger way, the newspaper lets us know of all that is doing in wars and rumors of wars that are going on, the sounds of martial music that are blown about the world, the patriotic deeds which are being done everywhere, and the story of invention and progress. We must have a margin in our home life for our daily papers, weekly papers, and also for some one or other of the magazines, which furnish entertainment and instruction to the family group.

---

## A New Year's Tale.

We had drawn our chairs around the fire, and made the circle a close one, for the night was bitterly cold. The wind howled in the forest as if a pack of wolves were loose and famished for food. The sky had been low hung and gray since early morning. At dusk the white flakes began to fall—the thick, heavy kind in which several clusters cling together. By the time father came in from milking, and bedding the horses and cows comfortably for the night you could not see the fence nor the bars at the end of the lane. Father was red with cold as he unwound his great woolen comforter that came up well above his ears, and hung his shabby old overcoat on the nail in the entry.

"It's well for them that have no house to go to this night," he said, quoting a family proverb. It meant "well for those already in the house."

"Yes, John, dear," said our sweet mother, adding, "I've made oat scones and fried sausages for supper. I knew you'd need something hot."

"And coffee, mamma; you'll have coffee, won't you?" cried Louis. "Tea is so sloppy on a very cold night."

"Coffee, if you want it, my boy," said mother. "One's as little bother as the other, if Sadie will grind the coffee, or if you will, Louis, as you are the pleader in the case, and Sadie is busy with her fancy work."

Well, we had supper, and a jolly one it was, and then on the last night of the year we settled down to a quiet, homely evening with fun and songs and stories. What cared we for a bitter storm with our own all safe, and not a jar in the sweet melody of our beautiful love-life as a household to whom God had been good far beyond all deserts.

We had just finished "Annie Laurie," and the echoes had hardly died away, when Sadie declared she heard a call for help out there in the snow. Nobody else heard any sound except the twisting and whirling of the bending boughs, tormented with the wind, and the wail of the wind itself, rioting like a fiend around the rattling panes and clattering like a dragoon on horseback against the eaves. There are silent snow storms and angry snow storms, and this was one of the furious sort.

But whether Sadie heard anything or whether she did not, Leo, our old retriever, was sure in his mind that somebody was outside. Leo sniffed under the mat by the door and barked and whined. Then he came to father and tugged at his coat, and father got up, lighted the lantern, put on his hat and muffler and went into the storm, Leo at his heels.

Presently they returned. Father was dragging what looked like a great bundle behind him. Leo rushed after it, barking with the greatest excitement. The snow followed them all in a white whirling cloud and the cold came in with the fierceness of an invading army. We hurried to shut the door, and then mother and the girls undid the bundle.

It was a slip of a maiden not much beyond childhood. She was so pretty as she lay unconscious before our eyes that Louis held his breath with wonder and pleasure. Father began to rub her cold hands, Sadie chafed her temples, mother pulled off her soaked and sodden shoes and stockings. Soon she opened her blue eyes and gasped twice, then in a faint, flute-like voice asked, "Where am I? Is this heaven?"

"No, my dear," said mother, holding a glass of warm milk to her lips and putting her strong, gentle arm under the girlish head, "it isn't heaven. Its Flyaway Farm, that stands on the hill near Oakhurst."

"And it's not so far from being a heaven-like place," said father, as he sat down behind the hearth again.

Who was this girl and how came she to be alone in such a storm? None of our neighbors but would have known better than to venture forth in such weather as had threatened since morning. But this was a stranger, and when she came to herself she proved to be of a graceful bearing and of an air seldom seen in our plain countryside. As to her looks, she was not fashioned of common clay, but of the finest porcelain, the loveliest thing you ever dreamed of, and not past twenty years old.

"I am Dorothy Lester," she told us, "and I've come from Honolulu, where I lost my parents, to stay with my uncle, James Quincy. Uncle did not expect me so soon, but he knew I was on the way. I left the railroad at noon and came in the stage to the Corners. There I got out and the driver told me how to go on, but I lost my way in the snow."

"Abominable conduct in William Scott," said my father, "to let a girl, and a stranger, start on such a road with such a storm brewing."

"Well," said mother, soothingly, "you are here now, and God watched over you, dear child. Here you'll remain till the weather changes, and then we'll take you to your uncle's."

"'Tis an ill wind that blows nobody good," said Louis, who was uncommonly pleased with the addition to our party.

Well, we had Dorothy with us four splendid shut-in days, when the snow walled us away from the world, and nobody came in or went out. She shared our happy New Year festivities, and joined our family prayers, and we treated her as if she were Noah's dove that had fluttered out of the tempest into the ark. We all felt sorrowful when the time came that father harnessed the gray horses to the old sleigh, piled in the robes, put a glowing foot-stove in the bottom for Dorothy's little feet, and then glided away with a guest we had learned to love.

"I wouldn't mind it so much," said Louis, as he turned mournfully from the door, "if her aunt, Miriam Quincy, were like anybody else—like our dear mother, for instance; but she is so cross and hateful!"

"Oh, well!" said Sadie, cheerfully, "Dorothy won't have to stay there always. Girls marry and go to homes of their own."

15

Which was precisely what Dorothy did in another new year. Ask Louis what he thinks of the wife God brought him from over the sea, and sent to his arms on the wings of the wind. "A prudent wife," however you find her, "is from the Lord."

## A Chat With Country Girls.

The brightest, cleverest and wittiest girl I ever met in my life was brought up in a remote hamlet among the Virginia mountains, a whole day's journey from the nearest railroad. Her own family, a few scattered neighbors, and the books she read and loved, had been her teachers, for she had never attended a school other than a very small one conducted by her mother. No young girl ever surprised and charmed me more than did this graceful and refined Salome, whose manner of entering a room would have done credit to the most finished belle. I mention entering a room, because one's ease in this common, every-day action, or one's awkwardness, show the observer to what degree of social training one has attained, and unthinking people sometimes fancy that social training or *savoir faire*, the knowing what to do and how to do it, is an affair of the town rather than of the country.

Salome would have impressed any one by the cordial and sincere gladness of her greeting, if you were a guest, and she stepped forward to welcome you. If it happened that a half-dozen kinsfolk and friends had driven across country and stopped at her home, she would have tactfully spoken to each, saying just the right word, asking for Aunt Mary and Uncle Thomas, remembering the ailing grandmother, and the babies. And when it came to serving refreshments, hers was the deft hand and the light foot; she knew how to set out a luncheon invitingly, she gave the right touch, she knew the values of little things. For jest and fun and repartee, few girls I have ever met have surpassed my mountain maiden, Salome.

Country girls have the advantage over their city cousins of an acquaintance with Nature in her several moods. They see great spaces of sky where we of the town are confined to little patches of blue, with here and there a star. They may, if they choose, know familiarly all the flowers which grow in their region, may classify the plants, and study the stones and rocks for miles. They may ride, climb, wheel; in short, engage in every form of outdoor sport, with ideal freedom, especially if they join their forces, three or four, or six or eight, girls going far afield together.

In many places it is not well for a girl to venture out on solitary excursions. A dog which loves his mistress is a good protector, but it is wise for a group of friends to go on jaunts in company, or for a sister to have her brothers as a body-guard, when going a distance from home over lonesome roads.

Country girls very naturally turn with longing eyes to the city, when the time arrives in which they desire to take some share in the world's work for themselves, in which, to put it plainly, they are anxious to earn their own living. Perhaps they desire to relieve their parents, knowing that father and mother have had a weary, up-hill time of it, in bringing the children to the present point.

There may be brothers to educate, or the farm may not be clear of debt. On how many households a mortgage presses heavily, and how praiseworthy it is for a daughter to wish herself able to lift at least a small part of that burden.

Now, girls, let me very earnestly give you one bit of advice: Do not come from the safe shelter of your own home, and from your mother's side, into a great town filled with strangers, where you have as yet no foothold, and where your chances are uncertain, where it may be next to impossible to procure employment at a rate of payment at which you can be self-supporting. Do not be allured

LOOKING AT HER PICTURE.

by a weekly stipend which sounds large in a place where little actual money is required, but which will be very small when out of it must be squeezed room rent, and board, and car fare, and luncheon, and a nice well-fitting gown in which to

appear in office or salesroom.   Stay where you are until you have an assured position awaiting you, and through acquaintances or relatives, or the Young Women's
Christian Association, make full and definite arrangements as to the home in
which you will be received as an inmate, and the people who will be your
companions.

A young girl coming from her home for the first time should bring a letter of
introduction from her pastor to a pastor of her own denomination, so that she may
at once find friends in a Sunday-school or church.   Should a girl from the country
find herself in town alone after dark, and without previous preparation, so that she
is at loss what steps to take, she should ask a policeman to direct her to the clergyman whose house or church is nearest the place where she happens to be, and to
him she should frankly tell her story and ask his counsel.   If she can be directed
to the Young Women's Christian Association, she will there find safe and judicious friends who will wisely advise her.   Only an accident, however, should
place a young girl in this position.   As a rule, a girl coming to a strange place
from the country should arrange beforehand to be met at ferry or station, and her
friends at home should not trust anything so precious as a daughter to the chances
of fate.

My motherly heart yearns over homesick girls, waifs in a crowd of alien
people, none of whom care for them.   Shy, and alone and anxious, they are greatly
to be pitied, even when pluck and courage carry them on to victory.

Make ready for life by thoroughly mastering some art, or trade, or accomplishment, so that when the hour comes for entering the world's market they will
be found ready.   In every hamlet and village, in every home in the land, there is
the opportunity to acquire something.   Possibly it is not the thing we prefer, but
to learn anything well is to make for yourself a stepping-stone to something
better and higher.   The greatest trouble in life is that there are so many incompe-
tent and incapable people about, people who cannot be trusted to finish what they
begin, or to do the least task as it should be done.

The young girl who has learned, for instance, the art of good housekeeping,
who can make a loaf of bread, a cup of coffee, and a cake fit for the prize-table at
a fair, will, by reason of that very knowledge, fill a position of trust more creditably than the untrained girl, even though it be in quite another sphere.   Knowledge is power.

Dear country girl, do not hastily give up a place of honorable, though
perhaps slenderly paid, service at home for one which seems an advance in salary
and prestige among strangers.   The advance may be only apparent.   In an affair
so important as this you must be sure beforehand that you are not about to make
a mistake which may be irreparable.

## Little Girl's Life in 1782.

One hundred and fifteen years ago a little girl named Mary Butt was living with her parents at the pretty rectory of Stanford, in England.   She was a bright and beautiful child, and when she grew up she became Mrs. Sherwood, the writer of a great many charming stories for young people.

But nothing that she wrote is so entertaining as the story of her childhood, which, when she was an old lady, she told to please her grandchildren.   I wonder how the girls who read this would endure the discipline which little Mary submitted to so patiently in 1782.   From the time she was six years old until she was thirteen, she wore every day an iron collar around her neck and a back board strapped over her shoulders.   This was to make her perfectly straight.   Perhaps you may have seen here and there a very stately old lady who never was known to lean back in her chair, but who always held herself as erect as a soldier on duty.

If so, she was taught, you may be sure, to carry herself in that way when she was a little girl.   Poor Mary's iron collar was put on in the morning and was not taken off until dark, and, worse than that, she says: "I generally did all my lessons standing in stocks, with the collar around my neck.   I never sat down on a chair in my mother's presence."

Her mother and herself were great readers, but you can count on the fingers of one hand all the books they had to read.   "Robinson Crusoe," two sets of "Fairy Tales," the "Little Female Academy" and "Æsop's Fables," formed their entire library.   They used to take "Robinson Crusoe" and seat themselves at the bottom of the wide staircase, with two heads bent over the same page together.   Whenever they turned a leaf they ascended a step, until they reached the top, and then they began to go down again.

You will ask what sort of a dress this little girl wore over one hundred years ago.   In the summer she wore cambric and in the winter a heavy wool dress, and at all times a pinafore—which was a great, loose apron, worn over everything else, and enveloping her from head to foot.   It is pleasant to find that the iron collar did not take from little Mary the love of play and of dolls.   Her special pet was a huge wooden doll, which was her constant companion.   I think the little girls who compare their lives of to-day with that of the little girls of 1782 must be very glad they were not born in the last century.

---

## Unconscious Revelations.

The other day, as I sat by my window, I was the observer of a little incident which set in motion the train of thought reaching from my quiet home to you, wherever you are.  I live on a street which has a smooth asphalt pavement greatly in favor with wheelmen and women, and there are few hours between morning and bedtime when young people are not flying up and down its lengths on their magical machines.

A very pretty girl came sweeping along, managing her bicycle with the graceful ease of a confident and skillful rider.  Her face was glowing with health, her dress was most becoming, and her whole air was that of one accustomed to the courtesies of polite society, and used, on her own part, to much gentleness and consideration.  Yet, when another girl, evidently a novice, swerved awkwardly and narrowly escaped colliding with her, the pretty young woman shocked and amazed the elderly lady in the shadow of the curtains, by exclaiming angrily, "Great Scott! I wish you would look where you are going!"

There was a bit of wholly unconscious revelation of character.  I saw that my beautiful maiden was not like the King's daughter, "all glorious within." She had caught, perhaps from a schoolboy brother, the trick of slang; she was impatient, she was hasty of speech and temper, and she failed to make allowance for the inexperience of another.  I was saddened, and I wished with my whole heart that the young girl could realize how unfortunate for herself was the frame of mind and the habit of petulance which had made possible her impetuous remonstrance.  Life may discipline her by greater trials than the clumsy blunder of a fellow traveler on the road, and by and by she may learn to repress the vehement word of irritation.  But what I long for, when I think of her, and of thousands like her, is that they may not feel the impulse to needless vexation with the errors or even with the carelessness of others.  It is a splendid thing so to live that the face, manner, voice, and what the Bible aptly terms "walk and conversation," are the expressions of inward poise, serenity and sweetness.

"Such a one does not love her sister," said a friend not long ago, coming from a home where an invalid had been lying at death's door for weeks.

"Why do you think so?" was the inquiry, a very natural one in the circumstances.

"I notice," the reply came slowly, "that she has nothing to say of Jean's sufferings, or of Jean's marvelous patience and fortitude; that she is only impressed with Jean's occasional forgetfulness to thank her for a kindness, and that she dwells mainly on her own fatigue, and the number of invitations she has had to decline, owing to this ill-timed illness on Jean's part.  Love suffereth long, and is kind; love vaunteth not itself, is not easily provoked; therefore, love would lead the sister who is well, to take a different tone about the sister who is laid aside on a bed of pain."

"She would disclaim any lack of affection," said the other, "and there is the excuse for her, too, that she has had a long strain, and is tired."

"That last I grant; nevertheless, whether she is, or is not, aware of it, she is not in love with Jean. The revelation on her part is entirely unconscious; but it is a plain revelation."

Perhaps you have often heard people say that what one is, is of more consequence than what one does, and you have fancied the saying rather trite. It is, however, profoundly true. One who goes on his way living the Christ-life, brave, honest, fearless, unselfish and magnanimous, wins others to the Christ, because he shows forth the spirit of the Master. One who has not kept his soul a spotless chamber for the indwelling Christ, will constantly reveal, when he does not dream it, the insincerity of his professions. We must be good, if we would do good. We must reveal ourselves in a thousand ways, whether we mean to or not; and if Christ be in us, as the lamp that guides, we will reveal Christ.

## Wasting Our Time.

I am not about to recommend to my readers that exceeding thrift of time which keeps on hand a book or a piece of embroidery for odd minutes, and which from sun to sun never indulges in repose. The person who is most conscientiously and most constantly employed is often the person who wastes time, for employment is not invariably good economy, and it is sometimes the best saving which is also wise spending.

To most of us, day in and day out, it happens that we do waste, or at least misuse, precious hours. We start on a new day with a feeling that it is all too short for what we have to do. We lavish our strength on tasks which seem worthy of accomplishment and endeavor, and yet, were the whole truth known, neither we nor the world would have suffered had we let those things go by. The toil has been put in the wrong place and our time has been wasted.

For example, we spend a great deal of time in talking about what we mean to do, planning over and over what may as well be settled at once, and going into the minutiæ of things which are not sufficiently important to be thus regarded in detail. In domestic affairs we hesitate and change our minds, and cannot come to a decision about the parlor curtains or the kitchen closets, and meanwhile the day is slipping by, and our small boy is playing in the street, and growing familiar with companions we would not choose for him. After all, the mother's first work in life is her small boy, and compared with him carpets, curtains and kitchen plenishing are of the very smallest account.

We waste time in reading, for example, by trying to master the contents of the whole of the daily or weekly newspaper, whereas, in many instances, the summary of news made up by a hand skilled in condensing and selecting, an

editorial or two, and an article on some instructive topic would be quite enough
for us.   Our reading grows scrappy and does not feed us mentally because we
take no time for the strong and wholesome books which promote intellectual vigor.
We have the time, if we knew how to manage it, how to utilize it, if we steadily
every day spent some part of it in consecutive reading of a thoughtful kind, along
lines which we have deliberately chosen.   Time is well spent which is spent in

" We do not waste time when we take outdoor exercise."

resting when we are tired.   A lady past middle age, but with the fresh complexion
and clear eyes of a girl, told me the other day that this was her only secret:
" Early in our married life," she said, " my husband, who was a physician, urged
me to take an hour every day for myself.   Let that hour be absolutely uninter-
rupted, he said, by household cares, by children, by any one.   Do what you
please in it, lie still and shut your eyes, or read a book you like, or sit still in

your rocking-chair and knit, but don't do anything which taxes your strength, and always secure your hour of rest." That was wise advice.

We do not waste time when we take outdoor exercise. This, too, some of us need to remember. When we are ordered by our medical counselors to walk or drive every day, to get the air somehow and set the blood in motion, we are ready to obey, but a more sensible way would be to anticipate the prescription and take the exercise so that we may keep well.

We may set it down as without exception that time spent in worry is recklessly wasted. It is hard not to worry, particularly when we see the troubles and mistakes of those who are dear to us. Faith halts when we are anxious and distressed in behalf of our sons and daughters, whom we long to help and for whose good we sometimes long in vain.

But even here our worry is futile. Even here we should cast the burden on the Lord. Do thy best and leave the rest is a safe motto for the Christian.

---

## The Everlasting Love.

There is no rest for the weary heart, no balm for the sorrows of life, no ease for the back bowed with the daily burden like the realized thought of the everlasting love. Blessed thought which comes to us in the night watches, calming disturbance, and soothing the eyes which care holds from slumber. Sweet words of faith and dependence spoken by holy men of old sing themselves to the tune of our modern melodies, as our lips move softly and we say, "The Lord is nigh unto all them that call upon Him in truth. Hear my prayer, O Lord, give ear to my supplications. I stretch forth my hands unto Thee, my soul thirsteth after Thee, as a thirsty land. Lord, Thou hast been our dwelling place in all generations." Verse after verse from the Psalms rises in memory, as stars arise in the sky, and, though we may be grieving over our dead, or yet sadder experience, grieving over our living dear ones, we still can say, "Because Thy loving kindness is better than life, my lips shall praise Thee. Thus will I bless Thee while I live, I will lift up my hands in Thy name. Because Thou hast been my help, therefore in the shadow of Thy wings will I rejoice."

In the midst of the day's toil, as in the wakefulness of the night, it is blessed to call to mind the assurances given by our Heavenly Father that He will always support and sustain us. "As thy day shall thy strength be." "Fear not, little flock. It is your Father's good pleasure to give you the kingdom." "Behold, the Lord's hand is not shortened, that it cannot save, neither is His ear heavy, that it cannot hear."

The disciple of Christ need never be cast down nor discouraged, let circumstances be adverse or opportune. For the one cable which holds against all strain of our infirmities, our wants, or our yielding to temptation is the cable of the ceaseless love of God. We are kept by the power of God through faith unto salvation. We do not keep ourselves. We are kept.

When we look about us in the world we cannot help seeing that earthly love and human friendship are subject to changing conditions. The staunchest plank of human affection may give way in a storm. The wife may grow cold and indifferent to the husband of her youth; the husband may cease to show the tenderness and consideration which once made her life a dream of delight. The child going forth from the home and forming other relationships, apparently is weaned from the early loyalty and the fondness he once felt for the parents to whom he was all in all. The father and mother may be disappointed in the daughter and the son, and no longer treat them with the proud fondness of a happier time. Brothers and sisters drift apart, and perhaps for weeks and months together they do not mention the names which once were spoken every day. Mrs. Hemans made a true statement of fact in her poem, "The Graves of a Household," about the scattering of many a family who "grew in beauty side by side, and filled one home with glee," but we do not always wait for the cold hand of death to come and separate beloved kindred. Life wields a surer and sharper knife of division than death. The love that lasts is not the earthly love. It is a love of finer tissue and stronger fibre, and it is eternal, being hid with Christ in God.

Shall we not cling closer to that endless love? "O Love Divine, how sweet thou art!" Shall we not comfort ourselves with the knowledge that we cannot be lost from the clasping embrace of the everlasting arm which fainteth not, neither is weary? Shall we not by prayer, by study of God's Word, by meeting with God's children, by faithful means of grace, and by frequent contemplation, dwell more than ever in the blessedness of a life of entire trust, in the confidence of the Father's enduring love?

---

## How to Entertain a House Party.

In deciding to entertain a house party, the initial steps are taken in the mother's room, and she has the deciding voice in the matter. The trouble which is caused by the enlarged family, the setting aside of the ordinary family routine, and the breaking up of the family quiet, are affairs for the housekeeper's canvassing before a single invitation is sent. But granting that mother, bless her heart, sees no objection and will be happy to forward the plans of the young people, the next thing in order is to group the guests carefully. There should be a probability that they will be congenial, that if already acquainted they may like each other's company, and that if strangers, they will have enough in common to make the week they will pass under one roof a pleasurable event to remember.

School or college friends form desirable elements for a successful house party. So do a number of young business friends who belong to a Christian Endeavor Society, or a Bible class or to the same social set.

"School or college friends form desirable elements for a successful house party."

We will suppose these young people to live in town, and their invitation is from a friend who has a home in the country. They are asked for a definite number of days, the train or boat they are expected to take is mentioned, and any information as to a change of conveyances en route is given with clearness and precision. On arrival at their destination, their host meets and escort them to the house which is to be their home and the background of their varied pleasures during their visit.

While guests, well-bred young people will, as a matter of course, be considerate and polite in their manner toward the elders of the household in which they are received.  To ignore a friend's parents is to show a marked deficiency in one's own training.  The guests will notice and conform to the routine of the house about meals, prayers, etc., and will take pains to give pleasure as well as to get it.

The host or hostess will have arranged beforehand for whatever forms of entertainment will be most likely to fill up the measure of the party's enjoyment. There may be boating, tennis, or golf.  Picnics will be in order.  Charades and tableaux and music will have their turn in the evenings.  Whatever happens in the way of disappointment or reversal of plans, everybody concerned will accept gaily and without complaint.  In a house party everybody must be cheery; nobody must sulk; each must contribute something to the general account.  If an evening of story-telling be proposed, each must do the best in his power by way of enlivening the whole.

A house party, perhaps more than any other social opportunity, enables the youthful disciple to show his love and loyalty to the Master.  Not by preaching or even by talking, but by the daily walk, by the habit of conscientious reference of all things to Christ, by the style of the Sabbath-keeping, by the daily Bible-reading, and by what the manner of the life *is* before one's friends, and in Jesus' sight.

## When to Do Right.

Away with this idea that we would do right if people, surroundings and influences were different.

Ah! do we not know, have we not yet learned, that to do right just where we are, and just as we are, is the important matter for us?

What we should do is very plainly laid down for us in the Holy Word.

Now we are entreated, enjoined to be patient.  Not to be patient with the patient only, but with *all*, and with all circumstances as well.  We are told to be thankful.  No time specified for the exhibition of this grace.  We can be thankful if all goes well.  Yes, but we are to be thankful in adverse circumstances.  We are to overcome the obstacles to thankfulness.

If a dear one from sickness or other cause, good or bad, be fretful or trying, we are to overcome impatience and not give way to it.

It is easy to do right where there is no temptation to do wrong—"easy to keep a fortress that is never stormed;" but when are we wholly without temptation?

If we are waiting for an easy time to do right, that time will never come. Life is not soft, but hard," says one good minister.

It is indeed time; the word is, "fight." Fight what? Our own inclination to wrong. This day, just where we are, just with whom we are, just in what state mentally and physically, our duty is to do right.

How often do we when alone with God resolve to be all we should be to our dear ones; but when we come out from our place of prayer and good resolvings we find the dear ones with the same individuality as usual, and perhaps some of the traits of this individuality don't exactly dove-tail in with our ideas and feelings; and then, alas! we forget and sin by impatience, or censure, or by frowns and unpleasant demeanor. If we could only remember that we cannot make other people over, it would help us greatly. The task of remodeling may be successful if the work is spent on *self*.

It is not other people's fault that we sin by word or deed. No, it is *ours*. It is not that they provoked us, but it is that we were provoked where we should have borne. Prayer and watchfulness are of use because we are liable to temptation.

Oh! to remember to do right, to speak right, to think right. We have, with pain of heart, noted Paul's declaration concerning himself: "As touching the righteousness which is of the law, blameless."

Our dear maternal parent often exclaims, "It is a *great* thing to do right!" And we from the heart echo, "A great thing to do right.".

## Singing in the Rain.

Hear my happy little bird
  Singing through the rain—
Singing while the fitful showers
  Dash against the pane.
"Blue sky somewhere," carols he,
  From his fearless heart,
Though the clouds are gathering thick,
  And the chill winds start.

Sweet and shrill the silver notes
  Weave a wordless strain;
"Bly sky somewhere," in my thought,
  Is their glad refrain.
Always sunshine just beyond,
  Brief the present ill,
Trouble never long to last,
  Is their meaning still.

## SINGING IN THE RAIN.

Sing thy sweetest, merry bird,
    Comforter of mine,
Bringing in thy little way
    Help from love divine.

" Hear the happy little bird singing through the rain."

Thou hast given me the clasp
    Of a golden chain,
Let from heaven into my hand,
    Through the clouds and rain.

What though all my way be hedged,
  Love shall ope a door
For the feet that follow fain
  His that went before.
What though trials test my faith,
  Peace shall yet maintain
Right to rule in one who walks
  Singing in the rain.

More than I can count of good
  Aye has been my share;
Dearest hands to help me on,
  Having all my care;
Blessings marking every day,
  To the latest one,
And the shadow only proof
  Of the glowing sun.

Therefore, with undaunted front,
  Trusting in my King,
Shall I face whatever foe
  In the path may spring.
So I hear a note of cheer
  In the brave refrain
Of my merry little bird,
  Singing in the rain.

## Dancing in the Street.

The wind was piercing and bitter,
  And I hurried fast along,
When sweet in the street about me
  Came the lilt of a little song.

And a poor old organ-grinder,
  With a monkey dressed in red,
Laughed at my look of wonder,
  Nodding his grizzled head,

As out of the narrow alleys
  And tumbling down the stairs,
Came a quaint little throng of children,
  Dancing in merry pairs.

Their clothes were rags and tatters,
  With broken shoes they were shod,
But they sang with cheery voices,
  And danced to the player's nod.

They didn't mind the biting
  Of the nipping, frosty air,
They heard the sound of the music
  And danced away their care.

Sweet little lads and lassies,
  It comes to me as I look,
That we all might be the better
  For a leaf from your happy book.

---

## Thanksgiving.

"Oh that men would praise the Lord for His goodness,
and for His wonderful works to the children of men!"—
Psalm cvii. 31.

Dear Lord, are we ever so thankful,
  As thankful we should be to Thee,
For Thine angels sent down to defend us
  From dangers our eyes never see;
From perils that lurk unsuspected,
  The powers of earth and of air,
The while we are heaven protected
  And guarded from evil and snare?

Are we grateful, as grateful we should be,
  For commonplace days of delight,
When safe we fare forth to our labor,
  And safe we fare homeward at night;
For the weeks in which nothing has happened
  Save commonplace toiling and play,
When we've worked at the tasks of the household,
  And peace hushed the house day by day?

Dear Lord, that the terror at midnight,
  The weird of the wind and the flame,
Hath passed by our dwelling, we praise Thee,
  And lift up our hearts in Thy name;
That the circle of darlings unbroken
  Yet gathers in bliss round the board,
That commonplace love is our portion,
  We give Thee our praises, dear Lord!

Forgive us who live by Thy bounty
  That often our lives are so bare
Of the garlands of praise that should render
  All votive and fragrant each prayer.
Dear Lord, in the sharpness of trouble
  We cry from the depths to the throne!
In the long days of gladness and beauty
  Take Thou the glad hearts as Thine own.

Oh, common are sunshine and flowers,
  And common are raindrop and dew,
And the gay little footsteps of children,
  And common the love that holds true.
So, Lord, for our commonplace mercies,
  That straight from Thy hand are bestowed,
We are fain to uplift our thanksgivings—
  Take, Lord, the long debt we have owed!

# CHAPTER XXXII.

## Fault-finding.

"AKE us the foxes, the little foxes that spoil the vines," is an injunction of Holy Writ. Among the prowling foxes which ravage the vines of home comfort, first and foremost is that wretched habit of fault-finding, into which we drift almost without knowing how or why. It is like going down hill, this fault-finding—we start and there is no stopping us; we go on from bad to worse.

A fault-finding husband ruins the happiness of his wife; a fault-finding wife, nagging and scolding on every occasion, drives her husband out of the house. Fault-finding parents make about the children an atmosphere of a pitiless hail storm, and children soon catch the prevalent tone and in turn find fault with one another. The habit has its root, as most bad habits have, in selfishness. Once indulged it becomes easy to yield a second time to the temptation to say that this or that thing is not what we wish, to be querulous and hateful in manner, to be satirical and bitter in word.

Singularly, the table is often the arena for the persistent fault-finder. The steak is either tough in the first place, or else it is not the right cut, it is too well done or it is underdone. The potatoes are soggy, the bread is not up to the usual standard, the dessert is just what you do not like. I heard of a little girl not long ago who did not think rice pudding a dessert worth eating, and so one day when she was saying her prayers she thanked God for everything she had had that day except the rice pudding. Now there are people who not only do not thank God for rice pudding or for some other thing which they do not like to eat, but they also are so rude and ungrateful that they make everybody uncomfortable by objecting to the ill-timed or ill-chosen viand when it is quite too late to get anything else. All children should be taught at the outset to eat such things as are set before them, and it should be a fixed rule in home life that no one is to show irritation or anger at a meal.

Nothing is worse for digestion than a lack of cheerfulness, and cheerfulness is impossible where people are in a surly and morose mood. If anybody is to be reproved do not let it be at the table. The mother can speak privately to the child in a way that will not call attention to the little fault of manner; but by no means should a reproof be so administered that the attention of all at the table is turned upon the unfortunate offender.

If the carving knife is dull, as, alas, carving knives are often bound to be, let not the man of the house vent his displeasure upon the whole family because of this distressing occurrence. Rather let him carve as well as he can without interjecting remarks about the knife being as dull as a hoe, or the probability that somebody has used it to cut bread or saw wood, or do some other thing for which carving knives are not intended.

What folly it is to make life a burden for anybody by constant fault-finding! Once in a while friends say to one another, "Tell me my faults." Nobody does this conscientiously. The fact is, we do not want our friends to tell us our faults, and this is proved by the quick resentment with which people receive the candid announcement that a friend has discovered a fault in their character.

Occasionally a parent or a teacher must speak words of criticism, but when this is necessary let it be done in private and with the utmost kindness and gentleness; and on no account let any fault-finding to child, or servant, or friend, be done in public. The hasty word may leave a sting which will not soon be healed. We may quite wisely take to ourselves the lesson in the simple verses which follow:

If I had known in the morning
How wearily all the day
The words unkind would trouble my mind
That I said when you went away,
I had been more careful, darling,
Nor given you needless pain,
But we vex our own with look and tone
We may never take back again.

For, though in the quiet evening
You may give me the kiss of peace,
Yet it well might be that never for me
The pain of the heart should cease!
How many go forth at morning
Who never come home at night!
And hearts have broken for harsh words spoken,
That sorrow can ne'er set right.

We have careful thought for the stranger,
And smiles for the sometime guest,
But oft for our own the bitter tone,
Though we love our own the best.
Ah, lips with the curve impatient,
Ah, brow with the shade of scorn,
'Twere a cruel fate were the night too late
To undo the work of the morn!

It hardly seems worth while to say it, and yet I venture, because there is here and there the need of a sort of caution about finding fault with those older

" The one thing we cannot escape is growing old."

than ourselves.   Old people have their little ways, and sometimes these ways are
trying to younger ones who have not the traditions of the former generation, and
who have little patience with the fixed ideas of their predecessors.

Stop a minute, however, and think. The one thing we can none of us escape is growing old. To-day we are in the heydey of youth and activity, our energy confronts every obstacle, and we fear nothing, but day by day, week by week, by imperceptible steps and degrees, we are going forward to the time of silver hair and lessened strength on life's downhill slope. When that time comes we shall need consideration from our juniors, and we shall then feel that we have a right to our own lives, even though children and grandchildren wish to order them for us in their own way, and not after ours.

I have known old men and women, grandfathers and grandmothers, made very unhappy by the constant interference, or the perhaps gentle fault-finding of younger people in the home. Let grandmother potter about as she will; do not venture to order your mother around. Refrain from comment and criticism upon father and his methods of speech or somewhat conservative preferences. You have perhaps had advantages which your parents never had; you owe these advantages to their unfailing unselfishness, their hard work and their self-denial.

If they do not use the same kind of English that you do, if they occasionally have a lapse in grammar, or if their table manners are not quite up to the modern standard of etiquette, far be it from you to interfere. There is really no sin whatever in pouring tea or coffee into a saucer, as some old people like to do, yet I have seen young people inordinately distressed because of some such little act in their company.

I recall with shame some young people who apologized to me for their mother's lack of acquaintance with the conventionalities of the day. I blushed for them to think they were so ill-bred and crude, and my heart ached for the poor mother who was subjected to their foolish fault-finding.

Let me finish this chapter with a little bit of sensible verse by S. W. Foss. It is called "The Soul's Spring Cleaning," and it seems to me that it has a lesson for all of us. If we just take up the thought in this homely little poem we shall not be in much danger of finding fault with anybody. And fault-finding is an enemy to avoid.

> Yes, clean yer house, an' clean yer shed,
> An' clean yer barn in ev'ry part;
> But brush the cobwebs from yer head,
> An' sweep the snowbanks from yer heart.
> Yes, w'en spring cleanin' comes aroun'
> Bring forth the duster an' the broom,
> But rake yer fogy notions down,
> An' sweep yer dusty soul of gloom.

Sweep ol' ideas out with the dust,
  An' dress yer soul in newer style;
Scrape from yer min' its worn-out crust,
  An' dump it in the rubbish pile.
Sweep out the hates that burn an' smart,
  Bring in new loves serene an' pure;
Aroun' the hearthstone of the heart
  Place modern styles of furniture.

Clean out yer morril cubby-holes,
  Sweep out the dirt, scrape off the scum;
'Tis cleanin' time for healthy souls—
  Git up an' dust! The spring hez come!
Clean out the corners of the brain,
  Bear down with scrubbin'-brush and soap,
An' dump ol' Fear into the rain,
  An' dust a cozy chair for Hope.

Clean out the brain's deep rubbish hole,
  Soak ev'ry cranny, great an' small,
An' in the front room of the soul
  Hang pootier picturs on the wall;
Scrub up the winders of the mind,
  Clean up, an' let the spring begin;
Swing open wide the dusty blind,
  An' let the April sunshine in.

Plant flowers in the soul's front yard,
  Set out new shade an' blossom trees,
An' let the soul, once froze an' hard,
  Sprout crocuses of new idees.
Yes, clean yer house, an' clean yer shed,
  An' clean yer barn in ev'ry part,
But brush the cobwebs from yer head,
  An' sweep the snowbanks from yer heart!

# CHAPTER XXXIII.

## Our Aunt Mary.

OMEBODY once said that when conversation flagged you could always start it going by turning to your next neighbor and innocently inquiring ' How long is it since you heard from your Aunt Mary ; The person would usually fall at once into the trap and say Why, I did not know that you had met my Aunt Mary," or "Aunt Mary is very well, I thank you," or "Aunt Mary has gone to California," or "Aunt Mary is coming to see us next week," the fact being that everybody has an Aunt Mary.

The sweet word " Mary," name endeared to Christians because it is the name of the blessed Mother of our Lord, has woven itself into every life and placed itself in almost every home. Quite often we find out that a person whom we have always known as Jennie or Gertrude or Virginia has also the baptismal name of Mary, and it is perhaps an impossibility to find anywhere a large family connection in which Marys are not as plentiful as daisies in summer or ripe apples in autumn.

Aunt Mary when she comes to stay at our house is always a welcome guest. Once when I was a child there was a question eagerly discussed in the family councils as to whether a certain dear and intimate friend who often made visits at our house could be comfortably entertained during a winter when many other things were on foot and the house was more than ordinarily crowded. The elders were reluctant about making up their minds that they would have to put off the guest whom they loved, and who had hitherto always come whenever she chose and always been received with open arms. A solemn-eyed little child, sitting with his toys on a rug and apparently too young to have entered into the merits of the conversation, decided the matter by piping up in a very resolute voice "There is room enough for Aunt Mary." Little Jack's verdict carried the day, and Aunt Mary came and stayed as usual, making the house brighter by her cheery presence and adding an element of interest to all that was going on.

There is many a sweet Aunt Mary to whom children go with quite as much confidence as to their mothers. In communities where the trained nurse is not easily obtained, and where primitive neighborliness still lingers, it is Aunt Mary who goes, packing her little satchel with necessaries, to the household where measles has broken out, to the other household where they have scarlet fever, or to the other where death has entered bringing desolation and distress in his wake. Always she comes bringing comfort, joy and strength, this capable, efficient, charming Aunt Mary.

If there is a wedding on the carpet, it is she who is consulted about the great occasion itself, the bridesmaids, the maids of honor, the bridal gown and veil; it

AUNT MARY'S VISIT.

is she who has known all about it from the very first, who was first aware that Eugene had looked longingly at Betty, and that coquettish Betty had at last yielded her heart to a persistent lover. Very likely Aunt Mary has a romance of her own. It might make the youthful lovers smile to know that this staid and demure personage had in her own day had offers from courtly admirers, and that perhaps her heart was still faithful to one who for some reason or other never had the courage to offer her his hand.

One summer day long ago an elderly gentleman alighted at a little station in the mountains of Pennsylvania. In this village there was a school for young women, presided over by a gracious lady with silver hair and eyes still bright and keen, though she had seen her fiftieth birthday. Little reckoned she as she sat at her desk or presided in chapel, or listened to the confidences of the young girls under her care, that a stately and courtly judge who many years before had wooed her in vain, when her hair was golden and his brown, had in late life and widower-hood taken the pains to find out where she was and had come again once more to try his fate. To the great astonishment of all her friends, and to the consternation of the girls who had been her pupils, one day it was announced that this lady, Aunt Mary to any number of bright young kinsfolk, was about to enter the married state. Do not smile at elderly lovers. There is often a good prospect for happiness in the serenity of Indian summer, and life's late afternoon may be mellow and sweet to two who find it possible to unite their fortunes even in the waning day.

"My Aunt Mary," said a boy, "is as jolly as any other fellow in town." It was really a great compliment, and I quite understood it when I saw her, as eager and interested as anybody else, standing and watching a game of baseball, and absolutely shouting, in her interest, directions to her favorite players all over the field.

To another Aunt Mary came a motherless boy, a boy who had been neglected, who had few ideals, to whom no one had been specially kind or attentive. This boy had not been started right, and when he was taken under the wing of this gentle, yet spirited, woman, he had many faults and failings; but she knew how to reach a boy's heart, and before long there was the greatest change visible in Will. His school reports became steadily more and more creditable, day by day he made friends, the somewhat sullen and often boorish boy became transformed into a quiet-mannered, gentle and altogether agreeable lad whom everybody liked; and in years to come, when people shall find him in situations of honor and merit, it will all be due to Aunt Mary.

Sometimes Aunt Mary is very much discouraged. It seems to her that she has no special gift or talent, that she does not shine, and that people could get on very well without her. She is less apt than formerly to resent the title "Old Maid," because not only are old maids at preent as thick as blackberries in summer, and not only are they a most useful and excellent body of women without whom the community would fare ill, but the reproach once clinging to the term is entirely gone.

Spinsters have engaged in business on equal terms with men, they are to be found in every occupation, they are at the head of our schools and colleges, they go independently where they will, they add flavor and grace to society, and there is no place in which they do not fit. They might have been married, many of them, had they chosen, but they did not choose—they preferred their independence, and wherever they are they are recognized as quite as honorable as their married friends.

One dear spinster whom I know—why do I say one, for I know several, but one occurs to me at the moment—a woman who is so sweet and gracious, so beautiful, so full of tact, whose home is so lovely, and whose influence is so great, that around her young people flock, and her home is the centre of pleasure for all her acquaintances.

Aunt Mary carries on the missionary society, Aunt Mary presides at the tea table, she is in the Sunday School, she mothers the little ones while their mothers are off at clubs; in fact, what does she not do, this dear and beautiful Aunt Mary?

# CHAPTER XXXIV.

## The Art of Living Together.

THE art of living together is not one of the least among the fine arts. When we think of it, the ordinary intercourse of a refined family affords opportunity for many little daily sacrifices, for much exercise of self-denial, and for the development of some of the noblest qualities in human nature. The advice once given to a married couple by a sage, that they should take into their new home two bears—bear and forbear—is as important and useful as ever in this latter part of the nineteenth century.

Proverbially the first year of married life is a difficult one, because husband and wife cannot at once grow accustomed to each other's little peculiarities and ways. Also, in all home and social living people must take into account the caprices, the whims, the peculiarities of temperament, and the resultant training of different households, all of which have an effect on character, on manners, and on modes of thought.

This is why it is no light thing to take into one's home, in permanent relationship to the home, any one who is in some sense an outsider. A lady living by herself, and in somewhat infirm health, thinks that the wheels of life will move more easily for her if she have a companion or a private secretary, or some confidential friend who can take upon herself little duties and afford a certain amount of company to cheat time of its loneliness. Sometimes the experiment turns out well, again it is an utter failure; it all depends on whether or not the new element proves congenial.

So in the inevitable changes of life which bring aged or necessitous relatives beneath the roof, there are times when the coming of these adds greatly to the joy of life, and again their strange and odd individuality proves a source of unhappiness. For instance, in my early girlhood an aged connection of the family came to stay indefinitely as a member of our household. It was quite right that she should come, and we gave her the warmest and most cordial of welcomes. Yet I never look back upon the years during which this old lady—a gentlewoman through and through—was a member of our home without thinking sympathetically of the shadows her fretfulness brought to the youth of the home, and wonderingly at the great patience of my saintly mother.

(251)

I have told the story before, but I will repeat it now, of a certain morning when the dear lady did not descend at her ordinary time to breakfast.  As she was usually a pattern of promptness we naturally felt some anxiety on her account, and thinking that she had been  taken ill in the  night, a messenger was sent to her door and knocked.   Repeated knocks brought no response.   Again and  again we went. Finally in great fear and trepidation we concluded that she must either have had a stroke of paralysis and must be lying there speechless in her bed and helpless, or else that perhaps the Angel of Death had come in the night and carried her away.

There was nothing to do but to enter by forcible means, and after much trouble we broke the lock and made our way into the silent room.   There sat our stately step-grandmother completely dressed, her neckerchief crossed above her black gown, her beautiful white cap immaculate over her gray hair, her spectacles on, and her Bible in her hand.   She had taken a sudden determination neither to come down stairs nor to answer us, and as she looked up from her Bible she remarked placidly, " What is the meaning of this unseemly confusion?   It seems very strange that I cannot be allowed to attend to my morning devotions in peace."

One can easily see that a lady of this turn of mind was not an easy inmate, and it is much to the credit of our home training that none of the children and young people of the family retorted in any way, but, as our sweet mother told us, continued to be respectful and gentle in demeanor toward this querulous personality.

There are times when we must live with those who are not congenial, and when those who are not congenial must live with us.   Whenever this is the case the thing for us to do is to bear with their peculiarities, so that our common conduct presents no sharp occasion for criticism.   One rule may be laid down, and that is that in no circumstances should we ever yield to the temptation either to talk at people or to talk about them to one another.   If there is a disagreeable thing to be said, let it be said always directly to the person himself or herself, and let it be said in the gentlest and sweetest way possible.

If there is in the  home a spirit of entire and sweet confidence there will be little room for censure and criticism.   By no means let there be parties in the home, or one person made the butt of remarks.   Rather if there is in a family circle a child or a youth or any one who is jarring, let the others form around that one a wall of defence, shielding him or her from the criticisms and censure of others in every way, giving to the world a united family front.   This can be done; it is often done by those who make of life a study of serene philosophy, and who can thus be responsible to God for their social life as well as for every other thing which concerns them.

Respect for personal property is another factor in the art of living together agreeably. There are households in which nobody seems to have any individual possession which the others do not make free with at their pleasure. Sisters are quite apt to use each other's gloves and ribbons and hair-pins, and I once knew an instance in which a girl was very ill and it was feared she would not recover, when her sister rushed into the room and said, "Oh, Mary, get well, get well, and I will never take

LOVING ATTENTIONS TO THE AGED.

your collars and cuffs again!" The incongruity of the remark amused the invalid and made her smile, and from that moment she began to recover. It is to be hoped that her sister kept her word. Mothers, too, are pillaged by their daughters quite remorselessly, and it often happens that mother's handkerchief-box or work-box is regarded as a sort of common ground which everybody may invade. The sense of ownership in some homes is carried perhaps a little too far. Thus I have seen a certain chair regarded as the property of father or mother, and even in the absence of the owner the family hesitated to sit in it temporarily. This seems to carry the idea of ownership a trifle too far. We need to regulate our lives by common sense as well as by amiability.

In the interests of peace and harmony it is best that those who live together on intimate terms should be of kindred faith. People of widely diverging religious views will not usually enjoy comradeship on the journey of life so fully as those who are of one mind. It is not best, as a general thing, that husband and wife should have widely differing beliefs, and certainly children are better brought up where there is a unity in the religious life of the home.

What shall we say of truth telling? May we not judge that there is a candor which is misplaced, and that now and then it is just as well not to say everything that we think, even while we must in no circumstances evade or violate the strict obligation of truth? For example, if Jennie comes home from the milliner's with a hat which is the pride of her life, which has captured her imagination, and which she is sure she will look well in, where is the kindness in saying, "I never saw anything so lacking in taste as that hat; it is most unbecoming and does not suit your complexion in the least." Why should we meet a sister or brother in the morning with the remark, "I never saw you looking worse. Your color is pallid, and the way your hair is arranged gives me quite a turn." It is far better to say complimentary things, or else to say nothing at all.

Perhaps you have noticed that one must act with great tact in telling people about any mistake which they have made, or about anything wrong with their toilette. A lady is walking on the street and half a yard behind her trails a piece of her skirt binding. She is quite unaware of this accident and walks proudly on without the slightest feeling of discomfort in the matter. If in your desire to help her you step up and say, "Pardon me, madam, but your skirt braid is ripped," she may or may not receive the piece of information graciously. Quite often she will turn upon you in anger and receives what you have to say in freezing silence, and evidently does not thank you for having observed that something was wrong with her attire; and yet you have done her a kindness.

I believe in doing the kindness even if one is snubbed therefor, and I have often marveled why it is that people are so vexed at being told that some little thing is wrong with their costume. We must learn in life to receive criticism and reproof at need without disturbance, and with some slight appearance of equanimity. A friend certainly does not wish to wound us, and it is well for us to accept a suggestion even if it does not seem to be quite in the line of our own preconceived notion.

# CHAPTER XXXV.

## Stepmothers.

F all the world loves a lover, all the world seems by unanimous consent to hate a stepmother. I do not mean that stepmothers in individual cases are always treated with aversion or dislike. Many of these excellent women are exceedingly successful in the difficult work they have taken up, and they are rewarded for their labor and care by the fond love of the children in their homes and by the respect of all who know them.

A stepmother has three sets of people to please, if not more. She must commend herself to her husband and his children, to the husband's relations and the relations of his first wife, the children's own mother. After that she must run the gauntlet of criticism from her neighbors and townspeople, and even from strangers, for wherever she goes accompanied by her stepchildren the eyes of those upon her will take note of any defect in manner or any little irritability; above all things, of any difference she may happen to make between her own children and those to whom she is acting as mother in step relationship.

An own mother may be impatient and unjust and no one observes it, but the slightest dereliction on the part of a stepmother calls forth pity for the children, poor things, and pitiless comment upon the woman who is supposed to have married her husband only to regard his children as a burden. In all literature and in all nations hard measure is dealt out to the stepmother. In the fairy stories, in lyrical ballads, in the old-fashioned novels and the new, she is the type of whatever is despotic, of whatever is unkind, of whatever is unmotherly.

Yet there are stepmothers and stepmothers. No woman who undertakes the office of stepmother, if she do so with a full conception of the responsibilities it involves, is anything but a brave, true woman. Often the mother-heart is found in women who never bear a child of their own. There are blessed and lovely mothers who simply remember compassionately the one who has gone and do their very best to supply to those she has left the care and sweet tenderness she would have given had she lived.

One of the happiest homes I have ever known had in it three sets of children growing up together. Husband and wife had each been married before and each had a family of children. There came along by degrees a third little family, and the various boys and girls lived together in an ideal harmony. The respective rôles of stepmother and stepfather were carried on successfully by the parents, who seemed to show no partiality to the younger brood, but treated all alike.

Stepfathers are less unfavorably commented upon than stepmothers. They are, indeed, a rather popular set of people. A man's work taking him outside his home he is not expected to stay there and administer justice, discipline the children, or spoil them by over-indulgence. He does not have to wash the little hands and faces a dozen times a day, to sew on buttons or mend torn trousers, or settle little disputes, and therefore, whether he is father or stepfather, he gets along pretty well, occasionally acting indeed as the court of last resort in certain difficult cases, but ordinarily having a pleasant time with his children and escaping much of the triviality which makes woman's life a dull routine.

Children are often set against a stepmother by the thoughtless remarks of relatives and friends, or of heedless servants, who take pains to sow the seeds of jealousy and suspicion before the new wife comes upon the scene. This is certainly wicked work, and a little care on the part of those who have children in their hands to bring up would prevent it. Many a stepmother is doing all she can to educate and train the children whom she loves most dearly, and she should be helped and not hindered in this work.

\*        \*        \*        \*

Some years ago I was paying a visit in a beautiful old home on Long Island, where each summer as the month of August came round a widely scattered family grouped itself under the old roof-tree around one of the most beautiful women I have ever known. She must have been lovely as a girl and as a young matron, for I did not know her until the lines gently laid by time upon her face indicated three score years and ten.

But she had so young a heart, so sweet a disposition, such quick sympathy with youth and childhood, such tender comprehension of the troubles which come to people as they meet the problems of life, that in age she remained what she must always have been—a perfect queen. Around her gathered as long as she lived, which was until she had long passed her eightieth birthday, her children and grandchildren; and those to whom she had taken the place of stepmother were just as devoted, just as loyal and considerate, as were the others.

Her oldest stepson had been a young man when the fair young wife came into the house, and there were a number of children belonging to that first set. Then she had a large family of her own. One of these told me that she shall never forget the shock she felt when, as a growing girl, some meddlesome neighbor took upon herself to inform her that her older brothers and sisters were not really her own, but only what are called half brothers and sisters. She rushed home to throw herself on the maternal breast and sob, and that sweet mother told her not to mind anything that was said; that she loved the children all alike.

Many of us have similar memories which we recall, and we know that it is not the fact merely of bearing offspring, but the warm mother heart, true and sweet, the feeling of responsibility in undertaking the sacred trust, and the overflowing love which makes some women's hearts a sanctuary for all which needs shelter, that make the stepmother a true mother.

Occasionally one's heart is harrowed by tales of cruelty, but these do not spring from the fact of the rela-

"She rushed home to throw herself on the maternal breast."

tionship so much as from the fact of the narrow and selfish heart of the woman who has undertaken to care for children when she has no love for them. An own mother has sometimes been known to be injudicious, unjust and severe, and so far as in us lies it will be a good thing if we should all join hands hereafter in

17

opposing the senseless and foolish prejudice which makes the stepmother a butt for ridicule or a target for sneers.

Louisa C. Tuthill, alluding to extreme sensitiveness, once said something which stepmothers may find helpful:

"If your enemies misunderstand your motives, it matters little if they are such as you can lay open to the eyes of Him who sits as a 'refiner and purifier.' If you are led, by their severity, to a clearer discernment of your own motives, to a closer scrutiny into your own conduct, they in effect serve you better than your flatterers—even better than your friends. 'You will form your own character, nor can your enemies prevent it. Their calumny will injure you less than you imagine.'

"Injuries, real or supposed, are not to be met with a haughty and contemptuous spirit. Loathing and disdaining meanness and sinfulness, avoid transferring your hatred to the beings who are guilty of them. Hatred, malice, and all evil passions, burn themselves with the firebrands they throw, poison themselves with their own deadly mixtures. They whose bosoms are haunted by these demons should not meet with condemnation alone; they should call forth the deepest commiseration. When you can 'pray for those who despitefully use and persecute you,' not generally, but individually, it is the surest proof that they are entirely forgiven. The Christian's heart should bound to offer forgiveness, even to those offending ones who will not ask it. Blessed indeed is that spirit which, in humble imitation of the divine Redeemer, can say, 'Father, forgive them, for they know not what they do.'

"But not alone toward enemies is the spirit of Christian forbearance to be exercised. Such, alas! is fallen human nature, that the best and loveliest of earthly friends have their darker shades of character. We should be foolishly employed in endeavoring, day after day, to count the spots upon the glorious sun; to dwell upon the faults of those whom we love would be equal folly. Habitually to interpret their motives kindly, to make charitable allowances for their weakness, to use every favorable opportunity to draw forth their excellence, to endeavor to correct their faults by example and by advice, unostentatiously offered; this is the task of Christian forbearance.

"Excessive sensitiveness to unkindness or to dislike should not be suffered to mar your happiness. This may arise from morbid sensibility, or from pride. In either case, you will be disturbed by

> " ' A something light as air—a look,
> A word unkind or wrongly taken,'

from the friends whom you fondly love, and weeks of dejection be the consequence. No better remedy can be prescribed, than a cordial, wholesome kindliness of manner on your own part, which will most probably call forth the same manner from your friends, Practice that true Christian courtesy, recommended by the Apostle Paul, and so beautifully exemplified by our blessed Saviour in all His social intercourse. This courtesy exhibits itself from day to day, in those 'thousand decencies' that give to life its sweetness. If, notwithstanding your own kindliness, you have true friends who are deficient in courtesy, their want of suavity should not alienate you; with this unfortunate deficiency, their hearts may be kind and benevolent. Habituate yourself to their unpleasing manners, and steel yourself against them; a rough rind often encloses fruit that is sweet and nutritious."

Where, as sometimes happens, the stepdaughters are nearly the same age with their mothers, the problem grows more difficult of solution daily, unless on both sides there are good temper, common sense and conscience. These brought to bear upon any situation soon rob of its worst aspects. A man has a right to marry a second time. Let this be conceded and his family will accommodate themselves to the arrangement, even if they would have preferred it otherwise.

# CHAPTER XXXVI.

## Love of Country.

UR country! Do we love her? Will we at need yield for her our very heart's blood? Is she dear to us beyond any other, so that the sight of her flag streaming from turret or mast-head thrills us with joy, and, when seen in a foreign port, brings the quick tears to our eyes? When our country is threatened by a foe, are we ready to defend her, pledging her our lives, our fortunes and our sacred honor? Can we sing with all our souls,

> " Columbia, the gem of the ocean,
> The home of the brave and the true,
> The shrine of each patriot's devotion,
> Our heart offers homage to you;"

or,

> " Rally round the flag, boys,
> Give it to the breeze,"

or,

> " Hail, Columbia, happy land."

Best of all our national hymns do we count,

> " My country, 'tis of thee,
> Sweet land of liberty,
> Of thee I sing.
> Land where my fathers died,
> Land of the pilgrim's pride,
> From every mountain side
> Let Freedom ring!"

This is as it should be, but no one is a true patriot who is merely sentimental about his country.

In this great mother-land of ours, there are not a few men, older and younger, who are so indifferent to the country's welfare that they hold aloof from politics and lightly prize the freeman's birthright, the ballot. They explain that bribery and corruption have invaded legislative halls, that primary meetings are the resorts of the vulgar, that gentlemen stand aloof from elections. So charging their generation and their period, whether falsely or truly, with a great shame and sin,

(260)

they do nought to improve matters, but simply play the coward's part, and refuse to take a personal interest in the ruling of their own America. Cynical, hostile, or indifferent, it is all one; they are practically enemies to the land which calls them her sons. A share in her government is the birthright of every man born into a free country, and if he despise his birthright and shirk its obligations, he is to be pitied and condemned.

The Fourth of July used to be so kept by our people that it was an important educator in patriotism. Early in the morning we were awakened by the thunder of cannon from fort and fleet, or from the village green, then the children, rushing to the windows, saw everywhere the red, white and blue of our flag, floating from roof and spire. There was a sense of music in the air, jubilant, ecstatic, throbbing and pulsating, in drum beat and bugle call. By and by there was the parade, soldiers marching behind their banners, cavalry in stately procession riding down the street, and then came the fathers of the town, the ministers and elders and deacons, the city magnates, people of dignity and position, and the trade representatives, and by and by the Sunday-school children in white frocks and ribbon sashes, or in white trousers, and jackets with brass buttons, according as they were girls or boys.

The Declaration of Independence was read, and everybody listened and absorbed its lofty sentiments. Do our children still know the names of the signers of that immortal document, do they yet admire the bold screed of John Hancock, and the clear chirography of Samuel Adams, and sympathize with the spirit which induced Charles Carroll to add "of Carrollton" after his name? *We* studied those names as we did our alphabet. Patriotism was part of our education. Not less were we taught to look upon America as God's hallowed ark of freedom, the asylum for the oppressed of every land and nation. "God save the Commonwealth!" we were taught to add to our prayers.

"God bless our native land !
Firm may she ever stand !"

Let our flag stream from the schoolhouse and flutter from the ships and wave over our heads as we walk through our streets. Only a bit of bunting? Yes, but it means liberty, obedience to law, protection to the weak, freedom of conscience, and equal rights for all men. Only a bit of bunting? Yes, but it means what men would gladly die for; it is the flag of our country. God bless it and save it !

---

"EVERY American woman should be familiarly acquainted with the history of her own country, its constitution and form of government. She should know that the stability and permanency of a republic depend upon the intellectual, moral and religious character of the people; upon this broad principle she must act, and endeavor to induce everybody to act, over whom she exercises influence. To enter as a fiery partisan into the contentions of political opponents is unbecoming the delicacy and dignity of female character.    Men talk much of a conservative principle.    We trust we shall not be accused of presumptuousness if we name one: A high moral and intellectual character in the women of our country, that shall make them true patriots, preserving a consistent neutrality, and exerting their influence for the good of the whole.    Leaving government, and all its multifarious concerns, to those to whom the all-wise Creator has delegated authority, let us be content with that influence which is 'pure, peaceful, gentle, without partiality, and without hypocrisy.'

"Let not a meddlesome spirit, in matters that do not concern you, mar the pleasures of social intercourse.    Must they, who fly to your society for relief from the jarrings of men, be teased with the perpetual din?    Has the miasma of politics infected the whole moral atmosphere?    Is there no elevated ground, where they can breathe a purer air, and escape for a while into a serene and tranquil region?    We remember, some time since, hearing a gentleman say of a great statesman, who was his intimate friend, that, in the society of an amiable and interesting young lady whom he admired, ' he was like a great mountain by the side of a little flower, and forgot that he was a mountain.'

"A man possessing political influence is sometimes, in society, beset by a swarm of female philanthropists, urging their claims, or, as they call them, the claims of humanity, of benevolence, etc.    ' Now, sir, you cannot refuse me that slight favor.'    ' Do vote, for my sake, on my side; I shall be superlatively grateful.'    What is a gallant man to do?    If he drive off this swarm, like the fox in the fable, another more clamorous may succeed, until he is robbed of every drop of enjoyment in society.    And is it certain that every politician has principle enough to withstand these fair petitioners, when they urge him contrary to his own better judgment?    A sage and potent Senator, one of the most polite and elegant men in the world, once confessed that he left the Senate-chamber, when a vote was taken on a question in which a splendid woman of his acquaintance was deeply interested, because he could not vote against her while her dark eyes were fixed upon him from the gallery.    True, it was a question of no great importance to the welfare of the country, and involved no party interests; but his opinion and his vote were sacrificed to his chivalrous gallantry.''

## Through Death to Life.

Have you heard the tale of the aloe plant,
　Away in the sunny clime?
By humble growth of a hundred years
　It reaches its blooming time;
And then a wondrous bud at its crown
　Breaks into a thousand flowers.
This floral queen in its beauty seen
　Is the pride of the tropical bowers.
But the plant to the flower is a sacrifice,
　For it blooms but once and in blooming dies.

Have you further heard of this aloe plant,
　That grows in the sunny clime,
How every one of its thousand flowers,
　As they droop in the blooming time,
Is an infant plant that fastens its roots
　In the place where it falls to the ground,
And fast as they drop from the dying stem
　Grow lively and lovely around?
By dying it liveth a thousand fold
　In the young that spring from the death of the old.

Have you heard the tale of the pelican,
　The Arab's Gimel el Bahr,
That dwells in the African solitudes
　Where the birds that live lonely are?
Have you heard how it loves its tender young,
　And cares and toils for their good?
It brings them water from fountains afar,
　And fishes the sea for their food.
In famine it feeds them—what love can devise!—
　With blood of its bosom, and feeding them dies.

Have you heard the tale they tell of the swan,
　The snow-white bird of the lake?
It noiselessly floats on the silvery wave,
　It silently sits in the brake;

For it saves its song till the end of life,
    And then in the soft, still even,
'Mid the golden light of the setting sun
    It sings, as it soars into heaven;
And the blessed notes fall back from the skies,
    'Tis its only song, for in singing it dies.

Have you heard these tales? Shall I tell you one,
    A greater and better than all?
Have you heard of Him whom the heavens adore,
    Before whom the hosts of them fall?
How He left the choirs and anthems above
    For earth in its wailings and woes,
To suffer the shame and the pain of the cross,
    And die for the life of His foes?
O Prince of the noble! O Sufferer divine!
    What sorrow and sacrifice equal to thine?

Have you heard this tale, the best of them all,
    The tale of the Holy and True?
He died, but His life now in untold souls
    Lives on in the world anew.
His seed prevails, and is filling the earth
    As the stars fill the skies above.
He taught us to yield up the love of life
    For the sake of the life of love.
His death is our life, His loss is our gain,
    The joy for the tear, the peace for the pair

Now hear these tales, ye weary and worn,
    Who for others do give up your all;
Our Saviour hath told you the seed that would grow
    Into earth's dark bosom must fall;
Must pass from the view and die away,
    And then will the fruit appear;
The grain that seems lost in the earth below
    Will return many-fold in the ear;
By death comes life, by loss comes gain,
    The joy for the tear, the peace for the pain.

## A Patriotic Woman.

Miss Helen Gould has endowed the school of engineering, University of New York, with an additional $10,000, which brings her benefactions to a total of $60,000. This does not represent all that she is supposed to have contributed to the University of New York. A contribution of $250,000 was made on May 27, 1895, with the proviso that the name of the giver should be kept secret. It was generally rumored that the unknown contributor was Miss Gould, who wished in this way to make amends for the omission of any bequest to the university in her father's will. Miss Gould's benefactions to charitable and educational institutions have been countless, but so great has been her dislike to the association of her name with them that only a small part of her good work is known. Her sympathies have gone forth especially for the relief of poor children. Among the institutions under her special patronage are a home for tenement-house children, at Tarrytown, and the Kindergarten and Potted Plant Association, near that place, to which she recently gave a valuable tract of land. At the time of the great tornado in St. Louis, she immediately contributed $100,000 for the relief of the homeless sufferers. She presented a scholarship to Wellesley College a year ago, and last January gave $5000 to found a scholarship at Mount Holyoke College, in memory of her mother.

---

## A Gift to the Lord.

There is something the dear Lord wants on earth,
    That nobody else can give
Except yourself, to the blessed Lord
    Who came to the earth to live;
Who walked about in its crowded ways,
    And prayed in its hills alone,
Who had joyful days and sorrowful days
    On this earth where He sought His own.

The something on earth which the dear Lord wants
    And which only you can give,
Is the loyal love of your heart, my child,
    And your earnest will to live
Soldier and servant of Christ the King,
    To watch for the glance of His eye,
To cherish His honor and do His work
    While the flying days go by.

There's something the dear Lord wants in Heaven,
    And waits till it reach Him there,
The sight of a soul that turns from sin
    And uplifts the penitent's prayer.
And you may give to our Lord in Heaven
    That gift which will reach the throne,
And add a joy to the Blessed One
    Who would gather home His own.

In earth, in Heaven, the dear Lord sees
    Each of us quite apart
From the throng who are ever burdening
    The love of His tender heart.
And each of us to the Lord may give
    An offering He will take,
And prize through the ages ever more
    For the humble giver's sake.

## Frances Willard and the Reporter.

The Washington *Post* says that when Frances Willard lay dead in Chicago, among the flowers near her was a bunch of violets from a Washington newspaper woman. "I never saw Miss Willard but once," said the newspaper woman the day she sent the flowers. "It was in a Western city. I was reporter on a local paper, discouraged, overworked, blue, homesick, and altogether miserable, for I was only—well, I wasn't out of my teens, and I had been away from home only a few months. Miss Willard came to the city. I was sent to her hotel to ask her something impertinent. Miss Willard was ill, but sent word that I might come up. I found her sitting in an easy chair, very pale, but very sweet. I had only begun to tell my errand when she rose and came toward me. She put her hands on my shoulders. 'Why, dearie,' she said, 'how tired you look! Take my chair child.' And I—well, nobody had called me 'dearie' for so long, nobody had called me 'child,' that I—well, I put my head on Frances Willard's shoulder and cried it all out. I had never seen her before; I have never seen her since, but for the memory of those few kind words I say : God bless Frances Willard."

# CHAPTER XXXVII.

## College or Business?

T a certain point in his development the boy must decide, or his parents must decide for him, whether he is to leave school at fourteen or fifteen, learn a trade, or go into a factory or store, with a view to entering business life, or whether instead he shall proceed with his education, and go to college. The latter course means four years devoted to study under good instructors, and insures to the responsible sort of lad, an excellent foundation for the future. A college course is not indispensable to success. Some of our most conspicuous public men never went beyond a country school. William Dean Howells, our foremost American author, is the product of the printing office and the home library. A man may do without college, and still shine. And to some persons, not fond of study nor devoted to learning in any of its aspects, time spent in college is rather a waste. They would do better to go at once into the daily drill of counting-room or office.

College does not unfit a man for business, however. Granting that he has ability, accuracy, and the tendency to grasp the matter in hand, which is an essential of business success, his capacity will be enlarged, his mind will be a more facile tool, his powers will be broadened by the collegiate training. In certain lines of business college graduates are preferred to others, because their prolonged period of study has made them manlier, and has taught them how to cope with men.

Apart from their direct bearing on character, the college friendships are of great value indirectly to young men. A small college equally with a large one, brings together men from widely differing homes, and from various parts of the country. Angles are rubbed off, provincialisms are softened, and men are brought nearer to each other in the attrition of the college life, as well as in its agreeable social opportunities.

### Colleges for Women.

Nobody can visit a woman's college, Mount Holyoke, or Smith, Wellesley or Vassar, Wells or Baltimore, or Randolph-Macon, Barnard, Radcliffe, or any other college, without being impressed with the all-round training girls receive in these admirable institutions.     These young women will be better wives, better mothers, better daughters, for their years at college.     And, if they do not marry, they will be better business women, journalists, doctors, teachers, ministers, workers in all fields, because of their college associations.

### Co-Education.

A great deal may be said for co-education.   As we see it at Oberlin, Cornell, Syracuse and Ann Arbor, at Brown University, at Madison, Wisconsin, and elsewhere, it shows how natural is the arrangement which sets young people side by side in the classroom, as in the family or the church.   Very little flirtation is found in the co-educational college, for there is little temptation to flirt with a man or a girl, whose Latin may be better than your own, and whose demonstration on the blackboard may put yours to shame.

Says Hamerton pithily:

" Whatever you study, some one will consider that particular study a foolish waste of time.

"If you were to abandon successively every subject of intellectual labor which had, in its turn, been condemned by some advisor as useless, the result would be simple intellectual nakedness.   The classical languages, to begin with, have long been considered useless by the majority of practical people—and pray, what to shop-keepers, doctors, attorneys, artists, can be the use of the higher mathematics?   And if these studies, which have been conventionally classed as serious studies, are considered unnecessary notwithstanding the tremendous authority of custom, how much the more are those studies exposed to a like contempt which belong to the category of accomplishments !   What is the use of drawing, for it ends in a worthless sketch ?   Why should we study music when, after wasting a thousand hours the amateur cannot satisfy the ear ?   *A quoi bon* modern languages when the accomplishment only enables us to call a waiter in French or German who is sure to answer us in English ?   And, what, when it is not your trade, can be the good of dissecting animals or plants ? "

Thus, one must cultivate independence, and study what he wishes, in distinction from what is forced upon him.

# CHAPTER XXXVIII.

## Homes for Spinsters.

ONE of the greatest problems the self-supporting woman in our large cities has to face is the question of a home. How and where shall the working girl without home ties live? If she has a relative to assume the care and work, or if she has herself sufficient resources and self-reliance, there is no reason why she should not keep house. Or if this is not feasible fortunate is she who is taken into a congenial private family. Really homelike boarding houses do exist, but not every one who seeks can find or can afford to pay for when found. The modern apartment house has possibilities of a home for three or four banding together to share work and expenses. Any one of these methods of living may be within the reach of a woman who is earning twelve dollars a week and upwards. She may weigh the disadvantages and compensations of each and choose, yet even for her the choice is not always easy.

What about girls whose weekly wage is less than eight, or even less than five dollars? What becomes of these—the young, the inexperienced, the weak, the stranger in the great city, discouraged and perhaps tempted? Where shall such find shelter, protection and wholesome social life? This matter of clean, independent, self-respecting existence for working women on small pay in large cities is so important a phase of social economics that government has turned its attention to it. The latest bulletin issued by Hon. Carroll D. Wright for the Department of Labor is devoted in part to a study of homes and clubs for self-supporting girls, signed by Mary S. Fergusson.

Most of us are familiar with the boarding home as it exists in connection with the Women's Christian Associations, but it is not generally known how many similar homes exist on a smaller scale in various cities, under both Protestant and Roman Catholic auspices. The first organized effort in this country to offer a comfortable and attractive home to self-supporting women, at rates within the means of those earning small wages, was made in 1856 by the Ladies' Christian Union in New York City. Baltimore came next, with its Female Christian Home established in 1865. The Labor Department reports statistics of ninety boarding homes and clubs existing to-day in forty-six cities. But even in New York, Boston, Chicago, Philadelphia, Baltimore, St. Louis and Cincinnati, where the best provision for women wage-earners is made, the supply is entirely inadequate to the demand, while in some of our other populous cities little attention is paid to this matter.

The essential features of the boarding home are the protective supervision, personal interest and moral support afforded by the home roof, the house mother and association with other women similarly circumstanced. At none of these

"A comfortable and attractive home."

homes is the boarder an object of charity, although many of them owe their object to philanthropic effort. They are all founded upon the principle of mutual aid and co-operation and are wholly or partly self-supporting.

Of necessity more or less strict oversight is maintained. . Boarders are obliged to keep rules and adapt themselves to the order of the household. Not infrequently the working girl chafes against the restraints and complains of loss of freedom. But what is the alternative? A third-rate boarding house, or, worse yet, a cheap lodging house, in which she lives by herself, drifts about from place to place for meals, and receives her friends and acquaintances in her bedroom or meets them on the streets or in questionable places of amusement. If she refuses to avail herself of such opportunities of social intercourse, she lives a life of loneliness, detrimental to health and happiness. Our own acquaintance with such girls confirms Miss Fergusson's statement that for them "home has no meaning except, perhaps, as a memory, and all the restraining influences of home and home ties give place to an independence which is perilous and a freedom that only the strongest can safely use."

In some cities, where women have been unwilling to take either of these alternatives boarding clubs have been formed. These are co-operative enterprises which owe their origin to a revolt against authority as administered by a paid officer in the boarding home, as well as to an abnormal sensitiveness to receiving benefits which might be regarded as charity. The boarding club aims to become independent of outside financial help and to establish itself as an economic success. This has been done by the Jane Club, of Chicago, through a system of co-operative housekeeping. In other cases the plan is to furnish a home to a limited number in connection with a restaurant having large accommodations. The Working Girls' Club, of Buffalo, is a conspicuous example of this class.

This movement is still in its experimental stage. For the better paid worker, morally strong enough for the independence of such club life, yet glad of the protection and social opportunities afforded by numbers, this may be a solution of the problem of living. It is not to be denied, however, that such a movement strikes to some extent, at least, at the root of home life, of which the very essence is mutual dependence and willingness to sacrifice individual freedom. Neither the boarding home nor the boarding club may offer an ideal home for the working girl on small pay, but they are the best substitutes for a real home that we can offer her. Now that the commissioner of labor has called attention to the importance of this matter from the standpoint of social economics as well as that of humanity, it is to be hoped there will be increased effort to multiply and improve such institutions, and to add opportunities for social pleasures and self-culture.

An interesting writer tells in *Harper's Bazar* of her own experience in making comfortable and homelike her spinster dwelling, entering very fully into the several details of furnishing and managing the same, making the most of limited space and overcoming other difficulties. In her view her home is a growth, and the woman who wishes to make hers ideally attractive must let it develop by degrees.

She says, speaking of the ordinary flat, in small apartments no provision is made for the storing of unused articles. Chairs, step-ladders and tables have to be put away on top of the small trunk you would take away for a Sunday. But you learn after a little to have divans that open, window-boxes that will hold anything, dress-boxes that slide under beds like old-fashioned trundle-beds. You learn, in fact, to adapt yourself to conditions, and finally to eliminate the sense of confusion from the home. For all that, the spinster is strongly advised to get space when she can. She may be tempted into a small apartment by the idea of gaining coziness. But coziness has nothing to do with the size of a room. It depends upon the distribution of the furniture, upon the spirit of the mistress who arranges it. A tiled bathroom in a new flat can never compensate you for a dining-room too small for the comfort of your guests, or a parlor which allows no free movement around it.

Choose an apartment, if possible, with a back and front door; but if that cannot be accomplished, at least insist upon one with a hall that does not run through any room—even the dining-room. With two hall doors you have less confusion in the coming and going of guests and messengers, and the maid in the kitchen has much embarrassment spared her and her friends. I know that there are those who think it savors of the snob to make domestics use different doors and elevators from their point, but there are parlors without number in many small apartments—where, for instance, a mother and daughter have to live together and economize space—in which the bureau is found in the parlor or is to be seen from it. A bureau should always be concealed by a screen when out of a bedroom. The casual visitor should never even get a glimpse of it, for the whole meaning and purpose and beauty of a living-room are at once destroyed by it. When the exigencies of life demand that a parlor should not be kept intact, you could easily use a desk instead of a bureau, putting the toilet articles inside and keeping the desk closed. If a mirror is necessary, make it part of the decoration of the room; put it over the mantel-piece or arrange it as a corner mirror, but never let it give the impression of dressing by it. " In order to be beautiful it is necessary to suffer," says a French proverb, referring to the toilet of women, and in a small apartment in order to have a home that will lack in no refinement it is necessary to suffer even more at times.

Again, when one has to sleep in a parlor, use a divan, not a folding-bed. A folding-bed is a device of the economical, a trick through which any one can see. But a divan, while a little more trouble to arrange at night, is at least an honest bit of furniture by day, not pretending to be bookcase or desk, or even sideboard, as is sometimes the case. A folding-bed, moreover, is never of use except at night, while a divan can be used at all hours. With its heaps of cushions, it can be made quite the prettiest feature in a room. And just here it may be well to say that a scheme of color for a divan and cushions is of quite as much importance as for the walls of the room itself. If one is careless about this, or gathers cushions together of every color and hue, and is pleased only by the number, one produces at once distracting and jarring notes, and all the restful influence of the room is at once destroyed.

In a bedroom nothing is really accomplished in the furnishing unless a certain peace and serenity suggest themselves in it, unless daintiness and freshness and something more than mere cleanliness are felt. For here all the preparations for meeting the world are made; here the body and mind are refreshed by sleep, old garments are exchanged for new.

A bedroom should be the airiest, the sweetest, the prettiest room in the house. No woolen hangings or tablecloths should disfigure it. Scrupulous order should prevail. If there be space, there should be a sofa on which you can rest during the day.

Nothing is ordinarily more discouraging to a beginner than to see the wealth of another's full accomplishment. To the beginner in a spinster home, in which she enters unfortified by the host of wedding-presents that always accompany the bride who makes a similar start, it sometimes seems that the hideous bareness of her first venture will never be relieved. But it is well to remember that the tendency of most things when started is to grow. One has only to make a few sacrifices in the beginning, to exercise a little judgment, and the desire of one's heart is finally accomplished. If to-day your choice lies between a new hat and a sofa cushion, and your hat can possibly do for a little while longer, get the sofa cushion, for the sofa cushion will outlast a dozen hats and may become a part of the permanent furniture of your room, while your hat will be old-fashioned before two seasons have passed.

It is in the exercise of judgment in these directions, and by making little sacrifices when beginnings are made, that the problem of furnishing is simplified for the spinster and her task made easy. Her step into her new home is a voluntary one, and none of the cares which it involves should be a burden to her. One object of the suggestions made in this volume has been to simplify her task, to give her the results of others' experience, and to help her to avoid those mistakes which must mark the failure of any home begun upon a wrong basis.

Settle your kitchen first. It is right to do this for the sake of those who work for you, and greater content will be felt throughout your home. You do not make a contract with your domestics for personal sacrifices, but for certain services. It is you who must make the sacrifices when sacrifices are necessary, you who must go without one thing for the sake of others more essential to you. For yours is the home, yours the duty, the obligation, the privilege of making it. You can hardly have a right to demand sacrifices of your employe, or to murmur if you do not get them, unless you too bring something more to the bargain between you than a question of so many dollars a month. Your kitchen once furnished, your work in that direction is practically done. It costs little to replenish tins and china, after all.  Your table and refrigerator last for years, as do all the solid pieces.

When it comes to furnishing the rest of your apartment, pause before you begin.  Realize that nothing can ever be made perfect in it if the ground-work is bad, if the color of the walls lacks repose, or your carpet has a figure in it that jumps at you whenever you look at it.  Decide quietly on some scheme of color—whether your dining-room shall be rose-pink and green, or blue and white, with china entering in as part of the decoration.  Think a long time before you commit yourself to a red and white parlor, or one of white and gold; but if you do decide on gold, never get a gilt paper, unless you want your nerves eternally distracted by the constant changes in tone and color which a gilt paper undergoes in different lights.  Avoid also all conspicuous figures in your paper if you want your pictures to look well.

Make all your rooms express the uses for which they were intended, and when necessity compels you to make certain combinations and compromises, guard yourself at every turn, preserve as many of your family traditions as possible, and always be careful to subordinate one use to another.  If, for instance, you must sit as well as eat in your dining-room, never let the sitting-room feature predominate over the other, or your dining-room will grow to look as if dining were a haphazard and accidental part of life, indulged in when other things were cleared away.  For dining ought always to represent a feast or a festival; ceremony ought to be associated with it, light and cheer, and the idea of refreshment.  More than all other places in the home, I sometimes think, the dining-room ought to be kept intact.  But sometimes a dining-room in an apartment has to be utilized for other purposes besides that of dining.  When that is the case call to your aid infinite tact.  Never let the sewing machine, for instance, be visible in it for an instant.  Conceal it with a screen if it cannot be banished altogether, or your whole room is destroyed.  If reading or writing must go on in it, make a corner for your books and papers—a northwest or a southeast corner, or whatever you may want to call it; only let it be a corner pure and simple. Never let it become an intrusive feature; never let it suggest any interference with the rightful purpose or true use of the room.  It is of vital moment that the spinster in her apartment remember this..

   The uses of a parlor when one has no other reception room are manifold. The same room may have to be used for reading and writing, for the entertaining of guests, and so much of the family life as a spinster is able to enjoy.  If she can have a study as well as a parlor her problem is simplified, but a study is hardly possible in an ordinary flat.  The primal use of a parlor is for the welcome of others.  There ought, therefore, to be good cheer expressed, comfort promised, repose suggested for the body and rest for the mind.  One should always be able to get to its central points easily, the chairs and tables not standing in the way. The fireside should be one of these points in winter, the windows in summer. Your most beautiful and most restful picture should hang over the mantel-piece, so that when you lift your eyes from the fire you always see it, as when you lift them from flowers or the sea you find the sky above you. There should be books within easy reach. No home is furnished without them, and no guest quite prepared for. Do not hang your pictures too regularly, yet preserve a certain balance. Let your lamps be placed near chairs that invite you at once to a book. Let your sofa be where the glare from a window does not strike full upon the eyes of one who lies upon it. Let warmth and sunshine prevail, and let hospitality be suggested, not prim and forbidding formality. Study comfort and repose. Color enters into a question of comfort as much as sofa cushions. Two yellows, one with the pink tone predominating and one with the green tone, will, when brought together, be more wearisome to the sensitive nerves than a sofa without springs to an invalid.

Avoid the cheap heavy woolen stuffs sold for curtains. If you must get an inexpensive material get something which will wash; it at least will suggest daintiness. You are apt to get bad colors in cheap woolens or in so-called silk hangings.

Another hint, apart from all furnishings, is applicable to the women who dwell in spinster homes.

In days gone by, before the new woman appeared upon the scene of action, girls were rigidly taught the good old-fashioned principle of tidiness. "Neatness" hardly expresses my meaning as well as does the quaint old time word. To be "tidy," Webster tells us, is to be "arranged in good order; neat; kept in proper and becoming neatness." Nowadays girls are neat to a certain extent and in a certain way. They bathe freely and wear clean clothes, but are they tidy? Frequently they are not. Their hair is often loose and prone to tumble down, their gloves are sometimes ripped at the finger-tips, and one or two buttons are lacking from their boots. The stock-collar is often fastened on with an ordinary white pin that is very obvious, and the veil has occasionally a hole over the nose or chin. Our girl is charming, but is she as careful as she should be?

The other day I was making a morning call at a friend's house, and there met another caller, a woman who made a most agreeable impression upon me. She was not elaborately dressed, but her black tailor-made gown fitted her well, and there was not a spot or a speck of dust on it. I knew that it had been brushed carefully before she left her room. Her linen collar and cuffs were snowy white, and did not twist or shift from their proper places. Her gloves did not wrinkle and buttoned smoothly over the wrists; her shoes were like the rest of her attire, dainty; and her bonnet rested firmly and straight on soft brown hair that, while wavy and fluffy, was neatly dressed, and so securely pinned that I fancy a high wind would not have caused it to come down. A thin veil covered a fresh complexion and bright face. The *tout ensemble* gave one the idea of daintiness and delicate finish. In speaking of this woman afterwards to a man who knows her I said:

"There is something about her appearance that charms one. What is the secret?"

"I will tell you," he said. "She is a well-groomed woman. There are never any rough or loose ends about her."

"You mean that she is tidy," I said to him.

"You call it 'tidy,' I say 'well-groomed.' We both mean the same thing."

However one may express it—in sporting terms or with the old-fashioned word—is the condition not well worth striving for? Nothing is so destructive to illusion, so detrimental to the fascination of beauty or personal charm as the lack of this quality.

The traditional spinster must have something to love, a cat, a bird, a dog, in her apartment, and so she will not lack for loving welcome when she comes home.

There are no pets, on the whole, so responsive and so satisfactory as the familiar house-cat and the dog, of whatever variety he may be. Long usage to the ways of civilized man has made these creatures most friendly and sympathetic, and, once admitted into the home life, they fit into their places, and become as essential as other members of the household to its daily round of duty and its measure of delight. The man or woman who regards a dog or cat with either aversion or indifference can never hope to understand the regard felt for these animals by their lovers. The dog is the more trustful pet, the readier to take good will for granted, and the more dependent on the companionship of man. Dogs there are of high degree and long descent, large and small, from the Great Dane to the toy terrier; but one thing they all share, and that is a fond clinging to their master and a liking for his society. A dog is the best of comrades, the most constant of friends, and to those who care for him he is the solace of lonely hours and the source of pride.

A cat, on the other hand, does not yield affection by instinct. Whatever may have been originally bestowed on the cat by his far-away savage ancestors, the untameable beasts of the jungle and the den, he still keeps part of the wild creature's subtlety, suspicion and stealth. His very step suggests the panther's—so soft, so padded, so sinuous, so dexterous.

For ages, too, cats have been maligned as witches, treated with cruelty by thoughtless boys, condemned to vagrant wanderings and prowlings by heedless owners, who could go off on pleasure trips, leaving a forlorn and neglected pet

DOMESTIC PETS.

(277)

behind them to seek its meat where it could find it, to starve, or to prey upon a neighbor's shelves.

Nothing on this earth is more pitiful than a hungry, gaunt and attenuated spectre of what should be a well-fed, sleek and prosperous-looking pussy.

Cats show the effect of good treatment in their coats, which grow soft and silky, in their finely groomed appearance, and in their air of pride and serenity. A cat should have a good bed on which to sleep at night; it should have plenty of food at the right times, daintily served, and it should never be frightened or struck. Cats are intensely nervous, and they have long memories. A cat once abused does not soon forgive nor forget to stand on guard.

A dog should be fed twice a day; not on mere leavings and scraps, but on food nicely prepared, and containing some variety—perhaps a cereal, perhaps some cooked vegetable with portions of meat, and a bone or two on which the dog may gnaw. Give the dog his meals on a clean platter, and for both cat and dog provide drinking-water in a convenient place.

Quarrelsome householders will have quarrelsome pets. Only the loving soul can have loving natures about it, whether of the lower or of the higher orders. Probably our little dumb friends know far more than we imagine of what is going on around them, and understand our speech and language in a way which would surprise us if we were in the habit of observing them. Little Fanchette, a spaniel brought from Paris to New York, moped and pined with homesickness, until it occurred to somebody to speak French to her, when she speedily plucked up courage and grew sprightly again. Juno, a huge mastiff, was given away by her mistress to a friend in the same town. The change of homes and owners puzzled the dog at first, and she could not be reconciled to it. From the hour that she comprehended the transfer she treated her original owner with the utmost indifference, verging on disdain, never responding to a caress, never lifting her head when the lady spoke to her. Juno's resentment was royal and unmistakable.

By all means let us treat our pets as though they had natures in some degree akin to our own, and then let us watch and discover what fine traits they show when trained with care and treated with uniform kindness.

A phase of our present life which has escaped the attention of some of us, is the desire for independence on the part of our girls. Self-supporting as they often are, and looking forward to a career, they do not wish to remain under authority, and their mothers, dearly as they love them, do not command their entire obedience, as mothers once did, where unmarried daughters were concerned.

"Marriage gives a woman freedom from parental authority; gives her scope and opportunity, a house to manage, new interests to pursue. She finds her development in it. The single state robs her of these opportunities, and she misses her development, unless she has work to do, interests, responsibilities, and

FEEDING THE PETS.

activities in which to forget herself. She is often, in consequence, the most uncomfortable, restless, irritable, and misunderstood member of a family.

" ' Everything is done for you,' she is told, ' and yet you are not happy.' Sometimes she hears she is ungrateful, and grows self-conscious under an accusation she does not know how to deny.. Those who have reared her have never understood that something besides that of their own planting has grown up in the girl whom they have watched and shielded for years. They also fail to see that a full nature denied all normal outlets must grow to be the turbulent nature, unless wisely guided in right channels. The young daughter will not understand. The mother must. She must realize that self-absorption and restlessness do not necessarily indicate an evil nature so much as a strong nature balked by being denied opportunity for expression.

" We are apt to think that until women, our own especially, are invited to express sentiment and affection, or until they are presented with an opportunity for the exercise of their deepest instincts and emotions, these instincts and emotions ought not to exist, forgetting the great spiritual forces that play into all human souls, and which, unexpressed in one direction, must breed storm and confusion, restlessness and discontent, or break into new outlets for themselves.

" Then why not permit the daughter at home some of the privileges and opportunities she would have in the house of her husband—a certain authority, some one domain in which she would reign supreme? Why not expect and demand less from her to you as an individual, and give her more in the way of those very opportunities for activity which you and nature have been helping her to be ready for?

" A mother, in all her experience, never needs so much unselfishness, so much wisdom, knowledge, and prudence, as when her daughters are full grown and still under her control."

The happiest girls I know, or some of them, are those who have combined, several girls together, with an elderly or middle-aged friend to act as housekeeper and chaperone, and have made for themselves a spinster-home, in which they have entire freedom to work and rest as they will. They go to their own roof-tree from this retreat, with a feeling of holiday gladness, and are friends with the dear home people in a new sense.

---

## Returning Spring.

Says Carlyle, " From a small window one may see the infinite." My pot of hepaticas have shown me all the handiwork of spring.

"The restitution of all things;" that is nature's spring song, and no wonder that it is dear to man.  All the lost things torn from us by autumn winds and frost have come again; not new things, but those we loved last year.  We cannot miss one lovely line, nor fragile bit of color; the faint fragrance has not changed its delicate refreshment, but lures us with the selfsame woodland sweetness.  High hopes of dearer things, lost to his sight, cheer man's heart as he notes this.

Happy are they who, in the time of nature's revival, turn toward country homes.  Nothing more refreshing comes into a tired man's way than his first visit to his country place after the tide has turned and the stir of spring is in the air.  The newly upturned sod sends up an odor that God surely meant should be grateful to his senses; the sense of preparation, the look of restoration are delightful to his weary brain.  If his dog welcomes him, and his horse is in good condition, he feels himself far richer than he did yesterday, when he rushed from his office to his club.  The uncovering of the strawberries and the asparagus is an event of importance; the violet frames are worth any Fifth avenue florist's gorgeous display; the hotbeds are full of promise, and a brood of young chicks, irrespective of their strain, is full of charm.

But he loves spring best who has hibernated in some solitary hillside farm, with nothing but the daily routine of feeding his cattle, the arrival of the weekly newspaper, and the Saturday visit to the country store to vary a life in which the body ages from disuse, and the mind grows dull from lack of contact with the world.  To such a one the sight of the first bluebird perched on the top of the pump, where it has gone in search of a chilly drink, is a positive thrill of delight.  Not long will it be before wholesome activity and work which is useful to his fellowmen will be within his reach, and the cattle, aimlessly chewing the scattered cornstalks in the barnyard, cropping the young grass.  A man like this may not, with spiritually enlightened eyes, watch with admiring wonder the ephemeral beauty of the woods, coloring as their life-blood stirs in their hearts, but he is apt to look long and happily over the scene that has been so wearily asleep, and to take off his hat that the wind may blow across his forehead.  And his voice has a ring of good cheer as he returns to the house and calls out, "Mother, I've seen a bluebird!"  It always strikes me with a pleasant recognition of what the husband thinks his wife's highest title when he calls her "Mother."—*Evening Post.*

## A Child's Service.

What if the little Jewish lad,
  That summer day, had failed to go
Down to the lake, because he had
  So small a store of loaves to show?

"The press is great,"—he might have said;
  "For food the thronging people call;
And what were my few loaves of bread,—
  My five small loaves among them all?"

And back the mother's word would come,
  Her coaxing hand upon his hair;
"Yet go, for here be food for some
  Among the hungry children there."

If from his home the lad that day
  His five small loaves had failed to take,
Would Christ have wrought—can any say?—
  That miracle beside the lake?

## When Saint Chrysostom Prayed.

'Twas not enough to kneel in prayer,
  And pour his very soul away
In fervid wrestlings, night and day,
  For those who owned his shepherd care;
But faith and works went hand in hand,
  As test of each petition made,
And saints were helped throughout the land
  When Saint Chrysostom prayed.

Within the closet where he knelt,
  A box of Bethlehem's olive wood—
"For Christ," engraved upon it—stood;
  And ever as he daily felt
The pressure of the Church's need,
  Therein the daily gift was laid;
For word had instant proof of deed
  When Saint Chrysostom prayed.

Beneath his folded hands he placed
  Whatever gold was his; and when
He travailed for the souls of men,
  So long by pagan rites debased,

The more he agonized, the more
  The burden of his spirit weighed;
And piece by piece went all his store,
  When Saint Chrysostom prayed.

O golden-mouthed, let this thine alms
  Rouse us to shame, who daily bow
Within our secret places now,
  With outstretched yet with empty palms!
We supplicate indeed; but has
  Our faith brought answering works to aid?
Have words by deeds been proven, as
  When Saint Chrysostom prayed?
                    —*Margaret I. Preston.*

## Heaven.

'Tis a time of war and conflict,
  A time to strike with might,
A time when peace herself must arm,
  And take the sword and fight.
In the light of blazing fires,
  In the sound of booming drums,
To her waning hour, with war and woe,.
  The latest century comes.

Earth, dyed in blood, and ghastly
  With crimes that shame the sun,
Looks up and finds her sentence
  The old imperious one
By the god of battles written
  In days of God's right hand,
Not peace, but war is needed,
  To save Jehovah's land.

Yet, sweet upon our discords,
  The thought of heaven falls,
Soft wafts the breath of heaven
  Down from the jasper walls;

There stand victorious ever
    The saints beyond the flood,
There never sounds of evil
    Or clash of strifes intrude.

Sweet fields beyond the river
    All dressed in living green,
Sweet country of the blessed,
    Where life is all serene.
To that thrice-joyous heaven
 .   Our longing eyes are turned,
Where all earth's grief is ended,
    And all earth's tasks are learned.

## I Knew Thou Wert Coming.

I knew Thou wert coming, O Lord Divine,
I felt in the sunlight a softened shine,
And a murmur of welcome I thought I heard,
In the ripple of brooks and the chirp of bird;
And the bursting buds and the springing grass
Seemed to be waiting to see Thee pass;
And the sky, and the sea, and the throbbing sod,
Pulsed and thrilled to the touch of God.

I knew Thou wert coming, O Love Divine,
To gather the world's heart up to Thine;
I know the bonds of the rock-hewn grave
Were riven that, living, Thy life might save.
But, blind and wayward, I could not see
Thou wert coming to dwell with me, e'en me;
And my heart, o'erburdened with care and sin,
Had no fair chambers to take Thee in:

Not one clean spot for Thy foot to tread.
Not one pure pillow to rest Thy head;
There was nothing to offer, no bread, no wine,
No oil of joy in this heart of mine:

And yet the light of Thy kingly face
Illumed for Thyself, a small, dark place,
And I crept to the spot by Thy smile made sweet,
And tears came ready to wash Thy feet.

Now, let me come nearer, O Lord Divine,
Make in my soul for Thyself a shrine;
Cleanse, till the desolate place shall be
Fit for a dwelling, dear Lord, for Thee.
Rear, if Thou wilt, a throne in my breast,
Reign—I will worship and serve my guest.
While Thou art in me—and in Thee I abide—
No end can come to the Easter tide.
                          —*Mary Lowe Dickinson.*

## Rise, Flowers.

Rise, flowers, arise,
    Out of your weary prison !
Open your joyful eyes,
    He hath arisen !

Lilies that He called fair
    Come in your virgin glory;
Your stainless lips prepare
    To sing His story.

Rose that have borne His name,
    On hills of Sharon springing,
Open your heart of flame !
    Arise with singing !

Flower with the passion-cross
    That quivers on your bosom,
Tell of our Lenten loss !
    Arise and blossom !

All in the dust of earth,
    Hear in your dreaming !
Shout for the glad new birth
    Easter is beaming.

Hear ye its angel choir
　　Exulting o'er us;
Creatures of earth, aspire !
　　Join the loud chorus !

Rise, every mortal voice, ·
　　Praise Him with singing,
Sea, earth and sky rejoice;
　　Set joy-bells ringing.

Death is forever dead,
　　Broken its prison;
Lo ! from the tomb our Head,
　　Christ hath arisen !
　　　　　　　　—*Rose Terry Cooke.*

## Overcometh.

To him that overcometh !
　　O word divinely strong,
The victor's palm, the fadeless wreath,
　　The grand immortal song.
And his the hidden manna,
　　And his the polished stone,
Within whose whiteness shines the name
　　Revealed to him alone.

To him that overcometh—
　　Ah, what of bitter strife
Before he win the battle's gage,
　　And snatch the crown of life !
What whirl of crossing weapons,
　　What gleam of flashing eyes,
What stern debate with haughty foes,
　　Must be before the prize !

To him that overcometh
　　Shall trials aye befall,
The world, the flesh, the devil,
　　He needs must face them all.

Sweet sirens of temptation
  May lure with silvern strain,
And cope he must with subtle foes,·
  And blanch 'neath fiery pain.

To him that overcometh
  A mighty help is pledged;
He wields a sword of purest mould
  By use of cycles edged.
And prophets and confessors,
  A matchless, valiant band,
Have vanquished earth and stormed the skies,
  With that triumphant brand.

To him that overcometh—
  O promise dearest dear!
The Lord Himself who died for him
  Will evermore be near.
Here, dust upon his garments,
  There, robes that royal be;
For, " On my throne," the King hath said,
  " Mine own shall sit with me."

To him that overcometh—
  O word divinely strong !
It weaves itself through weary hours
  Like some rejoicing song.
For him the hidden manna,
  And his the name unknown,
Which Christ the Lord one day of days·
  Will tell to him alone.

## . God Is Good.

The days are so full of pleasure,
  The nights so bright with cheer,
Thou hast heaped so high the measure
  Of life in the passing year,

That, Master and Lord, we bless Thee,
    And bring Thee thankful praise;
Our reverent lips address Thee
    At this parting of the ways.

Many a time, and often,
    Thou hast pardoned our foolish pride,
Hast tarried our griefs to soften,
    Hast our selfish prayers denied.
The kinsman and the stranger
    Alike have known Thy grace,
And the sword of the unseen danger
    Has fled before Thy face.

Many a time Thy vision,
    Clear in the light of love,
Hath aided our slow decision,
    And pointed our eyes above.
Thy hand hath poured the chalice
    And broken the daily bread,
Till the hut has been as the palace,
    And as princes we have fed.

From the gins and traps of error
    Thou hast turned our feet away,—
Hast saved our hearts from the terror
    Of the unbegotten day.
Our lot in Thy land has ever
    In fairest ground been cast;
Thou hast left us lonely never,
    Though our dear ones hence have passed.

For into Thine own sweet heaven,
    Home of their souls and ours,
They have entered, sin-forgiven,
    To praise with fuller powers;
And therefore now we praise Thee,
    With all who have gone before,
The endless hymn we raise Thee,
    And bless Thee, and adore.

## GOD IS GOOD.

And still Thou art always with us,
   Even unto the end;
Thyself, our strength, art with us,
   Ever our guide and friend.
How can the life be dreary
   In the sun of Thy ceaseless care,
Or the path be aught but cheery,
   When Thou art everywhere?

# CHAPTER XXXIX.

## What Has Become of the Old Ladies?

WAS reading that sweet idyl of homely life, "Margaret Ogilvy," this morning, and I said to myself, "What has become of the dainty old ladies we used to meet?"

My mother never varied the form of her dress for forty years. She was comparatively a young woman when she adopted gray and black dresses, never deviating from those quiet and sombre colors. She was an old and venerable woman when she fell asleep and put on garments of immortality. To the last she wore a soft fleecy cap, a muslin kerchief about her neck crossed in front, a gown with the skirt gathered in fullness and fastened to the waist, with no flounces or furbelows. Other women of her period dressed as she did. But to-day the aged matron draws her thinning locks into a tight little knot at the back of her head, or wears false hair, with never a softening cap about her sweet and faded face. She is dressed as her juniors are, and not to her advantage.

This is how Margaret Ogilvy was dressed. It is early in the morning, mind, and she has just come out of her room.

"She is up now and dressed in her thick maroon wrapper. Over her shoulders is a shawl, and on her head a mutch. Oh, that I could sing the praise of that white mutch (and the dirge of the elaborate black cap), from the day when she called witchcraft to her aid and made it out of snowflakes, and the dear worn hands that washed it tenderly in a basin, and the starching of it, and the finger-iron for its exquisite frills that looked like curls of sugar, and the sweet bands with which it tied beneath the chin. The honored snowy mutch, how I love to see it smiling to me from the doors and windows of the poor; it is always smiling, sometimes may be a wavering wistful smile as if a snowdrop or a teardrop lay hidden among the frills. My mother begins the day with her New Testament in her hands, an old volume with its loose pages beautifully refixed, and its covers sewn and resewn by her, so that you would say it can never fall to pieces. Other books she read in the ordinary manner, but this one differently, her lips moving with each word as if she were reading aloud and her face very solemn. The Testament lies open on her lap, long after she has ceased to read, and the expression of her face has not changed."

(290)

It seems to me that nobody who has not had that kind of a dear old saintly mother, the presence as of an angel ever in the house, can win to heaven as easily, as those whose mothers were like mine, and like Margaret Ogilvy. Mothers, dear mothers, do your children see you reading the Bible and brooding over its tender and rich promises? Mothers, dear mothers, are you as simple and true and sincere, and God-fearing as mothers ought to be?

---

## Politeness in Children.

A mother writing in *Harper's Bazar* prefaces her "talk" under the above heading by telling of reading, not long ago, of a discouraged and despairing mother who said to her children, "You ain't got no manners, and I declare I can't beat none into you."

Now, the course pursued by this mother was not more unwise, and but little more vulgar, than that pursued by some parents in the higher walks of life in their attempts to teach their children to be polite. As politeness is the expression of kindness and good will, it cannot be whipped nor scolded into children. It cannot be put on or off at will, like a garment. It must be largely the result of example in the case of children. The imitative faculty is strong in a child, and, if father and mother are habitually polite to each other and to every one else, the child will imitate this beautiful trait and be polite also.

The writer recalls without pleasure a visit in a home in which the mother very properly classed good manners among the cardinal virtues of life, and she was determined that her children should be "little ladies and gentlemen." Her methods of achieving this result were astonishing, in view of her intelligence and of her position in life. No sooner were we seated at the dinner table than she began to instruct the children in this wise:

"Edith, sit up straight. It is vulgar to lounge at the table, above all places. Harry, take your elbows from the table. How often have I told you that it was rude to put your elbows on the table? Is it possible, Harold, that you are eating mashed potatoes with a spoon? I have told you over and over again just what was the proper use of the spoon at the table."

In the parlor it was: "Edith, sit erect! Harry, don't pass in front of Mr. H—— without an apology! Harold, you forgot to say 'Thank you.' Mamma wants her little boys and girls to be polite."

Now we are all more or less familiar with this painful method of instructing children in the art of politeness. It is possible that it was the misfortune of some readers of this to have received this sort of instruction in the days of their own childhood. If so, they can testify to the sense of humiliation and anger that filled

POLITENESS IN CHILDREN. (292)

their childish breasts when the attention of strangers was directed to them. They felt shy, awkward, and painfully self-conscious in the presence of visitors, and the arrival of guests was looked forward to with fear and dread, because it meant public exposure of the child's defects.

This method would imply that good breeding was confined altogether to the external things of life, and that if children ate properly and gave proper replies when spoken to, and bowed at the right time, and in the right way they had achieved the highest forms of politeness.

Henry Ward Beecher said that "politeness is a religious duty, and should be a part of religious training." The law of politeness applies to men and women quite as much as to children; and if courtesy and kindness and sweetness are the natural expression and attitude of the parents, these graces will naturally manifest themselves in the child.

One evening I happened to enter a room where several young people, with books and work, were sitting around the lamp. The young man with the lexicon and the grammar on the table before him, was the busiest of the group, but he instantly arose and remained standing until I had taken my seat.

The little action was automatic; the habit of this family is to practice small courtesies, and the boys have been trained from childhood to pay deference to a woman. They always rise whenever a lady, their mother, sister, friend or the guest of the house, comes into the room where they are at work; they place chairs gallantly and gracefully for ladies at the dinner table; and take off their hats when they meet their mother on the street, and never kiss her with a hat on; in saying good morning or good evening to her, it is hat in hand. Her bundles are carried, her way is made easy, a beautiful politeness waits for her word in the domestic discussion, and refrains from interrupting her even in the most heated argument.

Neither mother nor sister goes out after dark without an escort. One of the boys can always go out of his way, or find it in his way, to see her safely to a friend's door, or to the meeting which she wishes to attend. Most winning and sweet is the air of good breeding which these young men have acquired, which they wear with an unconscious grace.

Equally charming are the girls in the home I speak of; gentle, soft-spoken, appreciative, considerate, reverential. To old people they are tender, to children kind, to each other lovely.

One cannot too sedulously look after the small courtesies in one's conduct, and, if one be charged with the management of the household, in the accustomed ways of the family. Habits count for everything here, and example is better than precept.

Forty years ago all small people were carefully instructed in the formalities of life, and one of the things especially insisted upon was that they should invariably, in addressing their elders, say " Yes, ma'am," " No, ma'am," " Yes sir," and " No, sir."

A well-bred child in a later period than that always rose when older persons entered the room, and remained standing till told to take a seat.   It is observed by Augustus Hare in his lately published autobiography that his mother in her girlhood not only stood when in the room with her father, but even accorded that honor to his empty chair if she were in the room with it.   In our period a well-trained boy rises when his mother or other woman enters a room, and stands till she is seated.   A little girl, too, is taught to be soft of voice and gentle in movement, and to slip a cushion behind the back of a friend, to urge on a guest the most comfortable seat, to adjust screens against window glare and fire-light, and to avoid interruption and contradiction.   But "sir " and " ma'am " are not now in vogue for children, being considered the appropriate form of address for servants and for those of inferior position.   Children are in no sense inferiors in their homes.   They are socially on the same plane with their parents, and it is fitting that they should be treated with courtesy as well as practice it.

A child should be taught to say " Yes, mother," " Yes, father," " Yes, Mrs. Smith," " No, Mr. Jones."   It is always elegant to repeat the name of the person you address.   " Mother " and " father " are preferred at present to any affectionate diminutive for the speech of even little children, and " mamma " and " papa " (not momma and poppa) are in the second place in favor.   Singularly, " daddy " and " mammy " have just now established their claims to be heard in the drawing-room, though of old the laborer's cottage was their accustomed place.

To train a child in the conventionalities of his own generation is certainly advisable.   Only by the automatic practice of every-day forms during the years of childhood can man or woman hope for the unconscious ease which in maturity is the first flower of good manners.

---

## Reciprocity.

Two ladies settled themselves comfortably at a small restaurant table and prepared to enjoy their lunch together.

" It is always a treat to lunch with you, Louise," the older woman said, " because you are sure to be here on time, and you never seem tired to death, even after a morning of shopping."

" But I'm tired to death this time," Louise replied, " shopping isn't a circumstance to servant hunting."

" You don't mean that Maggie is leaving?" Mrs. Rust asked, sympathetically.

"Yes, that is exactly what I do mean. After getting me to raise her wages twice, give up my spare room to her, favor her in every way, and allow her a week's vacation, she had the ingratitude to tell me this morning that my work was wearing her all out, and she must go without even a day's notice."

"How many does this make since you were married?" Mrs. Rust asked, with the familiarity which relationship sanctions.

"Seven, I believe," Louise answered, smiling, "and I have only been married two years. I wish you would tell me, aunt, how you keep your girls until they marry or die."

"By putting myself in their place," Mrs. Rust replied. "I don't mean that I do their work for them, but I always plan to make work light on their hard days, and to allow them some time for themselves, for only a machine can keep on working with no time for rest."

"I fairly dread making another round of the intelligence offices," the younger woman said. "I am sure they all know me and think me a perfect shrew to change girls so often."

"They don't know me," Mrs. Rust said, good naturedly, "and if you are willing to exchange work with me I will spend an hour this afternoon in getting you a girl, and you in return can take this memorandum to the stationer's for me; my visiting cards are all out, and I haven't paper enough left to write a letter."

The two friends separated, agreeing to meet later in the afternoon, and each started out on her self-imposed mission.

Mrs. Rust reached the nearest intelligence office a few minutes before one o'clock, and finding the attendant gone she began to question a tidy looking girl who was the only other occupant of the room.

"Are you looking for a place?" Mrs. Rust startled her by asking.

"Indeed, I am that, ma'am," the girl answered respectfully.

"Where have you been working, and why do you leave?" Mrs. Rust asked kindly.

"Well, ma'am, it's the truth I'm telling ye. I'm leaving because it's not flesh and blood at all that they think I'm made of, but they kape me going night and day till the life's about wore out av me."

"Perhaps it is a large family where you have been working," Mrs. Rust said, after a little pause.

"Only three av 'em, ma'am, but one's a baby and no nursemaid for him aither, and what with runnin' afther him by day and walkin' the flure wid him by night, besides the scrubbin', and the cookin', the washin' and the ironin' it's about dead I am entirely, so I give my notice this marnin' and am afther findin' a new place where the wurruk's aisier."

"Can you cook?" Mrs. Rust asked, wishing to change the subject.

"Ye may well say that I can cook," answered the girl, "that is if I have the likes av anything to cook wid, but Mrs. Eastman wud expict ye to get a male out av the boords av the refrigerator, and a good male too, and they's not a girl living cud do that, ma'am."

"Mrs. Eastman"—could it be that this was Louise's girl, Maggie, who had given her notice this morning?

"What did you say is your name?" said Mrs. Rust, who in spite of her amusement could not help feeling a good deal of sympathy for the young girl.

"Maggie McLean is my name, ma'am, and I am sure I cud suit a nice, motherly-lookin' woman like yourself. Thim young ones ixpect too much intirely; they think one girl can do the worruk of three."

"If Mrs. Eastman would be willing to get a nursemaid for the baby, and to send a part of the washing out, and if she would be more careful to provide supplies for the kitchen would you be willing to stay with her?" Mrs. Rust asked the astonished girl.

"That I would, ma'am, and for a dollar a wake less, for it don't pay to be killin' yourself for big wages," said Maggie.

Imagine if you can the feelings of Mrs. Eastman when Mrs. Rust told her the result of the search for a servant.

"Of course Harry will grumble a little over the extra expense of another maid and of laundry bills," Louise said, after hearing her aunt's plan, "but if we must we must, and really Maggie is a fine cook and capable waitress. But it is we mistresses who are the real servants nowadays."

---

THANK God every morning that you have something to do that day, which must be done whether you like it or not. Being forced to work and to do your best will breed in you a hundred virtues which the idle never know.—*Charles Kingsley.*

---

IT was Napoleon's custom, even when emperor of France, to inquire the price of every article used for his household, and to make accurate calculations with regard to the necessary quantity to be consumed. It may be said that this was royal meanness; nevertheless it prevented fraud and dishonesty. Many think it a mark of gentility, as well as of generosity, to be regardless of economy. They think that spending money with reckless freedom proves that they have always been accustomed to wealth. It is proverbial, that the sons of misers are spendthrifts, and men who have acquired wealth suddenly generally spend it rapidly; while they who have lived year after year in the same respectable style, usually impart to their children their own habits of regular systematic economy. It is said with much truth, that the Americans are not an economical people. Money-making and money-loving even to a universal monomania, that which is acquired with such mighty effort they spend with lavish profusion. We know nothing about economy as practiced in Europe, by men of high-sounding titles, that would delight ears democratic. The Frenchman's invariable practice of taking up his two or three remaining bits of sugar, wrapping them in paper and carrying them from the *café* in his pocket, is only one example of the minuteness of their economy. The French women are wonderfully "good managers;" the care they take of their furniture and wardrobes can scarcely be imagined, even by a notable Yankee woman. An excessive love of display, and the tormenting desire to rival European luxury and elegance, have brought already so much misery upon our country, that it is high time that American women should inquire how far the blame comes deservedly upon them; and what measures they must pursue to avoid such ruinous extravagance.

Having learnt the prices of articles of home consumption, and the quantity necessary for an ample supply, you may be able to regulate your expenses. You will know how your table should be furnished on ordinary and extraordinary occasions, avoiding the extremes of niggardly frugality and wasteful superfluity. You will find that a skillful manager purchases most articles by large quantities, as they are thus reduced in price; besides, it is a saving of time.

The better to understand what to order for the table, acquire some insight to the mysteries of the culinary department. If your delicate fingers have hitherto only been familiar with the piano and harp, embroidery and letter-paper, can you bring them into contact with vulgar butter and sugar, eggs and flour? Horrible! Yet you may go to the far West and be without "helps," as the Trollopes, etc., aver that we call servants; or, in town, they may leave without "giving warning." And it should ever be remembered, that the varying tide of fortune may leave many who now ride triumphantly at the top of the wave upon a barren strand.

The American ladies of lang-syne were exceedingly notable; their pride in pastry, puddings, pickles, preserves, and the rest of the category, was certainly more palatable than the boasted ignorance of their degenerate daughters.

---

How many lessons of faith and beauty we should lose if there were no winter in our year! Sometimes in following up a watercourse among our hills, in the early spring, one comes to a weird and desolate place, where one huge wild grape-vine has wreathed its ragged arms around a whole thicket and brought it to the ground,—swarming to the tops of hemlocks, clenching a dozen young maples at once and tugging them downward, stretching its wizard black length across the underbrush, into the earth and out again, wrenching up great stones in its blind, aimless struggle. What a piece of chaos is this! Yet come here again, two months hence, and you shall find all this desolation clothed with beauty and with fragrance, one vast bower of soft green leaves and graceful tendrils, while summer birds chirp and flutter amid these sunny arches all the livelong day.

EVERY one knows that there is a certain magnetic power in courage, apart from all physical strength. In a family of lone women, there is usually some one whose presence is held to confer safety on the house: she may be a delicate invalid, but she is not afraid. The same quality explains the difference in the demeanor of different companies of men and women, in great emergencies of danger. Read one narrative of shipwreck, and human nature seems all sublime; read another, and, under circumstances equally desperate, it appears base, selfish, groveling. The difference lies simply in the influence of a few leading spirits. Ordinarily, as is the captain, so are the officers, so are the passengers, so are the sailors. Bonaparte said, that at the beginning of almost every battle there was a moment when the bravest troops were liable to sudden panic; let the personal control of the general once lead them past that, and the field was half won.

THIS influence of the social transition bears upon all women; there is another which especially touches wives and mothers. In European countries, the aim at anything like gentility implies keeping one or more domestics to perform household labors; but in our United States every family aims at gentility, while not one in five keeps a domestic. The aim is not a foolish one, though follies may accompany it,—for the average ambition of our people includes a certain amount of refined cultivation;—it is only that the process is exhausting. Every woman must have a best-parlor with fine furniture and a photograph book; she must have a piano, or some cheaper substitute; her little girls must have embroidered skirts and much mathematical knowledge; her husband must have two or even three, hot meals every day of his life; and yet her house must be in perfect order early in the afternoon, and she prepared to go out and pay calls, with a black silk dress and a card-case. In the evening she will go to a concert or a lecture, and then, at the end of all, she will very possibly sit up after midnight with her sewing machine, doing extra shop-work to pay for little Ella's music lessons. All this every "capable" American woman will do, or die. She does it, and dies; and then we are astonished that her vital energy gives out sooner than that of an

Irishwoman in a shanty, with no ambition on earth but to supply her young Patricks with adequate potatoes.

Now it is useless to attempt to set back the great social flood. The American housekeeper will never be killed by idleness, at any rate; and if she is exposed to the opposite danger, we must fit her for it, that is all.

## The Pleasant World of Books.

There are those who find their happiness in strolling near and far,
As if perchance their birth had been beneath some errant star.
The trackless desert beckons them, they scale the mountain peak,
And ever just beyond them see some gladness coy to seek.
For me, I sit beside my fire, and with benignant looks
From dear familiar shelves they smile—my pleasant friends, the books.

A world of sweetest company, these well beloved ones wait
For any mood, for any hour. They keep a courteous state,
Serene and unperturbed amid the ruffles of my day.
They are the bread my spirit craves. They bless my toiling way.

A pleasant world is theirs, wherein, though battles wax and wane,
There rolls the sound of triumph and there dwells surcease of pain,
On pages sparkling as the dawn forever breathes and glows
Through ages red with patriot blood, white freedom's stainless rose.

In this fair world of calmest skies I meet the martyr's palm,
There float to it dear melodies from coasts of heavenly balm.
All comfort here, all strength, all faith, all bloom of wisdom lives,
And be the day's need what it may, some boon this wide world gives.

The freedom of the city, where one walks in crowds alone,
The silence of the upland, where one climbs anear the throne,
The blitheness of the morning and the solemn hush of night,
Are in this pleasant world of books for one who reads aright.

Here, pure and sharp the pictured spire its cleaving point uplifts,
There, swept by stormy winds of fate, time's sands are tossed in drifts,
And I who sit beside the fire am heir of time and sense,
My book to me the angel of God's sleepless providence.

Who will may choose to wander far over sea and land.
For me the table and the lamp extend a friendlier hand,
And I am blessed beyond compare while with benignant looks
From home's familiar shelves they smile—my pleasant world of books.

---

## Why?

But why do I keep Thanksgiving,
  Did I hear you aright, my dear?
Why? When I'm all alone in life,
  Not a chick nor a child to be near,
John's folks all away in the West,
  Lucy across the sea,
And not a soul in the dear old home
  Save a little bound girl and me.

It does look lonesome, I grant it;
  Yet, strange as the thing may sound,
I'm seldom in want of company
  The whole of the merry year round—
There's spring when the lilac blossoms,
  And the apple trees blush to bloom,
There's summer when great moths flit and glance
  Through the twilight's starlit gloom.

Then comes the beautiful autumn,
  When every fragrant brier,
Flinging its garlands on fence and wall,
  Is bright as a living fire;
And then the white, still winter time,
  When the snow lies warm on the wheat,
And I think of the days that have passed away,
  When my life was young and sweet.

I'm a very happy woman
  To-day, though my hair is white,
For some of my troubles I've overlived,
  And some I keep out of sight.

I'm a busy old woman, you see, my dear,
   As I travel along life's road,
I'm always trying as best I can
   To lighten my neighbor's load.


That child? You should think she'd try me?
   Does she earn her bread and salt?
You've noticed she's sometimes indolent,
   And indolence is a fault?
Of course it is, but the orphan girl
   Is growing as fast as she can,
And to make her work from dawn to dark
   Was never a part of my plan.


I like to see the dimples
   Flash out on the little face,
That was wan enough, and still enough
   When first she came to the place.
I think she'll do, when she's older;
   A kitten is not a cat;
And now that I look at the thing, my dear,
   I hope she'll never be that.


I'm thankful that life is peaceful;
   I should just be sick of strife,
If, for instance, I had to live along
   Like poor Job Slocum's wife;
I'm thankful I didn't say "yes," my dear—
   What saved me I do not see—
When Job, with a sprig in his buttonhole,
   Once came a-courting me.


I'm thankful I'm neither poor nor rich,
   Glad that I'm not in debt;
That I owe no money I cannot pay,
   And so have no call to fret.
I'm thankful so many love me,
   And that I've so many to love,
Though my dearest and nearest are all at home,
   In the beautiful land above.

I shall always keep Thanksgiving
    In the good old-fashioned way,
And think of the reasons for gratitude
    In December, and June, and May.
In August, November, and April,
    And the months that come between;
For God is good, and my heart is light,
    And I'd not change place with a queen.

-----

## God's Providence.

"God's providence is mine inheritance!" I read
    The quaint old legend on a rainy day,
When gray and thick the clouds hung overhead,
    And mists were folding close about my way.

God's providence? Then, wherefore should I fear?
    My Father's love is roof and inn for me;
Forever, since my Father holds me dear,
    His goodness shall my guard and shelter be.

Another, heaven-endowed with worldly gain,
    May count his wealth and gaze his acres o'er,
May reap his harvest fields on hill and plain,
    And heap in barn and bin his fragrant store;

And I may own no inch of tilth or foot
    Of fallow in this great wide earth I tread;
Yet am I rich, and need no pledge to boot,
    Save God's clear stars above my lifted head.

God's providence is mine inheritance. Come loss
    Or change or grief, whatsoe'er God send,
All things shall work for blessing, and the cross
    Be gladly borne, if shared with Christ, my Friend.

THE OLD SWEETHEARTS.

## The Old Sweethearts.

HUSBAND—" The prettiest lass, with the lightest foot,
    And the merriest laugh in town,
With a laugh so gay it drove away
    The very thought of a frown;
A girl so fair and debonair,
    There was none as sweet as she.
You are winsome and white, my little maid,
    But you're not like my Marie."

WIFE—" The bravest lad, with the courtly speech
    And the bow a prince might own,
With a strong right hand, a look of command,
    A brow of truth the throne;
A man of men was this one when
    He first came seeking me.
You are bright and quick, among lads the pick,
    But you're not like my Henri."

The two old dears, their heads are gray,
    They are old enough to be young;
For them the bells in jubilant swells
    Of the golden wedding have rung.
Fourscore is one beneath the sun,
    The other fourscore and five,
But the true, true love that made them one
    Is to-day and for aye alive.

The old sweethearts, the fair Marie,
    The snow is on her hair,
And her eyes are dim, but not for him,
    He deems her fairest fair.
His shoulders stoop, his head may droop,
    But change she does not see.
To the sweet old wife, to the end of her life,
    Her hero he will be.

# CHAPTER XL.

## Our Love of " Things."

OES a man live who understands how a woman clings to her "things," her furniture, her chairs and tables, her carpets and her curtains? I was talking a while ago with an elderly gentlewoman who has arrived at great estate, and she was somewhat wistfully recalling her day of small things, of modest beginnings. "When John and I set up our house," she said, "I did my own work, and kept everything as neat and dainty as a new pin. Later when we had larger means and I kept help, I found that I could not compel Bridgets and Gretchens to do the work so exquisitely as I had—it needed the lady's touch for that—but I yielded a little for peace, and tried to possess my soul in patience and equanimity, even though china was nicked, and pots and pans were ruined." She paused for breath and then proceeded:

"My good Betsey married and left me and I did not hasten to supply her place. The fact is, I am enjoying more than you would fancy, making acquaintance over again with my things; my tea caddy, and my oat-meal boiler, and my egg-whip and my sieves. It is a real pleasure to handle them, and arrange the closets in my own way."

A woman can understand this; any woman can. And a woman knows how fond she grows of the old desk where she writes her letters, of the rocking-chair in which she sang lullabys to her babies, of the old clock which has ticked away the happy hours of all her life. Inanimate things, but so interwoven with the very woof of our memories and the very fibre of our hearts, that they seem as if endowed with sense and emotion.

I read a pathetic story of an old lady, and it brought the tears to my eyes. Perhaps you have read it too. She was a Vermont woman, and she had dwelt for fifty years in a tiny farmhouse in the shelter of a valley in the Green Mountains. Then her good man died, and her children said that mother could not go on living there alone. So Katharine carried her off to *her* great beautiful home in Boston, and gave her a wide sunny chamber furnished sumptuously, and appointed a maid to wait on her, and asked her to do nothing except rest and fold her hands and be quiet and go out for drives in an elegant carriage.

Was the old lady contented? Not in the least. She was desolate and home-sick, and pined for the old-fashioned home and the familiar things: her rag carpet, her braided rugs, her stove, her cane-seat rocker with the chintz covered cushions. She pined and fretted and dwindled away and would have died before long, if a big-hearted, breezy and sensible daughter-in-law, arriving on a visit from the dear old country home, had not seen how the case stood, and taken her home again. Established within sight of her own old house, with her old things around her, she plucked up courage enough to live and be happy.

I have a little round pine stand, not one bit pretty, and old beyond belief; a thing which came to me from my great-great-grandmother, and it keeps com-pany with my old old clock and that belonged to my grandfather's father, and money could not buy either of these treasures. They have stood faithfully by me in every vicissitude, always part of the household plenishing, and I love them. So you, dear lady, whose eyes fall on this page, have your own things which you prize more than silver or gold.

Laces, fragile as cobwebs, yet so strong that they survive dynasties and changing empires, fans which have been bequeathed by mother to daughter, and above all jewels which are ever enduring are among the things which women love. A ring, a brooch, a trinket, a string of pearls, but their very touch thrills you, their loss fills you with a sorrow too deep to pass easily away.

# CHAPTER XLI.

## A Duty to the Community.

ONE of our manifest obligations to the community in which we live is to do whatever lies in our power to prevent the spread of infectious diseases. If we have diphtheria or scarlet fever within our doors, we owe it to our neighbors to obey every precautionary edict and rigidly to quarantine the patient and his nurses, so that there shall be the minimum of danger, that the trouble will spread. Thoughtless people sometimes overlook this duty, and suffer visitors to enter their households, or themselves go forth and mingle freely with those to whom the malady may be a menace. In no such instance can a willful transgressor be held guiltless. Death may not ensue from his action, but pain and illness may, and in any event he has threatened society by indiscreet and selfish behavior.

When a child in any home has shown symptoms of a disease which is probably infectious or contagious, the proper course is to isolate him until you are sure that it is safe for the other children in the family to be in his company. If a child in your household is ill with any dangerous or dreaded malady, notify his teacher and withdraw from school the remaining children in your home. Do all that in you lies to keep the disease from spreading. This is your bounden duty to the community.

Equally, if there is anywhere near your home a well or stream or cesspool, or any place which may breed disease, you as a householder must at once take measures to purify it, and you must not protest if you are held responsible in case of negligence on your part, which is followed by evil consequences. In this world no man liveth to himself and no man dieth to himself, but we are bound in one bundle irrevocably.

It may not be amiss here to acknowledge our great debt of gratitude to one profession, that of the trained nurse. Formerly in every town and in our country villages and rural farming communities, there were always notable women, kind and self-sacrificing, who would go to a friend or neighbor in her extremity and help to nurse the children through an epidemic of measles, watch by the fevered patient and soothe the last moments of the dying. Blessings on their capable hands and their compassionate hearts! Still, wherever these friendly helpers are

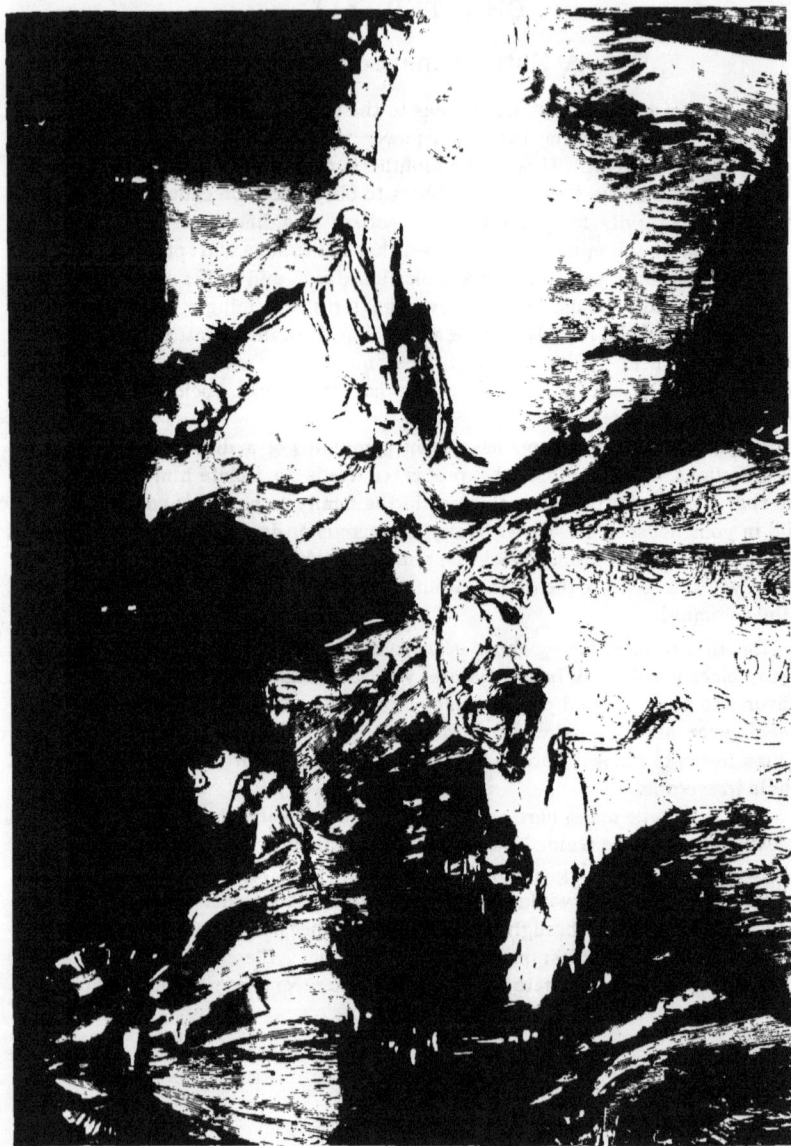

WATCH BY THE FRYER PATIENT.

(308)

found, they are uncanonized Sisters of Mercy, God's own angels of rescue and relief. In our more complex city life, where you may live actually under the same roof with a neighbor and know nothing of her except her name, and that only because it is over her doorbell, this old neighborly exchange of kind offices is now unknown. Therefore in critical and serious illness we send a messenger for

the trained nurse, and she comes to us, serene, efficient, gentle, and equipped for her campaign, doing quite as much for her patient and the family, as the physician does.

Trained nurses are obtained by application to a bureau where their names are registered, or to the hospital where they have received their training. A nurse takes a course of two or more years before she receives her diploma. In order to be accepted at the hospital where she desires to study, she must present a certificate of proficiency in ordinary English branches from her teachers at school, and a letter from her pastor testifying to her moral character;

THE TRAINED NURSE.

also a letter from her doctor, witnessing that she is in good health and has sufficient stamina to endure the hardships of her novitiate.

She is paid a small sum, increased at intervals, while she pursues her studies. She wears a uniform of cambric gown, apron and cap, while at her duty, and she submits to rules as a soldier to discipline. When she has been graduated, she *knows* what she has been taught.

The private hospital is, for those who can afford it, another boon of our period.   A woman, needing to undergo a surgical operation, is not forced to enter a public hospital, nor obliged to endure deprivations in her own home, where the appliances for her comfort are few.   She may go to a private hospital, receive every attention and be ministered to most carefully and intelligently, surrounded by every condition for improvement, and by much luxury.

No one should now entertain an old-fashioned prejudice against hospital treatment in illness.   A man or woman taken ill away from home, and in hotel or boarding-house, should at once seek admission to the nearest hospital, confident of receiving there the best medical attendance, and the best nursing, and being as judiciously treated as if among dear friends.

" Help to nurse the children."

# CHAPTER XLII.

## Notable Examples of Happiness in Wedded Life.

VERY one is familiar with the name and fame of Lord Palmerston, the renowned English statesman and diplomat, whose career was prolonged to a ripe age, and whose bow abode in strength almost to the very end of his days. Few men have ever been more fortunate than Lord Palmerston in his choice of a wife, and in a married experience of unalloyed bliss.

Lord Palmerston was married December 11, 1839, to Lord Melbourne's sister, the widow of Earl Cowper, "a lady whose benign influence" was perceptibly felt, and "who surrounded his political existence with a social charm which gave to his hospitality an attraction that at once enthralled his friends and softened his opponents." Shortly after her death, Earl Beaconsfield—then Mr. Disraeli—in a speech at Glasgow, while alluding to the happy circumstance of public life in England, that we do not, as a rule, permit our political opinions to interfere with our social relations, recalled in the following words one of his reminiscences: "If you are on the continent, and wish to pay your respects to a minister, and go to his reception, you are invited by the minister. The consequence is that you find no one except those that follow him. It is not so in England. I remember some years ago meeting, under the charming roof of one of the most accomplished women of the time, the most celebrated diplomatist of certainly half a century; and he said to me, 'What a wonderful system of society you have in England! I have not been on speaking terms with Lord Palmerston for three weeks, and yet here I am; but you see I am paying a visit to Lady Palmerston.'"

She was a woman, indeed, of whom he might well be proud; as polished in her manners as she was considerate and kind in heart. Even to the last Lord Palmerston was anxious to avoid adding to her anxiety, assuming a cheerfulness in her presence. "I remember that only a few days before his death," writes the Hon. Evelyn Ashley, "when, so far as the aspect of his face could betoken illness, he appeared as ill as a man could be when about and at work, Lady Palmerston at breakfast alluded to the cattle-plague, which was then making a great havoc in England. He at once remarked that all the symptoms of the disorder

were described by Virgil.  He then told us a story of a scrape he got into at
Harrow for throwing stones; and the excess of laughter, which he was unable to
restrain, with which he recalled the incident, was the only token that could have
betrayed to Lady Palmerston how weak he was."

It has been remarked that the same ardor which distinguished the intellectual temperament of William Whewell belonged in an even greater degree to his affections.  This was conspicuous throughout his life; and the most indulgent tenderness was ever displayed alike to those "from whom he differed in opinion on almost every point, as well as to younger relations, who could contribute nothing but love and gratitude to the unequal friendship."  What could be more charming, too, than the affection he had for his sister, to whom for so many years "all his home letters were

SYMPATHY AND ENDEARMENT.

written—all his home thoughts expressed?"  To a man with such a deep-rooted,
lovable nature marriage meant the closest union of sympathy and endearment;
and hence his married life was marked by a beautiful unreserve and communicativeness which knew not what secrecy or dissimulation meant.  Accordingly,
one of the trials of the loneliness which ultimately fell upon him was that, as

he was wont to say, "There is no one now to whom I can say whatever occurs to my mind at once, as the way of giving reality and meaning to all that passes before me." A wife with an uncongenial disposition would have been a bitter disappointment to a man like Dr. Whewell. But he was fortunate in Cordelia Marshall, for she possessed the very qualities he needed—"a warm and tender heart, a calm, strong sense, a wise and boundless sympathy."

Writing to his sister, he playfully announced his engagement to her, remarking that his Cordelia was "not the daughter of King Lear, but of Mr. Marshall, of Leeds." And a few days later on, in a letter to Archdeacon Hare, he thus alluded to the important event:

"When I wrote to you last I was not half grateful enough for the blessing I have now in prospect. I was to a certain extent under the influence of bewilderment, which has now, I trust, passed away forever. I think of my fortune with unmingled hope and comfort, and of Cordelia as my good angel."

The marriage was solemnized on October 12, 1841, at New Church, and the honeymoon, which had been anxiously anticipated by Whewell as a prolonged season of calm and repose, owing as he supposed to his final separation from Trinity College, Cambridge, was interrupted by news which brought the prospect of an appointment which had been the summit of his ambition.

On the very day of his marriage Dr. Wordsworth, the Master of Trinity College, wrote to him announcing his intention of resigning, at the same time expressing a wish that he might be "appointed as soon as possible to this important concern." Five days afterward he received a letter from Sir Robert Peel, intimating that Her Majesty had approved of his being offered "the succession to Dr. Wordsworth as Master of Trinity College, Cambridge."

The appointment was highly popular, and it was not long before Mrs. Whewell endeared herself to all around, increasing, if possible, her husband's influence in the university by her own calm, dignified manner, and by her hearty co-operation in his labors.

Their days flowed on in the calmness of domestic tranquillity, without a flaw or break, but in 1853 this good wife's health was the cause for the gravest anxiety; and in the close of 1855 the dark cloud, which had been long impending, burst, for on the eighteenth of December Mrs. Whewell died. Thus closed a happy union of fourteen years; and she who had shed a bright lustre in the brilliant home of which she was so graceful an ornament was gone.

How great her influence was we have ample testimony from his own words, for in a letter to his sister he says: "She shared our thoughts from hour to hour. And if I did anything good and right and wise it was because I had goodness and right-mindedness and wisdom to prompt and direct me." Writing to Professor Sedgwick he tells him: "It is a satisfaction to think that you saw in some degree how kind and thoughtful she was. The riches of her goodness, wisdom and love no one could know whose whole life was not united with hers. I must go on with a life emptied of all its value."

Lydia Mackenzie Fraser's attachment to Hugh Miller, the poor mechanic, was highly romantic. The mere fact of a young lady falling in love with a poetic stonemason was sufficient of itself to arouse the anger of her mother, who had no doubt thought, like most mothers, that no one was too good for her daughter. A girl of her position, in her nineteenth year, very pretty, with a clear waxen complexion which resembled that of a fair child rather than of a grown woman, would attract attention in any society. Added to this, she was a young lady of great natural ability, and could not fail with her intellect and beauty to create an impression.

But Hugh Miller, despite the fact of his being a stonemason, was no ordinary man, for in a letter addressed from Cromarty by Mrs. Fraser to her daughter we find this passage: "You may guess what are his literary pretensions when I tell you that from my window at this moment I see a stonemason engaged in building a wall. He has just published a volume of poems and likewise letters on the herring-fishery, both of which I send you."

Little did she think when writing these lines that she was about to excite a curiosity in her daughter, the effects of which she would have no power to control. An unconscious interest Lydia Fraser at once took in the stonemason, and on seeing him for the first time she was struck by the intense thoughtfulness of his face, and impressed by the color of his eyes, " a deep blue tinged with sapphire." Equally was he struck by her appearance, and from that hour a feeling, hitherto unfelt, sprang up in each heart—the consciousness of being in love. It is true that, like most young girls, Lydia Fraser had admirers with whose attentions she was flattered, but, although these might be younger and better trained socially, they had not for the young girl the attractions which were possessed by her lover, a man of great genius and sterling worth. A girl situated as Lydia was might anticipate opposition to a marriage which was in the view of her friends a misalliance, and such opposition came. Only after an engagement of five years were the young people married. Then followed years of happiness and mutual respect and regard, while Hugh Miller reaped literary laurels without stint. Alas! for the sorrowful conclusion of the story. In a fit of insanity the gifted husband finally took his own life, but his widow was comforted by remembering the gladness which had so long been hers without a cloud.

Courtship and marriage have often been conducted in a somewhat unconventional manner. Kepler, the astronomer, it may be remembered, when contemplating marriage, made a catalogue of twelve ladies, with a description of their qualifications; and Mason, the poet, is commonly reported to have proposed to the lady he married because "during a whole evening he had been in her company with others, she had never uttered a single word." She was, notwithstanding her reticence, possessed of intellectual and conversational powers, and made the poet a sympathetic wife. Abernethy acted in a similar manner.

He had a very quick perception of character, his profession affording him ample opportunities for the exercise and cultivation of this quality. Hence, in his choice of a wife he was not likely to ally himself to any lady who appeared deficient in what he considered the necessary qualifications for this position. When visiting some friends near London in his professional capacity, he was introduced to a Miss Anne Threlfall, and was much gratified with her kindness and attention. Possessing considerable personal attractions and agreeable manners, he quickly formed a high estimate of her character, and without much further consideration fixed on her as his future wife. Accordingly he wrote a note expressive of his wishes, pleading the nature and variety of his occupations as an apology for the method of making them known, and requesting the lady to take a fortnight to consider her reply. Her answer was favorable, and the marriage took place at Edmonton January 9, 1800. One circumstance on the occasion of his marriage was thoroughly characteristic of Abernethy; he did not allow it to interrupt, even for a

COURTSHIP.

day, a duty with which he rarely suffered anything to interfere—his lecture at the hospital.   Many years afterward, when he was entering the hospital one day, just before lecture, he met going out one of the young doctors gaily attired and with a flower in his coat.   The young man explained that he was taking a holiday as it was his wedding morning.

"Ah!" said the old surgeon, "I lectured as usual on the morning of my marriage day."

About the year 1839, some one, supposed to be the St. John of "Jane Eyre," and like him a clergyman, had the good sense to recognize the greatness of Charlotte Brontë, and to propose marriage.   But she, at the time a poor hard-worked teacher who hated her business, would have nothing to do with him.   She thus writes:

"I had a kindly leaning toward him, because he is an amiable and well-disposed man, yet I had not, and could not have, that intense attachment which would make me willing to die for him; and if ever I marry, it must be in that light of adoration that I will regard my husband.   Ten to one I shall never have the chance again; but n'importe.   Moreover, I was aware that he knew so little of me that he could hardly be conscious to whom he was writing.   Why! it would startle him to see me in my natural home character; he would think I was a wild, romantic enthusiast indeed.   I could not sit all day long making a grave face before my husband.   I would laugh, and satirize, and say whatever came into my head first.   And if he were a clever man, and loved me, the whole world, weighed in the balance against his smallest wish, should be light as air."

Her chance of matrimony thus rejected, she settled down as a governess; and not long afterward was much amused by another offer she received from an Irish curate, whose "declaration of attachment and proposal of matrimony" she received with laughter and ridicule rather than seriousness, remarking, "I am certainly doomed to be an old maid.   Never mind.   I made up my mind to that fate ever since I was twelve years old."   Then, as time went on, a certain Mr. X—— wanted to marry her—a good man, and kind and substantial withal. But she did not like his manners and habits, or his "dreadful determined nose in the middle of his face."   Indeed, when the unfortunate man came into her presence her veins ran ice, and although Mr. Brontë took to him, she could not tolerate him.   "No! if X—— be the only husband fate offers me, single I must always remain.   But yet at times I grieve for him."

In 1852, Charlotte Brontë was wooed and won by the Rev. Arthur Bell Nichols, to whom, however, she was not married till 1854.   One short year of joy was theirs, and then, succumbing to a malady incidental to pregnancy, Charlotte Nichols, perhaps the most gifted woman of her time, fell asleep, leaving her husband and father desolate in the little Haworth Rectory.

# CHAPTER XLIII.

## Religion in the Home.

GRACE before meat is the common way of recognizing that constant goodness of God which gives us our daily bread. "Lord, Thou openest Thine hand and satisfiest the desire of every living thing," said one of old, and again, "My table Thou hast furnished in the presence of mine enemies; my cup runneth over."

Let us never give up the good custom of asking a blessing before beginning our meals. The head of the household, the father, is the priest of his family, and the proper person to conduct its devotions; but, if from self-consciousness, or because of not being a professing Christian, or, for any reason, he does not like to assume this office, the wife should take it on herself. There are forms of grace which are convenient for those who cannot compose a little prayer and thanksgiving with ease, as, for instance:

"Bless, O Lord, we beseech Thee, this food to our use, and us to Thy service;"

or else,

"For what we are about to receive may the Lord make us truly thankful;"

or,

"Lord, bless this food and accept our grateful praise;"

or,

"Bless these mercies to our use, and keep us, Lord Jesus, in Thy dear love."

A little child may learn such a form and say grace, and it is well to accustom children to such service, so that any child called upon may reverently utter the words, and thus consecrate the meal.

An old English blessing, very quaint and sweet, runs after this manner:

"Some hae meat and canna eat,
Some can eat and hae no meat;
We hae meat, and we can eat.
May the Lord be thanket."

GRACE BEFORE MEALS.

There is, too, always the option of the silent grace, with bowed heads and uplifted thoughts, and no spoken words.

Family prayer, once universal in the homes of Christians, has almost been forgotten in thousands of homes. The urgency of trains, the fierce pressure of business, the differing engagements of people in the family, children going to school, men to their offices and shops, and one this way, the other that, called off by the world and its insistent clamor, that people fancy they cannot take time for morning prayer, and at night they are tired or scattered, and friends call, and there are meetings to attend, and the result is, we do not have family worship as we used to, and it is a great pity.

The reading of a short portion of Scripture, the singing of a hymn, the short, fervent prayer, followed by the Lord's prayer uttered in concert—how easy is this brief home service, and how elevating. What a strength it is in hours of weakness, what a rest when we are weary, what a consolation when we are sad!

And the son or daughter afar from the old home, it may be wandering among scenes of sin and peoples who hate God, how the recollection of the daily worship in the father's house holds the distant child to the Father in heaven as by an invisible cable. There may be trouble, there may be temptation, there may be sore distress, but they are praying at home—father, mother, the sisters and brothers. The piety of the home insures that of the Church. A nation of God-fearing women and men can be expected to come from homes wherein there is an altar to God and daily incense offered there.

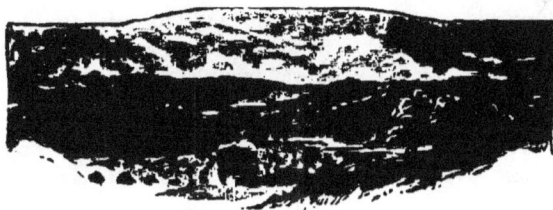

# CHAPTER XLIV.

## Odds and Ends for Everybody.

HILE you are getting ready to undertake an enterprise, weighing pros and cons and considering the difficulties in the way another and less timid person has carried the enterprise, through.

Fear has a certain paralyzing and benumbing effect on one's faculties. Never be afraid. Simply trust God and do your best. If suffering be appointed you, bear it bravely, but not in fear of anything worse. "Sufficient unto the day is the evil thereof."

Habit is like a highway. First there was the passing along of some pioneer and the path was broken. Then followed others and the path was widened. At last the road was laid and now the traffic of the countryside is carried on there. So with habit. It makes its own highways in the brain, its own ruts and by-paths, its own appointed ways in character.

Do not lose time in lamenting that certain talents and capacities which you discern in yourself are still undeveloped. Never mind if you have not yet had an opportunity to study in certain attractive fields. Begin to-day. Attack the new study. Develop your talents now. There is no "too late" while life remains for the brave and earnest soul.

If the curtain could be lifted from the lives around us we should find that many of the days we call so dull and commonplace are full of heroic deeds. We read in the newspapers of crowned heads and brave warriors afar, and learn to know them at least by name, but we do not know the hero who daily passes our window carrying his dinner-pail, nor the angel of patience prisoned in the invalid's room in the next block. Souls that are strong and brave, unselfish and true are all around us, even while we wail over the wickedness of the world.

Everybody has influence. The babe that never has spoken or stood alone nevertheless has an influence great enough to transform lives. Nobody ever was without influence. Nevertheless, in a larger sense, there is a greater influence that is to be acquired, and that does not come without effort. This is the influence that Christians should seek ; the influence that is strength and sweetness and

light, and that spreads abroad the sweet savor of Christliness.

Who is there that hath not a burden, who that stands in no need of relief? The burden of ignorance weighs heavy on one man. He finds himself so lamentably in the dark with regard to many most important things. The burden of responsibility weighs upon another. The burden of some secret frailty, some unconquerable weakness, oppresses another. The burden of doubt is crushing to this sin-tormented soul. The burden of mortality, the fear of death, is more than another can bear. The burden of levity and thoughtlessness is heavier

THE INFLUENCE OF A CHILD.

to some than is generally supposed. To one and all the command is " Cast thy burden upon the Lord." He will not remove your burden so that you will

21

have nothing to do—no more need of Him—but He will sustain you, He will administer support.

Eating heartily when overfatigued is an invitation to dyspepsia. A rest of only five minutes before a meal, when the system is exhausted, is beneficial. It will pay a woman to remove her dress, take down her hair, bathe her face in quite hot water, pressing the washcloth against the eyes and back of the neck, and follow this treatment with a dash of cold water in which a little cologne or toilet vinegar has been sprinkled. Then if she can lie down a few minutes and on rising put on a different dress she will feel decidedly refreshed.

How to strengthen the memory is an interesting question. I think the best way is to use it constantly, making it serve you by giving it definite facts and events to carry, as a pack-horse might on a journey. There are many phases of the problem, some people finding that they cannot fix dates in their minds, others forgetting the faces and names of friends, and others still having great trouble in committing anything by rote. Devices of rhymes and associations help some persons, and others simply depend on memoranda, and do not tax their memories at all. As a rule, the more we give the memory to do, however, the more quickly and faithfully it will respond to our wishes. In little children memory is very retentive, because their minds are at the stage when impressions are easily made; you know the line which says that in childhood our minds are "Wax to receive, and marble to retain." So that we should be very careful indeed about what we say, what we do, and what we teach, where the dear little ones are concerned. Some girls have a great deal of trouble in remembering the rules of syntax, the Latin conjugations, and the pages of history which their teachers require to be recited exactly as they are in the book. Try the method of studying aloud. Go away by yourself to commit your lessons to memory, and then, over and over, slowly, carefully, with your mind and attention fixed on what you are doing, read phrases, sentences and formulas, over and over, and over and over, and by and by you will have them by heart. I have often done this when I have wished to learn a hymn or a poem, and I know that hearing what one is studying assists the mere seeing. Then having other people in the room, talking and laughing, is very distracting to the attention. Try my method and report results.

Said little Johnny Green,
This is the funniest world I ever seen;
A fellow is sent off to bed
When he hain't got a bit of sleep in his head.
And he's hustled out of it, don't you see,
When he's just as sleepy as he can be.

Growing girls and boys do not always appreciate that it is while they are growing that they are forming their figures for after life. Drooping the shoulders a little more every day, drooping the head as one walks, standing unevenly, so that one hip sinks more than the other—all these defects, easily corrected now, will be five times as hard in five years, and twenty-five times as hard in ten years. A graceful, easy carriage, and an erect, straight figure, are a pleasure to beholder and possessor, and are worth striving for.

An easy way to practice walking well is to start out right. Just before you leave the house walk up to the wall and see that your toes, chest and nose touch it at once; then in that attitude walk away. Keep your head up and your chest out, and your shoulders and back will take care of themselves.

A Southern school teacher used to instruct her pupils to walk always as if trying to look over the top of an imaginary carriage just in front of them. It was good advice, for it kept the head raised. Don't think these things are of no value. They add to your health and your attractiveness, two things to which everybody should pay heed.

I think one of the most common forms of incivility as seen in daily life is the failure to show interest in what people are saying to you. This lack of interest, excused on the score of preoccupation, or absence of mind, or inattention, throws an effectual chill on family or social intercourse, and acts as a wet blanket wherever it is found. The fact is that when people are together they should be interested in each other's talk and each other's concerns. Letters, the morning paper, one's own thoughts and plans, should be put aside in the family, and whether in the sitting-room or at the table, a common life shared should make possible common conversation and polite intercourse.

I was a very little girl when my father gave me a rule for conduct which has never ceased to have with me the force of an obligation. ''Always look at the person who is speaking to you. Always look straight at the person to whom you are speaking.'' The practice of this rule makes one a good listener, and a good listener is as essential to pleasure in conversation as a good raconteur.

The whole secret, or nearly the whole secret of personal magnetism and popularity, is in this habit of giving deferential attention to what is going on about you. Next to this comes, and it has a high place in family amenities, the keeping in the background your grievances.

Where people are sensitive, and the greater the scale of refinement, the greater is apt to be the sensitiveness to others' moods and to praise or blame, it is inevitable that feelings will be hurt.

But my grievance, even if it be positive and well grounded, is my personal affair, and must not be permitted to intrude upon the peace of the household. It is mine, and therefore it is my privilege to put it with other unpleasant things quite out of sight. No personal slight, no personal sorrow, no individual infirmity, should be allowed to cloud the general happiness.

Among the neglected amenities of life, one finds often the scarcely veiled indifference of the young to the old. Younger people are so full of vitality, so occupied, so *rushed* in these busy days with their engagements and their pleasures that they too frequently have scant consideration for their seniors. But age has its rights as well as its privileges, and it has a claim on the courtesy, the patience and the respect of those who, however young they may be now, will, if they live long enough, in time be old themselves.

Among the needless brutalities of daily life is a habit of brusque and indiscreet candor. "What a hideous bonnet you have; pray, where did you get it? You look like a fright!" I heard one sister say to another, and I felt most indignant. The bonnet may or may not have deserved the comment; that was a matter of preference, but the young woman capable of so rude a remark should have been made to wear a penitential sheet with holes for her eyes until she had learned better manners. "You are looking very ill," if repeated often enough, will make even a well person a temporary invalid, and, where disagreeable truths will do no good, and no principle is involved in their expression, it is best not to utter them. Silence is sometimes, not always, but often, golden.

A friend writes asking in what way a number of ladies may unite to show honor to a person of distinction who happens to be visiting in their neighborhood. No single family is at present conveniently situated for the giving of a reception to this personage; yet all wish to do her honor. Why not have a composite luncheon? To this all the ladies might contribute something, either in the way of viands, flowers or menu cards. One lady might have the luncheon at her house; the oldest or most prominent woman in the place chosen to preside, the guest of honor being at her right hand, and all might thus take part in showing their pride in and regard for the author, artist or traveler, whichever she may be, who has won their admiration. In New York a number of ladies often combine in this way, and each contributes one dollar or two dollars, or more or less, as the case may be; then arrangements are made with one of the hotels, where an elaborate luncheon with all needed service is provided at a moderate cost per capita. There will be included in this charge a parlor in which the company may receive their guests, and a dressing room where ladies may leave their wraps. It is simply the method with which our women's clubs are familiar, applied temporarily to a few friends who gather for an occasion. Such a luncheon was given at the Fifth Avenue Hotel to a very charming woman who was going abroad for a rather prolonged period. In her case, the affair was so nicely managed that it was a surprise to her. All guests were invited to assemble at one o'clock; at half past one they were seated in a spacious dining room, where tables were laid for twenty-four persons. The decorations of spring flowers were exceedingly beautiful; the bill of fare, consisting of a number of courses, had been arranged with much care. All guests were seated at the tables, when a lady, who had been appointed to do so, ushered in the guest of honor. At her entrance everybody rose; handkerchiefs were waved and she was received with great eclat! Everybody does not like to be surprised, and it requires a good deal of self-possession to face even a pleasant surprise without embarrassment; so that, as a rule, it is much better to take the guest of the day into your confidence; allow her to be present to receive her friends beforehand, and conduct her with ceremony to her place at the table; but, on the other hand, there is something very fascinating and exciting about a well-carried out surprise, and in either case the person who receives such a compliment should thereafter try to live so that her friends will continue to love her and be proud of her as they hitherto have. Such loving compliments leave upon one a great responsibility. It is like dressing up to one's gloves or one's best bonnet. One must live finely whose friends show that they have so much confidence in and respect for her.

## Laugh a Little Bit.

Cherish this as sacred wit:
" Laugh a little bit."
Keep it with you, sample it:
" Laugh a little bit."
Little ills will sure betide you,
Fortune may not sit beside you,
Men may mock and Fame deride you,
But you'll mind them not a whit
If you laugh a little bit.

## In Blueberry Time.

'Tis blueberry time, and the pasture
    High up on the hill-side is sweet
With the fragrance of hay, and the incense
    Of flowers you crush 'neath your feet.

# A PRAYER FOR LITTLE THINGS.

The stone wall is crimsoned with briers,
  The clematis tangles its spray,
The deep, wine-red plume of the sumac
  Uplifts like a soldier at bay.

Bob White, with his silvery whistle,
  Sings shrill from the heart of the corn,
And clear over fir-top and elm-top
  The caw of the black crow is borne;
And night falls in shadow and silence,
  Save only the katydid's strain,
And the hoot of the owl from the thicket,
  Or the whippoorwill's plaintive refrain.

'Tis blueberry time in the mountains,
  The time of the quiver of heat,
The time of the sudden down-slashing
  Of rain that is welcome and sweet.
The bare-footed, brown, dimpled children
  Troop out with their baskets and pails;
The rabbits are scared at their laughter,
  And, startled, forth flutter the quails.

---

## A Prayer for Little Things.

A little light, O Father, that my feet
  Along life's devious ways may stumble not,
That I may give to virtue praises meet,
  Nor all too harshly scan the sins that blot
And darken many a life that seemeth fair
But hides some blighting sin, some cankering care.

A little love, but changeless, pure and true,
  That, when my soul faints 'neath life's heavy load
And yields the race with victory in view,
  Shall, like the fount that in the desert flowed,
When Israel's prophet smote the frowning rock,
Still give me strength for sorrow's rudest shock.

And one more boon, O Father, let me gain
When these worn hands are folded in repose,
And this sad heart, so often thrilled with pain,
Shall lose in death its trials and its woes;
Grant me, before Heaven's praises I begin,
A little space to rest, Thy courts within.

*—Louise W. German.*

## Frances Willard's Counsel to Girls.

Miss Willard was constantly impressing it upon her hearers and readers that every woman, rich or poor, married or unmarried, should cultivate individuality and independence. One of the most characteristic chapters in her breezy, helpful book for girls, "How to Win," is the one in which she urges every young reader to cultivate a specialty. "By this means," she writes, "you will get into your cranium, in place of aimless reverie, a resolute aim." And she goes on to say:

"This is where your brother has had his chief intellectual advantage over you. Quicker of wit than he, far less unwieldy in your mental processes, swifter in judgment, and every whit as accurate, you still have felt when measuring intellectual swords with him that yours was in your left hand, that his was in his right; and you have felt this chiefly, as I believe, because from the dawn of thought in his sturdy young brain he has been taught that he must have a definite aim in life if he ever meant to swell the ranks of the somebodies upon this planet, while you have been just as sedulously taught that the handsome prince might whirl past your door ''most any day,' lift you to a seat beside him in his golden chariot and carry you off to his castle in Spain.

"And of course you dream about all this; why shouldn't you? Who wouldn't? But, my dear girls, dreaming is the poorest of all grindstones on which to sharpen one's wits. And to my thinking the rust of woman's intellect, the canker of her heart, the 'worm i' the bud' of her noblest possibilities has been this aimless reverie; this rambling of the thoughts; this vagueness, which when it is finished is vacuity. Let us turn our gaze inward, those of us who are not thoroughgoing workers with brain or hand. What do we find? A mild chaos, a glimmering nebula of fancies, an insipid brain soup where a few lumps of thought swim in a watery gravy of dreams, and, as nothing can come of nothing, what wonder if no brilliancy of achievement promises to flood our future with its light! Few women, growing up under the present order of things, can claim complete exemption from this grave intellectual infirmity."

## Gifts to God.

The wise may bring their learning,
   The rich may bring their wealth,
And some may bring their greatness,
   And some bring strength and health.
We, too, would bring our treasures,
   To offer to the King;
We have no wealth or learning—
   What shall the children bring?

We'll bring Him hearts that love Him,
   We'll bring Him thankful praise,
And young souls meekly striving
   To walk in holy ways.
We'll bring the little duties
   We have to do each day;
We'll try our best to please Him
   At home, at school, at play.

And these shall be the treasures
   We offer to the King.
And these are gifts that even
   The poorest child may bring.

---

## Summer in the Soul.

Since I have learned Thy love,
   My summer, Lord, Thou art;
Summer to me, and day,
   And life-springs in my heart

Thy blood blots out my sin,
   Thy love casts out my fear;
Heaven is no longer far,
   Since Thou, its sun, art near.

Summer! life-fountains! day!
   Within—around—above,
Where we shall see Thy face,
   Where we shall feel Thy love.

## Some Time.

Some time, when all life's lessons have been learned,
  And sun and stars forevermore have set,
The things which our weak judgments here have spurned,
  The things o'er which we grieved with lashes wet,
Will flash before us, out of life's dark night,
  As stars shine most in deeper tints of blue;
And we shall see how all God's plans are right,
  And how what seemed reproof was love most true.

But not to-day.   Then be content, poor heart!
  God's plans like lilies pure and white unfold;
We must not tear the close shut leaves apart,
  Time will reveal the calyxes of gold.
And if, through patient toil, we reach the land
  Where tired feet, with sandals loosed, may rest,
Where we shall clearly see and understand,
  I think that we will say, '' God knew the best!''

  *—May Riley Smith.*

---

## A Love Song.

So near, so very near to God,
  I cannot nearer be;
For in the person of His Son
  I am as near as He.

So dear, so very dear to God,
  More dear I cannot be;
The love wherewith He loves the Son—
  Is the love He giveth me.

Why should I ever careful be,
  Since such a God is mine?
He watches o'er me night and day,
  And tells me, '' Mine is thine.''

## Saved by Grace.

I found this very remarkable instance of parental faith in the "Interior."
It was written by one who knew whereof he testified:

It happened more than seventy years ago, in an humble Christian home. A
boy only six years old was sick with typhoid fever. His name was not Samuel,
and his mother's name was not Hannah, but she had given him to the Lord as
soon as he was born, and her daily wish and prayer had been that he might be a
minister of the gospel. But now the doctor, who stood with the parents by the
little bed, felt the fluttering pulse, and told them that the boy was dying. At
once the father, a man of indomitable energy, began to rub the limbs of the
sufferer with alcohol, hoping to quicken the ebbing circulation, and the mother
knelt in prayer. In a few minutes the doctor said: "You may stop rubbing and
praying for the child is dead." They heard him, but kept right on as before.
The doctor was a personal friend as well as a skillful physician. He sympathized
with the anxiety of these parents to save their darling, and yet he was indignant
at their want of faith in him. He waited some minutes, and then said again,
"What is the use of your fussing and your prayers, I tell you that there is no
hope. The child has ceased to breathe, his pulse is still, his extremities are cold,
he is dead." The father did not reply at once, but after another interval of
intense attention and effort, he said, "Doctor, put your finger in this arm-pit, and
tell me what you think?" The doctor did so, and exclaimed: "Why, there is a
throbbing here, rub on, rub on." And he hastened to prepare a stimulating draft
to be put into the patient's mouth as soon as there was any possibility of its being
swallowed. Now father and doctor worked together, while the mother still
prayed, and in half an hour, or less, the child was pronounced out of danger.

I talked many times with the actors in that scene, and knew what their
thoughts and feelings were. The doctor said that the child for ten minutes had
given no sign of life, and yet in some mysterious way a spark of vitality must
have lingered somewhere, and the rubbing quickened it. He was certain that
without that severe friction there would never have been any animation. Then,
after this attempt at a professional explanation the good man would shake his
head and say: "If this was the age of miracles I could believe in that child's
recovery as one."

The father did not say much. He had heard of cases where even doctors
were mistaken. He never gave up as long as there was the remotest possibility
of success, and while his good wife, in whose piety he had the fullest confidence,
kept on praying, he felt that it was his duty to keep on working.

But the mother told me, again and again, that she knew God had accepted
lrer consecration of her child to Him and to His service, and she could not believe

that He had been mocking her. She was sure that He was only trying her faith, and she told Him so, reverently but earnestly. The Holy Spirit inspired her to continue in prayer notwithstanding the doctor's declaration. She had more faith in her Heavenly Father than in the most skillful human physician. In her case it was not rash or indiscreet presumption, but a simple, childlike confidence. That boy grew to manhood and in time became a minister. He has now been preaching the gospel for nearly fifty years, and though far beyond three-score and ten he is not yet superannuated or "honorably retired."

I have thought of this scene many times when reading the criticisms of rationalists and conceited scientists. They call our Christian faith a senseless superstition. They don't believe in anything but the phenomena of nature. But if there is a great all-pervading and all-controlling Spirit, as we believe, what, they ask, is the use of prayer? Can we induce Him to change His governmental policy by our petitions? We do not stop to argue with such cavilers, as those parents did not stop to argue with the doctor. We have no time to waste in that way. Millions are dying, and hence we just keep on praying and working. God has told us to ask and we shall receive, to ask in faith and to show our faith by our works. As obedient children we do just what our Father tells us to, though we can not know just how our feeble supplications can move the arm that moves the world. From the Bible standpoint, nay, from that of the dust even, how foolish is all this prating about nature and miracles. If there is a God who is over all and in all, a God who doeth His pleasure among the armies of heaven and the inhabitants of the earth, nature can mean only the way in which He chooses to work, and what we call miracles are only the results of such natural processes as are new to us or such temporary departures from those processes as the All-wise and All-mighty one chooses to make. A finite creature cannot comprehend the Infinite. It is therefore his duty and should be his joy to trust and obey. Much of what men call wisdom is foolishness with God. Nothing in human experience is so sweet, so full of comfort and hope as a simple, childlike faith—a faith like that of the mother at the bedside of her sick boy. Perhaps her prayers did more than her husband's efforts to retain and quicken the feeble, fluttering pulse.

And here I am reminded of a story. Some children were playing on the bank of a stream. A little boy fell in. The older boys rushed to the rescue. They joined hands and waded out to where the child was drowning. With their living life-line they brought him to the shore. And then his four-year-old sister knelt beside him, and thanked God that they had been able to save her brother. One of the boys said: "You had better thank us, for we did it." "I do," she replied, "but I thank God too, for while you were wading I was praying." That baby-believer was right. She was taught of God, and hence understood the philosophy of salvation.

## Camp Echoes.

"Rally round the flag, boys! Give it to the breeze!"
  Bless the dear old fiddle that wakes the gallant air.
Once we thundered it in chorus like the booming of the seas,
  Wives and sweethearts joining in, with an "Amen" to the prayer.

We're a lot of grizzled fellows, not so much to look at now!
  Young and full of vigor when the war began,
Some behind the counter, and some behind the plow,
  But we rallied for the country, enlisted to a man.

Counting not the cost, boys, never sordid aims
  Dimmed our record, hasting to the conflict's brunt;
Each to serve the nation, we answered to our names,
  And the flag before us, we hurried to the front.

Can't you see it waving, the banner of our love,
  Where the Shenandoah loops and twists like mad?
Can't you hear the shouting, the dying groans above,
  When we'd won a battle, and—lost the best we had?

Blessings on the music of "Tramp, tramp, tramp!"
  How it rang its challenge down the serried lines,
Cheered us when like hounds a-leash, we strained through days in camp,
  Or crashed with Sherman's storm-cloud, through Georgia's solemn pines

Here, like useless hulks, boys, we doze the days away—
  Doze and dream and spin our yarns; but when we come to die,
Lights out, some true hand for us let "taps" the last time play,
  Then wrap the flag about us in the bed where last we lie.

----

## The Little Red Stamp.

I'm the little red stamp with George Washington's picture,
  I have the right of way;
And the mail train thunders from under the stars
  And rattles into the day.

Now clear the rail for your Uncle Sam's mail;
  Ye freight trains stand aside!
Spur your iron-lunged horse to his fullest speed,
  For the little red stamp would ride.
So vomit your flame on the startled night
  And your smoke in the face of the day;
For the little red stamp with George Washington's picture
  Must have the right of way.


The engine plows, when I start on my ride,
  Through the drifted banks of snow;
But we hasten to climes where the rivers melt
  And climes where the roses blow.
First the pines of Maine, then the Kansas plain,
  Then whiffs from the western bay,
Till I drop in the hands that have reached for me
  A thousand leagues away.
Pull open the throttle and loose every brake,
  And dash through the night and the day;
For the little red stamp with George Washington's picture
  Must have the right of way.


I'm the little red stamp with George Washington's picture;
  And I go wherever I may,
To any spot in George Washington's land;
  And I go by the shortest way.
And the guns of wrath would clear my path,
  A thousand guns at need,
Of the hands that should dare to block my course
  Or slacken my onward speed.
Stand back! Hands off of Uncle Sam's mail!
  Stand back there! Back! I say;
For the little red stamp with George Washington's picture
  Must have the right of way.

              *—From "Dreams in Homespun."*

# CHAPTER XLV.

## Trouble and Sorrow.

OD does not willingly afflict His children, but God sends sometimes trouble and sorrow. In one or another form men's souls are tried. Loss of fortune comes. Riches take wings. Bereavement comes. Our loved ones lie down in the cold grave. Plans are defeated. Sometimes we walk softly through the valley of the shadow; sometimes the gloom is very deep, and we grope in vain for light. But courage faint heart!

> "Thy shepherd is beside thee
> And nothing shalt thou lack!"

His rod and His staff will guide us all our journey through, and "in heavenly love confiding, no change our heart shall fear."

So long as we love and trust God trouble may bend, but it will not break us. The storm will perhaps rock our barque over rough waves, but after all it will but quicken our journey home.

Says the Rev. Dr. T. L. Cuyler: "I am often impressed by the different ways in which different persons are affected by sorrows. Some seem to have no rallying power after a great affliction; the wound never heals. On the other hand, trials that consume some persons only kindle others into greater exertions. 'This financial gale has carried away all your spars and swept your decks,' I once wrote to an eminent Christian merchant, after his bankruptcy, 'but you have got enough grace stowed away in your hold to make you rich to all eternity.' That brave servant of Christ repaired damages, resumed business, rallied his friends, and 'at evening time it was light.' Smitten down he was not destroyed.

"The afflictions which are sent of God or permitted by Him are never intended for His children's destruction, but for their discipline. The Shepherd casts His flock into deep waters to wash them, not to drown them. 'You will kill that bush if you put that knife into it so deep,' said a gentleman to his gardener. 'No, sir; I do this every year to keep it from running all to leaves; pruning brings the fruit.' We pastors often find God's faithful ones bleeding under the knife, but afterward they yield the peaceable and precious fruits of

(334)

SORROWS.

(335)

righteousness and triumphant trust.   It is that 'afterward' that God has in His mind when He sends the trial.   Affliction is the costly school in which great graces are often acquired, and from which grand characters are graduated.

"How is it that a genuine Christian recuperates after being stricken down by a savage adversity or a sharp affliction?   Simply because his graces survive the shock.   For one thing, his *faith* is not destroyed.   When a ship loses her canvas in a gale she can still be kept out of the trough of the sea by her rudder; when the rudder goes she still has her anchor left, but if the cable snaps she is swept helplessly on the rocks.   So, when your hold on God is gone, all is gone.   The most fatal wreck that can overtake you in times of sorrow is the wreck of faith. But if in the darkest hour you can trust God though He slay, and firmly believe that He 'chastens you for your profit,' you are anchored to the very throne of love and will come off conqueror.   *Hope* also is another grace that survives. Some Christians never shine so brightly as in the midnight of sorrow.   I know of good people who are like an ivory dice, throw it whichever way you will it always lands on a square, solid bottom.   Their hope always strikes on its feet after the hardest fall.   One might have thought that it was all over with Joseph when he was sent to prison, or with John when he was exiled to Patmos, or with John Bunyan when he was locked up in Bedford jail.   But they were all put in the place where they could be most useful."

## Remembrance.

My cup is the cup of sorrow,
    And, turn it as I will,
The breath of the myrrh and aloes
    Clings to its sharp edge still;
But if ever I fain would leave it
    With the bitter dregs unquaffed,
Jesus, I try to remember
    Thine was a harder draught!

My path is beset with briers;
    They tear my lagging feet;
Dark are the ways I wander,
    Cruel the foes I meet;
But if ever I fain would linger,
    Then comes that face divine
Jesus, I try to remember
    A wearier road was Thine!

My cross is of fire and iron,
    It wounds to the very bone;
But if to the top of Calvary
    I needs must climb alone,
When the soul that I would have died for
    Turns, ice and stone, from me,
Saviour of all, I remember
    A world rejected Thee!

---

## Hide Thy Grief.

Bury thy sorrow, the world hath its share;
Bury it deeply, hide it with care.

Think of it calmly, when curtained by night;
Tell it to Jesus, and all will be right.

Tell it to Jesus, He knoweth thy grief;
Tell it to Jesus, He'll send thee relief.

Hearts grown aweary with heavier woe
Droop 'mid the darkness; go comfort them, go.

Gather the sunlight aglow on thy way;
Gather the moonbeams—each soft silver ray.

Bury thy sorrow, let others be blest;
Give them the sunshine, tell Jesus the rest.

---

## The Aloofness of Grief.

Our Lord was alone in Gethsemane. Then, as all through His earthly life, was fulfilled the word of the prophet that He was a Man of Sorrows and acquainted with grief. In those experiences of trial and suffering which come to His followers there is great comfort in the thought that He is aware of the loneliness and desolation of those who are led by grief into the wilderness, there to wrestle with the tempter, there to struggle or to bend beneath the pressing load, there to await the relief of heaven in the hour of utmost need.

We are often impressed anew as we sit in homes under the shadow with the aloofness of grief. It has a certain awesome dignity. Into the mystic circle

22

which it draws about the sufferer no alien may intrude. Even friends and kindred walk softly and touch with gentlest care the hand of her whose whole being
is absorbed in one intense yearning for that which has gone, in one baffled heartache over the mistakes of the past, in one agonized endurance of the conditions
of the present.  It seems strange that just beyond that hushed and darkened
spot, where the mourner's slow tears fall, the world is going on just the same as
it did before, with cheerful sounds of activity, the stir of business, the whirl of
gayety, the comings and goings of eager and happy people not affected by the
heartbreak which has set its seal on the bereaved.  To them life is shorn for the
moment of its usual interests, they feel stunned or benumbed, or else acutely
alive to the suffering in every vein and nerve, but the world does not care, and
nature goes smilingly on in its procession of day and night as if nothing had happened.

The aloofness of grief, while it apparently adds to the intensity of its sadness,
is really a blessing, for it surrounds the mourner with a sanctuary.  As of old
one in peril clung to the horns of the altar and was safe, so in the extremity of
mortal pain and the bitterness of the anguish-cup the wounded heart is shut
away from the world and shut in to heaven.  At first the cloud is so dark that
heaven itself hardly penetrates it, but by degrees there comes the rifting light.
The voice that could not frame coherent petitions falters out its "Oh, my Father,"
and back through the gloom, thrillingly, tenderly, returns the answer, "Here,
my child."  Bit by bit faith resumes its control, never lost, but perhaps for a
little while shaken, and the promises, one by one, rise and glow, like stars in the
firmament.

One can do little for friends in deep sorrow by the way of direct counsel; spoken
comfort is inadequate.  The ordinary consolations, accepted in ordinary times,
fall on deaf ears.  To love one's own, to cling to them, to feel with them, to pray
for them, is the most that sympathetic and affectionate friends can do in the hour
of the aloofness of grief.

Friends and relatives do not always see this necessity of letting the grief-
stricken remain in the sanctuary.  With well-meant, but clumsy, endeavors they
force food on those who are not hungry and drink on those who are not athirst.
They speak of recreation to those who can think of nothing beyond the desert
place in which they must abide till the tender Shepherd Himself find them and
lead them into the light.  It would be better in most cases to forbear attempts
which do little good, and to wait with patience for the healing touch of time and
the return of healthy life and vigor.  These come when God has done what the
sorrow was sent for, and from the sorrow's hour of darkness the sufferer arises,
stronger to comfort others, with a new experience of the divine love, and sometimes with a revelation, never forgotten, of the nearness of heaven to earth.

The day grows lonelier; the air
  Is chiller than it used to be.
We hear about us everywhere
  The haunting chords of memory.
Dear faces once that made our joy
  Have vanished from the sweet home band,
Dear tasks that were our loved employ
  Have dropped from out our loosened hand.

Familiar names in childhood given
None call us by, save those in heaven.
We cannot talk with later friends
Of those old times to which love lends
Such mystic haze of soft regret;
We would not, if we could, forget
The sweetness of the bygone hours,
So priceless are love's faded flowers;
But lonelier grows the waning day,
And much we miss upon the way
Our comrades who have heard the call
That soon or late must summon all.

Ah, well! the day grows lonelier *here*.
Thank God, it doth not yet appear
What thrill of perfect bliss awaits
Those who pass on within the gates.
Oh, dear ones who have left my side,
And passed beyond the swelling tide,
I know that you will meet me when
I, too, shall leave these ranks of men
And find the glorious company
Of saints from sin forever free,
Of angels who do always see
The face of Christ, and ever stand
Serene and strong at God's right hand.

The day grows lonelier, the air
  Hath waftings strangely keen and cold,
But woven in, Oh, glad, Oh, rare,
  What love-notes from the hills of gold!

Dear crowding faces gathered there,
  Dear blessed tasks that wait our hand,
What joy, what pleasure shall we share,
  Safe anchored in the one home-land!

Close up, O comrades, close the ranks,
  Press onward, waste no fleeting hour!
Beyond the outworks, lo! the banks
  Of that full tide, where life hath power,
And Satan lieth under foot,
  And sin is killed, even at the root.
Close up, close fast the wavering line,
  Ye who are led by One divine.
The day grows lonelier apace,
  But heaven shall be our trysting place.

---

## "Practice What You Know."

  "And it came to pass, that, as they went, they were cleansed." Deliverance cometh in the course of obedience. The faith was adequate to the duty set before them. If the ten lepers had not in a measure believed they had not gone at all. The desire to be relieved of their dreadful malady was doubtless a supreme longing. But they did not stop at desire. The hope, perhaps only a possibility in their minds, determined them to make the venture, and immediately they acted upon the Master's direction. "And it came to pass, that, as they went, they were cleansed."

  The fact involved in this narrative, in as far as it concerns personal duty, is a simple but practical one. Its sphere is far-reaching, extending to numerous emergencies, to every instance, indeed, in which the individual has a part to bear, and in which the result depends upon human conduct. We frequently distinguish between that which God accomplishes for us and in us, without our co-operation, blessings which come to us as the sunlight to the earth, and those events in which He works through our faculties. The illustrations of the latter, in the natural world, are apparent on every side. From the harvest ripening on the hillside, to which the plowman and sower have given their toil; from the forces of nature, to be tamed and controlled for material ends; from mental faculties to be developed through personal application; from the rich resources of the physical world to be garnered for our gain comes the lesson, too evident to require the impression of words, that these shall be to our advantage just to the extent that we employ our powers in co-operation with Providence.

Our Saviour gave to this truth the emphasis of His own method. He demanded the exercise of force where apparently there was no force. To the man whose right hand was withered He said, "Stretch forth thine hand!" To others, from whom faith seemed impracticable, He said, "According to your faith be it unto you." "Believest thou that I am able to do this?" No resistful consciousness of impotence, in those who came to Him for help, was permitted to defeat the infinite wisdom of the arrangement by which men are yet to participate in the benefits of His grace.

Very wise was the advice given by an experienced Christian who, in his religion, as in other things, was accustomed to exercise his common sense. A young man, in the days when it was beginning to be deemed a token of profanity to question, and to magnify doubt, was speaking to an admiring circle of the difficulty to understand and reconcile certain doctrines of revelation. It appeared to him to justify his delay to become a Christian, if not to dismiss the whole matter as one of no personal concern. With ill-concealed impatience the veteran heard him through, and then said: "Young man, practice what you know, practice what you know; when you have done all that you know, you may begin to speculate in mysteries." Had the counsel been followed, probably the occasion to question never would have recurred.

Our Saviour has said: "If any man will do His will (the Father's) he shall know of the doctrine." It is as true that obedience in every other duty will bring conviction and will verify the truth of the Divine promises. Without corresponding action, aspiration is worthless sentiment, a self-persuasion of interest where no sincere interest exists. Believing and doing go hand in hand. Knowledge and obedience are twin spirits. We are taught in order that we may do; else all our knowledge is vanity. Upon these, in their just relation, hangs the entire system of morals and religion. Irreligion divorces them; for sin is always separative. It divides the heart from God. It renders acquaintance with the truth unfruitful. It makes our own inclination the standard of what is to be done, what left undone, and conforms the life to that which is pleasing to self. Knowledge in such a case informs the soul, but does not stimulate to duty. It is an aurora flash, light without heat, or, as the cold beams of the moon, a reflection from a frozen heart.

Therefore the Great Teacher always couples hearing and doing, believing and obeying, and attaches the responsibility which knowledge owes to every sphere in which it is present. "He that heareth my words, and doeth them." "If ye know these things, happy are ye if ye do them." "If any man love me, he will keep my commandments." Going forward in the way of Christ's command gave healing to the lepers.  It could not be otherwise.  The command involves the end. It pledges the saving grace.  " He that believeth shall not be confounded."  That which withstands our spiritual peace and progress is merely the failure to obey; for all the promises of God are yea and amen in Christ Jesus.

We perceive at once how applicable this truth in the spiritual realm.  What numbers fail to get beyond the point of desire, desire for salvation, desire for clearer views of their acceptance, for the assurance of their calling and election. For years they linger upon the threshold, and get no farther, until at length they conclude that these things are not for them.  Some apprehend that, in a way unknown to themselves, they may have grieved the Spirit; others allow themselves a little comfort in the fact that God must know how intense is their desire, and that this may be accounted to them for righteousness.

Now no one can overestimate the blessedness of devout aspiration.  The longing for holiness, for a closer walk with God, is none other than the Holy Spirit in our hearts, crying Abba, Father.  But aspiration that does not seek opportunity and obey direction is as forceless as the steam that issues from the spout of the kettle.  Aspiration condensed into purpose is the mighty power capable to almost all results.  Then it becomes as the prayer that lays hold upon the very strength of God, pleads His promises, makes things invisible realities in possession.—*Rev. Edward P. Terhune, D. D.*

# CHAPTER XLVI.

## The Futility of Worry.

ORRY is the most wasteful thing in life, yet few of us escape its baleful effects. We lie awake in the dead of night and worry haunts us, stares us in the face like a ghost in the darkness, frets at our hearts, gnaws us like a rat in the wainscot, and eats out the very core of our strength. And never a bit of good do we get from it when all is said and done. Worry does not make your child well when he is ill, nor bring back safe to shore the ship which is overdue, nor pay your note in the bank, nor put a new breadth in your worn and faded gown, nor secure you against a fall on the ice, nor convert any soul from the error of his ways, nor do a single thing of the ten thousand things for which we women pine and sigh, for which our men, less patient than we, storm about the world, and work till their heads are gray and their shoulders are bowed. Worry sends people to the insane asylum, but it never yet wrought a cure in mental or physical disease. The Don't Worry Club of the hour is a move in the right direction, only, my friend, you need not join a club to keep from worrying. You can begin the life of peace and freedom and sweetest composure and serenity here, in your own home, now, as you read this page.

Let me give you an old receipt for ease of mind and poise of brain: "I will trust and not be afraid." Trust whom? Why, the mighty God, the Everlasting Father, and the Prince of Peace. The God who says "As thy days thy strength shall be." The God whose book is one long train of promises, whose hand is not shortened that it cannot save, nor whose ear heavy that it cannot hear. "I will trust and not be afraid," and "What time I am afraid, I will trust," are texts worth your laying up in memory as most precious treasures.

Look in the Book, and see how many times peace is mentioned. Over and over, the Lord pledges us peace, promises us peace. The Saviour's last gift to the disciples He was leaving, was just this, peace, and peace means freedom from agitation, freedom from fear, and freedom from worry.

Don't worry about your health. It might be firmer, it is true, but rest, and forget pain, and believe that it will be better, because it is the nature of disease to get well, and because God is perfectly able to give you the measure of health you need.

(343)

(344)                    DON'T WORRY, BROTHER.

Don't worry about your children. You are doing the best you can for them, and giving them the best advantages, and you must leave the future to the dear

"Don't worry about your health."

Saviour. When you have done your best for your boys and girls, according to the light you have, it is to the last degree senseless and absurd to sit down and grieve and lament and fume because perhaps some other course would have been a better one.

Don't worry over business. It has its fluctuations. Times are hard to-day, but courage, they will be better to-morrow. Don't incur unnecessary expense, but keep within the safe and narrow path of strictest honesty. Live within your income. But if there comes a period of calamity, if days of disaster overtake you, still do not worry. It won't help, and it will hinder, and it will make you less able to meet the evil day, than you will be if you will maintain your composure.

Don't worry over the length of your life; you will live long enough to do whatever tasks the Lord has appointed you; in fact, you cannot die while God has anything in this world for you to do.

> Because in a day of my days to come
>     There waiteth a grief to be,
> Shall my heart grow faint and my lips be dumb
>     In this day that is bright for me?
>
> Nay, phantom ill with the warning hand,
>     Nay, sense of impending ill,
> I am traveling on to my Father's land
>     And His grace is with me still,

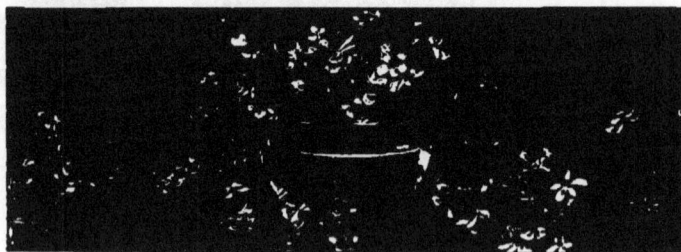

# CHAPTER XLVII.

## Our Dear Ones Gone.

"There is no flock however watched and tended
But one dead lamb is there;
There is no household howsoe'er defended
But has one vacant chair."

ENDERLY familiar these sweet lines of America's dearest household poet recur to memory whenever we think of our dear ones gone. Few households there are which do not show missing darlings from the fireside group; few families have the felicity of maintaining an unbroken circle from childhood to maturity. Hearts must know loss as well as gain in this world, and most of us understand only too well what it is to mourn "for the touch of a vanished hand, and the sound of a voice that is still."

When a baby dies unthinking friends and acquaintances are very apt to minimize the grief of the event, saying: "Oh! it is only the baby!" *Only*, as if a grave a span long could not blot the very heavens with blackness and shut out the glory from the sky, and crush the father's heart and almost break the mother's. For, when a baby dies, it isn't only to-day you bury, it is to-morrow and to-morrow, and next year, and twenty years to come. A thousand possibilities are bound up in a baby, whether it be a man-child who shall carry on the old name and represent the family in the days to be, and stand in his father's room, and reign in his father's stead, or a woman-child, whose fair face and sweet grace shall repeat the beauty of her mother before her, and make blithe the home, and proud the kindred. The dust falls on the tiny coffin, and the parents plant violets on the sod, and go home to their desolate house, where the very silence aches.

After a while comfort will come in the remembrance that God knows best, that God always cares, that the child is safe and sheltered with the All-loving Father. But there must be time before the bereft can realize this in its fullness.

When a mother dies, or a father, when a grown-up son is suddenly snatched away, when any terrible weight of anguish falls on the household, for a season we are benumbed. We cannot understand how life can go on; we are beside ourselves with the wonder and amazement of the shock.

(347)

(348) THE DEAD CHILD TO HEAVENLY REST.

But why do we drop out of the speech of the family the beloved name? Why do we shrink from any mention of her who was our daily joy, of him whose very presence was to us an unspeakable benediction? Are we not weak and foolish, and in a way unjust to the dead when we so treat them?

Do you recollect Rossetti's lyric about the blessed damozel who looked out over the gold bar of heaven? It seemed to *her* she had been one day in that glory; to those she had left below it was *ten* long years.

> "The wonder had not yet quite gone
> From that still look of hers."

When there has been a death in a family it is customary for intimate friends to call and express sympathy at once. Others send cards or letters of condolence.

" As for the coffin, it is simpler than formerly; and, while lined with satin and made with care, it is plain on the outside—black cloth, with silver plate for the name, and silver handles, being in the most modern taste. There are but few of the 'trappings of woe.' At the funeral of General Grant, twice a president, and regarded as the savior of his country, there was a gorgeous catafalque of purple velvet, but at the ordinary funeral there are none of these trappings. If our richest citizen were to die to-morrow, he would probably be buried plainly. Yet it is touching to see with what fidelity the poorest creature tries to ' bury her dead dacent.' The destitute Irish woman begs for a few dollars for this sacred duty, and seldom in vain. It is a duty for the rich to put down ostentation in funerals, for it is an expense which comes heavily on those who have poverty added to grief.

" In dressing the remains for the grave, those of a man are usually ' clad in his habit as he lived.' For a woman tastes differ: a white robe and cap, not necessarily shroudlike, are decidedly unexceptionable. For young persons and children white cashmere robes and flowers are always most appropriate."

The days immediately following a death in the family are more or less filled with excitement. Arrangements must be made for the funeral and the interment, perhaps mourning must be procured in haste, and relatives who live in other places arrive and must be entertained. The blank, cold loss does not settle down on a home until the return from the cemetery. Then, the absence of the dear one, the desolation of the house, and the strange solitude of it all are terribly poignant.

It is an open question which is the harder to bear, a sudden death, or one which is the close of a wasting sickness. The first is no doubt easier to the one who goes, than is the second. To be well and strong and busy to the very latest moment, then to slip softly and swiftly out of this life into the next, with no instant's loss of conciousness, could anything on earth be more desirable, when God is ready to call His servant to heaven? But, such a death is a great shock to survivors who have no preparation to encounter it. When they have watched by a dear one's bed, and seen the breath ebb faintly away and cease, they are grieved but not stunned.

Mourning is a matter of taste and is to some extent regulated by arbitrary rules. Mrs. John Sherwood, in "Manners and Social Usages," says:

"For the first six months the dress of a widow should be of crape cloth, or Henrietta cloth covered entirely with crape, collar and cuffs of white crape, a crape bonnet with a long crape veil, and a widows' cap of white crape if preferred. In America, however, widow's caps are not as universally worn as in England. Dull black kid gloves are worn in first mourning; after that *gants de Suède* or silk gloves are proper, particularly in summer. After six months' mourning the crape can be removed, and grenadine, copeau fringe, and dead trimmings used. After twelve months the widow's cap is left off, and the heavy veil is exchanged for a lighter one, and the dress can be of silk grenadine, plain black gros-grain, or crape-trimmed cashmere with jet trimmings, and crêpe lisse about the neck and sleeves.

"All kinds of black fur and seal-skin are worn in deep mourning.

"Mourning for a father or mother should last one year. During half a year should be worn Henrietta cloth or serge trimmed with crape, at first with black tulle at the wrists and neck. A deep veil is worn at the back of the bonnet, but not over the head or face like the widow's veil, which covers the entire person when down. This fashion is very much objected to by doctors, who think many diseases of the eye come by this means, and advise for common use thin nun's-veiling instead of crape, which sheds its pernicious dye into the sensitive nostrils, producing catarrhal disease as well as blindness and cataract of the eye. It is a thousand pities that fashion dictates the crape veil, but so it is. It is the very banner of woe, and very few have the courage to go without it. We can only suggest to mourners wearing it that they should pin a small veil of black tulle over the eyes and nose, and throw back the heavy crape as often as possible, for health's sake.

"Jet ornaments alone should be worn for eighteen months, unless diamonds set as mementoes are used. For half-mourning, a bonnet of silk or chip, trimmed with crape and ribbon. Mourning flowers, and crêpe lisse at the hands and wrists, lead the way to gray, mauve, and white-and-black toilettes after the second year.

"Mourning for a brother or sister may be the same; for a stepfather or step-mother the same; for grandparents the same; but the duration may be shorter. In England this sort of respectful mourning only lasts three months."

For children, mourning is worn for nine months, though many women have not the wish to remove it at the end of so brief a period.

In wearing mourning, or the reverse, one should be independent. The person who elects to go without it misses the shelter and sanctuary it affords her at first. People not aware of her loss, or forgetful of it, treat her with a lightness and lack of compassion, to which her sombre robes would entitle her. On the other hand it is often a very serious expense for a woman whose means are limited to go into mourning, and her example is followed by other poor women to whom it means both debt and anxiety. The rich and well-to-do may deny themselves the luxury of mourning for the sake of those whose purses will not endure so great an outlay.

Flowers are sent to the house of mourning and to funerals in testimony of our sincere regret. There is no particular sentiment in large and costly set pieces, doves surmounting broken columns, gates ajar, pillows on which legends are written. A few flowers, long-stemmed and fragrant, a palm branch, a sheaf tied with white ribbon, a cluster of lilies, a simple wreath, have each and all a significance beyond that of mere display. I have seen a coffin covered with a pall of purple violets, and a grave lined with roses. These were tokens of sorrow, which children displayed at the burial of their parents.

In recent fiction there is no tenderer scene than the description by Ian MacLaren of the funeral of Doctor Maclure in " The Bonny Brier Bush." The snow lies deep and white in the glen, the drifts are high, the wind is cold. But the shepherds, the farmers and the lord of the manor make nothing of the winter nor the tempest. They attend the good man's funeral, follow him to his grave, and stand bareheaded while the minister prays.

> " The while my pulses faintly beat,
>   My faith doth so abound,
> I feel grow firm beneath my feet
>   The green, immortal ground."

So, anticipating the hour of her departure, sang dear Alice Cary, her strain akin to that triumphal hymn of her sister Phœbe, familiar to us all:

> " One sweetly solemn thought
>   Comes to me o'er and o'er,
> I'm nearer my home in heaven to-day
>   Than ever I've been before.
>
> " Nearer the bound of life,
>   Laying my burdens down,
> Nearer leaving the cross,
>   Nearer wearing the crown."

Christina Rossetti, in a poem on Good Friday, exclaims:

> " Am I a stone, and not a sheep,
>     That I can stand, O Christ, beneath Thy cross,
>     To number drop by drop Thy blood's slow loss,
>     And yet not weep?
>
> " Not so those women loved,
>     Who with exceeding grief lamented Thee,
>     Not so fallen Peter, weeping bitterly,
>     Not so the thief was moved." '

In Bishop Westcott's remarkable book, "The Revelation of the Risen Lord," he dwells on the return of the Master after the three days in the grave, the same yet different, and shows by a convincing argument from the Scriptures how the " thought of that life, of that Providence, of that presence, of that communion, of that mystery of pain, has passed into the world and become part of the heritage of mankind." Good Friday and Easter belong to us and are our treasures beyond price. The old hymn sung by God's people for centuries cries out exultingly:

> " He who bore all pain and loss
>     Comfortless upon the cross,
>     Lives in glory now on high,
>     Pleads for us and hears our cry."

The very core of the Easter consolation is in that simple line, " Pleads for us and hears our cry." For our Christ is the Lord of the living, alone able to say, " I am He that liveth and was dead, and behold, I am alive forevermore." The Easter music, the Easter flowers, the Easter joy are comprehended in that statement that our Brother, our Redeemer, our Master, daily sees our needs and daily presents our prayers and pleads for us, too, and never a moment of any day forgets one of us whom He loves.

Easter is to Christmas as the flower to the bud. Between the two great holy days there stretches the whole of the Christ-life on the earth, the healing of the sick, the giving of sight to the blind, the going about on the hills and through the vales of Galilee, the words He spoke, the deeds He did, from the hour that His ministry began until He cried, " It is finished," upon Calvary. The most amazing period in the story of time, those three years in which God tabernacled in human flesh, is commemorated in two small places, Bethlehem and Easter—the one with the star-beam, the other with the day-dawn, the one with those who worshiped at the cradle, the other with those who sought the garden tomb, and both with the help and song of the angelic visitors who came to serve their Lord.

In Bunyan's " Pilgrim's Progress " there is a passage which I think especially suitable to the Eastertide. Christian and his fellow-pilgrim, Hopeful, have arrived at the gate over which is written, in letters of gold, " Blessed are they that do His commandments, that they may have right to the tree of life, and may enter in through the gates into the city." And as, at the word of the King, they entered in and were transfigured, there were those that met them with harps to praise withal, and with crowns in token of honor. Then, says Bunyan, "I heard in my dream that all the bells in the city rang again for joy, and that it was said unto them, 'Enter ye into the joy of your Lord.'" One more radiant glimpse is vouchsafed to the dreamer, and he adds, "After that they shut up the gates, which when I had seen I wished myself among them."

The comfort of Easter is largely in the closer union it gives us with heaven. A great company of our friends and kindred are there. For some of us the number on the other side is much in excess of the number here. And Christ is there, the Christ of Nazareth, of Galilee, and of this waning century and this country of ours as well. Often we are amazed at our insensibility to the suffering Christ. Often we are vexed at our lack of loyalty to the reigning Christ. Yet there are days when the stony hearts melt and we have throbbing hearts of flesh. There are days when our love goes joyously out to greet our King. And evermore, not at Eastertide only but in all tides of time,

"He who bore our pain and loss"

lives for our redemption.

---

## An Easter Idyl.

Many a year the Easter came, laughing o'er land and sea,
    Wafting the perfume of lilies wherever its dawn light fell,
Kindling the flames of the roses, and waving their torches free,
    Far over hill and mountain, and deep in the lonesome dell.

And many a year at Easter I sat in the old church loft,
    And lifted my voice in Te Deums, and sang like a mavis clear,
Sang of glory and triumph, and my voice thrilled sweet and soft,
    Oh! many a time in the Easter of many a cloudless year.

Till there fell a season of anguish, when the stars went out in the sky,
    When I covered my face, and bent my knees, and beat with a hopeless prayer
At the golden gates of heaven that were shut to my bitter cry,
    While the Angel of Death at my threshold was deaf to my love's despair.

Then, straight on that wild, bleak winter there followed the fairest spring,
    With snowdrops and apple blossoms in riotous haste to bloom,
With the sudden note of the robin, and the flash of the bluebird's wing
    And all that was mine of its beauty was the turf that covered a tomb.

23

Oh ! the bells rang out for Easter, rang strong and sweet and shrill,
  And the organ's rolling thunder pealed through the long church aisle,
And the children fluttered with flowers, and I sat mute and still,
  I, who had clean forgotten both how to pray and to smile.

And I murmured in fierce rebellion : "There is naught that endures below,
  Naught but the lamentations that are rent from souls in pain;"
And the joy of the Easter music, it struck on my ears like a blow,
  For I knew that my day was over, I could never be glad again !

And then—how it happened I know not—there was One in my sight who stood,
  And lo ! on His brow was the thorn-print, in His hands were the nails' rough
      scars,
And the shadow that lay before Him was the shade of the holy rood,
  But the glow in His eyes was deeper than the light of the morning stars.

"Daughter," He said, "have comfort ! Arise ! keep Eastertide !
  I, for thy sins who suffered and died on the cruel tree,
I, who was dead, am living; no evil shall e'er betide
  Those who, beyond or waiting, are pledged unto life with Me."

Now I wake to a holier Easter, happier than of old,
  And again my voice is lifted in Te Deums sweet and strong;
I send it to join the anthem in the wonderful city of gold,
  Where the hymns of the ransomed forever are timed to the Easter song.

And I can be glad with the gladness that is born of a perfect peace;
  On the strength of the Strong I am resting; I know that His will is best.
And who that has found that secret from darkness has won release,
  And even in sorrow's exile may lift up her eyes and be blessed.

## The Sweet, Long Days.

The sweet, long days when the morning breaks
  Over the mountains in rose and gold,
When the shadows linger on vale and lakes
  And the afterglow tints field and wold.
The summer days when the pasture land
  Lies dappled with daisies beneath the sun,
When the waves wash up on the pebbly strand,
  And the little ripples leap and run.

# THE SWEET, LONG DAYS.

THE PASTURE LAND.

The sweet, long days when the children play
  Merry and sweet as the day is long,
Driving the cows, and tossing the hay,
  And singing many a snatch of song.
When mother is busy from morn till eve,
  And father is earning the children's bread;
In every task when a prayer they weave
  For blessings to rest on each little head.

The sweet, long days when though trouble may come,
    We bear the trouble in trustful cheer,
For ever in God is our constant home,
    A refuge and shelter from grief and fear.
The sweet, long days which our Father sends,
    Foretaste and pattern of days to be,
In the time when the measure by days shall end,
    On the fadeless shore of the Crystal Sea.

## Our Lost.

They never quite leave us, our friends who have passed
    Through the shadows of death to the sunlight above;
A thousand sweet memories are holding them fast
    To the places they blessed with their presence and love.


The work which they left and the books which they read
    Speak mutely, though still with an eloquence rare,
And the songs that they sung, and dear words that they said,
    Yet linger and sigh on the desolate air.


And oft when alone, and as oft in the throng,
    Or when evil allures us or sin draweth nigh,
A whisper comes gently, " Nay, do not the wrong,"
    And we feel that our weakness is pitied on high.


In the dew-threaded morn and the opaline eve,
    When the children are merry or crimsoned with sleep,
We are confronted, even as lonely we grieve,
    For the thought of their rapture forbids us to weep.


We toil at our tasks in the burden and heat
    Of life's passionate noon.   They are folded in peace.
It is well.   We rejoice that their heaven is sweet,
    And one day for us will all bitterness cease.

## OUR LOST.

We, too, will go home o'er the river of rest,
　As the throng and the lovely before us have gone;
Our sun will go down in the beautiful west,
　To rise in the glory that circles the throne.

Until then we are bound by our love and our faith
　To the saints who are walking in Paradise fair.
They have passed beyond sight, at the touching of death,
　But they live, like ourselves, in God's infinite care.

# CHAPTER XLVIII.

## The Sunshiny Household.

SUNSHINE saves the world. If you want to kill a plant or a human being you need only shut either up in a crypt and rob it of the life-giving influences of heat and light. No wonder that in all ages by stairways of sunbeams our thoughts have climbed to heaven; no wonder that men, ignorantly seeking a God to worship yet knowing Him not, have found in the sun His best type and symbol. A sunshiny household is the abode of good-natured people. It is not the residence of the churl or the miser, not the home of the cross or the despotic, or the morbid, or the gloomy. Only brightness and cheer may dwell in the sunshiny house.

The young people in this home are not afraid of their father. His countenance is not frowning and repellent, his presence is no signal for silence. The mother is the queen of her realm, and where she is there can be only pleasure and delight!

In the sunshiny home the mother is not crowded out by her young folk from her true place. There are homes wherein the mother has no rest to the sole of her foot, so aggressive are the juniors. Elsie and her young friends monopolize the parlor, Louise and her lessons occupy the sitting room, Jack and his arithmetic and geography quite fill the vacant spaces in the dining room, and mamma must sit in her own chamber or go to bed. Truth to tell, her own room is not the least charming refuge in the household, for father comes there to sit in his old dressing gown and shabby slippers, Kitty and Mamie would rather stay with mother than in their own room or with their sisters, and the mother's room is the rallying place for the family in their hours of ease and enjoyment.

In the sunshiny household there are certain stock stories which everybody knows, certain anecdotes which everybody enjoys, certain allusions and reminiscences which are part of the general family fund, and which they would remember and share though they were divided by the width of the globe.

The sunshiny household is a loyal one. The family bond holds. The family stands by its several members and by its absent ones, and if there be one who has *ways* and must be protected that one is surrounded by the rest and most gently cared for. "The youngest Miss Archer," said my friend, " is not very bright and has a very bad temper." "Indeed!" I replied; "why she seems to be the special favorite." "Yes, they all regret her infirmity and shield her from herself and from criticism."

In Miss Muloch's charming novel of "Mistress and Maid" there are several very admirable lessons for us, among them the devotion of Miss Leaf and Miss Hilary to the very fretful and irritable Miss Selina, who had "ways." And the bearing of the sisters with their stupid, unformed servant Elizabeth, who develops under the tutelage of love and gentleness into a treasure of skill, good sense and absolute loyalty, is worth our studying. Few women may not derive help in the management of their domestics from the perusal of this account of Elizabeth Hand and Miss Hilary Leaf.

Elizabeth did not know how to write and the bright little lady, with infinite pains, undertook to teach her— no easy task.

"She is stupid enough," Hilary confessed, after the first lesson was over, "but there is a dogged perseverance about the girl which I actually admire."

"I hope she will do her work, anyhow," said Selina, rather crossly. "I'm sure I don't see the good of wasting time over teaching Elizabeth to write when there's so much to be done in the house by one and all of us from Monday morning till Saturday night."

Selina, poor thing, was doomed always to be the stumbling-block in the peace of this family. When Hilary proposed to give Elizabeth writing lessons on Sunday, because there really was so little time through the week, this sister was much offended. She opposed the plan as usual, vehemently, and with stubborn anger, but Hilary interposed amiably:

"I might say that writing isn't Elizabeth's week-day work, and that teaching her is not exactly doing my own pleasure; but I won't creep out of the argument by a quibble. The question is, What is keeping the Sabbath-day 'holy?' I say—and I stick to my opinion—that it is by making it a day of worship, a rest day—a cheerful and happy day—and by doing as much good in it as we can; and, therefore, I mean to teach Elizabeth on a Sunday."

"She'll never understand it. She'll consider it 'work.'"

"And if she did, work is a more religious thing than idleness. I am sure I often feel that, of the two, I should be less sinful in digging potatoes in my garden, or sitting mending stockings in my parlor, than in keeping Sunday as some people do—going to church genteelly in my best clothes, eating a huge Sunday dinner, and then nodding over a good book, or taking a regular Sunday nap, till bedtime."

"Hush, child!" said Johanna, reprovingly; for Hilary's cheeks were red, and her voice angry. She was taking the hot, youthful part, which, in its hatred of shams and forms, sometimes leads—and not seldom led poor Hilary—a little too far on the other side. " I think," Miss Leaf added, "that our business is with ourselves, and not with our neighbors. Let us keep the Sabbath according to our conscience. Only, I would take care never to do anything which jarred against my neighbor's feelings. I would, like Paul, 'eat no meat while the world standeth' rather than 'make my brother to offend.' "

Hilary looked in her sister's sweet, calm face, and the anger died out of her own.

"Shall I give up my academy ?" she said, softly.

"No, my love. It is lawful to do good on the Sabbath day, and teaching a poor ignorant girl to write is an absolute good. Make her understand that, and you need not be afraid of any harm ensuing." ·

"You never will make her understand," said Selina, sullenly. " She is only a servant."

"Nevertheless, I'll try."

Hilary could not tell how far she succeeded in simplifying to the young servant's comprehension this great question, involving so many points—such as the following of the spirit and the letter, the law of duty and the compulsion of love, which, as she spoke, seemed opening out so widely and awfully that she herself involuntarily shrank from it, and wondered that poor, finite creatures should ever presume to squabble about it at all.

But one thing the girl did understand—her young mistress' kindness. She stood watching the little delicate hand that had so patiently guided hers, and now wrote copy after copy for her future benefit. At last she said:

"You're taking a deal o' trouble wi' a poor wench, and it's very kind in a lady like you."

The day arrived when Elizabeth Hand more than repaid, full measure, pressed down and running over, the great kindness of Miss Hilary, and this leads me to say that one great element of sunshine in any home is the maintenance of cordial relations between the employer and the employed, the mistress and the servant or servants. In our country many women get on very comfortably with no help—many more keep one maid, others maintain an establishment, but these are in the minority. The household is far from sunny where a ceaseless warfare is going on, suspicion on the one side and surveillance on the other. Fair and just dealing between the two contracting parties, work clearly indicated, and duties precisely defined, and wages promptly paid, with always the recollection that servants are human, will do much toward keeping home-life calm and beautiful.

Parents, too, must observe that children sometimes fret at needless restraints, and must not too readily say no to innocent and reasonable desires for amusement and pleasure. Children grow up and are beyond authority sometimes, while parents still fancy them in a state of pupilage. Hence may arise needless friction and pain which should never have been allowed to creep into sensitive natures. Take short views. Make the best of existing circumstances. Envy no one. Be not covetous. Look not every man on his own things, but every man on the things of others. For, even Christ pleased not Himself.

Thinking of the fullest sunlight we must rise to a higher level.

Thank God that in this world of mingled experiences there comes to us now and then the day when we carry the full cup ! Our hearts are brimmed with gladness, and for the time we forget that we have had burdens to bear and that

" You're taking a deal o' trouble."

sorrows have set their stamp upon our faces. Out of the shadows we emerge into the sunlight, our plans are successfully completed, our hopes are fulfilled, our homes are delightful, our way is smooth and straight before us—it is our happy day of victory and of joy.

But we do not need to be reminded that it takes a steady hand to carry a full cup. We are in danger of slipping, of stumbling, of becoming over-confident and heedless in the elation which naturally follows a signal triumph or an unex-pected accession of good fortune. Many a man has been saintly in reverses who

grows arrogant and arbitrary in his period of success, and poverty is less trying
to the spiritual life than wealth.   The full cup requires special grace that none of
its sweetness be changed to bitterness, that its possessor remain loving and unselfish,
that about its silver rim may be wreathed the white blossoms of faith and charity.
In the day of adversity consider, was written by one of old.   Equally in the day
of prosperity should we draw near to the throne, keeping our eyes fixed on the
kindly face of the Master, endeavoring more than ever to do His will in our
hours of freedom, ease and contentment, making our very happiness a votive-
offering at His feet.

    God never gives to man or woman the full cup, except that he or she may
make of it a benediction.   All the rivers run into the sea.   All through nature
there is continual giving in return for constant receiving.   When the cup is full,
it is so that it may overflow in kindness and abundant blessedness upon others,
itself then being replenished, like the horn of Thor, from an inexhaustible fountain.   There are always opportunities of service for those who have the will and
the ability to accept them, and so no one need stand helplessly holding a full cup in
hand, wondering what God's meaning is and what would best be done for His
praise.

    In our own household there may be a dear one, a child perhaps, who is mis-
understood, an invalid to whom weary days are appointed, an aged one who is in
sore need of ministries of affection, or a servant who is homesick in a strange land,
a veritable stranger within our gates.   To any or all of these our appointed work
may be to give of our store of gladness.

    Always we should begin with our Christian work at the Jerusalem of our own
homes, but from thence we should broaden out in ever-widening circles of kindness and love.   A neighbor, a friend, a mission near us, an orphanage or a hospital, may be the better for our conscientious care.   One cannot be sure that a
tangible gift, as of money or service, is the only thing required.   A "gift without
the giver is bare," and she who bestows only alms, without personal interest and
affection added thereto, does not carry out God's intention when He puts in her
hand the full cup of revenue, of success, or of earthly bliss in any of its innumer-
able forms.

    I know a beautiful woman who has never in her life had anything to give
except the overflowing grace and friendliness of a beautiful and consecrated soul.
This soul, a temple for the indwelling Christ, glows in her lovely face, thrills in
her invariably sincere and gentle speech, and makes a visit to her or from her a
rare and uplifting delight.   Her cup is ever full, because she is innately happy,
because she accepts without a murmur all of God's appointments, and bears, with
unbroken serenity, every care and burden which comes to her from His hand.
One is truly living the blessed life who has attained to that condition where a

consciousness of heaven pervades one's mortal days.   This is to have a cup of
perennial fullness, even when the skies are darkened.

> 'Tis but the meagre crust, love,
> 'Tis but the scanty cup.
> On homely fare we breakfast,
> On homely fare we sup.

Never mind!   When the King meets us on the road and condescends to our
fare it becomes a royal feast, and the supply of heavenly manna is pledged never
to fail the pilgrim who accepts the old conditions and is fain to gather just enough
each day for that day's demand.

You see we cannot expect that the full cup shall always be ours.   It may
come to pass, because it is God's will, that in a moment everything earthly for us
shall be changed—everything in our home and our environment be so altered that
we hardly recognize it or ourselves.   Sorrow comes upon us like a flood, like an
invading army, like a great wind from the wilderness, "Even so, Father, for so
it seemeth good in Thy sight," and, "If this cup may not pass from me, Thy
will be done," our hearts will cry if their lifelong habit has been one of agreement
with the divine ordering.   For in the day of the full cup and in the day of the
empty one alike we belong, do we not, to the Lord who bought us, whose we are
and whom we serve?

## At the Parting of the Ways.

"Go forth in thy turn," said the Lord of the years, to the year we greet to-day—
"Go forth to succor my people, who are thronging the world's highway.

"Carry them health and comfort, carry them joy and light,
The grace of the eager dawning, the ease of the restful night.

"Take them the flying snowflake, and the hope of the hastening spring,
The green of the leaf unrolling, the gleam of the bluebird's wing.

"Give them the gladness of children, the strength of sinew and nerve,
The pluck of the man in battle, who may fall, but will never swerve.

"Send them the lilt of the singer, the sword that is swift to smite
In the headlong rush of the onset, when the wrong resists the right.

."Pour on them peace that crowneth hosts which have bravely striven.
Over them throw the mantle they wear who are God-forgiven.

"Shrive them of sin and of blunders; Oh, make my people free!
Let this year among years be thought of as a time of jubilee,

"Throbbing with notes triumphant, waving with banners fair,
A year of the grace of the Highest, to vanquish human despair.

"For sorrow and sighing send them, O Year, the dance of mirth,
And banish the moan and the crying from the struggling, orphaned earth.

"Go forth in thy turn, O blithe New Year," said the Lord of the passing days;
And the angels in heaven heard Him and lifted a pæan of praise.

## The Mother's Room.

The core of the house, the dearest place, the one that we all love best,
Holding it close in our heart of hearts, for its comfort and its rest,
Is never the place where strangers come, nor yet where friends are met,
Is never the stately drawing room, where our treasured things are set.
Oh, dearer far as the time recedes in a dream of colors dim,
Breathing across our stormy moods like the echo of a hymn,
Forever our own, and only ours, and pure as a rose in bloom,
Is the centre and soul of the old home nest, the mother's darling room.

We flew to its arms when we rushed from school, with a thousand things to tell;
Our mother was always waiting there, had the day gone ill or well.
No other pillow was quite so cool, under an aching head,
As soft to our fevered childish cheek, as the pillow on mother's bed.
Sitting so safely at her feet, when the dewy dusk drew nigh,
We watched for the angels to light the lamps in the solemn evening sky.
Tiny hands folded, there we knelt, to lisp the nightly prayer,
Learning to cast on the Loving One early our load of care.
Whatever the world has brought us since, yet, pure as a rose in bloom,
Is the thought we keep of the core of the home, the mother's darling room.

We think of it oft in the glare and heat of our lifetime's later day,
Around our steps when the wild spray beats, and the mirk is gathering gray.
As once to the altar's foot they ran whom the menacing foe pursued,
We turn to the still and sacred place where a foe may never intrude,

And there, in the hush of remembered hours, our failing souls grow strong,
And gird themselves anew for the fray, the battle of right and wrong.
Behind us ever the hallowed thought, as pure as a rose in bloom,
Of the happiest place in all the earth, the mother's darling room.

We've not forgotten the fragrant sheaves of the lilacs at the door,
Nor the ladder of sunbeams lying prone on the shining morning floor.
We've not forgotten the robin's tap at the ever friendly pane,
Nor the lilt of the little brook outside, trolling its gay refrain.
How it haunts us yet, in the tender hour of the sunset's fading blush,
The vesper song, so silvery clear, of the hidden hermit thrush!
All sweetest of sound and scent is blent, when, pure as a rose in bloom,
We think of the spot loved best in life, the mother's darling room.

Holding us close to the best in life, keeping us back from sin,
Folding us yet to her faithful breast, oft as a prize we win,
The mother who left us here alone to battle with care and strife
Is the guardian angel who leads us on to the fruit of the tree of life.
Her smile from the heights we hope to gain is an ever-beckoning lure;
We catch her look when our pulses faint, nerving us to endure.
Others may dwell where once she dwelt, and the home be ours no more,
But the thought of her is a sacred spell, never its magic o'er.
We're truer and stronger and braver yet, that, pure as a rose in bloom,
Back of all struggle, a heart of peace, is the mother's darling room.

----

## Sage! Thyme! Sweet-Marjoram!

"Sage! thyme! sweet-marjoram!"
    Down the crowded street,
    O'er the trampling feet.
Of the myriad throngs of men,
    'Neath the brilliant sky,
    Rings out the cry.
I hear it now and then,
    Vibrant and clear,
    As far and near
    O'er the noises all
    The vender's call,
"Sage! thyme! sweet-marjoram!"

"Sage ! thyme ! sweet-marjoram !"
  Of the purple hills
  Where the lone thrush trills
In his hermitage at eve;
  Of the soft gray mists
  And the amethysts
The looms of the morning weave;
  Of acres sown,
  By the four winds blown
From the heavens wide and free—
  I think at the fall
  Of the vender's call,
"Sage ! thyme ! sweet-marjoram !"

"Sage ! thyme ! sweet-marjoram !"
  Was it yesterday
  Or an age away,
When a child at my mother's knee,
  In the dim old space
  Of a garden place,
Where these dear things used to be,
  I gathered rue,
  Rosemary, too,
  And the herbs she loved,
  And her skill approved ?
"Sage ! thyme ! sweet-marjoram !"

"Sage ! thyme ! sweet-marjoram !"
  No drawing-room
  Cares for their bloom;
They are kitchen herbs, no doubt.
  Just simples three
  For the mystery
The cook knows all about.
  And their very name,
  In the hearth-light's flame,
Stirs the rhyme that the kettle sings,
  As down the street,
  With its myriad feet,

And over the hoof-beat's fall,
   Over and over—
   Daisies and clover—
   I hear the vender's call,
" Sage ! thyme ! sweet-marjoram '"

## Polly's Coming Home.

Tell the neighbors, Lish, as you drive to-night,
   That Polly, my Polly, is coming home,
That's why the place looks alive with light,
   That's why I've put on my silver comb
And my best black silk, and have set the table
   With honey and chicken and yellow cream,
And have gathered roses and ferns and heather,
   And made her room like a fairy's dream.

Polly, my Polly ! I've watched all day,
   Doing my work in a happy maze,—
I've traveled down from that great hot town,
   And counted the mile-stones, glad to gaze
On the dear old birches all a-quiver,
   And the fields with the daisies gold and white,
And the tangle of green on the edge of the river.
   I've laughed to see them with Polly's sight.

Down the hollow and up the rise,
   The old stage coach has rumbled along,
Climbing our hills that melt in the skies,
   Skirting our brooks so swift and strong.
Polly, my Polly, home from college,
   Coming back to her Dad and me !
Lish, as you drive, just tell the neighbors,
   They'll all be glad as glad can be.

Father, here, quick with the lantern, please,
   The stage is turning in at our lane,
I feel the blood growing weak at my knees,
   I'm dizzy with joy, 'tis love's sweet pain.
Oh ! here is my girl, she flies to mother,
   Straight as ever a bird to her nest,
Darling, my Polly, 'twas lonesome without you,
   Welcome to them that love you best.

# CHAPTER XLIX.

## What to Do, and How to Do It.

MUCH reading of the best manual of etiquette in the world, never yet, by itself, made any woman familiar with social forms, or gave any man ease of manner in company. Good manners constantly practiced at home, refinement of thought and speech, courtesy, consideration for others, common sense, and association with polite people, will make any of us fit to stand in Her Majesty's palace, or to wait in the courts of kings.

Here are a few Don'ts, and a few Dos:

Don't slam a door.

Don't interrupt conversation.

Don't forget to lift your hat to a lady in the street, to your wife, your mother, or your daughter, to women in an elevator, to women anywhere indoors.

Don't eat with your knife.

Don't use slang, or profanity.

Don't stare at strangers.

Don't fidget in church, or consult your watch when the sermon begins to weary you.

Don't use double negatives.

Don't misplace your pronouns. It is not right to say, "Aunt Lucy has invited Emily and *I* to dinner to-morrow," though hosts of people do put it in that way.

Don't look over the shoulder of a fellow passenger and read his morning paper.

Don't push or crowd rudely anywhere.

Don't think first how a proceeding will affect yourself.

Do be kind and amiable in the family.

Do be punctual at meals.

Do attend social meetings where your presence will give an additional pleasure.

Do promptly and in good condition return a borrowed article.

Do introduce people who may be mutually agreeable acquaintances.

Do make welcome strangers to your pew, and practice hospitality in your home life.

Do praise your wife or your husband.

Do take pains to have your dress attractive, and your usual demeanor genial.

Do listen with patience to an oft-told tale.

Do restrain yourself when you feel an inclination to set somebody right when the case is of an anecdote in which details are trivial and unimportant.

Do hesitate before you accuse any one else of being inconsistent.

Do acknowledge invitations promptly, accepting or declining at once.

Do keep punctiliously an engagement once you have made it.

Do pay attention in society to the older people.

Do rise and give a seat in a public conveyance to a woman, a mother carrying an infant, or an elderly gentleman.

Mrs. Sherwood tells us that the young married woman who comes to New York, or any other large city, often passes years of loneliness before she has made her acquaintances. She is properly introduced, we will say by her mother-in-law or some other friend, and then, after a round of visits in which she has but, perhaps, imperfectly apprehended the positions and names of her new acquaintances, she has a long illness, or she is called into mourning, or the cares of the nursery surround her, and she is shut out from society until it has forgotten her; and when she is ready to emerge, it is difficult for her to find her place again in the visiting-book. If she is energetic and clever, she surmounts this difficulty by giving a series of receptions, or engaging in charities, or working on some committee, making herself of use to society in some way; and thus picks up her dropped stitches. But some young women are without the courage and tact to do such a thing; they wait, expecting that society will find them out, and, taking them up, will do all the work and leave them to accept or refuse civilities as they please. Society never does this; it has too much on its hands; a few conspicuously beautiful and gifted people may occasionally receive such an ovation, but it is not for the rank and file.

There is no necessity for calling after a tea or general reception if one has attended the festivity, or has left or sent a card on that day.

For reception days a lady wears a plain, dark, rich dress, taking care, however, never to be overdressed at home. She rises when her visitors enter, and is careful to seat her friends so that she can have a word with each. If this is impossible, she keeps her eye on the recent arrivals to be sure to speak to every one. She is to be forgiven if she pays more attention to the aged, to some distinguished stranger, or to some one who has the still higher claim of misfortune, or to one of a modest and shrinking temperament, than to one young, gay, fashionable, and rich. If she neglects these fortunate visitors they will not feel it; if she bows low to them and neglects the others, she betrays that she is a snob. If a lady is not sure that she is known by sight to her hostess, she should not fail to pronounce her own name. Many ladies send their cards to the young brides who have come into a friend's family, and yet who are without personal acquaintance. Many, alas! forget faces, so that a name quickly pronounced is a help. In the event of an exchange of calls between two ladies who have never met (and this has gone on for years in New York, sometimes until death has removed one forever) they should take an early opportunity of speaking to each other at some friend's house; the younger should approach the elder and introduce herself; it is always regarded as a kindness; or the one who has received the first attention should be the first to speak.

In the matter of entertaining guests—distinguished or otherwise—there are two sides, the guest's and the entertainer's. It is doubtless true that family life, in its present complex organization and busy arrangements, does not lend itself to the entertainment of visitors for any length of time without much added care and anxiety on the part of the mistress of the home. In the olden time when the friendly guest came early in the morning to stay all day, it was not unusual for her to "take hold" and help the mistress of the house in whatever work might press. There are many of us who can recall the welcome kinswoman or neighbor, who in the days of our childhood made the hearts of the whole family glad by her coming for a day. She would nestle so harmoniously into the circumstances and needs of the family; she would finish hemming the set of napkins so much needed; she would dispatch a whole darning basket of stockings or buttonless garments; she would go right out into the kitchen and make a new kind of dessert which all would enjoy for dinner. And all the while the friendly flow of neighborly talk would murmur on, to all of which the children would listen with unfeigned delight. Perchance the friendly guest's husband came also, and he would make himself equally agreeable, picking the peas for dinner, or hulling the strawberries for tea. Oh, those simple, homely, loving visits of bygone days! We shall never see them more. They have vanished from home and society before the advancing march of railroad time-tables, electric cars, foreign domestics in our homes and clubs and reading circles for women with their necessary exactingness of time and place. No one dares now to drop into the family life of the nearest and dearest friend or kinsman. We do not know what arrangements we may upset. We can no longer "help out" in family occupations, for all are gone —delegated to the seamstress or the cook or the autocratic Bridget who wants neither the mistress nor her guests "bothering round." What shall ever supply to us those good old days of kindly entertaining and being entertained?

*    *    *    *    *    *    *    *    *

The best entertainment we can offer to our guests in our homes to-day is conversation—ourselves. Every other kind of entertainment palls or becomes a weariness. The pleasures of the table, looking at pictures, riding or rowing,

THE RECEPTION.

meeting other invited guests—all these may be pleasant incidents of a visit, but they are mere incidents. The first consideration then when we would invite a guest is—would he or she really enjoy the companionship we have to offer? has he or she sufficient interests in common with us to make it worth our while to spend our time or theirs in entertaining and being entertained? What a disappointment in this respect is many a guest—especially many a distinguished guest! Especially if he (or she) is a writer, and therefore accustomed to express thought through the pen rather than orally, is he apt to be silent, lacking in personal magnetism, absent-minded and unsatisfactory!

There are, however, distinguished guests, writers, orators, musicians, artists, whom to entertain is to have forever after a red letter day in memory. There are such guests who overflow with kindly and interested conversation; guests who do not ignore with cool indifference the children or the aged—both of whom have such especial interest and pleasure in the diversion of a guest. There are guests who can come into the family like a tone of music sounding in harmony with family chord. They do not keep meals waiting; they do not order the servants; they do not presume upon the hospitality shown to cause inconvenience or in any way interrupt family life. They do not mar the beauty of the guest room by unseemly splashings or personal disorder; their presence is a benediction; their going causes heartfelt regret. Such guests do not accept hospitality and afterwards speak slightingly or critically of their entertainers. How unfortunate then that such guests are so frequently the visitors of "tuft hunters" whose only object in entertaining them is to distinguish themselves or their families. What discoveries of inanity and presumption do such guests sometimes make in accepting hospitality! It is not without reason that distinguished guests so often declare their preference for a hotel. It is a disappointment to a refined man (or woman) to be importuned away from a hotel and then to find that he is expected to share the room of a younger member of the family, or that all his time is laid out for him without any special regard for his own convenience or preferences. Truly there is wide opportunity for the exercise of the finest sense of propriety, the finest good breeding as well as good sense, both in the matter of entertaining and being entertained.

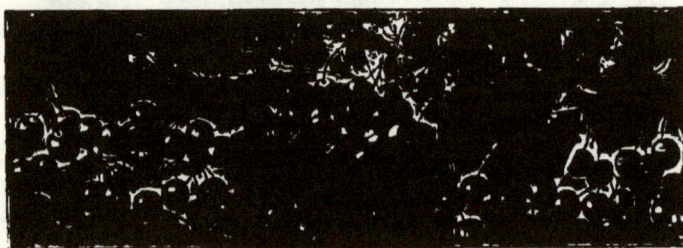

# CHAPTER L.

## Church Work.

HURCH work falls more than it ought on a few, there being in most congregations a select number who bear the burdens for the majority, on whom the pastor depends, and to whom he Church authorities turn in time of need. Help these women who labored with me in the Lord, may be the rayer of the modern minister, as it was of the ancient Apostle. Women, taking their full share of Church work, find it largely made up of visiting the stranger and the sick, of carrying forward foreign and home missions, and of raising money for the present needs, or future exigencies of the parish. Is a parsonage to be built, either at home or on a far western frontier, it is the women of the Church who will contribute the funds to do it with. Is a medical missionary to go to the zenanas of India, or to Yokohama, or Amoy, the Ladies' Aid Society will send her forth. Whatever is to be done as an extra, as *plus* to what the Church has done already, it will be the women's part to undertake, most heartily, cheerfully and ungrudgingly. In the face of the fact that women have a very slight personal hold as a rule on the family exchequer, that, unless they are wage-earners, they have little direct command of money. They can and do and always will, largely increase the sum of the Church's liberality.

Women have proved by harmonious and valuable organized effort that they can sink the individual preference and act for the good of the whole. That they can labor without regard to personal recognition, that with them Christ is the Supreme Dictator, and the grand motive power. As King's Daughters, as members of the Young Women's Christian Association, and as professing Christians, they are nobly helping forward God's Kingdom.

That they must work by means of fairs and festivals, suppers, and concerts and entertainments, is in a measure, their misfortune, but it should not be forgotten that the social side of all these functions has its excellent aspect, bringing together people who would else never know one another, except superficially, and thus unifying the work of the Church, and making its families acquainted. In a city congregation this is an especially happy circumstance.

(373)

Women and men too undertake Church work, aggressive and enthusiastic, in their Sunday Schools and Christian Endeavor Societies.

The obligation laid on us every one is to do our full share, not to shirk anything, not to leave for others what we should ourselves undertake.

Bishop Potter, writing to " Christian Women," pithily observes:

" I can offer no better prayer for you, or for the work you are doing for our Master, than that, in that work, you may each one of you illustrate a whole womanhood, rounded and complete and symmetrical, healthy in body, acute and vigorous in mind, but above all upward-looking and expectant in Faith, trusting in the Leader who leads you, confident because of the strength which He alone can give.   Says the Apostle, ' Ye are complete *in Him !*' Expressive word.    It is the *whole* womanhood that we want.''

Church work very naturally focuses around the home of the minister, the manse, or parsonage.

I have an affection for the old word manse, designating the home of the minister, and bringing up a throng of beautiful domesticities and simple hospitalities whenever it appears on the printed page.   In our country, where the pastor lives in his own hired house, as a rule, and not in a house owned by the parish and set aside for the clergyman's use, the "manse" has only a poetical meaning, but the minister's wife is as dear and sweet a reality as in any moss-grown or ivy-mantled manse in the world.

We hear it stoutly affirmed in many quarters that the mistress of the manse, as we shall call her for the sake of convenience in this bit of talk, is of no more account in the congregation which her husband serves than is any other lady there.   She is not included in the contract, has no stipulated obligations, draws no salary, is in every way independent and free and, so far as the parish is concerned, is a mere private gentlewoman.   All of which is in a manner true.   At the same time, the truth is at best to be accepted with qualifications.   Let it be supposed, for example, that the minister, marrying in his youth, has fallen upon those evil days which are the portion of the man who marries for beauty only; let us fancy him with a vain, or silly, or petulant, perhaps with a poorly educated and ill-disciplined, wife.   Does anybody for an instant think that he will not be very much handicapped professionally, his career of usefulness impaired, by this unfortunate marriage?   Granting that in any social position a man's rank and value largely depend on the sort of a wife he has taken to himself, is not the man in the ministry, whose candle cannot be hidden under a bushel but must shine conspicuously in the sight of the whole town, in a worse condition if he have not a creditable and sensible helpmeet ?

Providentially, ministers' wives, as I have known them, have been usually women of rare loveliness, amazing tact and charming discretion.   They easily take precedence among gifted and agreeable women, and they take hold of their end of their husbands' work with wonderful command of resources and unfailing courage; for the instances are few in which something is not expected of them by the congregation, or else in which, expected or otherwise, they do not womanfully —I had almost said manfully, but the other word is better—share the crosses and the losses of the day, conciliate the offended, soothe the irritated, and in many a quiet, unsuspected way sustain their husbands in their work of love and constant toil.

A popular minister's wife makes very secure her husband's position in a difficult parish. A beloved minister's wife helps to win love to her husband.

In a certain parish, where there were peculiarly inharmonious elements, several pastors in turn did their best, but retired vanquished from the field. Finally a man accepted the post, fully aware of the various causes of trouble, the jealousies between the young people and the older people, the feuds between certain families, and the clashing of interests which had made the church in question a reproach and a by-word. Meeting the brave pastor after he had held the position with increasing success for several years, I asked him how it was that he had not been defeated too.

"Under God," he said, "I owe everything here to Lizzie. She captured all hearts from the first. There isn't a home in the parish where her influence is not felt. The women adore her, the young people consult her. She is the confidante of the whole congregation. I never could have gained a foothold here had I not been aided by my wife."

It is not every husband, nor even every clergyman, who is candid and discerning enough to see and own how large a debt he owes to the unselfish and gentle comrade who stands gallantly by his side in all life's emergencies and vicissitudes. I liked the man who acknowledged so ungrudgingly the debt he owed to "Lizzie."

The manse sets a pattern for many another household. Invited to tea at the manse table, the young visitor notes the simple courtesies and delicate politeness of the lady whom she admires, and absorbs something of the latter's loveliness and charm. Advice given by the pastor's wife is accepted and prized where it would be resented if offered by another.

The parish has no right to exact anything from the wife of the minister, it is true. But she can no more help being influential than a rose can help diffusing its fragrance, and her natural qualifications for leadership, if these she have, cannot be hidden in this sphere of activity. If she does not wish to take the lead officially, she can still, by her own excellence and in virtue of the fact that her husband must be a leader, largely modify the social life of the congregation. She is its first lady, and all are glad to accord her the place of eminence.

## A Blessed Opportunity.

God gave me something very sweet to be mine own tnis day;
A precious opportunity, a word for Christ to say;
A soul that my desire might reach, a work to do for Him;
And now I thank Him for this grace, ere yet the light grows dim.

No service that He sends me on can be so welcome aye
To guide a pilgrim's weary feet within the narrow way,
To share the tender Shepherd's quest, and so by break and fen
To find for Him His wandering lambs, the erring sons of men.

I did not seek this blessed thing: it came a rare surprise,
Flooding my heart with dearest joy, as, lifting wistful eyes,
Heaven's light upon a dear one's face shone plain and clear on mine:
And there, an unseen third, I felt was waiting One divine.

So in this twilight hour I kneel, and pour my grateful thought
In song and prayer to Jesus for the gifts this day hath brought.
Sure never service is so sweet, nor life hath so much zest,
As when He bids me speak for Him, and then He does the rest.

## The Children's Day.

How beautiful this summer's day,
When June repeats the runes of May !

By silver slant of falling showers,
By fragrant breath of blooming flowers,

By velvet slopes of verdant sod,
Where time slips past with feet unshod,

By ripple of the lilting brook,
By nests in many a cunning nook,

By stars that let heaven's glory through
The sky above our dusk and dew—

By wayside stone, by vale and hill,
The loveliness is round us still.

THE CHILDREN'S DAY IN SUMMER.

But fairer than earth's fairest flowers
Are these dear little ones of ours,

Who fill our homes with voices sweet,
Who rush our wearier selves to greet,

And in their tender love and thought
For older hearts are heaven taught.

Sweet is their faith that upward turns,
And toward the blessed Saviour yearns.

We listen, and we hear Him say
Again, as in that elder day,

"Except you come as these to Me,
You cannot My disciples be!"

Ah! Lord, as children we would meet
To-day about Thy piercèd feet.

To-day would with the children give
Our service unto Thee, and live

Henceforth, through all the coming days,
Devoted to Thy work and praise.

# CHAPTER LI.

## Merry Christmas at Home.

THE happiest time of all the year. The clasp that binds the twelve months and fastens them with a golden key is Christmas, a day which never loses its power to charm the world; the day all children love and all grown people, too; the day of our Saviour's birth. Art and literature have done their best to make Christmas day memorable. It is the motive of song and story, the music of the sage, the star of hope for the whole earth. As the years roll on the joy of Christmastide is always extending, and the Babe of Bethlehem is worshiped by sages and kings, by poor and needy, by angels and men. Listen to the angels' song:

"Still through the cloven skies they come
With peaceful wings unfurled,
And still celestial music floats
O'er all the weary world."

There are good people who have their doubts about the propriety of keeping Christmas with Santa Claus as the central figure. They argue that there is really no such person as Santa Claus, and that when we tell children that a mythical personage, with bells and reindeer and laden sleigh comes down the chimney and fills their stockings with gifts, we are teaching them to deceive, since Santa Claus is only a name for fathers and mothers and other kind friends. But let us be quite sure that we are not ourselves in the wrong if ever we have joined the great company of these conscientious objectors to Christmas keeping, with a tree, and a saint, and Kriss Kringle and all the pretty lore of the period.

"Imagination," said Hans Andersen, "is a leaf from the sky." When we cultivate the imagination we cultivate the faith faculty and help our children to comprehend the invisible. Because of the poverty of human invention and of human language, there are a thousand great truths which men and women can only vaguely and feebly grasp, can never fully understand, for now we see through a glass darkly.

But there are experiences and verities which are made truer to us by means of symbolism, and the symbolism of Santa Claus helps our children to climb

upward to the place where they know that though actually the old saint does not
exist, yet in a very real sense, as the spirit of love and good feeling he is abroad

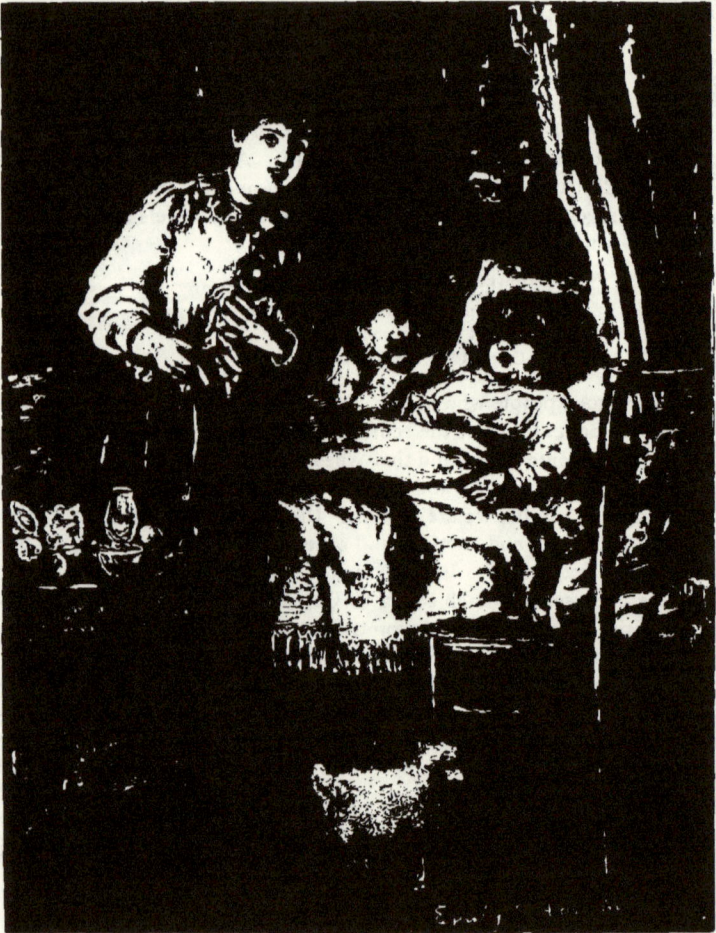

CHRISTMAS AT HOME.

in the world everywhere, making it blithe and gay. He converts by his magic
touch such a miser as old Scrooge, and his sweet goodness breathes in the prayer

of Tiny Tim, "God bless us every one!" In the mission schools, in the farm lands, in the great cities, in the tenements, in the crowded squares and the lonely fields, in and to these Christmas has come, the dear, the divine, the merry Christmas.

We learn how joy belongs to heaven when we join in the Christmas anthems, so loud, so resounding, and so thrilling with rapture. We return to the simplicity of our own early days when we gather around the Mother and the Child, bringing, too, our spices and myrrh, our gifts of love, our small self-sacrifice, our homage to the Christ. Wherever there is a baby in the house, wherever there is helplessness and sweetness and innocence, and the delight of bending over cradle and crib, there is the thought of Jesus, the Child who came to save us all. For

> " The star rains its fire
> And the beautiful sing,
> In the manger of Bethlehem
> Jesus is King."

No other shopping compares with this in fascination, in cheery good-fellowship with a host of people bent on a similar errand, in temptation, let it be added, to spend more than one can afford. The list of friends whom one wishes to surprise or delight at Christmastide is usually a formidable one, and the money in the purse is not always easily equal to the strain made upon it by one's affections, But whether one buys much or buys little, it is still a joyous thing to go a-Christmasing, and to watch the blithe faces of children, to feel the thrill of pleasure which is in the air, and to give one's own heart up to float along the tide in sympathy with the general feeling. For it is the spirit of the Child that is abroad on the earth, the Child who came from heaven and slept in Mary's arms, the Child whom the angels announced and the shepherds saw as they followed the star to Bethlehem. At Christmas, as at no other period, we again become simple-hearted and easily pleased and unaffectedly humble as children are; and even if world-hardened and narrow and selfish, we get some faint gleam of what Jesus meant when He said: " Except ye be converted and become as little children ye cannot inherit the kingdom of heaven."

I don't know which shops attract you most, my reader, in this holiday time, but I confess that I linger longest over the books. My idea of entire earthly bliss at this hour would be liberty to buy all the books I want, for a borrowed book, or a book merely to read and return to a library, is not like a book in possession. What rapture, the mere lingering, loving touch of the paper, the clearness of the type, the exquisite grace of the binding! Here is an edition of that volume of essays, that poem, that biography I've longed for so long, and wouldn't it be happiness beyond belief to purchase it and send it to my friend

——, who is as madly in love with books as I am myself! I never know when to leave when I stray at Christmastide into one of my favorite book stores.

But the fairyland of cut glass and china is very alluring, too! What miracles of grace in shape, what glory of color, what satin smoothness to the hand, what crystalline and prismatic transparency in the shelves which groan beneath cups and platters fit for the palaces of Christendom! It would savor of vulgar profusion to give an unlimited order here. One finds it refined and aristocratic and altogether becoming to consider the day of small things, and to buy sparingly but judiciously where everything is so charming to the eye of woman. The smallest bit of china makes a present worth offering and receiving, and a great deal of love may go with a very small bundle selected here.

I spent a day in early September at a country house where the daughters were making Christmas gifts. Fine linen was the basis and exquisite embroidery the superstructure, and the work of their deft needles was as that of the artist's brush. Doilies and centrepieces and bags and sachets had been growing under their hands all summer, for they preferred doing their Christmas planning and sewing and shopping a long while before the time itself. There is much to be said in favor of this method, particularly when one's gifts are one's own work, but one should take her share even then in the overflowing felicity of the season, be out in the street, go to the Christmas markets, carry to the hospital, the asylum, the homes of the needy and the shut-in, and even to the jail and the prison, some bit of the Christmas spirit.

The finest one can give is always himself. "The gift without the giver is bare." You may not have one dollar to spend, but you can carry sunshine if your face is bright and your manner is sympathetic and your heart is genuinely loving. Not in purple or fine-twined linen, not in silver or gold, not in any perishable earthly commodity inheres the elixir of the Christmas joy; it is finer, subtler, sweeter than aught money can buy; it is distilled from a heart "at leisure from itself," and over it angels have chanted "Glory to God in the Highest, peace on earth, good will to men."

When Christmas is over, the tree dismantled of its toys and its twinkling tapers, the gifts discussed and laid away, and the hour of sober reaction arrived, in too many households there is a sigh over what may be christened Christmas folly; for fast in the wake of Christmas follows the pursuing train of the Christmas bills, and fathers struggling to support large families on slender salaries, mothers accustomed to the drill and the discipline of a thousand small and obscure economies, suddenly awaken to the fact that the beautiful season has left them to drag through weary weeks a ball and chain of harassing indebtedness. Than this nothing can be more depressing, nothing more fatally sure to wreck domestic peace, and to age men and women prematurely, and well would it be for us all if a few rules could be laid down and resolutely observed, so that Christmas should never cause us to indulge in reckless spending far in excess of the income.

In the first place, if people cannot deny themselves the great pleasure of gift-making, let them limit the number of those who are on their list. The widening circles, which, beyond the immediate group at the fireside, include aunts, uncles, cousins nearer or farther in degree of kinship, friends and acquaintances, run up in some cases into the hundreds.

To send even a letter—which, by-the-bye, is an admirable Christmas gift in itself, so personal, so intimate, so fragrant with affection it may be—to send even this to everybody one wishes to compliment means a large investment of time, thought and trouble, and to those who must count very frugally, indeed, the stamps mean an outlay which may be formidable. For some of us any recognition of the Christmas joy, beyond our verbal expression of goodwill, is really a phase of Christmas folly.

But it is not the crowning folly. This is reached in the giving of what may be described as the composite present—the present sent by pupils to their precep-tors, by congregations to their pastor, by teachers in Sunday-schools to their superintendent. In every assemblage of people who thus bestow a united gift there are not a few who cannot easily and comfortably afford to give anything at all, but who have not the moral courage to decline, and so, with smiling faces and reluctant hearts, they add their grudging and hardly earned dollars, wondering the while what they can do without to make up for the useless sacrifice. Pride, that insatiate Moloch of the human heart, urges them on, and they simply do what they prefer not to do because they are afraid either of being thought mean and stingy or of having their poverty suspected. This is the coronation of Christ-mas folly.

Christmas is so dear and sweet a season, so full of jollity, so radiant with loving thoughts, that it seems a pity it should ever be spoiled or shadowed by a misconception. A truer self-respect, a finer feeling for the meaning of the day, a greater delicacy and discernment, would save us from clouding our sunshine, or wronging our creditors, or defrauding ourselves of the ease of mind which should be our right, or making our homes unhappy because of anxieties induced by wasteful spending during the holidays. By all means the open hand where it can be afforded. But never the expenditure which transcends honor and honesty, and is weak and ill-judged, and leads one not to Christmas merriment, but to Christmas folly. There is but one class of persons who, in every station in life, hail the arrival of the holiday season with unalloyed satisfaction. To the children Christmas comes fraught with joy. They live essentially in the present. For them there is no Past; they exist in a glorious Now, rich in visions of Santa Claus, reindeers, sugar-plums, Christmas trees and toys.

With us older people it is different.   In some homes Christmas is received with many festive preparations.   In others it is regarded in a cold, practical fashion as a must be—like Washington's birthday or the Fourth of July.   To others, and this is by far the larger class, Christmas is loved and dreaded for what it once was, and for what it can never be again.   It is a day on which we are forced to pause and gaze on the empty chair, and miss with a yearning that is physical pain one who is not here now.   There were times when we too had virtually no past, and when the Yuletide was all merriment.   Then, as we grew older, it lost some of its brilliancy as one after another home that we knew was saddened.   And at last the sorrow came to us, and since then Christmas has never been just the same

A friend once said to me, reproachfully, " But would you forget those who are gone?''

We cannot forget them.   And if they could speak to us now, would they not urge us to be happy?   The mother who shadows her child's life by her own sorrow has much for which to repent.   Said one child to another, in a moment of confidence, " I often wish I had died instead of my little sister, because then perhaps mamma would love me as much as she loves her.''

In another family, in which one of the little girls had died four years before, one child exclaimed to her older sister, " Let's have a jolly time this Christmas !'' Then, bitterly: " But of course we can't, because mamma won't want any jollity. It disturbs her thoughts of Mary.''

The young son of the house here broke in with his opinion : " I don't see why, just because our sister is happy in heaven, we must have such horrid Christmases here on earth.''

We cannot expect the children, who are, mercifully for them, ignorant of death and sorrow, to grieve with us.   Nor do we want them to do so.   They sympathize as far as they are able.   We should be glad that they can go no farther. The mother must remember that she is the standard by which her child judges the world.   To her the little one looks to set the mood of the day.   If mamma is always sad, it affects the child's spirits at once.   At first he may be frightened. Then, as he becomes accustomed to the doleful visage, he is either cowed by it, or, what is worse, is hardened into indifference.   One noble mother, who has had sorrow upon sorrow, has always made Christmas day bright for her children.   They do not guess at the heartache she hides from them, nor that, the holidays past, she says, from her aching heart, " Thank God ! the Christmas season is over !''

In years to come these same little folk will remember, and, remembering, will appreciate the heroic self-sacrifice of the brave mother.

" I could not bear to keep Christmas in my home," said a sad-eyed woman, " if it were not for the children.''

But it is for the children. And, through them, for the Babe of Bethlehem; for did He not say, " Inasmuch as ye have done it unto one of the least of these— ye have done it unto Me ? "

And not is such self-forgetful love the theme upon which the angels touched when they sang, on the first Christmas eve, of " Peace on earth, good will to men ? "

The giving of holiday presents varies from year to year. Sometimes it is the fashion to give indiscriminately, even lavishly, to everybody, far and near. Again custom decrees that only a favored few dear ones shall be the recipients. At times "useful" presents are in vogue, and again we are enjoined to let people buy useful things for themselves, and give for presents only pretty ones.

One of the first essentials of a gift seems to be its appropriateness. It may be very beautiful and costly, yet if the receiver does not know what it is for, much less have an opportunity to use it, the present is but an incubus, and confers a burdensome obligation. Such a giving over people's heads savors of a sarcasm more cruel than neglect would be.

Yet, when you select for your friend's need or pleasure, it is well that your gift should have a degree of daintiness which the friend would not get for himself. He wants a footstool, yet he would not buy such a handsome one as you buy for him. You know his favorite colors, too, and it is well to think of them at the right moment.

In short, your affection should not only meet his need, but it should give the little touch of "something more" which he would not otherwise have secured.

## A Christmas Carol.

Come, children, with singing,
With sweet voices ringing,
Come kneel to the Babe that in Bethlehem lies,
While angels a-choir,
With pinions of fire,
Are filling with music the listening skies.

Repeat the dear story
How, leaving His glory,
The Hope of the ages came down to the earth.
Oh, worship Him lowly,
The lofty and holy,
Our Star of the Morning shone out at His birth.

25

See Mary unfold Him
While shepherds behold Him,
And sages are bent at His beautiful feet,
Come, haste to adore Him,
And, bowing before Him,
The Christ who redeems you in reverence greet.

This wonderful Stranger,
His couch is a manger,
His cradle is made with the cattle in stall;
Yet God of creation
In blest incarnation,
He stoops to our nature to ransom us all.

Rock, bells, in the steeple,
Shout loudly, good people,
And, children, oh, merrily, merrily sing !
O'er land and o'er ocean
With joyful commotion
Send forth the glad tidings that Jesus is King.

## The Christmas Stocking.

Most of us, searching memory for our earliest association with rapturous joy
in possession or in bestowal, find that away in the dim and mysterious recesses of
the brain, there hovers a dreamy thought of the Christmas stocking.

It is Christmas eve. The children are on tiptoe with happy anticipation. In
a row, about the chimney piece, hang the stockings, larger and smaller, from the
father's to the baby's. When the little ones fall asleep it is with a thought of
Santa Claus tugging at the harp-chords of the heart, which vibrate thenceforth to
glad and silvery melody.

There are people who have scruples of conscience about our dear old Saint
Nicholas. They fear to inculcate falsehood when they talk to the children about
Santa Claus. But if they could see with my eyes, they would perceive that the
symbolism of Santa Claus is the garment of a profound truth, that the reindeer,
and the stealing down the chimney with the gifts while we sleep, and the whole
poetical machinery of the Christmas pageant are the husks, beneath which, safe
and sweet and forever true, abide the solemn realities of the Christmastide, the
love, the self-denial, and the abundant good will of the annual festival of the

blessed Lord's incarnation. The children will gradually discover for themselves what is truth to our material perceptions, and what is the everlasting truth beyond them.

Till they do thus differentiate and decide for themselves, let Santa Claus be to them a stepping-stone to the knowledge of the great love which keeps the world in its grasp.

On Christmas morning, when the stockings have been explored, and the gifts apportioned, when there comes a moment of quiet, read with the children once more the beautiful story of the Babe who was (and is) born in Bethlehem, of the Shepherds, of the Star, of the Wise Men, of the Angelic Song. Then tell the children that this Child shall be named Jesus, because He saves His people from their sins.

----

## The Indwelling Christ.

Wonderful and precious beyond words is the thought of the indwelling Christ, the Christ living in our souls and expressing Himself through us, His light in our faces, His power in our endeavors, His grace in our smallest actions. Not coming to us now and then, as comes the wayfarer who knocks at the door and is admitted for a transient stay; not even visiting us as does the dear and friendly guest, whose occasional tarrying under the roof is a benediction while it remains and a pleasant memory when it is over; not thus, arriving and departing, staying and going, but different and sweeter, and tenderer and more vital by far is the abiding with us of our Lord.

We do not always arise to the height of our privilege in having with us ever through life's journey, on the highways and the byways, by night and by day, the company of the unseen Christ, an inmate of our own household, strong to comfort, blithe to cheer, sympathetic in sorrow, our guard, our guide, our defender. We think of Christ as our Lord above, to whom we are traveling on pathways arched by the steadfast stars and fragrant with the flowers of love and hope. But Christ is our comrade on the way; in our walks and our talks, in our anxious hours and our weary hours, in our darkness as in our light, Christ is our comrade! Therefore we need never be desolate, though we may now and then be lonely. Therefore we may never fear the tempter, nor be conquered by the sin that doth most easily beset us. For our Christ, dwelling with us and shining through us, shall put the tempter to flight and enable us to trample sin under our feet.

The sense of dominion should come to us as we realize this vital abiding of the Christ in our lives. The child of the King, albeit in rags and squalor, should keep some memory of the Father's house and the Father's state. The child of the King in the palace, with the King smiling upon him should bear himself royally and give largesse of good to all he meets and overrule all which fights against the kingdom. What means our dear Lord when He tells us: " The kingdom of heaven is within you," but that wherever we are, we are to carry the light and the song of the palace, the joy of the festival, the power to dismiss doubt, to disarm enmity, to win those who are estranged and hostile, and bring them into peaceful harmony with the divine order ? Only as we are in tune with heaven, can we reach and bless those who are skeptical and lack vision, those who are grief-stricken and deaf to angelic melodies, those who are indifferent and need to be aroused.

We seldom reach as we would like to any of these classes, for the reason that we carry to them too little of the Christ. The little we do carry blesses and uplifts them, but we do not carry enough. For the clear shining of the light which our Lord gives us is obscured by our own selfishness, our want of humility, our faltering faith, or our disobedience to the orders which come to us from above. Half-hearted service so weakens us that we do not carry our light of love as we might into the dark places of the earth. Impatience and self-seeking and low ideals alienate those who are looking for the Christ, but cannot find Him, in the lives we show them.

You take your lantern and wrap a blanket around it and no one sees the flame though it may still feebly burn. You light your lamp and shade it with dark paper or thick horn, and the spark or taper sheds only a faint glow. But around the starry light let there be a pellucid porcelain shade, and the steady radiance is an illumination which penetrates the surrounding gloom and lights homeward the feet of the returning child.

----

## When the Holidays Are Over.

When the holidays are over, and the shopping bills are paid,
And the little lads and lasses with the brand-new toys have played,
When the pretty eldest daughter is the graceful debutante,
And the poor have had their harvest, sometimes all too bare and scant,
When the snow is on the mountain, and the sheen is on the lake,
And we settle down to winter, freezing blast and flying flake,
Somehow, then we draw the curtains, and at night the home is sweet,
With the fire upon the hearth, love, and outside the stinging sleet.

And we take account of stock then, here the labor, there the gain,
All for which we've toiled and striven, paid the price in joy or pain,
Gems and curios, lands and houses, treasures brought from West or East,
Warily we count and tally from the greatest to the least,
Are we richer, are we poorer, are we free, or slaves to debt?
Have we rosy dreams to beckon, sordid memories to forget?

When the holidays are over, and the evergreens are gone,
And the common days are ours, full of care from dawn to dawn,
Somehow, then we cling the closer, comrades on the uphill road,
Bound to share each other's fare, and bound to ease each other's load.
And the dearest things we own, love, are the things that no man sees,
Faith, and truth, and hope unbounded, courage, patience, things like these;
And, you know, a little grave, dear, on a hillside far away,
Where the violets bloom in summer, and the snow fleece lies to-day,
That small space of earth is ours, and the bliss we buried there
Is our holiest possession, none so sacred anywhere.

## Spring-Time.

My little bright-eyed darling,
  Pray did you ever see
The dainty flower-angels
  Who flit through bush and tree?
They come when April coaxes
  The baby leaves apart,
And to and fro on errands
  Of gentle haste they dart.

And oh! the joy they feel, dear,
  When, in a tender quest,
Some shining April morning
  They find a fairy nest.
A pretty birdie's cradle
  Just rocking in the air,
With pearly eggs close lying,
  Tucked in with fondest care.

SPRING-TIME.

The little cherub watchers
　　Have learned one secret well —
That songs and wings are prisoned
　　In every fragile shell;
But till the shell is broken
　　The melodies are dumb,
And so the flower-angels
　　To free the birdies come.

## His Only Friend

Long miles the two comrades have wandered together,
　From hot city streets over meadow and moor,
Till, wearied, one pillows his head on the heather,
　God pity him ! hungry and homeless and poor.

Forgetting his troubles, the worn feet extended,
　The aching limbs resting, his sleep is profound;
But he is not alone as he sits there—befriended
　By Waif, who is ready to spring at a sound.

No peril shall menace the form of the sleeper
　Unchallenged by one who is boldly awake—
A dear little sentinel, proud to be keeper
　Of him whose last meal it was his to partake.

The clumsy paw touches the hard hand, caressing
　Its brown knotted palm; and the shaggy head, pressed
Within the arm's circlet, lies soft as a blessing
　Against the true heart in the thin, faded vest.

They've been famished and chilly and tired together;
　Companions, have shared the sharp word and the blow,
Have faced a harsh world in the wildest of weather,
　And they know not to-day by what pathway to go.

Poor comrades, so faithful ! perhaps just before you
　Is shelter, a home that will open its gate.
All hardships have endings; kind heaven is o'er you;
　The brave and the honest may conquer their fate.

---

## The Angels' Watch.

　When golden stars are in the sky,
　　And all the earth has gone to sleep,
　God sends His angels from on high,
　　O'er little children watch to keep.

They fill the night with heavenly songs,
   Sweet dreams their blessed music brings;
Until at dawn in rising throngs
   They wake us with their rustling wings.

---

## The Portrait.

A throng of men and women,
   Gay, gallant, debonair,
No hint of burdening heartache,
   Or weight of sordid care
In the surging crowd of faces,
   The flutter of carven fans,
The courtly commonplaces,
   In that gathering of the clans.

But from the wall a portrait,
   With keen judicial eyes,
Surveyed the sea of people
   As a star might from the skies.
Apart, alone, unnoted,
   The portrait looking down,
Read the sorrow and the secrets
   Of half the smiling town.

---

## The Comfort at the Core.

There came to me a day of dole, when chill across my path
A wind of sorrow, smiting, swept; it seemed a wind of wrath.
So icy was its blighting, so sore and deep its pain,
That I bent before the blast, and thought I could not rise again.

But in the very secret of the anguish, as I lay,
My pillow wet with heavy tears, there broke a dawn of day;
Another day, another dawn, and life grew full once more
Of blessedness, for lo! I found God's meaning at the core

Of the great and weary trial; God sent the pang to me,
And gave Himself, that dreary time, my star of life to be.
Since when I lift my head and walk serene through care and loss;
The flowers of life immortal are garlanding the cross.

And aye, in hours of loneliness, my heart sets wide its door,
And God's strong angel shows me pain has comfort at the core.

## Comfort One Another.

Comfort one another,
For the way is often dreary,
And the feet are often weary,
    And the heart is very sad.
There is heavy burden bearing,
When it seems that none are caring,
    And we half forget that ever we were glad.

Comfort one another,
With a hand-clasp close and tender,
With the sweetness love can render,
    And the looks of friendly eyes.
Do not wait with grace unspoken,
While life's daily bread is broken—
    Gentle speech is oft like manna from the skies

# CHAPTER LII.

## Open Secrets.

ARY EMILY CLAYTON found it hard to realize that she was an old woman. She never did realize it in the least, even when her tall grandchildren, the prettiest girls in Massachusetts, clustered around her, and the only way she could be made to understand that she was on life's downhill grade was by compelling herself to think back, back, over the long, long past.

When she was a little maid in a blue checked gingham frock and a sunbonnet, carrying her dinner to school in a tin pail, she was the gayest, most heedless, most light-hearted lassie in the county. She was a vain little girl, for she remembered that she used to look in the glass, and think herself pretty, as indeed she was. Once a boy gave her a gold pencil case, and her mother said she must give it back, which she did to her intense mortification. That boy died fifty years ago, in his young manhood.

Then she looks back, and she sees herself a slim young girl, with bands of smooth hair, and bright near-sighted eyes, and a way that charms and pleases people and helps her to make friends. She isn't in love, except with being loved, so she makes a great mistake, and too early says yes to the wooer who comes, brave and debonair, and begs her to wear his name, and share his lot " for better, for worse till death us do part."

Nevertheless, though she discovers in part her mistake before she is married, she will not draw back, and Richard Clayton never dreamed that he was a disappointment, that he failed of being her perfect hero. She made him the most loyal, the most loving, the most devoted of wives, and on his dying bed he blessed her, and, so had their hearts by that time grown together, that never at any moment of her long widowhood, did she recall a time of incompleteness, never did she cease to idealize the husband of her youth, when he had passed on before her. But it was not in her temperament nor her disposition to grieve incessantly nor forever; she was elastic, and it was her fortunate fate to renew her strength after periods of depression.

At forty, at fifty, at sixty, Mrs. Clayton found it in her power to receive new impressions, vividly and joyously. At sixty-five she set about learning Hebrew, a difficult task, but not an insuperable one to a woman who had been a student more or less during life. At seventy she took a long and difficult trip across the continent, then by sea went to San Francisco, and concluded by a journey round the world.

"Will you tell me," said a friend, "of what fountain of youth you have the secret? How do you manage to keep well, and blooming, and beautiful, when other women have bent shoulders, wrinkled skins, and scant endurance?"

"I have only open secrets," she replied. "I rest when I am tired, I go early to bed, and if I do not sleep I close my eyes and lie quietly in the comfort of the darkness. During the day when I am at home, I take an hour's rest after midday, with my feet on a chair and an interesting book in my hand. I drowse if I like, I think of nothing fatiguing, and I stay alone. That is my own hour, and nobody is allowed to intrude upon it. I sometimes shut my eyes for five minutes at other times. It is wonderful how much good a brief bit of rest will do to a woman.

"As to my looks, I bathe my face in hot water every night and in cold water every morning. I take a daily bath. I eat fruit plentifully. I am in the fresh air at least two hours a day.

"I seek and enjoy the society of the young. As women grow old they should keep in touch with those who are less advanced on the road than they. Otherwise they are apt to grow crotchetty and queer, or they cling to their own opinions and are intolerant of their juniors, and of opposition. Young society keeps us fresh and young.

"Then, and more than all except one thing else, I do my work. It has never yet occurred to me that I can be laid on the shelf. I am occupied in many ways, and I do my daily task just as I always have, without seeking to be released on the score of age.

"And the one thing else? It is simply this: I trust wholly and without reserve to the goodness and mercy of my heavenly Father.

> "'I know not the way I am going,
> But well do I know my guide;
> With a child-like trust I take the hand
> Of the mighty Friend at my side.'

"Those are my only secrets."

---

## Thanksgiving.

To-day the fields are reaped and shorn,
    The fruits are gathered in,
And shines the golden light of morn
    On wealth of barn and bin.

Dun tints lie where the summer's green
  Waved at the south wind's breath;
Bare boughs are lifted, stripped and clean,
  By besom touch of death.

Along the brown and slumbrous tide
  Float down the withered leaves,
The fields are naked far and wide
  Where late were bound the sheaves.

A touch of frost is in the air,
  The nights are crisp and cold,
The Northern Lights like torches flare
  O'er wintry wood and wold.

And now we open wide the door
  And call the kith and kin
To throng beneath the roof once more
  Till all are gathered in.

The white-haired sire, the sturdy son,
  The blooming boys and girls,
Down to the latest little one
  With yellow clustering curls,

About the table meet to-day,
  And feast with joy and mirth;
And many a tender word they say
  Around the radiant hearth.

And thanks they give to God above
  Whose hand upon their way
Has been a hand of constant love
  And led them to this day.

For blessings more than tongue can tell
  The household praises rise;
The strains of music throb and swell
  And climb to pierce the skies.

" God save the commonwealth ! " they
In faith that God will hear,
Since never prayer was sent on high
To reach a loveless ear.

" God save and bless the dear home-land !
God save our flag from shame,
God keep us ever, strong to stand
A nation in His name."

So, from its dawn to sunset's hour,
We keep Thanksgiving Day.
For sheaf and seed, for bud and flower,
For life and death we say,

" All glory to the Lord of Hosts !
All glory, honor, praise ! "
The psalm is heard on all our coasts,
Our seas and inland bays.

A nation with its thousands brings
To God its homage meet,
And here its mighty choral flings
Low at Jehovah's feet.

# CHAPTER LIII.

## The Cost of Living.

EVEN when it is most economically administered, the cost of keeping up a home is never small. The late Prince Albert once said to his daughter, afterward the Empress Frederick of Germany, "My dear, in all your management of income take care that you leave yourself a margin." This excellent practical advice finds itself always in order to people of all ranks and conditions, because the joy of life is largely in having a margin beyond what we require for the present wants of the day. But it is not possible or practicable for every one to have much of a margin. Still, the person who values peace of mind, self-respect and length of days will rigidly keep within his or her income. The margin is needed for such expenses as doctors' bills, the payment, if necessary, of a trained nurse in cases of severe or prolonged disease in the family, the mounting up of drugs and prescriptions, and many things along that line of which we never count the cost until the enemy is upon us.

Then, too, carpets and curtains wear out. Even with the greatest care these yield to the incessant patter of children's feet and to the ordinary effects of household usage. After a while you find that you must slip the carpet away from the edge of the stairs to remove the strain of constant wear. You find certain breadths of your carpet growing shabby and threadbare, and you shift them round to go under a bed or under a table. By and by you have to put a braided rug or a mat over a thin place in the carpet to hide it.

Your furniture requires new covering. The springs of your bed sag in the middle; the mattress itself must be made over, and this periodically to keep it in perfect condition. Paper and paint grow dingy. The fences need repair. Outside and in it costs a great deal to keep up. Every week of her life the housekeeper must go into every closet and corner and fight not only dust but the predatory moth. Children are forever wearing out shoes and growing out of clothes. The cost of school-books is large.

The cost of food must be regarded as one of the things which the good housekeeper wil not consider the right field for economy. I once overheard a

conversation in a public conveyance.  Two women elegantly attired sat near me.
One of them said to the other, "You notice my silk gown and my sealskin cloak,
how beautiful they are."  And indeed they were; the silk was thick enough to
stand alone, and the sealskin was a dream of beauty.  "Yet," she said, "if I
have not saved and skimped and contrived to get them, nobody ever did.  We
have not had a beefsteak in our house for a year.  I have fed the children on picked
codfish, and it has done just as well, and in fact I have saved and scraped in every
direction.  But now, you see, it pays, because here I have these beautiful
garments."

I did not hear the friend's reply, but I thought at what a cost this woman
had adorned her person—the cost of her children's flesh and blood, very likely of
her husband's vigor and strength.  One must choose where to be frugal and
where to be lavish.  Money is not well saved which is taken from the table and
put upon one's back.  There is indeed a certain vulgarity in making everything
else yield to dress, since, after all, dress should be the expression of one's best
self and should never be fine or elegant beyond one's means.

But this was not what I started to say when I began, which was, rather, that
save as we may, the cost of a home is no slight thing.  There are many odd jobs
to be done that must be paid for, unless the children do them.  There are always
accidents happening on which we did not count, and the only way in which, for
most people, the home can be engineered safely through all its perils and made
and kept a cozy and beautiful nest, a castle to which the good people retire in all
emergencies, is by having everybody take hold together and work for it with
heart and hand.  Children should understand that the home is worth a great deal
to them, and they should be taught how to take care of certain parts of the
household work.

Some time ago, when visiting a beautiful school in New England, where the
work is carried on by the scholars themselves, I was struck with the sweet
atmosphere and the delicate consideration which prevailed there.  In the house in
which I was a guest the work was divided between twenty young ladies, each of
whom had her definite share.  Never have I sat at a table more beautifully
appointed, nor have I in any house eaten more delicious food.  The sweet composure of the young women who had cooked the dinner, and of those who
quietly rose from their places at certain times to remove the plates and bring on
the dessert, was a beautiful thing to see.  I found that it was possible for the
girls in this school to obtain an excellent, all-round education, because the cost
of housekeeping was minimized, and because they all took hold of it and merrily
helped it along.

So in our home, if the mother did not usually think it too much trouble to teach
the boys and girls how to help her, their help would be most willingly given; but it

"The most beautiful hands are those which work for others."

is often harder to show a person how to do a thing than it is to do the thing one's self. And there are not a few noble women who never succeed in training their daughters to follow in their footsteps, for two reasons—one, that they will not take the trouble, and the other that they are weakly unwilling to tax their young daughters. They think the pretty white hands of the maiden should be saved from any disfiguring task; they want the daughter to enjoy her day of youth in ease and luxury. They really put their daughters in a wrong light, since the good daughter is never so happy as when helping the good mother.

Then, too, there is no need why housework should ruin even a faultless hand. It is quite possible to save the hands by the use of mops, India rubber gloves, and such contrivances; and a little care taken either in doing housework, gardening, or any other manual occupation will keep the hands ladylike and fair. The most beautiful hands in the world are those which work for others, and in all our household labor we should reflect that we are giving of ourselves for others' need, and making others happy at perhaps a little cost to ourselves. But what of that! Love counts no service hard; love is of all things generous and self-forgetting.

In looking over our accounts for a year which has passed we may often see where we were injudicious in expenditure, and equally we may regulate affairs better for the year which is to come. No one should despise small savings. Five cents here, two cents there, a penny in another direction, and before one knows it a dollar is gone. Every one has noticed how quickly a dollar bill melts away once it is broken. Divide it up into silver and it is soon a vanishing quantity. We must not regulate our expenditures by the incomes of those who are endowed with longer purses than we. Each family for itself must consider what it can spend, what style of living it can afford, and then with true American pluck go to work to make the most of its resources.

I heard a lady the other day discussing the furnishing of a room with a woman whose sum set aside for the arranging of a parlor was quite small. The lady said, "Do not try to furnish your whole parlor at once, but, as you can manage it, by one piece at a time. A good lounge, a good chair, curtains of some dainty stuff which will wash, by and by a clock and a lamp—just as you feel you can get each of these—and after a while you will be mistress of a dainty, pretty room in which you will enjoy entertaining your friends. Above all things," said this wise counsellor, "do not delude yourself with buying furniture on the plan of buying by instalments.

"Nothing is more flattering and specious than the invitation held out at first for this kind of expenditure, but in the end it proves a millstone around one's neck. There may come, after months of careful saving and meeting the payment, a time when it is not easy to do this, and then, presto, you find yourself in debt, and the furniture man, if he chooses, may ignore all you have paid and resume his claim upon your property. Pay for things as you go, and never buy anything for which you cannot at the moment readily pay in cash."

26

The buyer who buys for cash has a great advantage over the buyer who purchases on credit. Merchants like to have credit accounts, but they reap a profit in the end by charging larger prices or in some way managing to get the interest on their money. They, besides, count on the fact that when a person is not paying cash down, he or she is apt to buy more lavishly and sometimes to purchase things which could very well be done without. In calculating the cost of a home, it is wise to make it an invariable rule to pay as you go, and to have no troublesome debts to keep you awake at night.

In buying dress goods there is an advantage in choosing those which will not go speedily out of fashion. Very marked plaids and stripes or colored effects which are the fashion of the moment are less economical than plain colors, quiet in tone and of good quality, which may be turned and twisted and renewed by different trimming for a long time. A woman who cannot afford many best gowns should choose something in dark blue or brown or black. A black gown always wears well if of good quality, and you are not remembered by it as you are by something more pronounced or of gayer hue.

I sometimes feel a little sorry for the younger children in a large family, because necessarily they are obliged to wear what the older ones outgrow. A young girl once said to me, "I have never had a new frock yet, and I am now thirteen. I always have to wear what Susie and Kitty are done with." The mother might occasionally plan to let the little girl enjoy the pleasure of something entirely for herself, even if the elder ones that season manage to go without anything particularly new.

# CHAPTER LIV.

## Correspondence.

ORRESPONDENCE forms an important part of our modern life. We take less time for letter-writing than people did formerly, and sometimes it seems as if the old leisurely epistle has gone out with the stage-coach of our fathers. When postage was a matter of very great moment and a letter cost anywhere from six to twenty-five cents, also when its conveyance was a matter of much labor on the part of those who carried it, one relay of horses after another being harnessed to the mail-coach, sometimes when an armed escort was necessary to convey it through a hostile country, or one infested with banditti, it seemed hardly worth a person's while to sit down and dash off a hurried missive. People somehow had more time in past days than there seems to be now. Consequently, we still find great enjoyment in the long letters which were written by people a hundred years ago, though we do not ourselves indulge our taste in correspondence in just the same way.

On the other hand, nothing can be done now without letter-writing, and the ability to write a good letter is the hall-mark of a fine education. Letters, of course, are of various kinds. There is the business letter, which must be short, concise and to the point, with no waste of words, and with the utmost clearness of explanation. There is the formal letter of invitation, which may be in the first person or in the third, and which requires an answer explicit and prompt, since society could hardly get on if people were careless with regard to the invitations which they receive. There is the letter of condolence sent to the house of sorrow. This should be sympathetic and sincere. There is the letter of congratulation, when some happy event has taken place in a friend's family. One always knows how to write a letter saying that one is glad of the birth of a little child, or of the announcement of a friend's engagement, or of any other thing which is making life dear for others.

But after all, the correspondence with which we have most to do is that which goes on between families when they are separated. Nothing so strengthens the family bond as frequent letters, and these should be gossipy and full of small details, and should concern themselves with just the sort of things which people talk about when they are at home. If your son has left home and is making his way in a town far from you, sitting at a boarding-house table, sleeping in a hall bedroom, finding his pleasure where he can, what a delight it is to him to get, every week, the long letter from home, mentioning the people he knows there, telling about the little doings on the farm, and keeping him in touch with all that life of which he was so lately a part, but which now seems far away from him.

It is a good plan in answering a letter to look over the one which you last received and see that you are not over-looking any questions which have been asked. Bear in mind, too, that a letter going abroad will take a week, two weeks, or a month, to reach its destination, and do not be too much troubled when you receive a letter from a friend in foreign parts if she tells you of illness or accident which may now be three weeks back, and from which she has probably emerged

THE LETTER.

by this time. Never write an angry letter. If you are distressed about anything, let it be what it will, or in any way troubled in mind, say to yourself, "I will wait till to-morrow," especially if you are resentful or vindictive, because the written word has a certain permanence. And while it may be to you an escape-valve to sit down and write out your indignation, the letter in the hand of friend or foe may be a destroying and wounding weapon.

Above all things, never write to anybody that which you would not be willing, in case of necessity,. to have shown to all your friends and blazoned upon the four winds. People should never carry on a clandestine correspondence, or lower themselves by writing that of which they should be ashamed were it known. Of course nobody who is decent in any conceivable circumstances ever sends an anonymous letter. The anonymous letter is a stab in the dark, and the sender of it is beneath contempt. The recipient of such a letter should immediately burn it up and pay no heed whatever to its message.

About children's letters people should behave with a high sense of honor. I have often been very much disturbed to see a mother open the little letter which has come to her child, as if the child, like every one else, did not enjoy breaking the seal of her own letter. It is well that a mother should supervise the corres-pondence of her children, should know to whom her daughter and son write and from whom they receive letters, but the letters themselves once sanctioned by parental consent should be the child's own property.

For ordinary correspondence one should use good white paper, unruled, of fine quality, with envelopes to match which are large enough to easily admit the paper. Eccentricities of note-paper are to be avoided, also tinted papers or those which have curious devices. If you can afford it, your monogram at the top of your sheet, or your residence in engraved script, is a finishing touch to the letter which adds a certain elegance, but these are by no means necessary. Also, one may seal a letter with her own individual seal if she chooses, though the only essential thing is to have good mucilage and enough of it, so that the letter may safely go on its way.

We begin a letter usually with "My dear Mr. Smith," or "My dear Mrs. Jones," if the letter is a formal one. A shade of greater intimacy is given by the use of "dear" without the personal pronoun. In writing to a business firm we say "Messrs. Hastings & Sons, Gentlemen," or else "Messrs. Howard & Co., Dear Sirs." A very formal note may be written thus, "Mrs. Elbert Carruthers, Dear Madam." To our intimate friends we say "Dearest Emeline," or "Dear Margaret," or any other term we please. We may sign a letter "Yours respect-fully," "Yours cordially," "Faithfully," "Truly," "Sincerely," or in almost any manner we please, avoiding very affectionate and demonstrative terms except to those who are our very intimate friends, exceedingly dear and beloved.

Always in sending a business letter which requires an answer be sure to enclose stamps for return postage. This is a little matter which is often neglected. One cannot be too careful about it, however, because if people have to pay postage on many letters which do not concern them it amounts in the course of a year to a very serious tax.

Always write your post-office address very plainly at the top of your letter. A business letter is also dated at the top. A letter of friendship or of ceremony is dated at the bottom, and the date is written, not given in numerals. The signature of a letter should be extremely plain and should be written out invariably in full. Your friends cannot be expected to remember the little details of your residence, and your signature means yourself. Do not sign your pet name, except to very intimate friends or members of your own family. Be always to the outside world Edward or Caroline or Frances or Charlotte, or whatever your name may be.

# CHAPTER LV.

## Ill-Temper at a Premium.

IT really seems sometimes as if the most amiable people are obliged in this world to go to the wall. Very often the one who has least claim to be considered is the one who gets her own way, simply because it is easier to avoid a fuss and to slip on quietly than to make a constant fight for one's rights. Which of us has not seen injustice in the household because some one person is aggressive and determined, and makes it uncomfortable for the rest if he or she is not indulged?

Sometimes, but very rarely indeed, it is the mother whose caprices and spells of temper are the terror of her family. I was deeply impressed and greatly shocked when quite young, a guest in the home of a school friend, to find that her mother simply scolded everybody from morning till night, the shrill voice seldom ceasing, and husband, children and servants alike the objects of her constant shower of abuse. Accustomed to my own gentle mother and to low tones and kind words as part of human nature's daily food, it astonished me to notice how calmly my friend's household went on its way, paying little attention to the termagant who sat at the head of the table, and who indeed was treated with great respect by every one. Later the poor woman became insane and ended her days in an asylum, the probability being that her malady was coming on at the time when I was under her roof.

Seriously, one should stop to think whether or not in the interest of one's reason it would not be well to lay a restraining hand upon violence of temper and upon its expression. Certainly the cross and disagreeable person does not always become insane, but there is no sanity in ungoverned passion, and this is a fact worth remembering.

In a very sensible little article by Mrs. Van de Water I find these observations: " Look at the mother and housewife as she goes about her tasks, and observe how often she utters an impatient exclamation, how often she sighs over her servants' shortcomings, how often she starts nervously at a noise from one of the children, and each time that she loses control over herself, her nerves, her temper, she loses just a little nervous force, just a little physical well-being, and moves a fraction of an inch farther on into the path that leads to premature old age and invalidism." The trouble with many women is that they waste emotion over trifles, and are as much distressed over a small accident as over a great casualty.

To return to our subject, it is occasionally the petted daughter of the house, the one for whom everything is done and on whose slightest wish everybody waits, who becomes what might be called the household monopolist. She does not exactly storm about, but she grows depressed, and when she is in a fit of the sulks she makes the atmosphere around her decidedly uncomfortable and blots the sunshine of the home. Let the sinner be whoever it may, father, mother, sister or brother, she gains or he gains an undue prominence and is far too well treated when, lest there should be trouble, a premium is put upon his or her moods and tenses.

Sometimes the only way to tranquillity in this world is by the way of battle. There are times and seasons when it is right to fight in order that one may have peace, and while we should be careful that we do not invite conflict and strife, yet if it must come it is better to have it than to give up everything and allow the person with violent temper to reign undisputed monarch of all he or she surveys.

People make light of little quarrels, overlooking the fact that no harmony is perfect which is frequently disturbed, and that no one can ever entirely forget the effect of broken relations. The strain has come once, it may come again. Life is so short and love is so precious, that it is far better always when we can to go on through life drawing only upon the heavenly forces, making the angels our ministers, and putting far from us whatever agitates and disturbs composure.

* * *

J. P. McCaskey, in an admirable essay, says:

"In the Russian Department, in the Art Building of the Chicago Exposition, at the north end of the gallery, there hung a picture that attracted much attention, and that has since been reproduced so often as now perhaps to be more widely known than any other of the fine paintings upon those walls. It told its familiar story simply and pleasantly, and one lingered, as loath to go, and came back day after day to look upon it, drawn by a spell deeper than the painter's art. And it has taken its place in the picture gallery of memory of untold thousands.

"She comes hurrying from the kitchen, where she has been eagerly and lovingly busy, hand and head and heart at the service of an honored guest — the most hospitable woman, shall we say, in all Bethany, and one of the best and most helpful to know, and to love, and to live with? So at least He seemed to think who knew to their depths the hearts of those about Him, and longed for human sympathy and affection. If we may judge from the record, as we read between the lines, He seemed to regard this family, two sisters and one brother, as very attractive people, and among the best He knew in Palestine.

" ' Master, bid her that she help me. Mary is a good enough girl, but she's leaving me to do everything just now. I don't know what you're talking about, but it seems as if she can't tear herself away from it. You are tired and hungry, and I want to have something for you to eat as soon as possible.' And, laughing, she kept on: ' Mary is a good cook and a good housekeeper, and always ready to lend a hand when anything is to be done, but now—well, I've called her two or three times and she doesn't seem to hear me. Bid her that she help me.'

"He smiled as He looked into her truthful eyes, noted her quick, half-impatient manner which He knew so well, and the tones of her pleasant voice that had in them, one can readily imagine, the faintest suggestion of fault-finding. ' Martha, sit down. You are one of the best women in the world; but Mary is better than you are.' ' I know that,' she said impulsively; ' I always knew that. But I would like her now to help me get this dinner.' And she laughed good-naturedly at Mary's pleasant disclaimer that Martha was the ' best woman ' she knew—for they were friends, you know, as well as sisters, and appreciated and loved one another. ' Don't worry about the dinner, Martha '— and in His fine eyes there beamed a light that spoke more than words might say —' nor much about anything else. All that in good time. We were talking of Eternity. But one thing is needful.' And the sisters together soon spread the generous table for their welcome guest.

"Christ was no far-off teacher, cold in manner, didactic in method, but a beloved, and trusted, and familiar friend, good to live with. What a compliment did He pay to those women and their brother in His habit of going to their pleasant home in Bethany !

"Good to live with ! Of all people in the world, let this be said of wife and mother, then of husband and father, sister and brother.''

---

THAT piety, devotion to one's Father in heaven and to one's spiritual nature, should ever have what may be described as a seamy side, a side of rough edges and tangled knots, seems at first an impossibility. Yet it is a matter of personal observation that many good people, pious to the very core of their being, are, unfortunately, so imperious, so exacting, or so unreasonable, that they do not commend their religion to others, that, in effect, their daily conduct dissipates the impression which their sincerity and enthusiasm in right beliefs ought to make on the minds of their associates.

"Living epistles, known and read of all men," is the pithy phrase which describes, as in a single strong picture, what the child of God should be to his own generation. Whenever one who is earnestly striving after a deeper intimacy with Christ, a more entire consecration of body, soul and spirit to that service which is perfect freedom, becomes aware that he or she is antagonizing friends rather than winning them, is growing irritable in the family and, therefore, showing a wrong example to childhood, it is time to see whether the piety has not, needlessly, a seamy side.

An autobiography, recently published, shows in what appears to be an almost unconscious revelation the effect on a boy of an unhappy religious ideal on the part of his elders. One of these, an aunt, concerning whose entire singleness of aim and devoted piety there cannot be a doubt, so misunderstood the sensitive little fellow, and so constantly snubbed him, that after the interval of a lifetime, in his deliberate judgment, the man grown old sets down his recollections thus:

"The hours after five o'clock in my much-longed-for, eagerly-counted holidays were now absolute purgatory. Once landed at the rectory (where with his mother the boy daily dined) I was generally left in a dark room till dinner at seven o'clock, for candles were never allowed in the winter in the room where I was left alone. After dinner I was never permitted to amuse myself or to do anything, except occasionally to net. If I spoke, Aunt Esther would say with a satirical smile, 'As if you ever could say anything worth hearing, as if it was ever possible that any one could want to hear what you have to say.' If I took up a book I was told instantly to put it down again; it was 'disrepect to my uncle.' If I murmured, Aunt Esther, whose temper was absolutely unexcitable, quelled it by her icy rigidity. Thus, gradually, I grew into the habit of absolute silence at the rectory, a habit which it took me years to break through and I often still suffer from the want of self-confidence engendered by reproaches and taunts which never ceased. For a day, for a week, for a year, they would have been nothing, but for always, with no escape but my own death, or that of my tormentor!"

Such a presentation of childish misery, acute and long-enduring, caused by the mistaken and repressive discipline of a good woman, leads to serious thought. In our day juvenile training is less rigorous than formerly, discipline, indeed, is very much relapsed, the pendulum having swung in the other direction, but there may be among the women who read this paper some who need to be reminded not to let their good be evil spoken of, not to provoke children or others dependent on their words for home sunshine, to wrath or to sorrow by displaying religion which has a seamy side.

If there is a seamy side, why not wear it within, ourselves bearing the fret and friction of our short temper, our folly, our errors, our regretted impulses, but never inflicting the results of these on the household or on our companions in society. Enter into thy closet and shut thy door, is a good rule for the Christian; there, in the secret of the Master's presence, confessing, repenting, gaining courage and strength to press on, with a light on the face and love in the speech and gentleness in every act.

HERE are some suggestive thoughts by Sallie V. Du Bois:

A little star, shining out in a dark night upon the world, seemed to find its silvery beams lost, and had almost decided it was not worth the effort any longer. "It is such a gloomy night and there is not another star visible anywhere, why should I shine? I cannot penetrate this folding gloom," said the star. "But then I may be a part in God's great plan, and if so I ought cheerfully to do the best that I can." So the star shone on all the long hours through, and the little beams it cast seemed lost, but not so. A mighty ship, tossed about upon the ocean bed, beset with danger, sought guidance by the star, and when the morning light dawned the captain turned to his first mate and cried in tones of cheer, "Thank God for the light shed by that star; it has taught me the lesson never to despise the sum of small things."

A tiny snowdrop, the first gem of spring, lifted its wee head through the soil and blossomed in obscure beauty. "How is this," it cried, "there are no other flowers blooming anywhere that I can see. Is it possible that I am the only one? The earth looks so drear and desolate I have a great mind not to stay." The north wind swept along with its cutting blast and bent the stem of the snowdrop until it touched the earth. "I might just as well have remained under ground," said the snowdrop, despairingly, "since I seem doomed to die alone and unseen." Just then a boy hurrying along the path paused suddenly, then then stooped and lifted the snowdrop tenderly. "Ah, how she loved these beautiful flowers," he said, "and now I can place it in her hand." Guarding it from the wind, he ran on, entering the door of an humble home, and there in the coffin, where one lay sleeping the sleep which knows no waking, he placed the spotless flower. He had not shed tears before, his grief had been too deep and full of anguish, but the flower was the symbol of death, and its spotlessness resembled the life his loved one had entered. Then the tears fell, the floodgates were opened and the snowdrop was bathed in the precious dew.

"What is the use," said a fleecy cloud; "I hold but a few drops of water at most, and they would be lost on the dry and parched earth. Why, I could scarcely bend the head of a lily, or revive the drooping daisy. Yet I am part of God's great plan, and what I can do I must do promptly and uncomplainingly." So a few scattered raindrops fell, then more and more, until mother earth put on new verdure and beauty and blossomed anew.

"The best that I can," and each one carefully and prayerfully following that rule, would cause the earth to resemble the primitive state and the kingdom of Christ would not be far removed.

# CHAPTER LVI.

## Domestic Training.

T is undoubtedly well for every mother to train her daughter in the arts of housewifery, beginning when the child is young and giving her some share in household tasks from the time the little one begins to pick up her own playthings and put away her own clothing after she comes in from play, until she is a grown woman. We are foolishly heedless often as regards this important part of a girl's education. While we spare no pains to give our daughters the most thorough school training, to open up to them avenues of pleasure and profit in various accomplishments, such as music, painting, and what used to be styled the ornamental branches, we take it for granted that a knowledge of housekeeping will come by itself without special effort on the part of any one. It is true that there are girls to whom cooking and managing appear less difficult than to others. Occasionally, one meets a young woman who seems to be a born cook or housekeeper; but this is the exception rather than the rule. I do not think there is anything so intricate or so subtle about the processes of the culinary art that they cannot be readily mastered by any intelligent girl in a comparatively brief time. I also hold that a thorough intellectual training assists one in manual arts of every sort. Mr. Beecher once observed that an educated man would light a fire better than an ignorant man; so that I am not advising any mother to abbreviate her daughter's school education. What I am pleading for is this: Let the daughter early have her share in managing, making, mending, and do whatever is to be done in the house. If necessary, let her now and then intermit a half-year or a year in her school course; staying at home, dropping books and helping mother; learning practically how to make bread; how to roast, bake, broil and boil; how to make puddings and pies and cake; something about the chemistry of food; nourishing diet for the sick; dainty desserts,—everything, in short, that a woman needs to know in order to properly nourish her family. I have seen a brilliant valedictorian of a college perfectly helpless and lost in the presence of a sudden illness, when there was the necessity to make so simple a thing as a dish of gruel for a patient who could eat no other food. This ought not to be. A woman should be capable and efficient and fitted for any emergency, and it is her mother's business to see that she is thus fitted for life, whether she marries or remains single.

A young girl should know how to direct her maids intelligently, whether she personally works in the departments which they undertake or not. She should

A CHILD'S TASK.

know, for instance, how to regulate an ordinary family washing; should understand that table linen is to be taken by itself; that fine clothes are to be separated from coarse ones; that flannels require very delicate and painstaking treatment if they are not to shrink up and become thickened and useless. The several parts of housekeeping cannot be learned in one day, although, as I have said before, any woman who gives her mind to them can acquire them without a very long novitiate. Little by little, day by day, the daughter growing up in the refined and well-ordered home and taking some share of its care, will become at an early age a good housekeeper.

There is an art in buying household goods to advantage, in marketing, in catering, and in keeping accounts. The latter is so important an affair that all women who wish to have happy homes should serve an apprenticeship to themselves or their parents in this one department. Let the girl begin when quite young with her own stated allowance. It may be very small at the outset, and she should know just what expenses it will cover. She should not be allowed to overrun it. If she foolishly spends the whole of it in one day or in one week, she should be obliged to feel the inconvenience of no cash the rest of the month. As she grows older her allowance may be increased and may be apportioned so that it will gradually enable her to buy her own clothing and to take entire charge of her own expenses.

The wife of a New York millionaire, presiding over a magnificent home with a very large establishment—coachman, footman, cook, laundress, waitress, chambermaid, seamstress, lady's maid, nursery governess, boy-in-buttons, etc., told me not long since that she had rigidly held her daughters to an economical management of money. She began when they were little tots, giving them a certain weekly amount for their spending, increasing this by degrees. At twelve her daughters were taught to make their own frocks and trim their own hats, and were given a certain amount to spend on their carfare, charity, books, and such items of dress as ribbons, gloves, shoes and belts. As they grew older the allowance became larger; but each girl in that family was more carefully trained as to her responsibility in the matter of money than are most girls in poor families. In fact, one usually finds that thrift and forehandedness are more conspicuous in the families of the well-to-do than they are in families where people are living from hand to mouth. Of course it makes a difference on this subject of spending of money whether one's home is in an obscure country district or in a large town. In town the temptation to spend money meets you on every side and is well nigh irresistible. In the country, remote from the shops, there is less need of money, and people, fortunately for themselves, can get along with very much less in the way of dress and of other articles which a city woman considers indispensable. Whether or not we have much or little, we are accountable to God for our use of it, and even more than a city woman does the woman whose home is in the country need to understand all the intricacies of household management.

"Taught to make her own frocks."

Away back in the days when David was fleeing from the face of Saul, there is an interesting story of good housekeeping which has always appealed very strongly to me. You remember that David was at that time an outlaw dwelling among the strongholds of En-gedi, hiding among the rocks of the wilderness in order that he might escape the jealous pursuit of the monarch who had once been his friend, but was now his enemy. David in those days had a following of several hundred young men, outlaws like himself, and they lived as Robin Hood in a later period, and as guerrilla warriors have done ever since, on the country in which they were in ambush. "Now there was a man in Maon whose possessions were in Carmel; and the man was very great. He had three thousand sheep and three thousand goats." The wealth of that day in a pastoral country was always in the number of a man's flocks and herds. This man Nabal was a miser and a churl; but he had a wife Abigail, of whom we are told that she was a woman of good understanding and of a beautiful countenance. The story, as told in the Bible, is very graphic. David heard in the wilderness that Nabal did shear his sheep. And David sent out ten young men saying, "Get you up to Carmel, and go to Nabal and greet him in my name: And thus shall ye say to him that liveth in prosperity, Peace be both to thee, and peace be to thine house, and peace be unto all that thou hast. And now I have heard that thou hast shearers: now thy shepherds which were with us, we hurt them not, neither was there aught missing unto them, all the while they were in Carmel. Ask thy young men and they will shew thee. Wherefore let the young men find favor in thine eyes; for we come in a good day: give, I pray thee, whatsoever cometh to thine hand unto thy servants and to thy son David." To this courteous request Nabal answered churlishly and rudely, "Who is David? and who is the son of Jesse? there be many servants nowadays that break away every man from his master. Shall I then take my bread, and my water, and my flesh that I have killed for my shearers and give it unto men, whom I know not whence they be?" David's little army at this time was composed of no less than six hundred hardy men, and at once four hundred of these girded on their swords and started with David to attack Nabal and make an end of him and his house. In the meantime, however, the lady of the manor, hearing of her husband's churlishness and gruffness, and being told that David and his men had been as a wall of protection and defence around the shearers for months past, determined to take the matter into her own hands. Indeed, her servants said to her very plainly, "Now, therefore know and consider what thou wilt do; for evil is determined against our master, and against all his household: for he is such a son of Belial that a man cannot speak to him." The story goes on to tell that this good housekeeper, Abigail, made herself and took a generous provision with her as she went forth to meet David—two hundred loaves, two bottles of wine—not our modern bottles, but great leathern bags filled with wine—five sheep ready dressed, five measures of parched corn, a hundred clusters of raisins and two hundred cakes of figs, and laid them on asses and thus went to meet the coming foe. We can see the lady riding on her own beast with her escort of retainers going before and surrounding her as she came down by the covert of the hill, and, behold, David and his men came down against her and she meets them in the way. Significantly it is said, "She told not her husband Nabal," but she intercedes for him and finds favor in the eyes of the youthful chieftain and saves her husband from destruction. Here in Abigail was exemplified all the qualities of the good housekeeper and the great lady, and one cannot do better than to turn back and read from beginning to end the twenty-fifth chapter of first Samuel, and there study her character.

Also in the last chapter of the Book of Proverbs we find set down by the pen of inspiration for all ages and centuries the description of a lady. "Who can find a virtuous woman? for her price is far above rubies. The heart of her husband doth safely trust in her, so that he shall have no need of spoil. She will do him good and not evil all the days of her life. She seeketh wool, and flax, and worketh willingly with her hands. She is like the merchants' ships; she bringeth her food from afar. She riseth also while it is yet night, and giveth meat to her household, and a portion to her maidens. She considereth a field, and buyeth it: with the fruit of her hands she planteth a vineyard. She layeth her hands to the spindle, and her hands hold the distaff. She stretcheth out her hand to the poor; yea, she reacheth forth her hands to the needy. She is not afraid of the snow for her household: for all her household are clothed with scarlet. Her husband is known in the gates, when he sitteth among the elders of the land. She maketh fine linen and selleth it; and delivereth girdles unto the merchant. Strength and honor are her clothing; and she shall rejoice in time to come. She openeth her mouth with wisdom; and in her tongue is the law of kindness. She looketh well to the ways of her household, and eateth not of the bread of idleness."

In this old chronicle one discovers a prophetic eye turned to the business woman of our own day. The manysidedness of the people is in no way more apparent than in the flashlight it turns from time to time on the possibilities and capabilities of womanhood in every age. This is not the Oriental woman living her slavish life as man's plaything, or her bitter life as his drudge, whom we have seen depicted by the pen of King Solomon of old. This ideal woman and splendid lady is a person versed in all domestic accomplishments and quite able to hold her own in any company, whether composed of men or of women.

While urging upon all women the most thorough and diligent study of the indoor arts, let me say that there is peril that the domestic woman shall be satisfied with her attainments and seek nothing further. This is a common mistake. One should be well aware that it is not enough to take prizes at county fairs, or to

27

keep a house up to the strictest and highest standard of excellence in its management. Also the good housekeeper must avail herself of the tonic of fresh air; must be able to hold her own with others in society, and must seek for her daughters the beauty and bloom of perfect health as well as the charm of a well-trained mind and deft hands which shrink from no toil.  One needs in these days all-around women to make home life ideal.

I cannot close this bit of talk without urging upon parents the propriety of allowing and, indeed, insisting upon their sons being useful and obliging in the home as well as the daughters.  There is no reason upon earth why a lad should not use his strength in helping out in household tasks.  I have been very much impressed with the manly way in which some of our New England boys take hold and help their mothers and sisters in whatever work is to be done.  It is not at all uncommon in Vermont and New Hampshire for the son of the house to take hold pleasantly and assist with the cooking or ironing or dishwashing or whatever the work is for the moment pressing, doing it quite as a matter of course—the same lad working his way or helping to pay his way through college, coming out after a while an honored man and very likely climbing so high in future life that he sits in the governor's chair or goes to Congress.

It is not a surprising thing at all that a man turning his attention to housework should do it well.  There is no housekeeping anywhere that surpasses in thoroughness that of sailors on board a man-of-war.  The whiteness of the vessel's decks, the brightness of its brasses and the accuracy about it shames our more careless home housekeeping.  Whenever men really master a thing they usually master it perfectly, and if your little son objects to assist you in making beds, or washing dishes, you have only to say to him that soldiers and sailors do that sort of thing as a matter of course.  We do not need to be told that men excel in everything which they seriously turn to do.  Our choice of tailor-made gowns is merely one straw which shows how we appreciate the excellence of a man's fitting and sewing.  A friend of mine has a man milliner who comes around at certain times in the year and trims all the bonnets of the household, doing it beautifully, and in India, the missionaries tell me that all their sewing is wonderfully well done by the men, who think nothing of making most beautiful gowns for the English and American ladies; taking them apart, altering them and doing whatever is necessary, with a skill and exactness unknown to our own dressmakers.

Surely in this age of the world we do not need to be told that men and women must stand abreast.  That if a man would be wholly fine and noble he must have in him something of the woman heart, and that the woman, to be complete, must share some masculine virtues.  Not in vain did our Father in heaven set children together in families—brothers and sisters side by side, that they might all together

CONSIDER THE LILIES OF THE FIELD HOW THEY GROW

learn the lesson of mutual daily self-sacrifice, their motto always being, "In honor preferring one another." It shows us beforehand what heavenly life will be. Alas, that it is so often low and pitiful; that we let creep into it the little trivialities, and discord and jealousness, cowardice, meanness and sins of ill-temper and other qualities which are sordid and contemptible. More and more we need to feel that if we would live after the Christian pattern and rise to the full standard of Christian womanhood and manhood, we must put self and sin aside and become more and more like our blessed Lord.

We cannot do better than to go back in our home life, in our social life, and everywhere, to the thought of the Sermon on the Mount. Our dear Lord said: "Blessed are the poor in spirit: for theirs is the kingdom of heaven. Blessed are the meek: for they shall inherit the earth. Blessed are the pure in heart: for they shall see God. Blessed are the peacemakers: for they shall be called the children of God." He told us, too, to lay not up for ourselves treasures upon earth, where moth and rust doth corrupt and where thieves break through and steal; but to rather lay up treasures in heaven, because where the treasure is there will the heart be also.

To those of us who are tempted to worry over the trivialities and troubles of the day, He said: "Take no thought for your life, what ye shall eat, or what ye shall drink; nor yet for your body, what ye shall put on. Is not the life more than meat, and the body than raiment? And why take ye thought for raiment? Consider the lilies of the field, how they grow; they toil not, neither do they spin: And yet I say unto you, That even Solomon in all his glory was not arrayed like one of these. Wherefore, if God so clothe the grass of the field, which to-day is, and to-morrow is cast into the oven, shall He not much more clothe you, O ye of little faith? Therefore take no thought, saying, What shall we eat? or, What shall we drink? or, Wherewithal shall we be clothed? for your heavenly Father knoweth that ye have need of all these things. But seek ye first the kingdom of God, and His righteousness; and all these things shall be added unto you. Take therefore no thought for the morrow: for the morrow shall take thought for the things of itself. Sufficient unto the day is the evil thereof."

# CHAPTER LVII.

## Education for Life.

O every youth and maiden there arrives a moment fraught with intense interest and most important in its bearing on the future. It is the moment of the first flight from the nest. Life, hitherto guided and guarded by parental care and wisdom, is henceforth to be a matter of individual responsibility and concern; the man is to do his own work and answer for himself, the woman is grown up and cannot longer be subject to authority with the docility of a little child. Parents are often slow to perceive the dawning of this pregnant hour, particularly in the case of daughters. Nevertheless, the hour strikes, and cannot be ignored.

Educators, professors and school masters and college presidents tell us that they have found in the course of their experience, that boys look forward to and prepare for this hour long before girls even think of it. A boy's profession or trade or calling is a matter of discussion in the family councils while yet the boy is in kilts and knee-breeches.

"What are you going to be?" asked Mr. Thackeray of the little Lawrence Hutton.

"A farmer, sir," replied the laddie, making his decision on the spur of the moment, as children will do, rather than be floored by the unexpected.

"Well, my little man," said the great author, laying his hand kindly on the small head, "whatever you are, be a good one."

The question at least was typical, and the natural inquiry to be addressed by a man to a boy. Less frequently are similar questions addressed to little girls. From the time when a boy begins attendance at school, through his college days, if he take his college course, and after that till he is fairly launched, his training is in one direction, it is intended to fit him for success in business, for making his mark upon the world, for standing in the ranks of men and hammering away at whatever task is set him to do. Therefore a boy's bent toward any particular thing is studied and he is assisted intelligently to gain his end. When it is time for him to go, the mother may shut herself up in her chamber to pray, and a few hot tears may drop on the pages of her New Testament, but she does not oppose his step.  She would be ashamed of a son who did not go forth and take his place and do a man's work in this stirring age.

If father and mother are wise they will not try to force their sons against their inclination into paths of parental choosing.  Will and John have a right to select for themselves.  If Will is an artist born, with music thrilling in his soul, or the power to paint mountains and seas, at the end of his fingers, it is folly to compel him to go and stand behind a counter and measure yards of cloth and weigh out bags of coffee, even if that is the father's business, to which Will ought to be the heir.

If John is a predestined merchant, or draughtsman, or lawyer, or doctor, don't bring argument and persuasion to bear on him to bring him into the gospel ministry.  Men are sufficiently handicapped in this crowded race of life without obliging them to carry clogs of a blundering choice from the initial start.  Help the boy to discover what he is fit for and then let the home training and discipline be of a character to assist him on his way.

Girls, these same educators to whom I have alluded tell us, are less steadily directed during their period of study and preparation, and are less strictly confined to straight and narrow lines.  A girl may be almost anything in these days, a journalist, a lawyer, a doctor, a minister, a business woman, a stenographer, a teacher; there is no door shut any longer in her face.  She is eager to earn money.  She is unwilling to stay at home in idleness.  Her mother does not always need her, and to do a little sewing, a little cake baking, a little church work, to spend her time in trivialities does not please our nineteenth century girl.  For her there is the hour of flight from the nest.

But nature is strong and will exact reprisals and penalties to the uttermost farthing, and, whatever may be our theories, the fact remains that a girl cannot enter the lists on exactly equal terms with a man.  Born to be the mother of the race, her physical equipment must not be overlooked.  That delicate machinery of her body, kept in order by "the rhythmic check" of a periodical condition, which renews her in strength and in beauty, is never to be ignored.  Whatever she may do or may omit to do she must take into account her physical organization.  And whatever harvests she may reap in the crowded fields of life, no sheaves can ever be gathered in her arms, one-half so rich and full and sweet, as those which are hers when she is wife and mother.  The queenship of home!  To no woman ever born, in any condition of society, from the highest to the lowest, can there be a fate so fortunate as to be loved and cherished in a true man's heart, to be a good man's honored wife.

For this vocation a woman has need of an all-round preparation, different from that which a man requires for his work.  If her flight from the home be a necessity, it is simply as a means to an end, in most instances.  She makes her excursion into the office, or shop, or factory, but it is an excursion only, more or less experimental, and by and by, if she be among the happiest of Eve's daughters, she finds her mate, and settles down with him to home-building of her own.

Having said this, even though it seem a trifle inconsequent and more than a trifle contradictory, let me go on to advise every girl to be the mistress of some bread-winning art which will be in her hand as a tool, or as a weapon, as a shelter and a defence when, if ever, the days come in which neither father nor husband can stand between her and want. A girl will none the less make a perfect wife because she is an accomplished typewriter or an admirable saleswoman, an efficient secretary, or a successful journalist. Should her husband die leaving his family without adequate provision against poverty, should he be ill and unable to work, should the wolf growl ominously near the door in a season of hard times, the wife will be the better off who knows her capabilities and who possesses something which can be utilized in the world's crowded marts. And if she never marry, and thousands upon thousands of most attractive women never *do* marry, she should have some ability to earn money, if hers is the need. A poor girl requires no more than a rich girl in these days of rapid and often unforeseen transitions to have thorough training in some definite direction.

If she is to teach, she must have her college diploma, if she would be a kindergartner, her certificate of fitness in a course of study creditably finished, if she would play or sing she must have devoted years to technique, if she would find a foothold anywhere, she must be able to show herself a proficient in what she has aimed to undertake.

A young man, as a rule, exceptionally charming in manner, and one whose advantages from early childhood have been of the best, said to me the other day: "It is no longer expected of a man that he shall rise and give his seat to a woman in a public conveyance. He gives his seat only to women whom he knows, or whom he is escorting. A man is a freak who rises every time he sees a woman standing and proffers her his seat."

A day or two later I was talking with a gentleman whose habits and manners were formed two generations ago. This man, considerably past seventy-five years of age, said to me, "Madam, during my stay in your city, now covering a fortnight, I have not once had a seat in any car or omnibus." I said, interrogatively, "I suppose you have happened to travel in the rush hours, or have found yourself in crowded conveyances." "Oh, no," he said, "but it is impossible for me to remain seated while I see women standing, and in every instance I have been obliged by my own sense of fitness to rise and give my seat to women both old and young, although I admit that I have seen many young and strong men quietly seated reading their papers. I think, madam, that there is a decline of gallantry, and that the young men of to-day are not brought up so well as we were in an earlier period."

My heart warmed to the courtly old man, on whose lips was the law of kindness, and in whose gracious suavity and elegant formality there lingered that peculiar grace which we denominate "courtesy of the old school." Yet as I mentioned the whole affair at my table at home, I found myself confronted by the younger people with the observation that this is an age of intense energy and competition, and that men who have been working all day in New York, or who are compelled much of the time by their business to stand on their feet, are really quite as much in need of seats as women, who, perhaps, are only out for a little shopping or an excursion of pleasure. This seemed to me a begging of the question, but it appeared to satisfy my juniors, who said that in these days women do not claim of men any special politeness on the score of sex; that all women ask is justice, and that gallantry has gone out of fashion.

Doubtless the entrance of women into multiform fields of business where they compete with men as wage-earners, added to the other fact that women have really crowded men out from places which they formerly considered their own, and this added again to the other fact that we are all too hurried and too worried and too flurried to be as polite as we ought, may be an explanation of the matter. But it is a fact to be regretted, that serenity and leisure and soft tones and gentle manners are no longer prized as once they were by thousands of people.

We would all do well to consider our ways in this regard. Wherever there is a place particularly designated as the property of women, as, for example, the ladies' cabin in a ferryboat, we might respectfully suggest to our brothers, husbands and sons that there at least mothers, wives and sisters should be permitted to take seats before they are pounced upon by the stronger sex. As it is, one does not find that the ladies' cabin, morning or evening, affords any resting-place for wearied women, or for the woman who has her day's work before her. Men crowd in there precisely as they crowd in everywhere else. They push and hustle and elbow and forget the decorum which one might expect when women are present, so that a football field in an animated contest is not very different from the terminus of the elevated railroad at the City Hall in New York about six o'clock in the evening, or any other point of crowded resort.

If there is a decline of gallantry, may we not hope for a reaction ? Will it not be possible for the mothers of to-day to so train the small boys who are now coming on, that they may excel in good breeding the grown men of the present time? Certainly something must be done, or Americans will soon lose the prestige and the fair fame which up to a recent date have been theirs, and they will no longer be able to claim the proud distinction of being always polite and deferential to women.

There is so much in daily life to try one's nerves and temper that it is not always easy to preserve one's cheerfulness. Moods are contagious; one unhappy person in a family without any active effort can destroy the pleasure of all the rest. We do not always remember this and so we give way to causes for depression, and we do not bear ourselves as bravely as we might when things are going wrong with us. It is a good rule to keep one's troubles in the background of life, in the background of thought, bringing to the front only that which is cheerful and sunny. To some temperaments buoyancy is not difficult. Whatever may happen to keep them down, they bob up again like corks. Others have inherited a tendency to gloom, or have cultivated in themselves an indifference to the comfort of those around them, the result being that they are not the most agreeable companions in the world.

The person whose outlook is cheerful always impresses others unconsciously and elevates the tone of all whom she meets. In my childhood, a little lady used to visit in my father's house. Her coming was hailed with acclamations by the children and grown people alike. We never knew beforehand about her visits. She simply would arrive; and whether she came on a bright day or a dark, she brought a cheerful atmosphere with her. I remember that she was married from our home; the first wedding I ever attended; and I still recollect my childish interest in the preparations and have in mind the shade of the bride's changeable silk gown. Her marriage brought her many new duties, among others the care of step-children; and in the course of a long and eventful life she had many sorrows; but she lived to a great age and a few days before the illness which carried her swiftly and gently away to the other life, she again paid me a visit in my home. The little old lady was still as erect as in her girlhood. She walked with a peculiarly quick step and her laugh was as ready and as spontaneous as in the earlier days. All her life she had known the advantage of a cheerful outlook, and cheerfully she went home when the appointed time came to the Father's house.

We may have observed that it is not always the young people who are most cheerful. One would think that girlhood, so bright and full of charm, would be always the happiest time in life and that a young man with his fortune all to make would be cheery and glad in the mere joy of living. Singularly, young people often give way to melancholy more readily than do their elders, who have had experience of life. This is a little selfish and very morbid, and its only excuse is that they have not yet known that discipline of patience and of trying experiences, out of which come the peaceable fruits of righteousness. By all means let us try to preserve in ourselves a cheerful disposition.

Ruskin says that the three great Angels of Conduct, Toil and Thought, are always calling to us and waiting at the post of our doors to lead us with their winged power and guide us with their unerring eyes by the path which no fowl knoweth, and which the vulture's eye hath not seen. These great angels are, indeed, leading us by unseen paths. But youth demands to see the way in which it must walk, whereas our Father has only promised us light for one step at a time. The urgent necessity for us all, older or younger, is to come out of ourselves, not to narrow the circle of sympathies, and not to live on too low a plane. The moment we can recognize the fact that we have responsibilities and duties toward all with whom we come in contact, and toward the great multitude whom we may never meet, but who are our Father's children as we are, that moment we shall be lifted into a condition in which unselfishness will become the natural and happy state of affairs. Christian life is easily summed up in entire consecration to Christ, and complete surrender of self in glad obedience to Christ's will and childlike faith.

## Jean's Clear Call

"Jean Eveleth is to speak this morning."

"Jean Eveleth? She addresses college girls, I suppose."

"Yes," said Mary Armstrong, who was folding the tablecloth in careful creases and talking earnestly, as with deft touches and pats she put the little dining room in order for the day. "Yes, Aunt Lucy, Jean has a way that takes with college girls, and, indeed, with all girls, whatever they may be doing. She's just back from a three months' trip to the West, and she's been at work among factory operatives and saleswomen and the girls who curl feathers, hand to hand work she calls it; visiting them in their homes, holding meetings every evening and getting right at their hearts and lives. She has a wonderful gift and a sort of thrilling, vibrating voice, which appeals to you and holds you fast whether you care for what she says or not; and then she's so dead in earnest. Jean has a clear call to this sort of work, and I'm told she's going in for it as her profession. I certainly hope so, for she'll be a success and a credit to our old class."

Mary paused a moment to take down the bird's cage and fill the little cups with seed and water. Her aunt, who was knitting a white crochet shawl, which lay in a great fleecy heap on her lap, kept on with her work, her needle flashing in and out of the soft wool. Aunt Lucy Erskine was habitually a silent person; but her silence was not of the grim, tombstone kind; it was sympathetic and made you feel that she was listening and thinking over what you said, taking it all in, even when she did not speak. There is a difference in silence as there is in speech.

When the bird was comfortable for the day, his cage swept and garnished, his bath removed and his rations provided, Mary returned to the topic which was

uppermost in her mind—Jean's plans for the future. The girls had been class-
mates and chums at Wanover College, and Mary had a girl's loyal admiration for,

"Visiting them in their homes."

and fervent championship of, a brilliant friend, whose discretion she somehow,
down in her sub-consciousness, felt might be questioned by conservative people.

She had always been defending Jean as long as she could remember, though Jean had never seemed aware of it.

"Jean is going to be a secretary of the State Association, Aunt Lucy," and Mary snipped off a dead leaf from a flowering plant. "She'll have her headquarters in some central place and give her whole time and talents to the cause. Aren't you coming to the hall to hear her, Auntie?" urged Mary, coaxingly.

"Not this morning, dear. I must finish my shawl and get it off for Cousin Harriet's birthday gift. You can tell me about it when you come home. Bring your friend back to luncheon. I don't see quite how Eleanor Eveleth can spare Jean. She must be needed at home, unless Eleanor is much stronger than she used to be."

This was a good deal for Aunt Lucy to say at once, and Mary thought of it as she tripped along, a gay little figure, the very type of the daughter at home, bowing to this one, smiling to that, pausing for a chat with an old gentlemen or a child, and reaching the hall just as the chairman called the meeting to order.

The hall was crowded with women of all ages, though youth predominated. Jean Eveleth, her dark eyes alight, her sensitive face pale but flushing with feeling as she warmed to her theme, needed no inspiration beyond that of a close-packed and responsive audience to kindle her to eloquence. To every corner of the building penetrated the sweet, cultivated voice; the words were well chosen, the argument convincing, for Jean was herself convinced, and that is half the battle when one deals with other people.

"I plead with you friends, sisters, daughters, mothers," said the speaker, with insistent emphasis, " to live the beautiful, noble, unselfish life. We are all striving for our own pleasures, our own ambitions, our own ends. Ever before us floats a radiant, divine ideal, beckoning us with the wing-sweep, the flute-note of an angel from the skies. But we refuse to see. Our eyes are holden. We will not hear. Our ears are deaf. What might we not be, what might we not do, if we could but heed the angelic intimation, if we would arise from the groveling present into the serenities of a future which the present can build? Let us trample self and ease and comfort and luxury under foot and go forth to the larger, fuller, sweeter life."

Aunt Lucy had slipped into the meeting after all. Needing more wool, she had gone down town to buy it, and then she decided to spend a half-hour in finding out what there was in Jean Eveleth which so bewitched Mary Armstrong, "For," she said to herself, " Mary is a very sensible girl."

Now, away in a shadowy corner under the gallery, the little old lady in the mouse-colored bonnet and Quaker shawl smiled with benevolent amusement as she listened to the eloquent peroration of the girl on the platform.

"Stuff and nonsense!" was her comment. "She's a pretty young creature and she's having a royally good time, but I'm sure Eleanor Eveleth could find something for her to do at home."

Aunt Lucy, walking soberly out of the door as the audience rose to sing a patriotic hymn, was joined by an old friend.

"That child has a clear call to speak in meeting, hasn't she, Lucy?" said this lady.

"So it would seem."

"But when it comes to unselfishness and trampling one's own wishes beneath one's own feet, I'm not so sure," the friend went on. "It's quite evident that Miss Eveleth is in her element, handling such crowds as hung on her words to-day."

"Well, yes," said Aunt Lucy, declining to give any further opinion.

Mary was a little late for luncheon, but she had been obliged to wait for Jean, who could not at once detach herself from the throng of delighted people who pressed up to congratulate her, to take her hand, to thank her, to ask her advice, after the session of the morning was over. There is something marvelously intoxicating in this brimming goblet of success, this cordial outpouring of thanks and pleasure, which is the meed of the attractive speaker. She walks on a flower-strewn path and the air around is sweet with the silvery throbbings of bugles inaudible to the duller ears about her.

When the two girls came in to luncheon at last, Aunt Lucy, just binding off the final row in her lovely, soft shawl, rose and greeted Jean affectionately.

"You look like your mother, my dear," she said, "though there's a hint of John Eveleth in that chin. I knew John and Eleanor in my young days, so I may be pardoned if I see them again in their daughter."

"Tell me about your parents, Jean," said the old lady, at the table, a little later.

"I'm afraid I cannot tell you very much, Mrs. Kathcart," said Jean, with the ghost of a blush. "I haven't been at home in three months."

"Jean's engagements keep her on the road most of the time, Aunt Lucy," said Mary, bountifully helping the guest to a delicious fricassee and passing her the white puffs of raised biscuit.

"But I suppose your mother's health is better than it used to be," pursued Aunt Lucy.

"No, Mrs. Kathcart," answered Jean, "mamma is as fragile as a bit of porcelain. She is almost never well, and the care of a large establishment tells on her terribly. Mamma is a very conscientious housekeeper, and, since you know my father, you won't think me undutiful if I say that, though the best and dearest of men, he is a little bit exacting. Papa won't tolerate an imperfection anywhere.  He expects mamma to run the house as he runs his business, and, with such help as she can get on the Fells, it isn't quite easy."

"Is your sister Carolyn at home?" asked Mrs. Kathcart.

"Oh! didn't you know?  Carrie is married and 1    home is in Kansas. Madge is studying medicine.  Aislie is a perfect fiend about music, and she practices literally every moment she can secure.  There are three boys growing up like weeds; the girls in our family came first."

"Eleanor has her hands full," said Mrs. Kathcart.  "She must miss Carolyn.  I think I've been told that she was rather domestic in her tastes, which is a good thing in an eldest daughter."

"Yes," said Jean, indifferently, " my sister Carrie is a born housekeeper and drudge.  She really enjoys mending and patching, sweeping and dusting, and making a good loaf of bread.  We always frankly called Carrie our commonplace sister, and she laughingly accepted the situation."

"Well," said Mary, who saw a glimmer of battle in Aunt Lucy's quiet eyes and wished to ward off the sharp word she feared, for the usually silent person can use a word like a scimiter on occasion,  "I answer to that description myself, Jean.  There. must be all sorts of talents, and mine are in the trivial round, the common task, which the poet says furnish all we ought to ask."

"But what if one's nature cries out for more, for a wider field," exclaimed Jean, hurriedly; "what if a girl cannot be contented unless she is doing good which she can see, attempting something which tells on the age, helping her period?  Then is she to hide her light under a bushel?  What if she have a clear call to do work in the world?"

Her eyes shone like stars.  The rose-hue sprang up in her cheek, she looked as she did when addressing her audiences.  Aunt Lucy smiled.

"One does not always discern the call of duty at once, there are so many voices in the air.  But I am sure your parents are glad they have such a lovely big houseful of girls and boys."

Mary carried Jean to her room to rest before the afternoon session.  "Aunt Lucy is old-fashioned," she said, half apologetically.

"Yes, she does not quite believe in new fields of action for women.  I can see that.  She is not sympathetic." Jean sighed and looked plaintive.  Then went on: "But, Mollie, I simply cannot vegetate at the Fells, doing work a servant can do, idling the days away in sewing and housework and managing. Mamma is a darling and I wish I could see her oftener and make things smoother at home, but I cannot give up my life work.  It would not be right.  Am I to fold my talent in a napkin and bury it?"

A peal at the doorbell, sudden, clamorous, urgent, startled the girls in the midst of their talk.  A moment later a white-capped maid appeared with a yellow envelope on her tray. "Miss Jean Eveleth, care of Mrs. Kathcart," it was addressed.

Jean opened it, but not with the frantic haste of one unused to telegrams. She often received them, and they did not make her nervous.

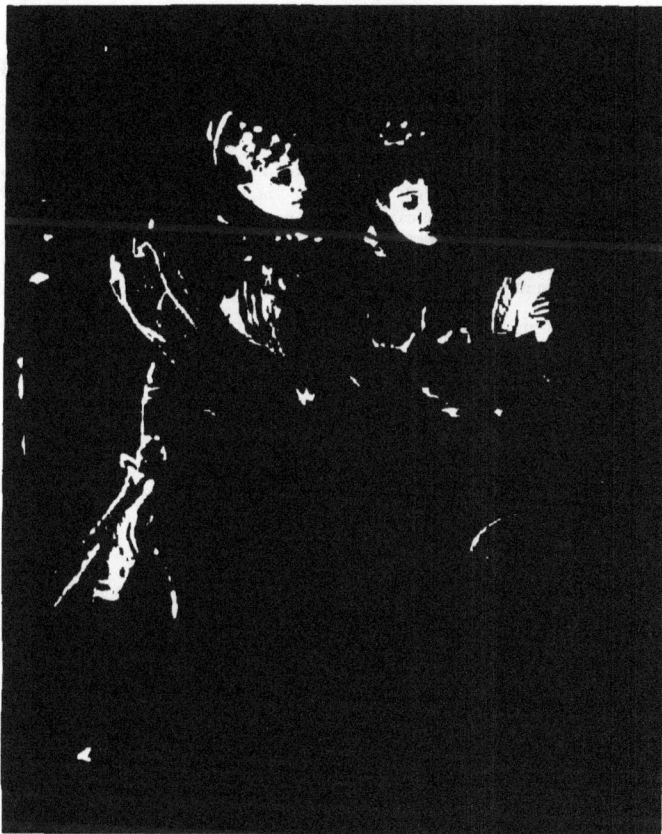

"Then came a brief letter."

Mary watched her, wondering at her composure. A telegram was an upsetting occurrence in her experience. But as she looked Jean's face changed and paled visibly. The little slip of paper quivered in her hands. She sprang to her feet, thrusting the despatch toward Mary, who read this laconic message:

Mother dangerously ill.  Madge has pneumonia.  Come at once.

JOHN EVELETH.

"Aunt Lucy," said Mary, "I will telephone for a cab, and take Jean to the station.  If she catches the next train she can be at home by nine this evening. We will send her things by express, and I will go to the hall and tell the committee that she has been sent for to go home, where there is severe illness."

Prompt, efficient, equal to the occasion, Mary did all that was called for, and saw Jean off, waving her hand cheerily as the cars whirled out of the station.

A week passed before she heard from her friend.  Then came a brief letter:

DEAR MOLLY:  My mother and sister are both better.  I have had a terrible fright. Madge was almost gone when I arrived, and mother did not know me.  We have two trained nurses, and they are jewels, but I am captain of the watch, and I've heard a clear call to stay at home and look after my loved ones.  I've been a selfish girl, Mary, but if God gives them back I'll try to make up for past mistakes.  Give my love to your Aunt Lucy, and pray hard for your devoted and penitent                                              JEAN.

"I knew there must be good stuff at bottom in Eleanor Eveleth's daughter," said Aunt Lucy, who had begun another shawl.

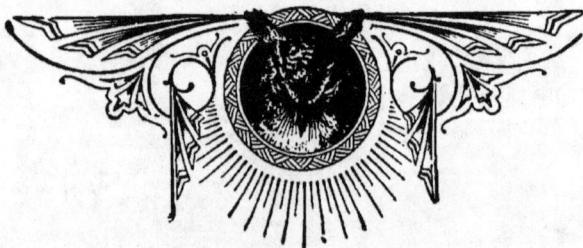

# CHAPTER LVIII.

## The Treatment of Casualties and Small Ailments.

AN English writer who has given much attention to the subject tells mothers how to deal with the small accidents and ailments which are inevitable in the bringing up of a family. She advises the matron to be provided against sudden emergencies, and to have on hand in a convenient drawer, or on a shelf in the closet, or else in a box of which she keeps the key, a supply of such requisites as a pair of scissors, three or four large needles ready with thread in them, some broad tape, some absorbent cotton, a roll of soft old linen, some flannel and muslin, some sticking plaster, mustard leaves, tincture of arnica spirits of camphor, etc.

Added to these simple precautionary appliances, the mother must lay in an ample stock of something not to be purchased at a chemist's or weighed in any ordinary balances. She must possess presence of mind, so that she will not become excited and frightened or frantic, in short will not lose her head, when her small boy is brought in limp and bleeding, or her little daughter burns her hand on the stove; she must exercise belief in Divine Providence and feel assured that her children will survive numerous catastrophes and accidents, and be none the worse for them in the end. That cuts and bruises and burns will sometimes occur is almost inevitable in a large and active household. Do not take your children so apprehensively that you and they shall fall under the tyrannical despotism of fear.

Cuts must be treated according to their position and character. A cut finger is best tied up in a rag with the blood; for blood is very healing. If a cut has any foreign substance, such as glass, gravel, or dirt, in it, this should be removed by being bathed in lukewarm water before the rag is put on. If a cut is severe, the blood should be examined. If it is dark, and oozes slowly from the wound, it comes from a vein, and is not serious; if it is bright scarlet, and spurts out of the cut like water from a fountain, it comes from an artery, and a doctor ought at once to be sent for. Until medical aid can be procured, the wound should be tightly bound, and the artery should be tightly pressed above the wound and nearer the heart. If the skin gapes from a cut, the edges should be at once brought to their

28                                    (433)

proper position with calendula plaster. If in a little time it begins to throb, the plaster should be removed, and a rag moistened with calendulated water laid on the place. This calendulated water is most useful for wounds where the flesh is deeply cut or torn. If a little lint is soaked in it and put upon the wound, it will in nine cases out of ten prove most beneficial. It is made by mixing thirty drops of the pure tincture of calendula, which may be bought of any chemist, with half a tumblerful of water. A cut on the head requires great care. The hair should be cut all round the place, and lint dipped in calendulated water be laid upon it. As long as the first dressing of a cut remains firm and gives no pain, it need not be touched.

For burns and scalds, lime and linseed oil makes an effective dressing, and they are often relieved by constantly repeated applications of cold water in which baking soda has been dissolved. Flour applied to a burned place is very soothing. The air must be excluded, and flour under soft cotton does this effectually. When one's clothes are on fire, lie down and roll on the floor, over and over, or let the person who sees the mishap cover the victim as quickly as possible with a rug or quilt, wrapping it closely to stifle the flames.

I heard a pretty story the other day. A man and a woman, entire strangers to each other, appeared at a city hospital carrying a child whom neither of them knew. An electric car was passing along the street and a lady passenger suddenly heard screams of agony, and saw a child on fire rush out of a house. To stop the car and fly to the child was the impulse and the work of a few seconds, and a man, also in the car, followed the woman. They caught up a blanket which was fortunately drying on a line, rolled the sufferer in it, and brought her to the hospital, a real work of mercy.

Bleeding of the nose looks alarming, but is seldom dangerous—indeed, it frequently proves beneficial, except in those cases where it is very excessive. To stop it, let the patient bathe his face and the back of his neck with cold water. If this is ineffectual, let him raise his face, lift his hands high above his head, rest them on the wall, and remain in this position for a few minutes. If after a little time the bleeding continues with unabated violence, procure medical aid as soon as possible.

*Choking.*—If a fish-bone or a portion of food sticks in the throat, and threatens to produce suffocation, first give a smart blow between the shoulders. This will most likely dislodge the substance. If the patient can make any attempt to swallow, put a large lump of butter in his mouth. This will help the offending substance to pass down the throat more easily. If he cannot swallow, put the finger as far down the throat as possible, and endeavor to pull the bone or meat out, or tickle the throat to produce immediate vomiting. Unless there is prompt action, life may be lost.

DON'T BE AFRAID, ONLY HOLD FAST.

*Stings from Insects.*—After being stung by a wasp or a bee, the first thing to be done is to remove the sting. This may be done with a pair of small tweezers, or the sides of the wound may be pressed with a small key, and so it may be squeezed out. Then apply to it immediately spirits of camphor, sal volatile, or turpentine, or failing of these, rub it with a little common salt, or a little moist tobacco or snuff. If a wasp or a bee stings the throat, a little turpentine should immediately be swallowed. If the place swells very much and looks inflamed, it should be bathed with arnica, or have a hot white-bread poultice laid upon it. The arnica may be made by mixing twenty drops of the pure tincture with half a tumblerful of water.

*Foreign Substances in the Ear.*—If an insect gets into the ear, hold the head on one side, and fill the hole with oil. This will kill the intruder and cause it to float, when it may be removed. If a bead or a pea gets into the ear, hold the head down on the other side, so that the occupied ear is under, and give the other ear two or three sharp blows. If this fails the ear should be syringed, but it should on no account be poked, as that is almost sure to do more harm than good.

*Foreign Substances in the Nose.*—Give a small pinch of snuff, and endeavor to make the patient sneeze. If this fails, put one finger above the substance, and gently press it to make it come down. At the same time put a small pair of tweezers into the nostril, and gently open it across. It may then be possible to draw the substance out. But ordinarily, when either eyes or nose have unfortunately any foreign body in them, send as soon as you can for the doctor.

*A Bite from a Mad Dog.*—Rub the point of a stick of lunar caustic (nitrate of silver) into the wound for fully eight seconds, and do this as soon as possible, for no time is to be lost. Of course it will be expected that the parts touched with the caustic will turn black. If, unfortunately, it should chance that any one is bitten by a dog that is said to be mad, it is worth while to chain the animal up, instead of shooting it instantly, for if it should turn out that it is not mad—and a false alarm is frequently raised—the relief to the minds of all concerned is indescribable.

*A Scratch from a Cat.*—A scratch from a cat is sometimes not only painful, but difficult to heal. When this is the case, the limb should be bathed with a hot fomentation of camomile and poppy-heads, and a hot bread-and-water poultice applied, to be renewed with the bathing every four hours.

*A Bite from a Venomous Snake.*—Suck the wound for several minutes. No danger need be apprehended from doing this, as venom of this sort does no harm when it passes into the stomach, but only when it gets into the blood. Of course the saliva need not be swallowed. Bathe the place copiously with hot water, to encourage bleeding, and tie a bandage tightly above the wound, between it and the heart. Procure medical aid as soon as possible.

*Accidental Poisoning.*—When poison has been accidentally taken, medical aid should be instantly sought.   As minutes may be of value, however, prompt measures may be adopted in those which must intervene until it arrives, and the following are recommended:  In poisoning from laudanum, opium, henbane, paregoric, soothing syrup, syrup of poppies, bad fish, poisonous mushrooms, poisonous seeds or plants, or indeed almost any vegetable substance, the first thing to be done is to empty the stomach with an emetic.   This may be done by mixing a tablespoonful of mustard or salt with a cupful of warm water, and repeating the dose until there is free vomiting.   In all narcotic poison the person should on no account be allowed to go to sleep, or he may never wake.   For all strong acids, such as oil of vitriol, muriatic, nitric, and oxalic acids, put an ounce of calcined magnesia into a pint of water, and take a wineglassful every two minutes.   If this is not attainable, dissolve half an ounce of soap in a pint of water, and give a glassful every four minutes.   Magnesia or chalk may be taken if lucifer matches are swallowed.   For arsenic, which is found in rat and vermin poisons and ague-drops, empty the stomach by an emetic of ten grains of sulphate of zinc, if it can be had; if not, mustard and warm water.   Give large quantities of milk and raw eggs, or failing these, flour and water, both before and after the vomiting.   For mercury in all its forms—corrosive sublimate, vermilion, red precipitate, calomel—the whites of twelve eggs should be beaten up in two pints of water, and a wineglassful given every three minutes.   If the patient vomits, all the better.   If the eggs cannot immediately be obtained, use flour and water or milk.   For prussic acid, which is often found in almond flavor, sal volatile and water and stimulants may be given.

*Boils and Carbuncles.*—These tiresome and painful excrescences are usually caused by poverty of the blood and weakness, and those who suffer from them should have plenty of wholesome food, fresh air and exercise.   The best and gentlest way of treating them is to keep warm linseed-meal poultices on them till they have broken, and the core has been removed; then lay a soft linen rag on the sore.   When the poultice cannot conveniently be applied, a little piece of sticking-plaster laid right over the boil, and renewed every two days, will keep it from being rubbed, and from being quite so sore.   The old-fashioned soap-and-sugar plaster is very efficacious, but rather cruel.   If the core of a boil is not removed, it is almost sure to come again.   Carbuncles require medical treatment. They may be distinguished from boils by being larger and flatter, and having a surface composed of cells.

*Fainting.*—Lay the patient on his back on the floor without any pillow under his head, and splash cold water vigorously on his forehead, rub his hands and feet, and apply strong smelling-salts to his nostrils.   As soon as he is able to swallow, give him a little wine or weak brandy-and-water.   Open the window, keep the room cool, and do not let three or four people crowd round him. Those who are subject to fainting should be careful to keep the bowels regular, the mind free from excitement, to avoid unwholesome food, and to take exercise.

*Earache.*—Put a hot linseed-meal poultice upon the ear, renew it when required, and when it has done its work, put a little cotton wool into the hollow for fear of cold; or, put into it a roasted onion, as hot as can be borne, and covered with muslin. If this fails to give relief, let the patient hold his head on one side, and drop into the ear a little warmed laudanum, or a drop of very hot water. The hot water bag as a pillow is very soothing.

*Taking Cold.*—Most people can tell the exact moment when they take a cold. A peculiar chilly, disagreeable feeling, more easily realized than described, gives the information. Now for immediate action. If possible, take a Turkish bath. If this cannot be had, take three or four drops of spirit of camphor on a piece of sugar every fifteen minutes, till five doses have been taken, and the cold will most likely take its place amongst the ills that might have been. If it still go on, drink a little warm tea or gruel, wrap up very well, and take a brisk walk until the skin is moist with perspiration; then return home and cool gradually. When bed-time comes, take a basin of gruel sweetened with treacle, and put an extra blanket on the bed. If these means are not successful, put the feet in mustard and hot water if practicable, take an aperient, a basin of gruel, a dose of nitre and sal volatile, and stay in bed an hour or two longer than usual, and so try to throw the cold off. Never have recourse to alcoholic stimulants, and never hover over a fire at such a time. Put on an extra garment, but avoid the stove.

Once let a man be thoroughly possessed by a cold in the head, and it is of no use his trying to be energetic, or virtuous, or dignified, or amiable, or beneficent: he will only fail utterly, and had better resign himself to gruel and blankets. It is my belief that when a cold has got into the system, there is nothing possible but endurance. It will have its time, and he is fortunate who can so deal with it that it shall not become more than a cold, and grow into bronchitis, inflammation of the lungs, or rheumatism. Nevertheless, the arrival of colds may be prevented, and their discomforts may be alleviated. They may be prevented to a very large extent by temperance, good living, warm clothing and regular exercise, daily bathing in cold water, and the use of common sense. The morning cold bath is a most valuable preventive to a cold, for it renders the body less liable to the effect of sudden changes; and I have myself met with several instances in which the proneness to take cold seemed to have been put to an end by a regular daily use of the cold bath. The way to prevent colds is to keep up the circulation by exercise, to avoid damp clothing, to wear good boots, to take plenty of wholesome food, and after getting either very warm or very cold, to bring the body slowly and gradually, instead of suddenly, to its proper warmth.

*Ringworm.*—Ointment of nitrate of mercury, 1 part; clarified hog's lard, 3 parts: to be mixed thoroughly, and applied in small quantity night and morning.

The above ointment, more or less diluted with clarified hog's lard, is an excellent application for the cure of many skin affections.

*Toothache.*—One drop of pure liquid carbolic acid upon a pillet of cotton wool, placed carefully in the caries of the teeth, will be found of great value both in allaying pain and arresting decay. When free from pain and sensitiveness, the tooth may be stopped either by a dentist, or, if the caries be too large, a temporary stopping of gutta-percha. The last-named may be found highly useful, and can be readily applied by one's own self as follows: Take a piece of either white or brown gutta-percha of the required size; immerse it in warm water, and when quite plastic, fill the tooth, and trim off before the filling hardens. The gutta-percha indicated may be obtained at any chemist's.

*A Speedy Remedy for Recent Colds.*—Ten drops of spirit of sal volatile, chloric ether, and red lavender, taken in a wineglassful of camphor julep, and repeated at intervals of a few hours.

*Lotion for Sprains.*—Sal ammoniac, half an ounce; rose water, half a pint; eau-de-Cologne, a tablespoonful. Rags wet with the lotion should be laid on the injured part, and changed when they get dry.

The above lotion will be found very useful and refreshing if applied as a wash for the face, neck, arms, etc., during warm summer weather, allaying much the inconveniences of profuse perspiration.

*A Good Pick-me-up.*—Dissolve as much bicarbonate of potash as will cover a five-cent piece and a small lump of white sugar in a wineglassful of cold water; then add a teaspoonful each of tincture of gentian and tincture of cardamoms, and half that quantity of sal volatile. Stir, and drink all.

*For Mosquito Bites.*—A mixture of menthol and camphor spirits, in equal parts, will be found very soothing.

Equal parts of menthol, camphor and cologne water are very soothing in headache. A hot compress laid on the head, and hot water applied behind the ears, will often drive away an obstinate nervous headache.

*Cold Cream for Chapped Hands.*—Take two ounces of oil of almonds, one ounce of spermaceti, and a piece of white wax as big as a hazel nut, and melt them together at the bottom of a basin. When these are melted and well mixed, pour over them a pint of cold spring water, and let them stand for twenty-four hours. Then pour away *all* the water, and pound the mixed residue in a mortar. Scent with a drop or two of the essence of bergamot, or a little lavender.

*Lip Salve.*—Alkanet root, one drachm; oil of almonds, one ounce; spermaceti cerate, two ounces. Add a few drops of any scent that you like, while warm.

Take care to let the alkanet root be put in a jar with the oil, and placed on the hob or in an oven till it is a beautiful red; then take it out and place it again on the hob with the cerate.

*To Prevent Chilblains.*—Wear flannel socks, or socks of chamois leather, when you go to bed.

*To Cure Chilblains.*—Wash them with tincture of myrrh in a little water.

*For Cold.*—Drink a pint of cold water when in bed.

*Windy Colic.*—Drink a pint of camomile tea, or parched peas eaten freely.

*Bilious Colic.*—Drink warm lemonade.

*Costiveness.*—Rise early, or take daily (two hours before dinner) a small teacupful of stewed prunes.

*Dry Cough.*—Immediately after your cough, chew a piece of Peruvian bark, about the size of a peppercorn. Swallow your saliva as long as

BRUSH THE HAIR THOROUGHLY.

it is bitter, and then spit out the wood. Do this every time you cough; it is invaluable.

*A Very Good Honey Soap for the Skin.*—Cut two pounds of yellow soap very thin; put it into a double saucepan, stirring it occasionally till it is melted, which will be in a few minutes if the water is kept boiling around it; then add a quarter of a pound of honey, a quarter of a pound of palm oil, and one-third of real oil of cinnamon; boil all together for six or eight minutes, then pour out and let it stand till the next day, when it is fit for use.

*For Preserving and Beautifying the Teeth.*—Dissolve two ounces of borax in three pints of water; before quite cold add one tablespoonful of spirits of

IN THE SICK ROOM.

camphor and one teaspoonful of tincture of myrrh, and put it into bottles ready for use. One wineglassful of this preparation added to half a pint of tepid water is sufficient for each application.

*Camphor Tooth Powder.*—Prepared chalk, one pound; camphor, one or two drachms. The camphor must be finely powdered by moistening it with a little spirit of wine, and then mixing it thoroughly with the chalk.

*Quinine Tooth Powder.*—Sulphate of quinine, six grains; precipitated chalk, twelve drachms; rose pink, two drachms; carbonate of magnesia, one drachm. Mix all well together.

*Hair Wash.*—For cleansing and promoting the growth of the hair. Oil of sweet almonds, one ounce; otto of roses, two drops; carbonate of ammonia, twenty grains; rosemary water, one-fourth pint; tincture of cantharides, two drachms; spirit of red lavender, ten drops. Mix as follows: Drop the otto of roses into the oil of sweet almonds; dissolve the carbonate of ammonia in the rosemary water; add to it the first-named articles; shake well the bottle; and lastly put in the tincture of cantharides and red lavender. A little of the above should be well rubbed into the roots of the hair every morning.

*To Fasten the Teeth.*—Put powdered alum (the quantity of a nutmeg) in a quart of spring water for twenty-four hours; then strain the water and gargle with it.

*The Sick Room.*—1. If possible, let it be large and sunny, and used only for illness.

2. Let there be very little furniture, no carpet and only rugs.

3. It should be very clean. The floor should be wiped over with a damp cloth every day.

4. As soon as medicine comes, read the labels and directions carefully. The medicines should be kept in one particular place, and all bottles, cups, etc., that are done with should be taken away at once.

5. The room should be kept very quiet. There should be no talking or gossiping; one or two people at the most, besides the invalid, are quite enough to be there at a time.

6. The sick person's face, and hands, and feet, should be often washed with warm water and soap, and the mouth be rinsed with vinegar and water.

7. When a person lies long in bed, take great care that the back and hips are kept clean and dry. If any place looks red or tender, dab it twice a day with some spirit, and arrange thin pillows so as to take the weight off the tender parts. If the skin comes off, apply yellow basilicon ointment.

---

Though you haven't gold or silver,
    Though you've neither lands nor name
Never dream you are not wanted,
    You are needed just the same.
In this world of change and sorrow
    You may take the valiant part;
And the world will love and bless you
    If you have a cheery heart.

# A CHEERY HEART.

Do not look at clouds and shadows,
  Watch for sunshine day by day,
Let your tones be full of courage,
  Scatter gladness on the way.
Up and down the teeming present,
  Learn the dear and precious art,
How to meet both haps and mishaps
  Ever with a cheery heart.

All forecasting of to-morrow
  In a mood of bleak despair,
All distrust of God's sure promise,
  All faint shrinking anywhere,
From a lack of faith and patience
  Takes the coward's foolish start;
Walk with God, with head uplifted,
  Bear about a cheery heart.

God forget you?  Never, never,
  He will keep you to the end.
If He sends a sudden tempest,
  Still His rainbow He will send.
Trust in Heaven, and make earth brighter
  For the trust, and let no dart
Of a transient pain bereave you
  Of God's gift, the cheery heart.

# CHAPTER LIX.

## Just Among Ourselves.

OWARD the end of August many city families who have had pleasant times in the country during the vacation feel that they must return to their homes in town. It is with profound regret that they turn their backs upon the green fields, the mountains or the seashore, remembering the closely-built streets and the lack of freedom which belong to a town environment. Still, the children must very soon begin their school year again. With September the school-room doors which have been closed, fly open; the teachers come back from their vacation; the children, brown and happy and rested, begin their routine of work once more, and we all know that home life for many years hinges principally upon the welfare of the children. For what else do parents toil and strive; what nobler end can parents have in view than the upbringing of their children in Christian nurture, than giving them the best opportunities possible, than preparing them to enter upon life fully equipped for its battles?

If the children have had the sort of outing they need, they will come back wonderfully fresh and strong, and for a while at least they will resemble pictures of health. A doctor once said to me about a little girl who had very bright eyes and red cheeks, ''Some children are well, but that child might have her portrait taken for the goddess of health.'' People make great mistakes if they do not allow their children a large measure of freedom in the country. There should be a truce to lessons, although it does no harm and really adds to a child's pleasure to have a daily hour of reading with mother or elder sister even during vacation. But what children need most of all when in the country is freedom to romp. They should not be hampered with the care of fine clothes; they should even be allowed at times to be dirty—a little surface dirt is easily washed off at night.

In coming home the mother feels that the freedom of the streets will have to be curtailed. Fortunately, all around our cities there are charming points which may be reached at a trifling cost, and for two car-fares, ten cents, one may have miles and miles of delicious sea breeze or mountain air by patronizing the trolley cars. On first coming home it is not a bad plan for the mother to plan frequent

THE END OF VACATION DAYS.

excursions for the children on Saturdays during the bright weather of the fall.   A
little care should be exercised over the house itself, that it be perfectly free from
germs of malaria, and very great care be taken that it be healthful for the returning
family.

One great advantage city people coming back from the country have,
strangely enough, over the dwellers in the inland farms.  Of course the vegetables
and fruits which are gathered where they grow have a delicious taste unknown to
those which have made long journeys and arrive at city markets; and yet,
acknowledging this, we must still admit that the person who resides in a great
city like New York, or Philadelphia, or Chicago, or San Francisco has a wonderful
advantage in the market to which she has access.  In August and September it is
an interesting thing to go through Fulton and Washington markets in New York
to see how the most delicious fruit of every kind and description is arrayed
temptingly on the venders' stalls, and to choose as one may from a great number
of vegetables and to find such choice of the sea-food as perhaps one finds nowhere
else.  Even if one misses to some extent the country table, yet if the marketing
and catering are judicious, there will be no dearth to the citizen when once city
housekeeping is again begun.

And yet the market which interests me most is not a city one; it is a queer
old-fashioned market in a Southern town, to which people from the country bring
green vegetables, and chickens, and eggs, and pot cheese, selling from the wagons
where they sit.  The old aunties in their gingham gowns, with their bright
head-kerchiefs put on like turbans, and the barefoot laddies who have flowers
to sell interest me very much.

## Occupations for Little Children.

An English writer says: "I am old-fashioned enough to think that children,
both boys and girls, should be taught to sew.  If they begin by making pretty
things, not humdrum, useful things, they will soon get to be fond of the work.
Many a man who has traveled far away from mother and sisters has felt the
desirability of knowing how to sew a button on or to put the necessary stitch in
linen; while girls of course ought to be taught needlework, and the sooner they
begin the more likely they are to become proficient in the art."

Wool work always delights children, especially if affection gives them a
motive for working.  How delighted a little girl is to make a pair of slippers for
her father.  Very pretty balls can be made with wool so soft that they will give
rise to no anxiety about the ornaments or the windows.  They are made as follows: Take two round pieces of cardboard and cut a hole in the centre of each

PLEASANT TIMES IN THE COUNTRY.

the size of a silver quarter. Wind wool through these holes around and around the cardboard till it is completely covered and the hole is filled up. Pass some string through the hole and tie it tightly in several places; then cut through the wool between the cards and gradually little by little draw the cardboard away. Trim the edges of the wool even to make the ball smooth and neat and it is ready for use. Wools of different colors should be used, and any little odds and ends of wool may be tied together and used instead of fresh wool. A few beads, with a needle and thread, will keep little children interested for a long time. They can make rings, chains, etc.

Very pretty water lilies may be made out of oranges. Take a sharp knife and cut the skin of the orange into sections, beginning at the top. Be careful not to pierce the fruit itself, and also to leave a small circle about a quarter of an inch in diameter at the stalk end of the orange untouched. Loosen these portions of skin from the orange so as not to break them; roll each one and leave it rolled at the bottom of the orange; divide the orange itself into sections and do not separate them, but leave them joined together near the bottom. Take the rolls of skin and place the tip of each one on the top of the orange, which will then assume an appearance somewhat resembling that of a half-opened water lily. A dish of oranges prepared in this way has a very pretty effect.

THE FIRST LESSON.

## How We Behave at Home.

Our manners in the family are very apt to be the sincere expressions, as they are the unconscious revelations, of our prevailing and dominant states of mind. Character is indicated by the tricks of speech and of gesture, the tones of voice, the politeness or the rudeness of daily deportment, and by a hundred small things which are automatic, things of which we take no note, perhaps of which we are quite unaware. Just as a habitually gentle and controlled person has a quiet and serene face, and as a tempestuous and unrestrained nature writes its record on the countenance, so the manners of a family set it apart as well bred or the reverse, and the family air stamps each individual of the clan.

Why do people residing under the same roof gain a certain resemblance? Originally, it may be, their features were cast in different molds, they started in being unlike, but time and familiarity, and an incessant process of unconscious imitation, has brought about a marked similarity, so that the loving husband and wife, after years of daily intercourse and common interests, actually look alike, with a subtler and more spiritual likeness than the mere surface resemblance of kinship. When the overwrought and overtired mother scolds her fractious child, allowing her fretfulness to sharpen her accents and speaking with the stormy emphasis of anger, she does not mean permanently to influence her little one's manner, but she is doing so nevertheless. The child grows querulous, reflecting the nervous susceptibility to strain which makes the mother unamiable. Placidity, serenity, a tranquil calm of strength and sweetness in combination seem to have vanished from many homes wherein people are hurried and worried, distraught and careladen.

Our manners may help to control our minds. So subtle is the connection between body and spirit whenever we can absolutely require of the former perfect repose, the repression of impatient movements and of irritated speech, the spirit gains time to conquer itself, and finds its lost poise. To go alone, sit perfectly still and refuse to allow even so much as a frown or a pucker upon one's face, to do this when circumstances are peculiarly trying, or when one is aware that weariness will presently degenerate to crossness, may save one from a humiliating outbreak, and add permanently to the stock of self-control which we all need as capital for life.

Family manners, apart from the relations of parents and children, which imply a reciprocal consideration, are apt to suffer from too much candor. We speak with great plainness in the circle of our own kindred; we comment too freely on foibles; we express the contrary opinion too readily and with too little courtesy. A slight infusion of formality never harms social intercourse, either in the family or elsewhere.

29

Beyond this too common mistake of an over-bluntness and brusque freedom in the manners of a household, in some of our homes there is a greater fault, even a lack of demonstration. There is the deepest, sincerest love in the home; the brothers and sisters would cheerfully die for one another if so great a sacrifice were demanded, but the love is ice-locked behind a barrier of reserve. Caresses are infrequent, words of affection are seldom spoken. It may be urged with truth and some show of reason that in the very homes where this absence of demonstration is most marked there is complete mutual understanding and no possibility of doubt or misgiving, and, so far as it goes, this is well. But often young hearts long unspeakably for some gentle sign

THE RECOGNITION OF AFFECTION.

of love's presence—the lingering touch of a tender hand on the head, the good-night kiss, the word of praise, the recognition of affection. Older hearts, too, are sometimes empty, and many of us, younger and older, are kept on short rations

# USEFUL AGE.

451

all our lives, when our right, on our Father's road to our Father's house, is to be
fed with the finest of the wheat, and enough of it, just as those who ate manna in
the wilderness had always an entire provision, not a stinted supply.

Another suggestion which should not be overlooked is the importance of
politeness to the little ones. To snub a small laddie needlessly, to order about a
child on errands here and there, instead of civilly preferring a request as one does
to an older person, in each case is an invasion of the rights of childhood. The
child to whom everybody practices politeness will in turn be himself ready to oblige
and agreeable in manner, for the stamp of the family is as plainly to be seen on
us every one as the stamp of the mint on the coin, and it is as indelible for time,
and why not, also, for eternity?

## Useful Age.

Rev. Dr. Field, writing in his own beautiful and venerable age, filled with
good works and kind words, has this suggestive thing to say to us about when to
stop work. I found it in the *Evangelist* and felt that you would like to see it—
you, woman, with the whitening hair and step a little less elastic than of old:

My neighbor was fully sixty years of age, but she had never thought of being
old till some new acquaintance suggested it to her.

"Of course you are not using your brush now," one of them said confi-
dently. They had just been admiring a fine landscape, some of her work.

The truth met her in the face like a blow. She was too old.

"Certainly I am using my brush now, just as I have done for years; not as
a business, but because I love it," she replied with spirit. "What should I do?
Why should I give it up?"

And yet in spite of this brave answer, she shivered, and shrank within herself,
and felt a cold wave of loneliness and discouragement creep over her being.

"I getting old!" she said inwardly. "And where is my life work? It is
not done; it seems scarcely begun. I have all my life been so anxious to do
something with my pen, but have always been so full of work and care, I am
ashamed of the little accomplished; and now, when my heart is desolate and my
hands empty, and I would fain fill up the remnant of life with the work which has
been so long knocking at my door, behold! I am old; and people think it wonderful that I ever use my brush. What would they say could they know that I
am still earnest and ambitious to use my pen to some effect in the world?"

She had been a devoted mother; but now, of her children, some were in
heaven, and some scattered over the earth, and she acknowledged to herself:
"Come to think, I am old; it may be my mental powers are declining, and perhaps

I am foolish to keep on trying. The results which I have longed to achieve need more years and more strength," she sadly admitted; for it is sad and hard to give up setting the fleshly feet upon the hills of the land of promise. So, with the discouraging conviction that it was too late in life to do anything of consequence, little by little, with many sighs and regrets, the struggle for improvement and excellence was, if not given up, carried on without much method or energy.

But, as it turned out, she lived on and on; and came to seventy bright and strong—brighter and stronger than at sixty, because her health was better, and she was also keeping pace with the times, her heart pulsing with the pulses of the world, and full of thoughts and helpful suggestions from the experience of years; but having given up effort in writing, she had lost facility and power in expression, and she sometimes thought regretfully: "If I had only known how well I was going to be, and kept right on, I might have made people listen to me by this time; and there is so much I would like to say; but now it is surely too late to start up afresh; it is certain I have but little time left."

So the years went on, and with undimmed intelligence and a pretty strong body came the dawning of her eightieth year.

"I am aged now," she told herself, "there can be no question about it; but only to think that twenty years ago, when I was only sixty, I was discouraged because people thought me 'old;' and now it is plain that I might have made all these years count for much more than they have done, had I kept right on, with method and determination, and not been influenced by the thought of age. Twenty years! but now—"

So the years went on again, and she was really aged before the Lord Jesus called her home; and the first thing when she reached heaven, He asked her: "What have you been doing these last twenty-five years to help My children on the earth, for whom I gave My life? I gave you those years, with some strength and talent, that you might use them in helping along My work. What have you done with those years?"

Then, full of regret, she had to tell over the story—of strong intent to go on with her work, and of finally yielding to discouragement because there was so little time left, and she might be called away or not have strength to finish. And the sorrowful answer came:

"Did you not read my order, 'Occupy till I come?' How did you know you would not have time? There is no world in the universe that needs help as does the earth, which was your scene of labor. Adverse pens keep busy; it is sad that yours should have stopped, for you little know the influence for good you might have exerted had you continued the effort."

Oh, my neighbor saw it all now. If she only had those twenty-five years to live over again!

In the extremity of regret she came to herself, and found it was a dream—or the twenty-five years were a dream. She was still on the earth, a woman of sixty; and joyfully she arose and went to her work with all the enthusiasm of youth, resolving never to lay down the implements of labor while her hands could hold them. She would go on with her pen, with her brush, and her music, and make them all serve the Lord, never asking whether there were time, never hesitating because she was old; she would not think of age.

What is "old" but the tabernacle growing frail and withered, while the dweller within may be growing more beautiful, with deeper sympathies and wider vision—yea, a vision that reaches on, beyond the clouds of earth, catching the radiance of the immortal hills and reflecting here their glory?

## Under God's Orders.

Hattie's earnest face glowed with enthusiasm, life was so full and rich in beauty, and lay all before her in possibilities. With a soul that had set out to grow eternally, she looked about for some work upon which to spend its force. Ah, how she wished she could be a missionary and sail over the waters into far-distant countries teaching benighted souls of the love of Christ.

Or she would like to become a trained nurse, gliding about in cap and spotless apron caring for the sick and wounded. What joy it would bring to soothe aching brows, and gaze into fevered eyes with a soothing quietness such as makes itself felt! There were exquisite moments when beautiful dreams of fame flashed before her mental eye, and she pictured herself the author of some great work of art, while the world smiled and looked applaudingly on. She would not attempt poetry, so many had been unsuccessful there; but why should she not write some little gem in prose, which, once read, would remain in the mind forever? "Under God's Orders," she looked startled as her eyes fell upon the words, they were so expressive with meaning. "After all," she humbly mused, "I can only be fitted for great tasks by performing faithfully the little duties about me. When I look at the commonest task as done for Christ, it assumes a sacredness which is not to be mistaken. I cannot serve the Master faithfully and follow out my own ends in life."

"No cross, no crown," is a motto applying to each individual, and every trust must be faithfully accepted. So, brave and faithful Hattie, whose duties closely held her within the walls of home, did not repine thereat. One task followed another in such quick succession that she had little time to think of her own ends and aims in life. Friends whispered together, and some tried to console her over the hard conditions of her life; but she sought consolation at the foot of the cross, and was more than comforted for all that she endured. Often she bowed in sweet communion at God's feet, and came away with a countenance radiant with beauty.

How sweet was this ! It was not the work she had sought, or had thought she could perform cheerfully; but here she found herself growing stronger each day, more able and willing to endure. This is one of the blessings of duty faithfully performed: the soul broadens and becomes fitted to fill lofty positions

" Under God's Orders ! " It is a beautiful thought, and the sacred joy once tasted makes us purpose never to slight or neglect a single task.—*Sallie V. Du Bois.*

---

## An Antique.

The other day in a country house I picked up an old school book printed in Albany in 1812, and bearing on its title page in childish hand the name of its owner, who, if living, is now a very old man ; who very likely may have passed on to the world where there is neither age nor death.

The book is a copy of Lindley Murray's English Grammar, and all through, in pencil marks, are the tasks which were set for the pupil to whom the book belonged. Reading it with a good deal of care, it does not seem to me that later grammarians have greatly improved on Lindley Murray. My own study of grammar in my school days was in the text-book of Goold Brown, who must have drawn very largely from the earlier author.

The rules, exceptions and remarks contained in this book are characterized by clearness, precision and common sense. Thus I note, '' Pauses in reading and public discourse must be formed upon the manner in which we utter ourselves in ordinary sensible conversation, and not upon the stiff, artificial manner which we acquire from reading books according to the common punctuation. It will by no means be sufficient to attend to the points used in printing, for these are far from marking all the pauses which ought to be made in speaking. To render pauses pleasing and expressive, they must not only be made in the right place, but also accompanied with a proper tone of voice, by which the nature of these pauses is intimated much more than by the length of them, which can seldom be exactly measured. Sometimes it is only a slight and simple suspension of voice that is proper ; sometimes a degree of cadence in the voice is required ; and sometimes that peculiar tone and cadence which denote the sentence to be finished.'' Again I read, '' In the use of words and phrases which in point of time relate to each other, a due regard to their relation should be observed.''

Evidently the child to whom this book belonged was required to memorize these rules precisely. Perhaps now and then a tear fell on these time-browned pages.

I fancy that the parsing which accompanied Murray's Grammar was done in Milton's "Paradise Lost," or perhaps in the works of Dr. Johnson. The child did not make diagrams as our children do to-day. His work was much less complex, I think, than the work now required of our little ones at school, but I have no doubt that the result was quite as satisfactory.

In his introduction, written at Holgate, near York, England, 1804, the author observes that the occasional strictures dispersed through the book, and intended to illustrate and support a number of important grammatical points, will not to young persons of ingenuity appear to be dry and useless discussions. He is quite sure that by such persons they will be read with attention, and he presumes that these strictures will gratify their curiosity, stimulate application, and give solidity and permanence to their grammatical knowledge.

I think my readers will not mind taking a peep with me at this treasure-trove of literature, which was in its pristine newness for sale in the early part of the century at the bookstore of Websters & Skinners, corner of State and Pearl streets, Albany, New York. The title page tells me that it was printed from the nineteenth English edition.

---

## The Summer Girl. .

Where are they—the reposeful Priscillas, the rare, pale Margarets, and the sweet Elaines? Do they dwell only in the minds of poets, and have we nothing between the clever girl busy with knotty questions, and Flora McFlimsy, given wholly to the superficial?

We realize, of course, that this is an age of burdens, not of the old-time sort; each generation has its own peculiar load to carry; to-day it is not the spinning-wheel and the loom, yet the present burdens for our girls seem to weigh more heavily than did Priscilla's care of the flax.

Ah, well! the tree of knowledge has had its price ever since the first woman took of its fruit, but we sometimes think that it is too great when we long for a sight of free, fresh girls, who have not been spoiled by the world's ambitions and conventionalities, and are not loaded with the woman's progressive purpose.

Yet it is not always the newer questions and responsibilities, relating to women's large field of effort, that occupy the attention of the young, but often the old ones of gowns and love, that seem to have an interdependence, and these have been given a place equal in importance to the other great questions, and have lost the old meaning in many cases, becoming simply means to an end. Dress is so often made an agent for the little god, Love, and Love a servant of power and position, that all the romance seems to have fled, and the sweet ministry of form, color and texture in the robing of a maiden, lost.

Sometimes in summer wanderings in nature's loveliest, most sacred spots, where her most perfect conditions are restful and satisfying, because full of simplicity, one cannot help comparing the natural beauty in earth and air with the artificial in society. If, then, there comes across the vision the sweet flower-like face of one who has arrived at the place "where womanhood and childhood meet," and finds that its owner has a nature in harmony with the natural conditions of life in the woods and in the fields, that like the blossoms it opens mind and heart to all the sweet developing influences, and is capable of surprise and wonder, what a delight the experience offers!

We have had far too many jokes at the expense of the "summer girl," and perhaps our Launcelots themselves are responsible for the extinction of the sweet Elaine species of maidenhood. In practicing their arts of fascination if they had held themselves always to the honor of true knighthood, they would not have made it necessary for the fair creatures whom they smote with the glances of their divine eyes, to learn the art of protection and to grow wary, and to devise schemes for laying traps, and so burdening themselves with things unworthy of a God-given womanliness. The summer girl should learn the fact that it is the burdened maiden who suffers defeat in her plans of attracting attention and winning the heart of a true man, and who is sure to miss the true benefits of an outing.

Naturalness has an attractiveness of its own; without it richness of attire, wisdom of speech, and the thousand little arts possible to women, can accomplish nothing desirable for the maiden of the summer resort.—*Mary R. Baldwin.*

---

## A Woman's Delight.

"What gathering flowers in a wood is to children," says Auerbach, "that shopping in a large town is to women." But the children do not run aimlessly from flower to flower, nor do they toss and tumble them in the search for some particular tint until they are in such a tangle that the gentlest of the fairies would have their tempers taxed in trying to straighten them out.

"I went shopping once with a lady," remarked a gentleman one evening when we were discussing this absorbing subject, "and ever since I have had a sincere sympathy for salesmen. I had heard her say before we started that she wanted to buy some black silk, and when she asked to see the goods she gave the impression that she intended to take a whole dress pattern, but after going to a dozen counters in as many different stores, and allowing the clerks to unroll piece after piece, she finally bought *one yard* for a basque lining.

"'Oh, half the pleasure of shopping is the privilege of looking at goods that we have no intention of buying,' she said, indifferently, when I ventured to commiserate the poor fellows whom she had put to so much needless trouble; and from all that I can learn in regard to women as shoppers I am inclined to think that the majority of them would agree with her."

Of course we had to admit that he was not far from right, for this sort of shopping is to many women as fascinating as a visit to a picture gallery is to others, and it is quite possible that on a dull day salesmen would rather be showing their goods, even though they sell nothing, than to stand idle; but at a busy season, when the rush is so great that customers must wait their turn to be served, and the hurried salesmen are having both strength and patience tried to the utmost, a lady will think twice before making any unnecessary request; and when she has finished her purchases, even though she may have to wait for change, she will promptly move aside and give her place at the counter to another.

"Without the rich heart, wealth is an ugly beggar," says Emerson; and the woman that snubs and overtaxes shop-girls and salesmen, though she be the "daughter of a hundred earls" and the wife of a millionaire, forfeits the right to be called a lady; while she who has a friendly care for the comfort and convenience of others, and a smile and a pleasant word for those that serve her, proves, whatever may be her nominal rank, her patent to nobility; and with such a shopper, whether rich or poor, the most sensitive of employes feels that "real service will not lose its nobleness," and is doubly eager to please her.

"A passion of kindness," quoting Emerson again, distinguishes "God's gentleman from Fashion's," and what is true of "God's gentleman" is equally true of God's lady. A kindly consideration for others is at the root of all genuine courtesy, and a woman has rarely a better opportunity to put the Golden Rule into practice than when shopping.—*Mary B. Sleight.*

## Requiescam.

[This poem is said to have been found under the pillow of a wounded soldier near Port Royal (1864). It is understood to have been written by Mrs. Robert S. Howland.]

I lay me down to sleep
　With little thought or care
Whether my waking find
　Me here or there.

A bowing, burdened head,
　That only asks to rest,
Unquestioning, upon
　A loving breast.

My good right hand forgets
　Its cunning now—
To march the weary march
　I know not how.

I am not eager, bold,
　Nor strong—all that is past:
I am ready not to do
　At last, at last.

My half-day's work is done,
　And this is all my part;
I give a patient God
　My patient heart,—

And grasp his banner still,
　Though all its blue be dim;
These stripes, no less than stars,
　Lead after him.

———

## Worth Remembering.

To pray to God continually;
To learne to know Him rightfully;
To honour God in Trinitie,
The Trinity in Unitie;

The Father in His majestie,
The Son in His humanitie,
The Holy Ghost's benignitie,
Three persons one in Deitie;
To serve Him always holily;
To aske Him all things needfully;
To prayse Him alway worthely;
To love Him alway stedfastly;
To dread Him alway fearfully;
To aske Him mercy hartely;
To trust Him alway faithfully;
To obey Him alway willingly;
To abide Him alway patiently;
To thank Him alway thankfully;
To live here alway vertuously;
To use thy neighbour honestly;
To looke for death still presently;
To helpe the poore in misery;
To hope for heaven's felicity;
To have faith, hope, and charity;
To count this life but vanitie—
Bee points of Christianitie.—*Thomas Tusser.*

## The Ministry of Angels.

I suppose it has occurred to us all in our reading of the Word that from beginning to end it is bright with the rustling of angel wings and sweet with the melody of angel harps. In these prosaic days we are slow to take the comfort we might from the assurances never revoked that the help of heaven is always ready to be given us in our hours of need. The age is material and prone to skepticism about many things which the dear Lord is ready to give His people and which we may have for the asking. One of these blessed things about which we care little and of which we seldom speak and for which we seldom pray is the help of the angelic host, and yet, as we read our Bibles we find that men of old were often met in the crises of their life by messengers from above; that the angels came to them for succor, for comfort, for warning, for strengthening, and that again and again they were sent to God's people in their very time of need. Thus an angel wrestled with Jacob the livelong night. In this case it seems as if it may have been our Lord Himself, who took this form before His coming as a babe in

Bethlehem, and once and again went to the relief of His servants for one or another reason. We remember Elijah as wearied and exhausted after his conflict with the prophets of Baal on Mt. Carmel, and threatened by Jezebel, he arose and went for his life and came to Beersheba, and after that went a day's journey into the wilderness, where he came and sat down under a juniper tree, and there he requested for himself that he might die; and as he lay and slept the sleep of exhaustion under the juniper tree, behold! an angel touched him and said unto him: "Arise and eat." And he looked, and, behold! there was a cake baked on the coals and a cruse of water at his head. Then he did eat and drink, and again he lay down, but the angel of the Lord came to him again and touched him and said: "Arise and eat, because the journey is too great for thee." Here we find an angel sent from heaven to minister to the material wants of one of God's tired children. A little later there is a beautiful story told of Elisha at the gate of Samaria. The king of Syria was at war with Israel, but constantly Israel prevailed over Syria, and at last the Syrian king became convinced that there were spies in his camp who revealed his plans to his enemy. One of his servants said: "Not so, but Elisha the prophet that is in Israel telleth the King of Israel the words that thou speakest in thy bedchamber." Then this king gave orders that Elisha should be sent for, and to capture the simple prophet of the Lord there were sent horses and chariots and a great host, and they came by night and compassed the city of Dothan, where the prophet was, and early in the morning when the servant of the man of God went forth, behold! a host compassed the city with horses and chariots, and the servant said: "Alas, my master, how shall we do?" and he answered: "Fear not; for they that be with us are more than they that be with them." And Elisha prayed and said: "Lord, I pray Thee open his eyes that he may see." And the Lord opened the eyes of the young man and he saw, and, behold! the mountain was full of horses and chariots of fire round about Elisha. I love to think that the same kind care which was over God's people in olden time is over them to-day; that still in our hours of distress and anxiety the angels whose place it is to minister come to us and give us, invisible as they are, the strong support of their presence. We know how they came to Christ, how they were with Him in His lonely hours. He said on one occasion, "Thinkest thou that I cannot now pray to my Father and he shall presently give me more than twelve legions of angels?" After the resurrection angels were sitting in the place where the Lord had lain, and after the ascension an angel said to the disciples, as they lingered looking upward where the cloud had received Him out of their sight, "Ye men of Galilee, why stand ye gazing up into heaven?" Let us take heart amid the vicissitudes and embarrassments and trials of life; let us take heart when around us the night gathers, when the temptations of the day seem more than we can bear, when we are watching by our sick or mourning beside our dead. Still, as in the old days, our Lord has His angel hosts who come to us messages of sweetness and strength.

> Still through the glowing skies they come
>   With peaceful wings unfurled,
> And still celestial music floats
>   O'er all the weary world.
> Above its sad and lowly plains
>   They bend on heavenly wing,
> And ever o'er its babel sounds
>   The blessed angels sing.
>
> Oh, you beneath life's crushing load
>  ·Whose forms are bending low,
> Who toil along the climbing way
>   With painful steps and slow,
> Look up, for glad and golden hours
>   Come swiftly on the wing;
> Or rest beside the weary wave
>   And hear the angels sing.

Better still, the Lord of the angels is always ready to come to us in our need. We have only to send one little prayer of faith to Him, and instantly in some way, not perhaps recognized by us, not perhaps just in the way we expect, but in some sweet way He will come to us, blessing us, giving us just what we need.

---

## If the Lord Should Come.

> If the Lord should come in the morning
>   As I went about my work,
> The little things and the quiet things
>   That a servant cannot shirk,
> Though nobody ever sees them,
>   And only the dear Lord cares
> That they always are done in the light of the sun,
>   Would He take me unawares?
>
> If my Lord should come at noonday,
>   The time of the dust and heat,
> When the glare is white, and the air is still,
>   And the hoof-beats sound in the street—

If my dear Lord came at noonday,
  And smiled in my tired eyes,
Would it not be sweet His look to meet?
  Would He take me by surprise?

If my Lord came hither at evening,
  In the fragrant dew and dusk,
When the world drops off its mantle
  Of daylight like a husk,
And flowers in wonderful beauty,
  And we fold our hands and rest,
Would His touch of my hand, His low command,
  Bring me unhoped-for zest?

Why do I ask and question?
  He is ever coming to me,
Morning and noon and evening,
  If I have but eyes to see.
And the daily load grows lighter,
  The daily cares grow sweet,
For the Master is near, the Master is here,
  I have only to sit at His feet.

---

## "Even So, Come, Lord Jesus."

Come to us, Lord, as the daylight comes
  When the darkling night has gone,
And the quickened East is tremulous
  With the thrill of the wakened dawn.

Come to us, Lord, as the tide comes in
  With the waves from the distant sea;
Come, till our desert places smile,
  And our souls are filled with Thee.

· Come to us, Lord, as the mother love
  Flows out to the babe new-born;
So come to us, Lord, as the mother's kiss
  That rouseth the child at morn.

Come to us Lord, as comes the bloom
  To the kindling heart of the rose;
Come, as the stir of a vivid life
  When from dreams our eyes unclose.

Come to us Lord, on our beds of pain,
  And soothe the fevered smart;
Come to our grief and our loneliness,
  And pillow our heads on Thy heart.

Come to us, Lord, when the tempter dares
  Our faltering faith to smite;
Come that the powers of Satan then
  May haste to take their flight.

Come to us, Lord, we watch for Thee;
  We shall never feel surprise,
If sudden we lift our eyes and see
  The day-spring o'er us rise.

Come to us, Lord, the hour is late,
  The night is slow and long;
Come to us, Lord, and bid us lift
  Redemption's endless song.

—*Margaret E. Sangster.*

FARE-THEE-WELL

*9 783743 407350 *